KEYSTONE TEN

= "Die Alte Zeite" =

GERMAN AMERICANA AND CLASSICS OF THE REFORMATION

Presented by

THE FAMILY ALBUM

RD 1, Glen Rock, PA. 17327 U. S. A.

Phone: 717 / 235 - 2134

KEYSTONE TEN

= *"Die Alte Zeite"* =

TERMS OF SALE

1. THERE IS NO CAVEAT EMPTOR.
ALL ITEMS ARE FULLY GUARANTEED AND RETURNABLE WITHIN FIVE DAYS, FOR ANY REASON. YOUR SATISFACTION IS ASSURED. OUR GUARANTEE ALLOWS YOU TO ORDER WITH COMPLETE CONFIDENCE.

2. PRICES ARE NET. INVOICES ARE DUE UPON RECEIPT.
INDIVIDUALS WHO HAVE NOT ESTABLISHED ACCOUNTS WITH US ARE REQUESTED TO INCLUDE REMITTANCE WITH THEIR FIRST ORDER. OVERAGES WILL BE REFUNDED. ACCOUNTS ABROAD WILL BE BILLED PRO FORMA, PAYABLE IN U. S. FUNDS, AND SUBJECT TO ADDITIONAL COLLECTION CHARGES, IF APPLICABLE. INSTITUTIONS MAY, UPON REQUEST, BE GRANTED EXTENDED PAYMENT TERMS TO FIT THEIR BUDGETARY NEEDS. VISA AND MASTERCARD ARE ACCEPTED ON ORDERS OVER $ 100.00

3. PLEASE ADD A MINIMUM POSTAGE ALLOWANCE ($ 2.00 / BOOK) TO YOUR REMITTANCE. INSURANCE AND ADDITIONAL POST WILL BE BILLED. AIR AND EXPRESS SHIPMENTS ARE AVAILABLE.

4. PENNSYLVANIA RESIDENTS PLEASE ADD 6% PA. SALES TAX.

5. FULLER DESCRIPTIONS, AND MORE DETAILED INFORMATION ABOUT ANY ITEM MAY BE HAD UPON REQUEST. THE MATERIALS LISTED IN THIS CATALOG ARE FROM OUR HOLDINGS IN THE LARGE SPECIALIST COLLECTING AREAS OF: *"GERMAN AMERICANA"*, *"CONTINENTAL AMERICANA"*, AND *"REFORMATION HISTORY"*. PLEASE NOTE THAT WE BUY, SELL, AND APPRAISE FINE BOOKS AND MANUSCRIPTS IN ALL FIELDS, AND OFFER A WIDE RANGE OF COLLECTION DEVELOPMENT SERVICES.

6. CODE WORD FOR THIS CATALOG IS: *"ALTE"*.

THE FAMILY ALBUM

RD 1, Glen Rock, PA. 17327 U.S.A.

Phone: 717 / 235 - 2134

First Edition - Limited to 1000 Copies **ISBN # 0-934630-18-6**

REFERENCES CITED

Adams = ***Books Printed on the Continent of Europe (1501-1600), in Cambridge Libraries.***

AI = ***American Bibliography. & A Checklist of American Imprints.***
Edited by Shaw, Shoemaker, Cooper, & Rinderknecht. Previously called: S & S.

Austin = ***Early American Medical Imprints, 1668 - 1820.*** By Robert E. Austin.

BMC STC German = ***Short - Title Catalogue of Books Printed in the German - Speaking Countries... 1455 to 1600, Now in the British Museum...***

Brethren Bib. = ***A Brethren Bibliography, 1713-1963.***
By Donald F. Durnbaugh & Laurence F. Schultz.

Bristol = ***Supplement to Evans' American Bibliography.*** By Roger P. Bristol.

Drake = ***Almanacs of the U. S.*** By Milton Drake.

Evans = ***American Bibliography. A Chronological Dictionary of All Books Printed in the U. S. 1639 - 1800.*** By Charles Evans.

GLP/USA = ***The First Century of German Laguage Printing in the U. S. A.***
A Bibliography Based on the Studies of Oswald Seidensticker and Wilbur Oda. Edited by Karl J. R. Arndt and Reimer C. Eck. Compiled by Gerd-J. Bötte, Annelies Müler, and Werner Tannhof. Pa. German Society & Göttingen: 1989. Two Volumes.
Ours is the first extensive catalog of German American imprints to employ, even in a modest way, this important new bibliography. We have coined the provisional reference name "*GLP/USA*" to stand for entries from this invaluable work.

Hild. = ***A Century of Printing. The Issues of the Press of Pennsylvania, 1685 - 1784.*** By Charles Hildeburn.

Karpinski = ***Bibliography of Mathematical Works Printed in America.*** By Louis C. Karpinsky.

Klinefelter = ***THE ABC Books of the Pennsylvania Germans.*** By Walter Klinefelter.

McDade = ***The Annals of Murder.*** By Thomas M. Mc Dade.

O'Callaghan = ***List of Editions of the Holy Scriptures Printed in America Previous to 1850.***

Parsons = ***Early Catholic Americana.*** By Wilfrid Parsons.

Repp = ***Luther's Catechism Comes to America.*** By Arthur C. Repp.

Rink = ***Technical Americana Printed before 1831.*** By Evald Rink.

Rosenbach = ***Early American Children's Books.*** By A. S. W. Rosenbach.

S & M = ***National Index of American Imprints through 1800. The Short Title Evans.***
Edited by Clifford K. Shipton & James E. Mooney.

Seid. = ***The First Century of German Printing in America, 1728 - 1830.***
By Oswald Seidensticker.

Shoemaker/L = ***Checklist of Imprints of the German Press of Lehigh County, 1807 - 1900.***
By Alfred L. Shoemaker.

Shoemaker/N = ***Check List of Imprints of the German Press of Northampton County, 1766 - 1905.*** By Alfred L. Shoemaker.

Welch = ***Bibliography of American Children's Books Printed Prior to 1821.***
By D'Alté A. Welch.

A MODEST DEDICATION

WILLIAM S. TROXELL

William S. Troxell (1893-1957), as The Allentown Morning Call's "Pumpernickle Bill", made the lore and dialect of the Pennsylvania Germans live for new generations. For more than thirty years (six times a week in the newspaper, and weekly on radio), he helped chronicle the daily experiences and anecdotes of the Lehigh Valley with sympathetic humor. Of the many "Pennsylvania Dutch" dialect writers, few have been so widely read. His efforts as a cultural historian did not go unnoticed. In 1952 he became President of the Pennsylvania German Society and continued in that office until his death. For many thousands, both rural and urban, "Pumpernickle Bill" became a beloved household name, which conjured up a vivid reality of their ancestral heritage as Pennsylvania "Dutch". We are proud to be able to offer, throughout this catalog, portions of his fine personal collection [which included many *unique* Lehigh County imprints]. As a tribute, and as a guide to modern collectors we indicate those books with: *WST.*

HENRY SNAVELY HEILMAN

Henry Snavely Heilman (1838-1911) was a Pennsylvania German Bibliophile from Lebanon County. His collection, in many ways, rivaled his more famous contemporaries Samuel W. Pennypacker and Abraham H. Cassel. It included the only copy, then known, of Franklin's 1730 "Mystische Sprueche", and many other treasures. The best account of H. S. Heilman was written by Dr. Robert M. Kline and presented at the Third Rose Hill Seminar in 1965. We are very pleased to offer in this catalog a small selection of books that were once in Heilman's library, or in the collections of kindred Lebanon families. As a tribute to this great bibliophile, and as a guide to modern collectors we indicate those books with: *HSH.*

PART ONE

KEYSTONE TEN

= "*Die Alte Zeite*" =

PART I

GERMAN AMERICAN IMPRINTS AND CLASSICS OF THE REFORMATION

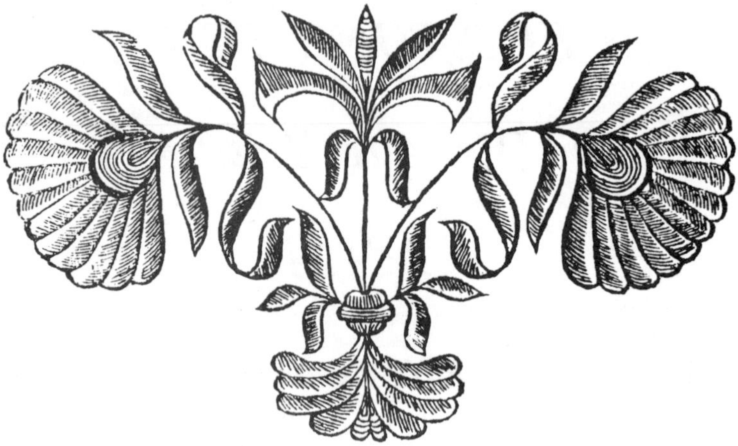

Device Used By Der Brüderschaft, Ephrata: 1748

KEYSTONE TEN = "Die Alte Zeite"
PART I

GERMAN AMERICAN IMPRINTS AND CLASSICS OF THE REFORMATION

1. ABC Book. **A B C = Buch für Deutsche Wochen und Sonntags = Schulen.** Neinstedt, Gettysburg: 1831. 24p. Original printed paper boards in crisp condition. *Apparently not in AI.* Kleinfelter 123. First Edition. In many ways, the German American ABC's were more cheerful and attractive to children than their English counterparts - such as the "New England Primer". A positively charming A B C. $ 150.00

2. ABC Book. **A B C = Büchlein für Kleine Kinder.** New Berlin, Circa: 1840. 8p. *Miniature in original printed wraps.* Soiled. Quite Rare. $ 125.00

3. ABC Book. **A B C und Buchstabir - Büchlein.** American Tract Soc. NY. Ca: 1860. 64p. Charming illustrations. Small 32mo. Flexible cloth. *WST.* $ 24.00

4. ABC Book. **A B C = Buchstabir und Lesebuch zum Gebrauch für Deutsche Schulen...** Verfasst von Johann Conrad Reissner. Miller for Orwig, et. al. and the Evangelical Association. New Berlin: 1838. 149p. Leather backed printed paper boards with some loss. *Ownership of Abraham Histand.* AI 52621, Klinefelter 133. Very Scarce. $ 140.00

5. ABC Book. **A B C = und Lese=buch zum Gebrauch für Deutsche Kathol. Schulen.** Scriba, Pittsburgh: 1845. 32p. Plain wraps. Scarce Catholic ABC. *Not in Klinefelter.* $ 75.00

6. ABC Book. **DAS ALLGEMEINE A B C = Buchstabier = und Lesebuch zum Gebrauch für Deutscher Schulen...** By Daniel Schmidt. Bär, Lancaster: 1840. 128p. Loss on one leaf. Attractive woodcut illustrations. Printed paper boards. Klinefelter 140. $ 50.00

7. ABC Book. **DEUTSCHES Buchstabir und Lesebuch zum Gebrauch Deutscher Schulen. Enthalend: Das ABC...** Billmeyer, Germantown: 1820. 128p. Some old paper repairs. Leather backed boards. *GLP/USA* 2416, Seid. p. 211, AI 1015. *Not in Klinefelter.* $ 80.00

8. ABC Book. **EIN WOHL EINGERICHTETES DEUTSCHES ABC = Buchstabir und Lesebuch zum Deutscher Schulen...** Billmeyer, Germantown: 1810. pp. 14, 120 + Very curious illustrations that may be type-metalcuts (one perhaps signed by Isaiah Thomas). Leather backed. XLib. *GLP/USA* 1732, Klinefelter 71, Seid. 178, AI 22077. *HSH.* $ 120.00

9. ABC Book. **ERSTES LESEBUCH FÜR KINDER.** Reprint ed. Raber, Baltic, OH. Ca: 1969. 160p. Library cloth. With / Another ABC reprint in wraps. $ 14.00

10. ABC Book. **HOCH-DEUTSCHES LUTHERISCHES ABC UND NAMEN BUCHLEIN FÜR KINDER...** G. S. Peters, Harrisburg. Cover: Sheffer & Beck, Harrisburg: 1852. 36p. Delightful woodcut illustrations. Stain. Printed paper boards. Klinefelter 163. $ 60.00

11. ABC Book. **HOCH-DEUTSCHES LUTHERISCHES ABC UND NAMEN BUCHLEIN FÜR KINDER...** Schafer & Koradi, Phila. Ca: 1858. 35p. Illus. Paper boards. $ 35.00

A PREVIOUSLY UNRECORDED ABC

12. ABC Book. **HOCH-DEUTSCHES REFORMIRTES ABC UND NAMEN BUCHLEIN, Fur Kinder, welche anfangen zu lernen...** Michael Billmeyer, Germantown: 1792. 31p. Quite worn and probably lacking 1 leaf, but extremely rare. Included are 3 leaves from an even earlier (unidentified) ABC. *Unknown to Evans, Seidensticker, and Klinefelter. This is apparently the same unique [incomplete] copy recorded by GLP/USA 848.* $ 320.00

13. ABC Book. **HOCH-DEUTSCHES REFORMIRTES ABC UND NAMEN BUCHLEIN, Fur Kinder, welche anfangen zu lernen...** Zentler, Phila: 1807. (30p.). Worn pictorial boards. Variant of *GLP/USA* 1566, Klinefelter # 62, AI 12766, Rosenbach 334. *WST.* $ 100.00

14. ABC Book. **DAS NEUE ABC = UND BUCHSTABIR = BUCH... Fur Deutsche Volkschul in Pennsylvanien und andern Staaten. Fur Kinder...** Benner, Sumneytown, Pa: (1861). 47p. Illus. Worn. Klinefelter 184. *WST.* $ 22.00

15. ABC Book. **DAS NEUE BUCHSTABIR UND LESEBUCH, zum Gebrauch Deutscher Volksschulen in Pennsylvanie und andern Staaten...** Benner, Sumnytown: 1860. 144p. Worn. *Not in Klinefelter. WST.* $ 40.00

16. ABC Book. **DAS NEUE DEUTSCHE ABC = BUCH, oder Erstes Buch für Kinder...** Blumer, Allentown: 1837. 36p. Nice printed paper boards. *Not in Shoemaker/L, nor AI.* Klinefelter 132. *WST.* $ 100.00

17. ABC Book. **DAS NEUE DEUTSCHE ABC = BUCH, oder Erstes Buch für Kinder...** Blumer & Busch, Allentown: 1851. 40p. Nicely illustrated. Printed paper boards. Klinefelter 162, Shoemaker/L p. 80. *WST.* $ 50.00

18. ABC Book. **DAS NEUE DEUTSCHE ABC = BUCH, oder Erstes Buch für Kinder...** Blumer, Leisenring & Co., Allentown: 1860. 42p. Plain paper wraps. Illus. Klinefelter 183, Shoemaker/L p. 100 *[Both recording this copy only]. WST.* $ 75.00

19. ABC Book. **DAS NEUE DEUTSCHE ABC = BUCH, oder Erstes Buch für Kinder...** Saeger & Leisenring, Allentown: 1862. 46p. Illus. XLib. Very worn but rare. *Apparently neither Klinefelter nor Shoemaker/L could locate a copy. HSH.* $ 75.00

20. ABC Book. Sanders, Karl W. **BILDER FIBEL...** (NY?) Ca: 1930. 100+p. Fine reprint of the 1846 edition. Printed wraps. Pictorial Primer in English & German. *WST.* $ 22.00

21. ABC Book. Schmauk, J. G. **ERSTES BUCH FÜR DEUTSCHE SCHULEN**. Phila. Circa: 1840. 156p. Nice woodcut illustrations. Disbound. $ 40.00

22. **ABRISS EINES UNTERRICHTS IN DER CHRISTLICHEN LEHRE G.T. L. St. für die Evangelische Jugend...** (Bruckman, Reading: 1820). 4p. Self wraps. Scarce. $ 45.00

a b c d e f g h i j
k l m n o p q r ſ
s t u v w x y z

THE MOST TRUSTWORTHY ACCOUNT OF THE EARLIEST PENNSYLVANIA SETTLEMENTS

23. Acrelius, Israel. **BESKRIFNING OM DE SWENSKA FORSAMLINGARS Forna och Narwarande Tilstand, Det sa Kallade Nya Swerige, sedan Nya Nederland, Men nu for tiden Pensylvanien... De la ware, Wast-Yersey, och New-Castle County uti Norra America...** Stockholm: 1759. pp. 20, 533 [ie. 503], 1 + *Bound with an unusual and very rare 1764 April Fool's poem (4p.).* Slight worming. 4to. Contemporary binding of leather backed paper boards, needs restoration. Early manuscript ownerships. Sabin 133, Howes A-34, Vail 528, "*This important work is hardly less scarce than that of Campanius... it has besides, the merit of being much more extensive and of reproducing a large number of documents, partly unpublished*" = Muller 1134. Rare first edition of the most trustworthy contemporary authority on the Swedish settlements along the Delaware, and the early colonization of Pennsylvania. $1500.00

24. Alleine, Joseph [1634=68]. **GRUNDLEGUNG ZUM THÄTIGEN CHRISTENTHUM...** William & Robert Dickson, Lancaster: 1796. 332p. Full leather. Ds. *GLP/USA* 1037, Evans 29965, Seid. p. 144. $ 50.00

25. Alleine. **WECKSTIMME FÜR DIE SUNDER...** American Tract Society. Fanshaw, NY. Ca: 1840. 480p. Cloth. 24mo. Allein's Alarm. $ 14.00

26. **ALMANAC COLLECTION.** A Lifelong Collection of Over 300 German American Almanacs; Including copies of Saur's *DER HOCH DEUTSCHE AMERICANISCHE CALENDER, 1764 to 1778*, and many other scarce and important Almanacs. For the early American "pioneer", Almanacs were the key to wit, wisdom, weather, wealth, law, literature, and learning. In the cities and on the frontier, they were "best sellers" - second only to the Bible. Read to tatters, they had to serve a family for at least a full year, and were frequently hung in the barn and consulted for decades. Consequently, many of those in this collection are extremely uncommon - but are also somewhat age and damp stained, with some loss of text or leaves. Many have interesting contemporary manuscript ownerships and annotations. See: Brendle & Unger - *Folk Medicine of the Pennsylvania Germans*. The retail value of the collection is over $2500.00, Please write for a brief, descriptive check list. *WST*. $ 1000.00

27. American Tract Society. **"JUNGEND = SCHRIFTEN"**. Unusual Collection of Eighteen German Chapbooks. NY, Ca: 1865. 32 mo. 32p. Each with charming little woodcut illustrations. Original printed wraps. It is getting increasingly difficult to gather a series of these German-American juveniles. Handsome group. $ 125.00

28. Arndt, Johannes. **...BUCHER VOM WAHREN CHRISTENTHUM...** Frankfurt am Main: 1739. 5 vols in 1. Disbound. *Manuscript register for the Wehr & Dorsheimer Families (Lehigh County?), 1744-59.* Arndt [1555=1621], was among the most significant of Lutheran mystical authors. He is sometimes referred to as the "father of German Pietism". $ 75.00

29. Arndt. **DER GOTTSELIGEN UND HOCHERLEUCHTETEN... PARADIESS = GARTLEIN...** Saur, Germantown: 1765. pp. (34), 531, (11). 24mo. Contemporary full leather. The Paradiesgätlein served as a major source for the first Swiss-Mennonite prayer book [Ernsthafte Christenpflicht]. *GLP/USA* 316, Evans 9907, Hild. 2304, Seid. p. 72. Very nice copy of an important book. $ 500.00

30. Arndt. **...PARADIESS=GARTLEIN...** Frankfurt am Mayn: 1777. 600+p. Hand colored frontis. Tall 24mo. 1843 Philadelphia manuscript inscriptions. $ 85.00

31. Arndt. ...**PARADIESS=GARTLEIN**... Halle: 1779. 268p. + Reg. *Manuscript ownership of Henry Heilman (Lebanon County, Pa.). HSH.* $ 120.00

32. Arndt. ... **SECHS BUCHER VOM WAHREN CHRISTENTHUM...** Bound with / **Paradiesgärtlein**... Blankenburg: 1741. Nearly 1500p. No plates in this edition. 4to. Full leather. *1791 Manuscript ownership of Samuel Weiser, Yorktown (Pa.).* $ 140.00

33. Arndt. ... **SECHS BUCHER VOM WAHREN CHRISTENTHUM...** With / **Paradiesgärtlein...** Halle: 1760. Nearly 850p. Ds. As in most of the editions listed below, there are ***many remarkable engraved plates, which include images of clocks, printing presses, rockets, fountains, sun dials, etc.*** The printing related illustrations are especially nice. The German rococo plates here are among the best of any 8vo. edition. 1/2 leather. "The most used devotional book in German Mennonite families" = Mennonite Encyclopedia. *HSH.* $ 150.00

34. Arndt. ... **SECHS BUCHER VOM WAHREN CHRISTENTHUM...** With / **Paradiesgärtlein...** Nürnberg: 1762. Over 1100p. + Remarkable engraved plates. The plates are each framed in florid rococo borders. Full alum tawed vellum, with clasps. *Nice (Mennonite?) manuscript ownership of "Michael Gross, April 10th, 1795".* $ 150.00

35. Arndt. ... **SECHS BUCHER VOM WAHREN CHRISTENTHUM...** With / **Paradiesgärtlein**... Nürnberg: 1806. Worn. Ds. These plates are among the very best. $ 95.00

36. Arndt. ... **SECHS BUCHER VOM WAHREN CHRISTENTHUM...** With / **Paradiesgärtlein**... Mentz & Sohn, Phila: 1832. 1173p. Woodcut mystical illustrations. Thick 4to. *Full leather binding, with a geometric design created by over 180 brass studs.* Original clasps. One of the most popular versions of this remarkable book. AI 11004. $ 100.00

37. Arndt. ... **SECHS BUCHER VOM WAHREN CHRISTENTHUM...** Mentz, Phila: 1834. 1172p. Well Illustrated. Thick 4to. Broken full leather. AI 23001[3]. *HSH.* $ 34.00

38. Arndt. ... **SECHS BUCHER VOM WAHREN CHRISTENTHUM...** With / **Paradies - gätlein**... Grater, Allentown: 1834. 928p. + Plates in fine state. Worn original embossed pigskin binding, with gilt tooled morocco labels. A more extended study of Grater's "imported" books and bindings would reveal much about the German American book trade. *WST.* $ 100.00

39. Arndt. ... **SECHS BUCHER VOM WAHREN CHRISTENTHUM...** Mentz, Phila. Ca: 1839. 1172p. Well Illustrated. Thick 4to. Worn full leather. $ 38.00

40. Arndt. ... **SECHS BUCHER VOM WAHREN CHRISTENTHUM...** Kurtz, Reutlingen: 1847. Several volumes in one. 1000+p. Illustrated. Full allum tawed pigskin. Unusual blind tooling. With clasps. Produced for the American market. $ 75.00

41. Arndt. ... **SECHS BUCHER VOM WAHREN CHRISTENTHUM...** Basel: 1867. pp. 1000, 272. Illustrated. 4to. Spine gone. $ 14.00

42. Arndt. ... **SECHS BUCHER VOM WAHREN CHRISTENTHUM...** Kohler, Phila: 1879. Illustrated. 4to. Attractive embossed leather spine. $ 28.00

43. Arnold, Theodore. **ENGLISCHE GRAMMATIK...** Jena & Leipzig: 1809. 386p. Homespun "sailcloth" covers. Interesting & scarce instructional language texts. $ 50.00

44. Arnold. **ENGLISCHE GRAMMATIK...** Jena: 1838. 382p. Marbled boards. Vellum gilt label. *WST.* $ 40.00

45. Arnold. **PRAKTISCHE GRAMMATIK DER ENGLISCHEN SPRACHE...** Phila: 1849. 336p. + Ads. Embossed leather backed boards. Edited by W. H. Furness. $ 38.00

46. Arthur, T.S. **BELL MARTIN, Ein Sittengemälde aus dem Leben der Vornehmen Welt in Nord-Amerika.** Translated into German by J.G. Reichman, Genoa, Michigan. Allentown: 1862. 173p. Shoemaker/L p. 106 *[Recording this copy only]*. *WST.* $ 50.00

FORTUNE'S WHEEL

47. Astrology. **GLUCKS = RAD, oder Würfel = Buch, Durch welches man nach Astrologischer Art...** Printed For the purchasers, (Reading?): 1833. 43p. + Folding Chart. Plain wraps. *Apparently Not in AI.* $ 140.00

48. **DIE AUFGEHENDE LILIE, ist ein Theosophischer Discurs...** Erste Auflage. William Hamilton, Lancaster: 1815. 204p. Bound With / **Das Kleine Jelängerjelieber...** Ehrenfried: 1816. 12p. 16mo. Printed boards with a repeated decorative (broadside type) border. Leather backed. *GLP/USA* 2087/2151, AI 33895 & 38021. Unusual. $ 125.00

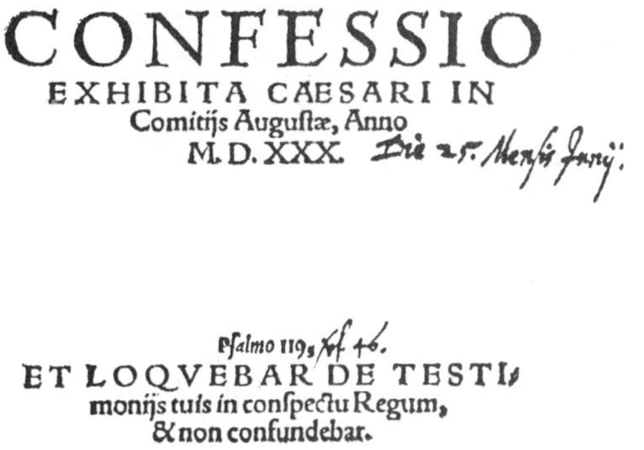
CONFESSIO
EXHIBITA CAESARI IN
Comitijs Augustæ, Anno
M.D.XXX.

ET LOQVEBAR DE TESTI-
monijs tuis in conspectu Regum,
& non confundebar.

THE FUNDAMENTAL LUTHERAN DECLARATION OF FAITH

49. Augsburg Confession. **CONFESSIO EXHIBITA CÆSARI IN Comitiis Augustae, Anno M.D.XXX. Et Loquebar de Testimoniis tuis in Conspectu Regum, & non confudebar.** (Froschauer, Zurich: 1530). 40p. 4to. Self wraps. Early manuscript annotations. The Augsburg Confession is not only a fundamental statement of Protestant doctrine, but a major historical document. In 1530, the newly crowned Emperor Charles V called for a diet of the German Estates. Charles intended to end the religious dissension which the Reformation had created in his empire, The initial text of the Confession was drafted by Melanchthon, from the material of the Schwabach and Torgu Articles. After many negotiations and revisions, there was a public presentation and reading on June 25, 1530. Even though the Emperor had strictly forbidden the publication of the Confession, there soon appeared six German editions, and this one, in Latin. The authorized "Editio Princeps" was not published until 1531, when Melanchthon issued it with the "Apology". This little pamphlet conveys an immediate sense of a compelling historical moment. The influence and importance of the "Confession" cannot be over-stated. ***We can locate no other copy in the United States. Apparently not in OCLC, NUC, & ARLIN, Etc.*** See: Adams A2132, Hartfelder p. 558, BMC STC German p. 51, Brunet II 218, and any good general encyclopedic reference, or religious history. A true monument of the Reformation. $6400.00

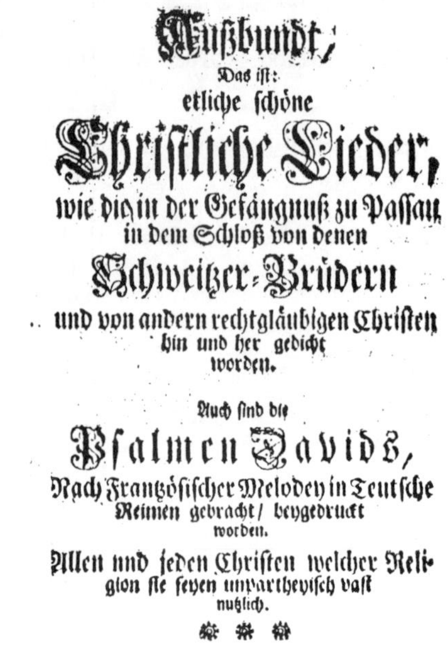
Außbundt,
Das ist:
etliche schöne
Christliche Lieder,
wie die in der Gefängnuß zu Passau
in dem Schloß von denen
Schweitzer-Brüdern
und von andern rechtgläubigen Christen
hin und her gedicht
worden.
Auch sind die
Psalmen Davids,
Nach Frantzösischer Melodey in Teutsche
Reimen gebracht/ beygedruckt
worden.
Allen und jeden Christen welcher Reli-
gion sie seyen unpartheyisch vast
nutzlich.

50 **AUSS BUNDT, DAS IST: Ettliche Schöne Christliche Lieder**... (Europe, Ca: 1700). pp. 11, 796, 6. Title with commas instead of diagonals. 137 Hymns. Contemporary full leather with decorated corner bosses and clasps & brass initials "N. J.". An impressive copy of this very rare early 18th century European Ausbund. First published in 1564, the Ausbund is the oldest hymnbook of the Swiss (Anabaptist / Mennonite) Brethren. These hymns are still in use and highly prized among the Amish and Mennonites. $1000.00

51. **AUSSBUNDT, DAS IST: Ettliche Schöne Christliche Lieder**... (Europe. Ca: 1700). pp. 11, 480, 4, 350 (of 351). Similar to the Hartzler copy, with Lobwasser's Psalter deliberately published with the Ausbund. Contemporary full leather with decorated corner bosses and clasps & brass initials "G. M. B." = G. M. Brandt? Rare early 18th Century European Ausbund. $1000.00

52. **AUSBUND. DAS IST: ETLICHE SCHÖNE CHRISTLICHE LIEDER**... Christoph Saur, Germantown: 1742. Lacks Tp. pp. 8, 812, 6, 20, 46. Some leaves worn. Contemporary brass trimmed Saur binding needs some restoration. *Manuscript ownership of Elizabeth Martin (1743). The first American edition of the Ausbund.* As well as being a major source of devotional songs, these Ausbunds contain valuable information on the persecution and sufferings of the Swiss / European martyrs. *GLP/USA* 25, Evans 4884, Seid. p. 14, Hild. 746. $ 340.00

THE SAUR AUSBUND OF 1751=2

53. **AUSBUND, DAS IST ETLICHE SCHÖNE CHRISTLICHE LIEDER**... Christoph Saurer, Germantown: 1751=2. pp. 9, 812, 6, 46, 40. The first title page in this copy really does seem to read *1752*. Contemporary full leather. Spine needs restoration. Ds. *Stamped Franklin County(?) ownership of Jacob Hege*. A colored fragment of an early fraktur is included. *GLP/USA* 139, Evans 6632 / 6847, Hild. 1205, Seid. p. 36. $ 400.00

54. **AUSBUND, DAS IST ETLICHE SCHONE CHRISTLICHE LIEDER**... Leibert & Billmeyer, Germantown: 1785. pp. (10), 812, (10), 103. "Standard" text of the German American Ausbund. Original full leather. *GLP/USA* 627, Evans 18919, Seid. p. 116. $ 145.00

55. **AUSBUND, DAS IST: ETLICHE SCHONE CHRISTLICHE LIEDER**... Bär, Lancaster: 1834. pp. 5, 812, 11, 24, 12, 52 (Bound without "Sechs Schöne Geistliche Lieder"?). Thick 24mo. *John L. Stoltzfus' copy. Exceptional contemporary leather binding decorated with tooled brass corners, head and tail Bands, + a central brass in a crude tulip design.* AI 23025. $ 255.00

56. **AUSBUND, DAS IST ETLICHE SCHONE CHRISTLICHE LIEDER**... Lancaster: 1856. Over 900p. Leather boards with later cloth back. *Amos K. Beiler's copy.* $ 45.00

57. **AUSLEGUNG DER CHRISTLICHEN LEHRE, mit Kurzen Heilsamen Ermahnungen in vier Hauptstücke Abgetheilet**. Lepper, Hannover, Pa: 1802. 256p. Ds. Leather backed wallpaper boards. *GLP/USA* 1301, AI 1790. *Not in Seidensticker.* Scarce. $ 125.00

58. Bacon, Paul V. **IM VATERLAND**. Boston & Chi: 1910. 414+p. Illus. $ 12.00

59. Ballmer, Daniel. **EINE SAMMLUNG VON NEUEN RECEPTEN UND BEWAHRTEN CUREN, Fur Menschen und Vieh**. Friedrich Goeb, Schellsburg: 1827. 40p. *GLP/USA* 2899, Seid. p. 235, AI 27940. See also Item # 175. $ 85.00

Eine

Sammlung

von

Neuen Recepten

und

Bewährten Curen,

für Menschen und Vieh.

Zusammengetragen und zum Druck befördert von Daniel Ballmer, bey Chambersburg. Anno 1820.

Schellsburg:
Gedruckt bey Friedrich Goeb
1827.

60. **BALSAM FUR DAS VERWUNDETE HERZ, Trost & Mahnungs Lieder...** Skippacksville: 1857. 80p. 24mo. Scarce little (Schwenkfelder?) song book. *WST*. $ 35.00

61. Barclay, Robert. **ROBERT BARCLAY'S APOLOGIE...** **Christoph Saur III, Germantown:** 1776. pp. 797, 26. Ds. Contemporary full leather. The first German translation of Barclay's defense of the Quakers. *GLP/USA* 479, Evans 14659, Seid p. 93-4, Hild. 3333. $ 325.00

62. Barth, C. G. **DIE RABENFEDER. Eine Erzählung für die Jungend**. Amer. Tract Soc. NY. Circa: 1860. 64p. + Ill. "The Raven's Feather". $ 12.00

63. Barth. **DAS FELSENKIND. Eine Erzählung für die Jungend**. Amer. Tract Soc. NY. Ca: 1860. 118p. + Ill. "Child of the Rock". $ 15.00

64. **DAS BAUERN = JOURNAL. Eine Monatschrift für Feldbau, Gärtnerei, Obstkultur, Viehzucht, Hauswirthschaft, Etc**. Vol. I #1 - II #7. Allentown: 1857-8. pp. 192, 160. Complete run of this very important monthly agricultural journal. Extremely scarce. *Shoemaker/L p. 91/94 was unable to locate even one issue. WST*. $ 200.00

65. Bausman, Benj. **SINAI UND ZION**... Miller, Reading: 1875. 448p. + Illus. Cloth. German - American's travels in the holy land. $ 20.00

66. Baxter, Richard. **ZURUF AN UNBEKEHRTE**... American Tract Society. Fanshaw, NY. Ca: 1840. 202p. XLib. Bright contemporary full leather. *HSH*. $ 20.00

UNUSUAL FRAKTUR BOOKPLATE

67. Becker, Christ. **DER ALLGEGENWARTIGE DEUTSCHE SPRACHLEHRER DES WORTES GOTTES**... Hütter, Easton: 1808. Four parts in one vol. 148p. Leather backed boards. *Full-page flyleaf fraktur bookplate for Susann Hendrick, 1810. Initialed by the artist "A. L." The bookplate is in a rectangular frame, and shows a 1/2 page drawing, in several colors, of a tree in leaf. GLP/USA* 1593, Seid. p. 172, AI 14462-3. $ 450.00

68. Becker. **DER DEUTSCHEN ALLGEGEN-WARTIGER ENGLISHER SPRACHLEHRER DES WORTES GOTTES**... Hütter, Easton: 1809-10. Three parts in one volume. 256p. + Woodcut frontis & foldouts. Leather backed boards. Includes a fine list of subscribers and an *unusual broadside ad telling where Hütter's publications are sold. German Manuscript on front flyleaf tells how George Sleeger (Schleeger) bought this book for 7/6 from Mr. Schnitor, his schoolmaster in Windsor Twp., York County*. See the long bibliographic entry in *GLP/USA* 1721, Seid. p. 174, AI 16970. Scarce and interesting. $ 75.00

69. (Becker, Christian?). **DAS UNENTBEHRLICHE BUCH FÜR DIE DEUTSCHEN BUERGER IN NORD AMERICA...** Hütter, Easton & Allentown: 1816. 391p. + Folding Charts. Some text in English. Ds. *Manuscript ownership = "Jacob Leibert, July 17th, 1829. Bought in Easton for $ 1.25."* *GLP/USA* 2138, AI 39138, Seid. p. 196. *WST.* $ 50.00

70. Becker. **DEINE SAMMLUNG NEUER GEISTREICHER PREDIGTEN...** Magill & Cleim, Baltimore: 1810. 264p. Full leather. *GLP/USA* 1712, Seid. p. 177, AI 19491. $ 36.00

71. Becker. **DAS 53 CAPITEL JESAIA...** Bremen: 1786. 48p. + 14p. *Supplied in manuscript, written by Rev. P. Gloninger (of Harrisburg, Baltimore, Lebanon, Etc.). With Gloninger's printed label.* Curious and uncommon mystical work. *HSH.* $ 100.00

72. Becker. **KURZER ENTWURF DER CHRISTLICHEN LEHRE.** Schäffer & Maund, Baltimore: 1817. 26p. 16mo. Lovely color printed floral wraps. *GLP/USA* 2194 [3 Copies only], AI 40160. *WST.* $ 75.00

73. Becker. **KURZER ENTWURF DER CHRISTLICHEN LEHRE, in Fragen un Entworten. Zum Unterricht der Jungend.** Blumer, Allentown: 1838. 60p. 16mo. *Apparently Not in AI.* Shoemaker/L p. 60. *WST.* $ 34.00

74. Becker. **KURZER ENTWURF DER CHRISTLICHEN LEHRE, in Fragen un Entworten. Zum Unterricht der Jungend.** Weber, (Hellertown): 1850. 63p. 16mo. $ 50.00

75. Beiler, David [1786-1871]. **DAS WAHRE CHRISTENTHUM. Eine Christliche Betrachtung nach den Lehren der Heiligen Schrift.** Bär, Lancaster: 1888. 302p. Original full leather. One of the few thoroughly Amish books. $ 60.00

76. Beiler. **DAS WAHRE CHRISTENTHUM. Eine Christliche Betrachtung nach den Lehren der Heiligen Schrift.** Gordonville, PA: 1976. 302p. 24mo. Library cloth. $ 12.00

77. **BEN HOLT'S GUTER NAME...** Amer. Tract Soc. NY. Ca: 1860. 96p. + Frontis. Chipped cloth. Very popular children's tale. $ 10.00

78. Benedict. **DER HEILGE BENEDIKT und Seine Orden...** NY & Cinn: 1874. 224p. Includes a catalog of German Catholic Books. Morocco cloth. $ 11.00

ARMBRUSTER'S FIRST BOOK?

79. Benkendorf, Henry. **SELIGER MARTER=STAND DER ERSTEN CHRISTEN...** Anton Armbruster, Philadelphia: 1753. 326p. *Plus a previously unrecorded 2p. Subscribers List. Contemporary full leather binding probably by David Limbeck.* Little known, but important martyrological handbook. Extremely interesting printed list of (German) American subscribers [showing only 83 names]. *Extensive 1784 German American manuscript ownership of Felix H. Dennbrant.* *GLP/USA* 159A, Evans 6924, Hild. 1290, Seid. p. 41. Rare. $ 450.00

80. Benner, Enos. **ABHANDLUNG UBER DIE RECHENKUNST, Practische Arithmetik.** Sumnytown, Pa: 1833. 152p. Full leather. Early manuscript ownership. Scarce school text. AI 17731. Benner was from Charleston, Bucks County, Pa. $ 30.00

81. (Bergleit, Joseph). **MARIANISCHES BLUMEN-GÄRTLEIN, Oder Vollständisches Gebet-Buch zu der Schmerzhaften Mutter Gottes, Maria...** Hartman, Lebanon: 1820. pp. 18, 432 (of 437?). Full leather. Worn. *GLP/USA* 2442, AI 2103. $ 100.00

82. Bernheim, Johann H. **DAS ABENDMAHL DES HERRN. Oder Betrachtungen uber Basselbe...** Baxter, Elizabethtown, Pa: 1834. 228p. Full leather. AI 23296. Curious text on the Lord's Last Supper. $ 20.00

83. (Bersch, Wilhelm). **ANEKDOTEN VON SONNTAGS=SCHULEN.** New Berlin: 1842. 120p. Woodcut on Titlepage. 24mo. Scarce children's book. Published for the Evangelical Association. *WST.* $ 50.00

BIBLES

PRESENTED TO MUHLENBERG

84. **BIBLIA, DAS IST...** Foreword by Hieronymo Burkhardt. Basel: 1741. Over 1150p. 12mo. Gilt tooled morocco. Boards detached. ***Warm Manuscript Presentation from John William Jäger (Yeager) to Dr. (Henry Melchior) Muhlenberg, Hannover, 14 April 1744.*** Rare. $ 250.00

THE GREAT SAUR BIBLE OF 1743.
THE FIRST BIBLE PRINTED IN AMERICA
IN A EUROPEAN LANGUAGE.

85. **BIBLIA, DAS IST: Die Heilge Schrift Altes und Neues Testaments...** Christoph Saur, Germantown: 1743. pp. (4), 995, (2), 277, (7). 4to. Ds. Title page printed in Red & Black. Contemporary full leather binding (hinges weak). Fine pointillé decorated copper or brass corner and center bosses, as well as a most unusual brass fixture for a center spine band. There are also remains of brass letters and numbers: (A. S.) 1 (7) 6 (1). An unusual copy of this very rare and important book. Long recognized as the first Bible in a Western language to be printed in North America. It is a book so rare & significant that copies sold in the 19th century brought $ 350.00, or more. Please note that this copy is new to the market, and has never been previously cataloged. *GLP/USA* 47, Evans 5127, Hild. 804, Seid. p. 20, O'Callaghan "*American Bibles*" p. 22, Wright "*Early Bibles in America*" p. 24-50. Additional details upon request. $ 4800.00

BIBLIA,
Das ist:
Die
Heilige Schrift
Altes und Neues
Testaments,
Nach der Deutschen Uebersetzung
D. Martin Luthers,
Mit jedes Capitels kurtzen Summarien, auch
beygefügten vielen und richtigen Parallelen;
Nebst einem Anhang
Des dritten und vierten Buchs Esra und des
dritten Buchs der Maccabäer.
Germantown:
Gedruckt bey Christoph Saur, 1743.

86. **BIBLIA, DAS IST: Die Ganze Heilige Schrifft...** Edited by Frantz Ludwig Sprünglin. Schaffhausen: 1743. pp. 1348, 372 + *Numerous finely engraved bibical and emblematic plates.* Many early Anabaptists settled in the Swiss city and canton of Schauffhausen; including this Bible's owner = Salomon Kramer. Apparently, Kramer emigrated to America in the 19th Century (perhaps with the Mennonite Sprungers). $ 375.00

87. **BIBLIA, DAS IST: Die Ganze Gottliche Heilige Schrift...** Nürenberg: 1747. 1100+p. Numerous Woodcut Illustrations + Plates of the Electors. Folio. Contemporary full leather binding with brass bosses. Spine perished. Early Manuscript ownerships. $ 225.00

88. **BIBLIA, Die Ganze Gottliche Heilige Schrift...** Basel: 1747. 1000+p. + Engraved Frontis. Numerous fine small woodcut Illustrations (many signed "C.M."). Some leaves repaired with slight loss. Folio. Early full leather. The boards are tooled with a distinctive floral and pine cone roll; and the raised bands are outlined with a palmetto roll. We believe the binding to be the work of a (still unidentified) Lancaster County artisan. $ 250.00

EPHRATA BINDING

89. **BIBLIA...** (Basel: 1747). Grossly incomplete. Thick 12mo. ***Full leather Ephrata binding. Head and tail bands intact, each with five squared brass bosses. Both boards with brass corner and center bosses; plus some tooling in blind.*** No clasps. Early manuscript Lancaster ownership. Handsome and characteristic example of the binding style attributed to the Ephrata Cloisters. Sold as a binding only. $ 250.00

90. **BIBLIA, DAS IST**... Nürenberg: 1755. 1100+p. Woodcut Illustrations. Very worn, with some loss. Folio. The contemporary pigskin binding with brass bosses, is apparently of American manufacture; and was executed, perhaps, in Ephrata. $ 200.00

91. **BIBLIA DAS IST**... Halle: 1761. pp. 1079, 300+. Suede-like binding. $ 40.00

92. **BIBLIA, DAS IST**... Christoph Saur (II), Germantown: 1763. pp. 4, 992, 227, 3. Mid-19th century full morocco. Printed on paper entirely of American origin. ***In German fraktur manuscript: "Bought in Lancaster on November 8, 1764 by Elizabeth Becker" + Extensive manuscript record of the Stahl/Stuhl family.*** Nice copy of the 2nd American Bible printed in a Western language. For details please see: *GLP/USA* 269, Evans 9343, Seid. p. 61, Hild. 1877, O'Callaghan p. 25. $ 950.00

UNIQUE EVIDENCE IN THE PRINTING HISTORY OF THE SAUR BIBLES

93. **BIBLIA, DAS IST**... Christoph Saur, Germantown: 1763. pp. 4, 992, 227, 3. Last leaf with slight loss. Contemporary full leather. ***This unique copy has a 1776 Saur titlepage overprinted, by type, with the (17)"63" date.*** The New Testament title, and most of the body text is that of the 1763 bible. ** For several years we have hypothesized that some few copies of the quarto Saur bibles were made up from sheets of different editions. We speculated that the Saurs, or their successors, even occasionally printed up missing sheets to complete bibles for patrons. This process of making up copies was not an uncommon practice - when printers and publishers were dealing with a large work, available "in print" over a period of years. This would explain the many anomalies of text, state, and legend that have been noticed within the Saur Bible corpus. We are very pleased to offer this remarkable copy as both evidence of these suppositions and fodder for future research. *GLP/USA* 269. $1600.00

THE PENNYPACKER / PANNEBECKER FAMILY BIBLE

94. **BIBLIA, DAS IST**... Christoph Saur, Germantown: 1776. pp. 6, 992, 277, 3. Thick 4to. Contemporary full leather. Hinges broken. Old repair to Tp. The first Bible printed with American type. ***Extensive 18th Century Decorated Manuscript Ownerships and Genealogical / Astrological Information Relating to the Märÿ, Pennypacker, Pannebecker, and Longenacker Families.*** The several 19th Century translations and notes include some by Governor Pennypacker. A fine association copy of the great "Bible of the American Revolution". For the story of how most of the edition was supposed to have been destroyed in the Revolutionary War, See: Rumball-Petre "*America's First Bibles*". *GLP/USA* 475, Seid. p. 93, Hild. 3336, Evans 13834, O'Callaghan p. 29. $1400.00

95. **BIBLIA, DAS IST**... Christoph Saur, Germantown: 1776. pp. 6, 992, 277, 3. Thick 4to. Contemporary full leather. Hinges broken. Boards tooled with a decorative frame (once sprinkled in contrasting colors). ***Manuscript ownership of George Miller [1794-1869].*** *GLP/USA* 475. *WST.* $ 950.00

96. **DIE BIBEL, Oder die ganze Heilige Schrift**... Halle: 1782. pp. 1079 + Fragment of New Testament. ***Important German Manuscript Birth and Baptismal note for the children of Theobald Gut(h): Carolina Elisabet and Jacob - in the hand of, and signed by (Gotthilf) Henrich (Ernst) Muhlenberg.*** $ 275.00

97. **DIE BIBEL**... Halle: 1797. pp. 1079, 312. Very worn. Extensive Luft (Light) family Manuscript genealogical record. *HSH.* $ 100.00

98. **BIBLIA DAS IST: Die Ganze Gottliche Heilige Schrift**... Basel: 1798. Over 1100p. Several large woodcut illustrations. Folio. Brass corner bosses decorated in a flaming heart motif. Needs some restoration. ***Colored 1889 American Manuscript presentation to David B. Seidel.*** Certainly, one of the Bibles most prized by the Pennsylvania Germans. $ 175.00

99. **BIBLIA, DAS IST**... Erste Auflage. Gottlob Jungmann, Reading: 1805. pp. 1008, 280. Thick 4to. Full Leather. Front board detached. The first quarto edition of the German Bible in America, after those of Saur. In the preface, Jungmann noted that the use of German was waning so quickly, that he wondered if there would ever be a need in America for another German Bible. *The Weigand / Schirk Family Copy. Probably owned by the famous Pennsylvania-Dutch author Conelius Weygant. GLP/USA* 1467, Seid. p. 166, AI 7984. $ 250.00

100. **BIBLIA, DAS IST**... Jungmann, Reading: 1805. Thick 4to. Full Leather. $ 140.00

THE SOMERSET BIBLE

101. **BIBLIA, DAS IST**... Die Erste Auflage. Friederich Goeb, Somerset, Pa: 1813. pp. 527, 66, 169. This copy lacks two leaves of Apocrypha, and has some old repairs. Worn full leather. Folio. *The first Bible printed West of the Allegheny Mountains.* Goeb wrote the preface, and annotated the first five books of Moses. Increasingly scarce. *GLP/USA* 2004, Seid. 190, AI 27883, Wright p. 153-4, O'Callaghan 114. $ 300.00

102. **DIE BIBEL**... Halle: 1815. pp. 1079, 310. Full leather. Thick 16mo. *Manuscript ownership of Maria Ensminger. HSH.* $ 40.00

103. **DIE BIBEL**... Halle: 1815. Approx. 1400p. Very worn full leather. Thick 16mo. *Attractive fraktur Manuscript ownership of "Eleisa Valentin, Maÿers=taun, Heidelberg Twp. [Lebanon County], 1817." HSH.* $ 100.00

104. **DIE BIBEL**... Halle: 1816. 1389p. Ds. Worn full leather. Thick 24mo. $ 25.00

105. **DIE BIBEL**... Basel: 1816. 666p. Ds. Nice Manuscript ownership. $ 24.00

106. **BIBLIA, DAS IST**... Bär, Lancaster: 1819. pp. Subscribers List (5), 100, 13, 738, 227, 92 + 2 Plates (Engraved by John Henry). Folio. *Outstanding contemporary full polished calf. Attractively tooled in gilt.* No clasps. Clean & handsome copy. *The first folio German Bible printed in America.* When new, this Bible cost ten day's wages. *GLP/USA* 2363, Seid. 207, AI 47206, Wright 154, O'Callaghan p. 146-7. $ 250.00

BIBLIA,
Das ist:
Die ganze
Heilige Schrift
Alten und Neuen Testaments.
Nach der Deutschen Uebersetzung
von
Doctor Martin Luther.
Mit lehrreichen Vorreden, und vielen nützlichen und seltenen Registern versehen.
Zugleich:
Eine kurz gefaßte Biblische Geschichte
und
Lebensbeschreibung Doctor Martin Luthers.
Lancaster, (Penn.)
1819.

107. **BIBLIA, DAS IST**... Bär, Lancaster: 1819. Same as above. Folio. *Full leather with a chained blind stamped roll crisscrossed on the boards.* This Lancaster, Pa. decorative binder's roll can probably be safely ascribed to Henry Miller. $ 275.00

108. **BIBLIA, DAS IST**... Lancaster: 1819. Same As Above. Full leather. Front board detached, but with the printed binder's label of Henrich Miller. $ 140.00

109. **DIE BIBLE**... Ritter, Phila: 1827. Very thick 4to. pp. 1560, 462. Tp. mounted w/slight loss. Worn full leather. *GLP/USA* 2878, AI 28112. *Not in Seid.* $ 65.00

110. **DIE BIBLE**... Howe for Mentz, Phila: 1828. Over 1000p. Full leather. Worn & Ds. *GLP/USA* 2963, Seid. p. 239, AI 32281. Early Manuscript ownerships. $ 30.00

111. **DIE BIBLE**... Mentz & Son, Phila: 1831. 1456p. + Woodcut illus. [One Signed by "Gilbert"]. *Manuscript Holsinger family record.* Contemporary full leather with clasps. $ 40.00

112. **DIE BIBLE**... Mentz, Phila: 1849. 1300+p. + Illus. Really pretty contemporary full mottled calf with clasps. $ 40.00

113. **DIE BIBLE...** Amerikanischen Bibel-Gesellschaft (American Bible Society), NY: 1844. Full leather. Worn. $ 18.00

114. **DIE BIBEL...** Stuttgart: 1846. pp. 1100, 327. Contemporary blind tooled alum-tawed vellum binding with clasps. Decorated with an unusual palmetto design similar to the tool used by Edwards of Halifax. *Extensive Manuscript ownerships of the Maÿer Family.* $ 80.00

115. **DIE BIBLE...** Amer. Bible Soc. NY: 1847. 1100+p. Leather. $ 20.00

116. **DIE BIBLE...** Amer. Bible Soc. NY: 1851. 1100+p. Embossed full leather. *Pretty fraktur manuscript record of the Hassler Family, Berks County.* Useful genealogy. $ 50.00

117. **DIE BIBLE...** Amer. Bible Soc. NY: 1867. 1100+p. Embossed full leather. $ 20.00

118. **DIE BIBLE...** Amer. Bible Soc. NY: 1893. 1100+p. Soft morocco. AEG. $ 16.00

119. **BIBLIA DAS IST...** Kimber & Sharpless, Philadelphia. Ca: 1840. 992p. + Plates. Full leather. Large 4to. *Curious Brand/Brandt family genealogical record.* $ 50.00

120. **BIBLIA DAS IST...** Kimber & Sharpless, Phila. Ca: 1840. 992p + Plates. Full leather. 4to. *Extensive Kaufman family (Lebanon County) genealogical record.* $ 40.00

121. **BIBLIA DAS IST...** Kimber & Sharpless, Phila. Ca: 1840. Boards detached. 4to. *Extensive Sprenkel / Landes / Sheets family (York County) genealogical record.* $ 40.00

122. **DIE GROSSE ALLGEMEINE VOLKS=BILDERBIBEL...** King & Baird, for Kohler, Phila: 1856. Over 1500p. + Illustrations + Chromolithographed title + Family Register. Each page framed in a decorative woodcut border. Thick 4to. Full leather very handsomely tooled in blind and gilt. Brass clasps. Marbled edges. In the Nineteenth Century, attractive bibles like this cost a week's wages. $ 120.00

BIBLES = NEW TESTAMENTS

123. **DAS APOKRYPHISCHE NEUE TESTAMENT...** (Bär) Lancaster: 1830. 484p. First American Edition. Unusual. *GLP/USA* 3106, AI 462, Seid. p. 246. $ 50.00

124. **DAS NEUE TESTAMENT...** Christoph Saur, Germantown: 1763. pp. 4, 646 [of 679]. Some other leaves with slight loss. Worn. *Manuscript ownership of Tobius Koch. GLP/USA* 270, Evans 9347, Hild. 1910, Seid. p. 69. Scarce. $ 200.00

125. **DAS NEUE TESTAMENT...** Hanau: 1795. 694p. Worn full leather. Early [1800]. Lancaster County manuscript ownership. *HSH.* $ 40.00

Das Neue
Testament
unsers
HErrn und Heilandes
JEsu Christi,
nach der Teutschen Uebersetzung
D. Martin Luthers.
Mit kurzem
Inhalt eines jeden Capitels,
und
Vollständiger Anweisung gleicher Schriftstellen.
Wie auch
aller Sonn- und Festtägigen
Evangelien und Episteln.
Zweyte Auflage.
Germantaun:
Gedruckt bey Michael Billmeyer, 1795.

126. **DAS NEUE TESTAMENT...** Michael Billmeyer, Germantown: 1795. pp. 537, 5. Old full leather with clasps. *GLP/USA* 977, Evans 28287, Seid. p. 141, O'Callaghan p. 50. $ 140.00

127. **DAS NEUE TESTAMENT...** Carl Cist, Phila: 1796. pp. 4, 525, 3. Full leather. Really clean and crisp copy of this scarce edition. *GLP/USA* 1039, Evans 30082. *HSH.* $ 140.00

128. **DAS NEUE TESTAMENT...** Billmeyer, Germantown: 1803. 542p. Nice full leather with clasps. *Interesting manuscript ownerships of Jacob Schmidt. GLP/USA* 1336, Seid. p. 160, AI 3794. $ 40.00

NORTHAMPTON COUNTY BOOKPLATE

129. **DAS NEUE TESTAMENT...** Schweitzer, Phila: 1805. 537p. Full leather with clasps. Front board detached. *GLP/USA* 1463, AI 7996. ***With the 1810 monochrome Fraktur ownership of Tobias Fieman, Lower Saucon Township, Northampton County - decorated with a bird perched on a folksy tulip in a vase.*** Though the ink has bled, and the design is rather crude, it is still an attractive and curious plate. $ 225.00

130. **DAS NEUE TESTAMENT...** Billmeyer, Germantown: 1808. 532p. Worn full leather. *GLP/USA* 1598, Seid. p. 172, AI 14489. XLib. *HSH.* $ 40.00

131. **DAS NEUE TESTAMENT...** Sechste Auflage. Billmeyer, Germantown: 1810. 540p. Lacks front bd. *GLP/USA* 1727, Seid. p. 178, AI 19519 $ 20.00

SOMERSET NEW TESTAMENT

132. **DAS NEUE TESTAMENT...** Die Erste Auflage. Friedrich Goeb, Somerset, Pa: 1814. pp. 537, 3. Full leather binding. ***First New Testament separately printed west of the Alleghenies. Messimore Manuscript Family Record.*** *GLP/USA* 2059, Seid. p. 193, AI 30871. $ 340.00

133. **DAS NEUE TESTAMENT...** Siebente Auflage. Billmeyer, Phila: 1815. 540p. Really nice full leather w/ clasps. *GLP/USA* 2098, AI 34075. ***Manuscript ownership of Anna Ranck.*** Thirteen pretty calligraphic lines written March 20, 1820. $ 80.00

134. **DAS NEUE TESTAMENT...** Billmeyer, Germantown: 1815. 540p. Nice full leather with clasps. *GLP/USA* 2098, AI 34075. $ 40.00

135. **DAS NEUE TESTAMENT...** Billmeyer, Germantown: 1819. 540p. Early Manuscript ownerships. Attractive full leather w/clasps. *GLP/USA* 2341, AI 47219. $ 35.00

MONTGOMERY COUNTY FRAKTUR BOOKPLATE

136. **DAS NEUE TESTAMENT...** Johann Bär, Lancaster: 1821. 523p. Full leather. ***Attractive Manuscript Bookplate / Birth Record for Hanna Dannehauer (Daughter of Elizabeth Gross), born 1813, Malboro Twp., Montgomery County.*** *GLP/USA* 2497, Seid. p. 214, AI 4684. $ 280.00

137. **DAS NEUE TESTAMENT...** Johann Bär, Lancaster: 1821. 523p. Full leather. Ds. XLib. *GLP/USA* 2497, Seid. p. 214, AI 4684. $ 24.00

138. **DAS NEUE TESTAMENT...** Neunte Auflage. Billmeyer, Germantown: 1822. 540p. Nice full leather w/clasps. Ms. ownerships. *GLP/USA* 2535, Seid. 216, AI 8025. $ 30.00

DOUBLE PAGE MENNONITE FRAKTUR BOOKPLATE

139. **DAS NEUE TESTAMENT...** Billmeyer, Germantown: 1822. 540p. Broken full leather. ***Delightfully decorated colored floral double page bookplate of Jacob Joder (Yoder). Drawn on February 23, 1821. A fine calligraphic plate bordered with vines and flowers. Though somewhat damaged by damp and wear, the colors and design are still impressive. The lettering and decorations are in black, brown, red, yellow, and blue-green.*** Please see also # 633 for another very attractive Yoder Book Plate. $ 1250.00

140. **DAS NEUE TESTAMENT.** Moser & Peters, Carlisle: 1825. 516p. Illus. Worn full leather. The Moser & Peters New Testaments were the first to be stereotyped in America. *Not in Seidensticker. GLP/USA* 2724, AI 19698. $ 40.00

141. **DAS NEUE TESTAMENT.** Moser & Peters, Carlisle: 1826. 516p. Full leather. *Manuscript Fraktur Bookplate of Mary Ann Teis, penned in 1826. Nice calligraphy framed in yellow drapery.* One small hole. *GLP/USA* 2788, Seid. p. 228, AI 23788. $ 150.00

142. **DAS NEUE TESTAMENT...** Ritter, Phila: 1828. 542p. Disbound. 16mo. *GLP/USA* 2970, AI 32318, Seid. p. 239. Possibly printed in Germany for Ritter, or from plates imported by him. *Manuscript ownership of Adelheid Dechant [1830].* $ 24.00

143. **DAS NEUE TESTAMENT...** Mentz, Phila: 1834. 504p. + Illus. Full leather with clasps. Spine taped. AI 23364. $ 32.00

144. **DAS NEUE TESTAMENT.** Peters, Harrisburg: 1834. 516p. Full mottled calf with clasps. Woodcuts in good state. XLib. AI 23363 *[1 location only]. HSH.* $ 50.00

145. **DAS NEUE TESTAMENT...** Grater, Allentown: 1835. 566p. + Engraved plates. Attractive full leather. Probably printed in Europe for Grater. *WST.* $ 40.00

146. **DAS NEUE TESTAMENT...** Paris: 1835. 365p. Ownership and ephemeral inserts of Louisa Kuntz (Lancaster or York, Pa?). Unusual German edition printed in Paris. $ 30.00

147. **DAS NEUE TESTAMENT...** Mentz, Phila: 1837. 504p. + Illus. Full leather with clasps. AI 43204. $ 22.00

148. **DAS NEUE TESTAMENT...** Mentz, Phila: 1840. 504p. + Illus. Full leather w/ clasps. XLib. *Lizzie Holstein's copy - Millbach. HSH.* $ 40.00

149. **DAS NEUE TESTAMENT...** Wyeth, Harrisburg: 1840. 472p. + Engraved plates. Pretty gilt decorated full leather. XLib. *HSH.* $ 20.00

150. **DAS NEUE TESTAMENT.** Amer. Bible Soc. NY: 1840. 24mo. Old worn full leather with the stamp of the "Young Men's Bible Society of Phila.". *Manuscript Fraktur Ownership of Jacob Spengler. HSH.* $ 40.00

151. **DAS NEUE TESTAMENT... Mit Erklärungen und Nutzanwendungen...** Daniel Dobler, Editor & Publisher. Miller, Lebanon: 1840. pp. 10, 428. Full leather. Unusual version that includes Mathew & Mark only. $ 40.00

152. **DAS NEUE TESTAMENT...** Mentz, Phila: 1841. 504p. + Illustrations. $ 16.00

153. **DAS NEUE TESTAMENT...** Bär, Lancaster: 1844. 537p. Full leather. $ 22.00

154. **DAS NEUE TESTAMENT.** Amer. Bible Soc. NY: 1844. 24mo. Worn. $ 12.00

LEHIGH COUNTY FRAKTUR BOOKPLATE

155. **DAS NEUE TESTAMENT.** Mentz & Rouvoudt, Phila: 1845. 504p. + Illus. Worn full leather. *With the 1845 bookplate of Sarah Miller. The unusual diamond and wave decorated border is penned in brown, red, and yellow.* A bright and really rather handsome example. $ 500.00

BRILLIANTLY COLORED FRAKTUR BOOKPLATE

156. **DAS NEUE TESTAMENT.** Mentz, Phila. Circa: 1850. 504p. + Illus. Full leather without clasps. *With the splendid colored fraktur bookplate of Mery Aenn Schnÿder (Mary Ann Snyder), Hilltown Township, Bucks County, 1853.* Though once damped, the glossy reds, yellows, blues and greens of the rising sun and decorative borders are still bright and handsome. $ 500.00

157. **DAS NEUE TESTAMENT.** American Bible Society, New York: 1851. Nice embossed morocco with clasp. 24mo. *J. H. Borneman's copy.* $ 20.00

BARBARA EBERSOL BOOKPLATE

158. **DAS NEUE TESTAMENT...** Bär, Lancaster: 1871. 537p. Worn full leather. *Though unsigned, this colorful (but worn) plate, with an octagonal central flower, was certainly drawn by the dwarf Amish artist Barbara Ebersol, for Lidia Stoltzfuss, August 19, 1887.* $ 325.00

159. **THE NEW TESTAMENT = IN ENGLISH & GERMAN.** American Bible Society, NY: 1854. 670p. Decorated morocco. $ 20.00

160. **THE NEW TESTAMENT = IN ENGLISH & GERMAN.** American Bible Society, NY: 1870. Full embossed morocco. $ 14.00

161. **THE NEW TESTAMENT = IN ENGLISH & GERMAN.** American Bible Society, NY: 1872. Full embossed morocco. Worn. $ 10.00

162. **DAUT NIEHE TASTAMENT.** Scottdale: 1988. 483p. The New Testament translated into Low German by J. J. Neufeld. $ 20.00

163. **HET NIEUWE TESTAMENT...** Bound With / **De Pslamen Davids...** Amsterdam: 1730. 700+p. Music in Shaped Notes. Ds. *Several early American Manuscript ownerships including: Jacob Ross (1777).* $ 75.00

=

END BIBLES

164. **BIBLISCHE GESCHICHTEN Alten und Neuen Testaments.** Allentown: 1883. 242p. 125 Illustrations. Probably printed in Philadelphia. Shoemaker/L p. 156. *WST.* $ 20.00

165. Biethe, W. **DER SCHLOSSER VON PHILADELPHIA...** Reading: 1895. 80p. + Illus. 24mo. Decorated cloth. Tale of a Philadelphia Locksmith. $ 12.00

166. **(BIOGRAPHIEN) BERUHMTE DEUTSCHE VORKAMPFER für Fortschritt, Freiheit und Friede in Nord=Amerika, 1626-1888.** Cleveland: 1888. 500p. + Illus. Interesting biographies of famous, and near-famous German Americans. *WST.* $ 40.00

167. Birmelin, John. **MAMMI GANS.** Dialect Nursery Rhymes [Mother Goose] Selected by Dr. P. A. Barba from a Group of 278 Children's Poems. Allentown. Ca: 1949. 28p. Original printed wraps. $ 12.00

168. Birmelin. **'S HEISEL IM HOF.** (Allentown, Ca: 1938). 7p. Printed wraps. 24mo. Warm inscription to *WST.* $ 22.00

169. **BLEIBET IN MEINER LIEBE, Lehr=und Gebetbuch für Katholische Jünglinge und Jungfrauen...** Einsledeln, NY, Cinn. & St. Louis. Ca: 1880. 537p. 32mo. Brass bound embossed leather. $ 15.00

170. **BLUTHEN UND FRUCHTE, Erzählungen für die Jugend = I.** Printed in Germany(?) for Brumder, Milwaukee. Ca: 1876. 63p. Printed boards. 24mo. *WST.* $ 20.00

171. **BLUTHEN UND FRUCHTE, Erzählungen für die Jugend = XI.** For Brumder, Milwaukee and Brobst, Allentown. Ca: 1876. 63p. Printed boards. 24mo. *WST.* $ 20.00

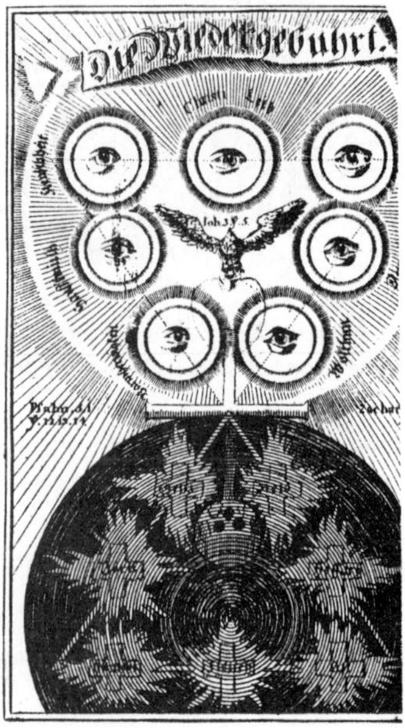

THE ONLY COPY KNOWN WITH SEVEN PLATES?

172. Böhme, Jacob . **CHRISTOSOPHIA, Oder Der Weg zu Christo...** Jacob Ruth, Ephrata: 1811-12. 396p. + ***Seven** Remarkable Engraved Mystical Plates.* Apparently, copies with the portrait and extra plate are almost unknown. Full leather. *1824 Ownership of Gottlieb Ottinger.* First American Edition. *GLP/USA* 1805, AI 22416, Seid. p. 181. Boehme's [1575-1624], theosophical works were very popular among the metaphysically minded Pennsylvania Germans. $ 200.00

173. Böhme. **CHRISTOSOPHIA...** Jacob Ruth, Ephrata: 1811-12. 396p. + Five Engraved Plates (As Usual). Leather backed boards. *Early Ownership of John Enck.* $ 130.00

174. Bogatzky, K. H. von. **GULDENS SCHATZ = KASTLEIN DER KINDER GOTTES...** Conrad Zentler, Phila: 1811. pp. 6, 365, 23. Oblong 24mo. Full leather. Bogatzky's [1690=1774], most popular work. Because of its sincerely warm piety, and simplicity of expression it stands among the best and most influential products of "Halle Pietistism". Widely read in Mennonite and Amish homes. *GLP/USA* 1853, AI 22419, Seid. p. 183. $ 70.00

Carl Heinrich von Bogatzky
Güldenes
Schatz=Kästlein
der Kinder Gottes,
deren Schatz im Himmel ist;
bestehend
in auserlesenen Sprüchen der heiligen Schrift,
sammt beygefügten erbaulichen Anmerkungen und Reimen.
Philadelphia,
gedruckt bey Conrad Zentler,
für Georg W. Menz, No. 71, in der Rehs=Straße, zwischen
der Zweyten und Dritten Straße.
1811.

VALUABLE COLLECTION OF CURES FOR MAN & BEAST

175. Bolmer, Paul. **EINE SAMMLUNG VON NEUEN RECEPTEN UND ERPROBTEN KUREN FÜR MENSCHEN UND THIERE.** Phila: 1838. 33p. Woodcut illustrated wraps. *Apparently Not in AI.* See also Item # 59. $ 140.00

176. Bösche, Edward Theo. **ALLGEMEINE BESCHREIBUNG DER ERDE...** Phila: 1840. 793p. Woodcut illustrations + *A rarely found Colored Map of the World (torn at folds) with text in German*, XLib. *HSH.* $ 90.00

THE GREAT EPHRATA MARTYR'S MIRROR

177. Braght, Tielman Jans van [1625=64]. **DER BLUTIGE SCHAU = PLATZ ODER MARTYRER = SPIEGEL DER TAUFFS GESINNTEN ODER WEHRLOSEN = CHRISTEN...** Bruderschafft, Ephrata in Pennsylvania: 1748=9. Two volumes in one. pp. 56, 478, 949, 11. Variation: + Engraved Baptismal Frontis; p. 72 = Four Flowers; p. 133 = Ephrata Lilly; No pagination error = 676-8. Full leather Ephrata binding (rebacked). With the original heavy brass corner bosses; two handsome brass center bosses; and studded head, tail and rarely seen center (!) bands. *Important early German manuscript ownership of Brethren elder Jonas Ürner which demonstrates how highly esteemed was this copy: "This book had belonged to our grand mother Anna Ürner / and after that it fell to our cousin Estes Schweitzer who presented it to me and my siblings / The price when new was 40 shillings / Now I paid David Reinhart 10 shillings / and to Abraham Ditlo 10 shillings / Now 3 quarters are mine and 1 quarter belongs to my brother Martin / My brother's part I finally also paid for".* Cornerstone text for the Pennsylvania German Sectarians, and a monument of the pioneer press in America. The largest and, in many ways, the most remarkable book of the entire Colonial period. For further details please see: *GLP/USA* 96, Evans 6256, Hild. 1050, Seid. p. 30, Sachse, Wroth, et. al.
$3600.00

Der Blutige Schau-Platz oder Martyrer Spiegel der Tauffs Gesinnten oder Wehrlosen-Christen,
Die um des Zeugnuß JEsu ihres Seligmachers willen gelitten haben, und seynd getödtet worden, von Christi Zeit an bis auf das Jahr 1660.
Vormals aus unterschiedlichen glaubwürdigen Chronicken, Nachrichten und Zeugnüssen gesammlet und in Holländischer Sprach heraus gegeben
von T. J. V. BRAGHT.
Nun aber sorgfältigst ins Hochteutsche übersetzt und zum erstenmal ans Licht gebracht.
EPHRATA in Pensylvanien,
Drucks und Verlags der Brüderschafft. Anno MDCCXLVIII.

178. Braght. **DER BLUTIGE SCHAU = PLATZ ODER MARTYRER=SPIEGEL DER TAUFFS GESINNTEN ODER WEHRLOSEN = CHRISTEN...** Bruderschafft, Ephrata in Pennsylvania: 1748=9. Two vols. in one. Title page repaired at margins. Variation: No frontis (as usual with copies owned by Mennonites); p. 72 = Winged Angel's Head; p. 133 = Basket of Flowers; No Pagination Error at 677-8. Later full leather with one clasp present. *Early Mennonite Manuscript Genealogy of the Kolb Family. Includes the birth of Jacob Kolb [1769-1858] who was the founder of several early Mennonite congregations in Ohio.* $2800.00

179. Braght. **DER BLUTIGE SCHAU=PLATZ, ODER MARTYRER SPIEGEL...** Ehrenfried, Lancaster: 1814. 2 vols in 1. Full leather. This 2nd American Edition is getting increasingly hard to find. *GLP/USA* 2023, Seid. p. 191, AI 30982. $ 220.00

180. Braght. **DER BLUTIGE SCHAU=PLATZ, ODER MARTYRER SPIEGEL...** Published by Shem Zook, Near Lewistown, Mifflin County, PA. Printed by King & Baird, Phila: 1849. pp. 340, 629, 6. 4to. Full mottled calf. No clasps. An important edition that is now infrequently encountered. $ 160.00

181. Braght. **DER BLUTIGE SCHAUPLATZ, ODER MARTYRER=SPIEGEL...** Aylmer, Ontario: 1973. pp. 635, 7. 4to. Modern reprint. Cloth. $ 32.00

182. (Braght). **KONKORDANZ ZU DEM MÄRTYRER=SPIEGEL.** (Elkhart: 1870?). 8p. 4to. A valuable index to the Martyr's Mirror. $ 25.00

183. Brastberger, I. G. **EVANGELISCHE ZEUGNISSE DER WAHRHEIT...** Grater, Allentown: 1834. Over 1100p. + Frontis. 4to. Attractive, stamped, alum tawed vellum binding. *WST*. Probably printed in Europe for Grater. $ 100.00

184. Brastberger. **EVANGELISCHE ZEUGNISSE DER WAHRHEIT...** Allentown: 1854. 32p. Plain wraps. 32mo. This little extract was certainly printed in Allentown, but it's *Not recorded in Shoemaker/L. WST.* $ 40.00

185. (Bredow, G. G.). **UMSTANDLICHERE ERZAHLUNG DER MERKWURDIGEN BEGEBENHEITEN AUS DER ALLGEMEINEN WELTGESCHICHTE... Fur Burger und Land Schulen...** Grater, Allentown: 1831. 640p. Leather backed boards. Interesting world history that includes America & Franklin. Shoemaker/L p. 52. Early Shaub ownership. *WST*. $ 55.00

186. (Brobst, S. K.). **CHRISTLICHE SCHUL - AGENDE für Sonntag = Schulen und den Kinder = Gottesdienst**. Erster Theil. Allentown: 1859. 30p. Self wraps. 24mo. Worn. Shoemaker/L p. 97. $ 20.00

187. (Brobst). **CHRISTLICHE SCHUL - AGENDE...** Allentown: 1872. 32p. Printed wraps. 24mo. Shoemaker/L p. 135. $ 12.00

188. (Brobst). **CHRISTLICHE SCHUL - AGENDE...** Allentown. Ca: 1880. 48p. Printed wraps. 24mo. *WST*. $ 10.00

189. (Brobst). **FRAGEBUCHLEIN UBER DIE ANFANGS=GRUNDE DER RELIGION...** Allentown: 1857. 31p. Printed wraps. 24mo. Shoemaker/L p. 93. *WST*. $ 22.00

190. (Brobst). **FRAGEBUCHLEIN...** Allentown: 1860. 32p. Crisp copy, in the original printed wraps. 24mo. Shoemaker/L p. 100 *[Locating this copy only]*. *WST*. $ 40.00

191. (Brobst). **FRAGE-BUCHLEIN...** Saeger & Leisenring, Allentown: 1865. 30p. Printed wraps. 24mo. Shoemaker/L p. 115 *[Locating this copy only]*. *WST*. $ 30.00

192. (Brobst). **FRAGEBUCHLEIN...** Allentown, Ca: 1867. 32p. Self wraps. 24mo. Shoemaker/L p. 182. *WST*. $ 20.00

193. (Brobst). **FRAGEN UBER DAS NEUE TESTAMENT...** Druckerei des "Jungendfreundes", Allentown: (1856). 36p. Printed wraps. Shoemaker/L p. 183 *[Recording this copy only]*. *WST*. $ 35.00

194. (Brobst). **FRAGEN UBER DAS NEUE TESTAMENT...** Ketterlinus, et. al. Allentown: 1858. 36p. Printed wraps. *Not in Shoemaker/L. WST.* $ 40.00

195. (Brobst). **DIE FUNF HAUPTSTUCKE DES KLEINEN KATECHISMUS...** Lippe for Brobst, Allentown. Ca: 1860. 32p. Plain wraps. 24mo. *Not in Shoemaker/L.* $ 20.00

196. (Brobst). **GEBETE FÜR SONNTAGS=SCHULEN...** Blumer & Busch, Allentown: 1847. 78p. 16mo. Leather backed marbled boards. 1st Ed. Shoemaker/L p. 74. *WST*. $ 26.00

197. (Brobst). **KINDER = SPEISE...** Allentown: 1864. 32p. Printed wraps. 32mo. Shoemaker/L p. 111. *WST*. $ 20.00

198. (Brobst). **KINDER = SPEISE...** Allentown: 1874. 28p. Printed wraps. 32mo. *Not in Shoemaker/L. WST.* $ 22.00

199. (Brobst). **LITURGISCHE GESANGE. Fur Singchore und Gemeinden...** Allentown: 1864. 16p. Oblong Pennsylvania German Song Book. No wraps. Shoemaker/L p. 111. Shaped Notes. Scarce. *WST*. $ 50.00

200. (Brobst, S. K.). **PRUFET DIE GEISTER...** Allentown: 1870. 96p. 32mo. Printed wraps. Manuscript notes. *WST.* $ 14.00

201. (Brobst). **SONNTAGS = SCHUL = GEBET = BUCH...** Allentown & Phila: 1862. 84p. 16mo. Cloth. Shoemaker/L p. 106. *WST.* $ 16.00

202. (Brobst). **TISCH; und Kinder = Gebete für Christlische Familien...** Allentown: 1868. 32p. Wraps. 32mo. Shoemaker/L p. 123. *WST.* $ 20.00

203. (Brobst). **200 FRAGEN UND ANTWORTEN Aus der Bibel, für Sonntags=Schulen...** Allentown: (1850). 28p. Plain wraps. 24mo. Shoemaker/L p. 79. *WST.* $ 32.00

204. **DAS BUCH ZUM TODTLACHEN, Erzählungen Lustiger Ränke und Schwänke für alle Altersklaffen...** Reutlingen & NY: 1870. 41p. Self Wraps. Humorous stories & jokes. $ 22.00

205. Buchanan/Fremont Presidential Election. **AN WAHRE DEMOCRATEN...** (Lancaster: 1856). 4p. Powerful arguments in support of Buchanan for U. S. President. $ 22.00

206. (Bückler). **LEBEN UND THATEN DES BERUCHTIGEN RAUBERS JOHANNES BUCKLER, GENNANT SCHINDERHANNES...** Zentler, Phila: 1818. Two volumes in one. pp. 124, 140. + Frontis. Ds. Sensational and riveting account of robbery, and the criminal life; including "Biblio-kleptomania". *GLP/USA* 2301, AI 43476/44551, Seid. p. 206. *WST.* $ 120.00

207. Buckshot War. **BERICHT DER ERNANNTEN COMMITTEE ZUR UNTERFUCHUNG DER VERANLASSUNG DER FRIEDENSTORUNG...** Harrisburg: 1839. 191p. + Folding charts. Original printed wraps. XLib. The bold, dangerous, and disgraceful dying gasps of Anti-Masonry Whigs in Pa. *HSH.* $ 75.00

16TH CENTURY TRAVELER'S GUIDE TO THE HOLY LAND

208. Bünting, Henric. **ITINERARIUM SACRAE SCRIPTURAE, Das ist Ein Redebuch, Ober die Gantze Heilge Schrifft...** Bound with / **De Monetis et Mensuris Sacrae Scripturae...** Donat/Kirchner, Magdeburg: 1584. 3 Volumes in 1. + Extraordinary maps and plates. Old repairs and slight loss. Lacks one leaf. Very popular practical, historic, and theological guide to the Middle East and the ancient world. Bound with / Huber, Caspar. **(SPRÜCHE JESU SYRACHS) SPIEGEL DER GEISTLICHEN HAUSSZUCHT. AÜSSLEGÜNG... das Buch Jesus Syrach...** Lechler, Frankfort am Mayn: 1569. Approx. 600p. Titles in red and black. Folio. Fine cut of Paradise, etc. All four works bound together. Worn alum tawed vellum. Important and very scarce artifacts of the Reformation. *These editions are not in Adams, nor BMC STC German.* Should be seen to be fully appreciated. $ 800.00

FIRST GERMAN AMERICAN EDITION OF "PILGRIM'S PROGRESS"

209.Bunyan, John [1628=88]. **EINES CHRISTEN REISE**... Bruderschafft, Ephrata: 1754. Two Volumes in One. pp. 280, 264. Age stained. Nice contemporary full leather binding, without clasps. *Several early German American manuscript ownerships, including: Mardin Bächtel (Martin Bechtel), Peter Schnebele (Snively), Etc. GLP/USA* 163, Evans 7162-3, Hild. 1343-4, Seid. p. 42. $ 600.00

210. Bunyan. **EINES CHRISTEN REISE**... G. S. Peters, Harrisburg: 1828. 2 vols in One. 322p. + Full page woodcut plates. Corners chewed. Full leather. XLib. *GLP/USA* 2934, AI 32516. *HSH.* $ 40.00

A MENNONITE BISHOP'S "ADDRESS TO THE YOUNG"

211. (Burkholder, Christian)[1746-1809]. **NUTZLICHE UND ERBAULICHE ANREDE AN DIE JUGEND, von der Wahren Busse**... Bauman & Cleim, Ephrata: 1804. 92p. Slight loss on p. 65. Leather backed boards. Early manuscript ownerships. Considered the foremost work ever composed by a Lancaster County Mennonite. *GLP/USA* 1370, Seid. p. 161, AI 6954. $ 180.00

212. (Burkholder). **NUTZLICHE UND ERBAULICHE ANREDE AN DIE JUGEND**... Ebner, Allentown: 1829. 96p. Full leather. Mennonite classic. *GLP/USA* 2993, Shoemaker/L p. 44, Seid. p. 240, AI 38005. *WST.* $ 50.00

213. Buschbauer, Hans. **AMERIKANISCHES GARTEN = BUCH, für Stadt und Land**... Milwaukee: 1892. 504p. Illus. Browned. Cloth. Scarce farm & garden guide. $ 40.00

214. Buschbauer, Hans. **POPULARES HANDBUCH DES GRASBAUS, FUTTER - PFLANZENBAUS UND DER MILCHWIRTHSCHAFT**. Milwaukee: 1883. 276p. Illus. Gilt embossed cloth. Extraordinary guide for German American Dairy Farmers. $ 40.00

215. Caesar, Johann Simon. **DER GESCHWINDE INTRESTEN-RECHNER**... Ritter, Reading: 1816. 44p. *GLP/USA* 2184, Seid. p. 199, AI 37148, Karpinski p. 207. $ 28.00

Eine
Kurze Nachricht
von dem
bösartigen Fieber,
welches kürzlich in
Philadelphia
grassiret;
Nebst einer Erzählung der Maasregeln, die desfals in den verschiedenen Theilen der Vereinigten Staaten genommen wurden.
Diesen ist hinzugefüget,
Nachrichten
von der
Pest in London und Marseille;
und
Eine Liste der Todten,
vom ersten August bis in die Mitte des Decembers, 1793.
Von Mathew Carey.
Nach der vierten verbesserten Auflage aus dem Englischen übersetzt, von Carl Erdmann.
Lancaster,
Gedruckt, für den Verfasser, bey Jacob Bailey, 1794.

CAREY'S ACCOUNT OF PHILADELPHIA'S 1793 YELLOW FEVER EPIDEMIC

216. Carey, Mathew. **EINE KURZE NACHRICHT VON DEM BÖSARTIGEN FIEBER**... Samuel Saur (Chestnut Hill): 1794. 176p. *Uncut and unopened in the original printed wraps. Of special note is the ad printed on rear wrap for Evans 26734.* Carey's important account of the Yellow Fever Epidemic, translated into German. *GLP/USA* 919, Bristol B8611, S&M 46996, Austin 405. See also Part I # 486, and Part II 1134-1135. Rare and remarkable in this condition. $ 550.00

217. Cassel, Daniel K. **GESCHICHTE DER MENNONITEN**... Phila: 1890. 551p. Illus. Fine copy from the Borneman Family. Cassel [1820-98] was an important Mennonite historian and genealogist. This German edition of his fine Mennonite history actually expands upon the first edition published in English (1888). $ 50.00

CATECHISMS

German American Catechisms not only reveal subtle changes in accepted theology, but must really be considered children's books. Their role in the education of youngsters was pivotal. In addition to moral training, they were used for Reading, Writing, and even Arithmetic. Some Catechisms in are listed under the several denominations, or their author's names.

218. **CATECHISMUS, Oder Kurzer Unterricht Christlicher Lehre**... Heidelberg: 1745. 272p. Full vellum. *Early manuscript ownership of Christian Grönwalt, Lebanon, Pa. HSH.* $ 100.00

219. **CATECHISMUS, Oder Kurzer Unterricht Christlicher Lehre, Für die Angehende Jugend... Samt de Haus=Tafel, Mit und ohne Biblischem Sprüch=Büchlein**... Cist, Phila: 1790, 124p. 24mo. *Pretty manuscript fraktur ownership of Susana Knabin, Oley, Berks County, 1796.* The version of the Heidelberg Catechism preferred among German Americas, and the "standard" of the German Reformed Church. *GLP/USA* 778, Evans 22830, Seid. p. 127. $ 195.00

220. **CATECHISMUS, Oder Kurzer Unterricht Christlicher Lehre**... Billmeyer, Germantown: 1796 118p. 24mo. *GLP/USA* 1019, Bristol B9569. *Not in Evans nor Seid. WST.* $ 155.00

221. **CATECHISMUS, Oder Kurzer Unterricht Christlicher Lehre**... Henrich Schweitzer, Phila: 1798. 110p. XLib. *GLP/USA* 1138, Evans 33866. *HSH.* $ 75.00

222. **CATECHISMUS, Oder Kurzer Unterricht Christlicher Lehre**... Zentler, Phila: 1807. 108p. XLib. *GLP/USA* 1564, AI 12274, Seid p. 170. Scarce. *HSH.* $ 40.00

223. **CATECHISMUS**... Ritter, Reading: 1811. 105p. Leather backed marbled boards. 24mo. *GLP/USA* 1865, AI 22488, Seid. p. 183. *WST.* $ 36.00

224. **CATECHISMUS... Reformirten Kirchenund Schulen**... Hütter, Easton: 1812. pp. 11, 288. Leather backed paper boards. *Manuscript ownership of Joseph Kelchner, 1821. GLP/USA* 1881, AI 26580, Seid. p. 184. $ 40.00

225. **CATECHISMUS**... Meyer, Phila: 1812. 108p. XLib. *GLP/USA* 1913, AI 26581, Seid. p. 184. *HSH.* $ 30.00

226. **CATECHISMUS**... Billmeyer, Phila: 1816. 118p. XLib. Leather backed paper boards. *GLP/USA* 2159, AI 37198, Seid. p. 198. *HSH.* Scarce. $ 30.00

227. **CATECHISMUS**... Schaeffer & Maund, Balt: 1817. 102p. *GLP/USA* 2198. $ 22.00

228. **CATECHISMUS**... Ritter, Reading: 1826. 105p. Ds. Leather backed decorated paper boards. *Not in Seidensticker. GLP/USA* 2830, AI 24035/25912. $ 24.00

229. **CATECHISMUS, oder Kurzer Unterricht Christlicher Lehre, die Angehende Jungend**... Zentler, Phila: 1827. 108p. + Frontis. 24mo. Crisp leather backed paste paper bds. XLib. *GLP/USA* 2884, AI 28421, *Not in Seid.* $ 35.00

230. **CATECHISMUS**... Zentler, Phila: 1830. 108p. + Frontis. 24mo. XLib. *GLP/USA* 3134, *Not in AI, nor Seid.* $ 36.00

231. **CATECHISMUS**... Mentz & Sohn, Phila: 1836. 108p. + Frontis. 24mo. Pretty original paste paper boards. $ 25.00

232. **CATECHISMUS**... Mentz & Rovoudt, Phila: 1843. 128p. + Frontis. $ 10.00

233. **CATECHISMUS...** Mentz & Rovoudt, Phila: 1846. 128p. + Frontis. Paste paper boards. We will soon see a time when these paper boards are eagerly pursued. $ 15.00

234. **CATECHISMUS...** Weisenburg (Lehigh County): 1852. pp. 69, 71. Scarce. $ 35.00

235. Catechism. **DER HEIDELBERGER KATECHISMUS, Sammt Auszugen aus der Kirchen - Ordnung... der Deutsch-Reformirten Kirche...** Victor Scriba for John Smith, Chambersburg: 1837. 94p. 24mo. AI 44735 *[1 copy only]. WST.* $ 32.00

236. Catechism. **DER HEIDELBERGER KATECHISMUS...** Chambersburg: 1863. pp. 69, 59. Embossed cloth. *WST.* $ 15.00

237. Catechism. **DER HEIDELBERGER KATECHISMUS...** (Cleveland: 1870). $ 8.00

238. Catechism. (Hermann, L. F.). **CATECHISMUS der Glaubenslehren und Lebenspflichten der Chrislichen Religion...** Hawrecht, Kutztown: 1847. 84p. Coth backed marbled boards. 24mo. *WST.* Unusual. $ 22.00

239. Catechism. (Jager, F. J.). **CATECHISMUS, der Christlichen Lehre...** Carl Benseman, Hamburg, Pa: 1853. 63p. *WST.* $ 20.00

240. **KATECHISMUS...** Jung, Doylestown: 1844. 64p. Mennonite Catechism. $ 40.00

241. **KATECHISMUS...** Schunemann, Skippach, Pa: 1848. 112p. 32mo. Full leather. Another scarce Mennonite Catechism. *WST.* $ 25.00

242. Catechism. **DER KLEINE CATECHISMUS...** Cist, Phila: 1791. pp. 4, 127, 1. Some slight defects. 18mo. XLib. Leather backed paper boards. The Pennsylvania Ministerium Edition of Luther's catechism. *GLP/USA* 820, Evans 23514, Seid. p. 130. *HSH.* $ 120.00

243. Catechism. **DER KLEINE CATECHISMUS...** (Bauman?), Ephrata, for Johnston, Phila: 1805. 139p. Worn. *GLP/USA* 1421, Repp p. 225, Seid. p. 164, AI 8808. $ 60.00

244. Catechism. **DER KLEINE CATECHISMUS...** Schnee, Lebanon: 1808. 140p. 32mo. Slight loss on 1 leaf. In this edition, Schnee took the liberty of changing the order of several sections, and inserted a variant Golden A B C = Repp p. 74, *GLP/USA* 1625, AI 15461. Scarce version of Luther's Catechism. $ 50.00

245. Catechism. **DER KLEINE CATECHISMUS...** Meyer, Phila: 1812. 139p. XLib. *Handsome color manuscript fraktur ownership of Magdalena Tellin (1814). GLP/USA* 1915, AI 25906, Repp p. 227, Seidensticker p. 186. $ 145.00

246. Catechism. **DER KLEINE CATECHISMUS...** Billmeyer, Phila: 1815. 132p. Pretty German leather backed paste paper boards, with decorated fore-edges. XLib. *GLP/USA* 2103, AI 35149, Seid. p. 195, Repp p. 228. $ 40.00

D. Martin Luther,

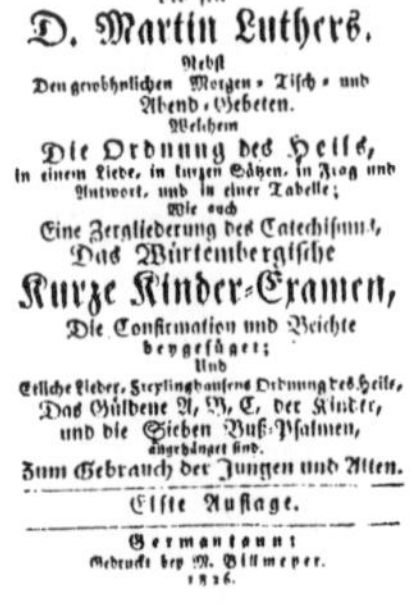

Der Kleine
Catechismus
des sel.
D. Martin Luthers.
Nebst
Den gewöhnlichen Morgen- Tisch- und
Abend-Gebeten.
Welchem
Die Ordnung des Heils,
in einem Liede, in kurzen Sätzen, in Frag und
Antwort, und in einer Tabelle;
Wie auch
Eine Zergliederung des Catechismus,
Das Würtembergische
Kurze Kinder-Examen,
Die Confirmation und Beichte
beygefüget;
Und
Etliche Lieder, Freylinghausens Ordnung des Heils,
Das Güldene A, B, C, der Kinder,
und die Sieben Buß-Psalmen,
angehänget sind.
Zum Gebrauch der Jungen und Alten.
Eilfte Auflage.
Germantaun:
Gedruckt bey M. Billmeyer.
1826.

247. Catechism. **DER KLEINE CATECHISMUS...** Bär, Lancaster: 1825. 122p. *GLP/USA* 2750. $ 22.00

248. Catechism. **DER KLEINE CATECHISMUS...** Billmeyer, Germantown: 1826. 128p. + Frontis. Paste paper boards. *GLP/USA* 2806, AI 25162. $ 32.00

249. Catechism. **DER KLEINE CATECHISMUS...** Neinstedt for the Theological Seminary, Gettysburg: 1828. 110p. Significant changes were made in the text of this edition. *Not in AI, nor Seid. GLP/USA* 2927, Repp p. 231. $ 40.00

250. Catechism. **DER KLEINE CATECHISMUS**... Bär, Lancaster: 1828. 126p. 16mo. Paste paper flower designed boards. XLib. ***Manuscript fraktur ownership of Joseph Schumm, 1831.*** *GLP/USA* 2949, AI 33931, Repp p. 231. *Not in Seidensticker.* $ 50.00

251. Catechism. **DER KLEINE CATECHISMUS**... H. W. Villee, Lancaster: 1828. 127p. 16mo. XLib. *GLP/USA* 2956, AI 33929, Repp p. 230. Great paste paper boards. $ 32.00

252. Catechism. **DER KLEINE CATECHISMUS**... Zentler, Phila: 1828. 142p. + Frontis. Leather backed paste paper bds. *GLP/USA* 2977, AI 33928, Repp p. 230. *HSH.* $ 30.00

253. Catechism. **DER KLEINE CATECHISMUS**... Mentz, Phila: 1833. AI 19811. $ 22.00

254. Catechism. **DER KLEINE CATECHISMUS**... Mentz & Sohn, Phila: 1836. 144p. + Frontis. Paste paper boards. AI 38608 *[Locating one copy only].* $ 28.00

255. Catechism. **DER KLEINE CATECHISMUS**... Mentz, Phila. Ca: 1840. 144p. $ 15.00

256. Catechism. **DER KLEINE CATECHISMUS**... Blumer, Busch & Leisenring, Allentown: 1850. 128p. Cloth. Shoemaker/L p.78. *WST.* $ 22.00

257. Catechism. **DER KLEINE CATECHISMUS**... Benner, Sumnytown, Pa: 1857. $ 12.00

258. Catechism. **DER KLEINE KATECHISMUS**... Brobst, Allentown: 1869. This is perhaps a false imprint. $ 15.00

259. Catechism. (Orwig, E. W. W.). **KATECHISMUS, Uber die Hauptlehen der Christlichen Religion**... Hammer, Cinn: 1863. 172p. Borneman family copy. $ 15.00

260. Catechism. **UNTERRICHT IN DER CHRISTLICHEN RELIGION. In Fragen und Antworten**. Allentown: 1853. 63p. 32mo. Plain wraps. Shoemaker/L p. 83. *WST.* $ 22.00

END OF THE CATECHISMS

261. **CHAUIROPFEN**. American Tract Soc. NY, Ca; 1860. 128p. Cloth. *Unusual German-American Miniature.* Prayers for each day. Scarce. $ 40.00

262. (Chemnitz, Martin). ...**LOCORUM THEOLOGICORUM... Quibus et Loci Communes, D. Philippi Melanchthonis**... Frankfurt: 1594. Two volumes. Over 1400p. Full contemporary vellum bindings, handsomely embossed with portraits of both Luther and Melanchthon. Gilt ownership = 1603 P. Z. S. Chemnitz [1522-86], was an influential German Lutheran theologian, whose popular and compelling lectures (1553) on the theology of Melanchthon, were published posthumously in 1591. This is apparently the scarce 2nd edition. $ 400.00

THE VISION OF ISAAC CHILDS

263. (Childs, Isaac). **DAS GESICHT DES ISAAC CHILDS, welches er gesehen hat, betreffend das Land seiner Geburt**. Barton & Jungmann, Reading: 1791. 20p. + 4p. Printer's ad. Plain wraps. 24mo. Rare German American edition of an extraordinary mystical Quaker work. Please see also the wondeful manuscript of this work [Pt. III #2158]. *GLP/USA* 827 *[2 Copies only]*, Evans 23257, Seid. p. 130. $ 250.00

264. **CHRISTLICHES GEDENKBUCH**. Printed in Germany for Wartburg Pub. Chicago. Ca: 1880. A prayer for each day with beautifully decorated borders + ***11 wonderful color chromolithographed floral plates.*** $ 30.00

265. **CHRISTLICHES VERGISSMEINNICHT**. Allentown: 1883. 372p. 24mo. + Five color chromolithographed plates. Prayers for each day. Shoemaker/L p. 157. *WST.* $ 22.00

266. Clarke, C. C. **DIE HUNDERT WUNDER DER WELT, und der Drei Naturreiche.** Translated from the English by G. H. Haumann. Ilmenau: 1831. 610p. + Plates. *Unusual printed paper binding showing the colossus at Rhodes. 1830's Lancaster Manuscript ownerships of Jacob Reis and Sebastian Fogel.* $ 75.00

267. **CLAVIS UNIVERSALIS ODER SCHLUSSEL DER GEHEIMNISSE, ZUR OFFENBARUND DES ALTEN UND NEUEN BUNDES!.** Joseph Bauman, Ephrata: 1818=19. 224p. With unusual woodcut vignettes and printer's devices (one signed "Durouchail"). Leather backed printed paper boards. *GLP/USA* 2339, AI 43636-7, Seid. p. 207. Curious Pennsylvania German mystical work from Bauman's Ephrata press. $ 100.00

268. Collier, David. **EINLEITUNG ZUM RICHTIGEN VERSTANDE...** Translated by F. E. Rambach. Printed by Reissner for the Evangelische Gemeinschaft, Neu=Berlin, Pa: 1845. 525p. Full leather. $ 50.00

269. **DIE CONSTITUTION DER VEREINIGTEN STAATEN VON AMERICA... und die der Republik von Pennsylvanien...** Bruckman for M'Williams, Reading: 1823. 156p. Handsome leather backed marbled boards. *From the Library of John Joseph Stoudt. GLP/USA* 2609, Seid. p. 220, AI 12244. $ 50.00

270. Cookbook. **DIE GESCHICKTE HAUSFRAU. Eine Sammlung Guter Recepte und Vorschriften zum Kochen, Braten, und Kuchen = Backen...** Lutz & Scheffer, Harrisburg: 1851. 38p. Printed wraps. Lowenstein #513. Scarce. *WST.* $ 125.00

271. **CORPORATION UND NEBEN = GEFETZE DER DEUTSCHE EVANGELISCH REFORMIRTEN KIRCHEN = GEMEINDE von Nieder Saucon Townschip, Northampton County.** Weber, Allentown, Ca: 1863. 16p. Plain wraps. 32mo. *Not in Shoemaker/L.* $ 30.00

THE "GROSS MARTYRBUCH"

272. (Crespin, Jean). **GROSS MARTYRBUCH, und Kirchen Historien...** Hanaw: 1606. 1726p. Some leaves mounted. Massive folio. Contemporary stamped binding lacks some of its vellum covering. The first edition in German. Translated by Paul Crocius from Crespin's huge historical record - "*La Livre des Martyrs*". Though Mennonites and Anabaptists are intentionally excluded, this remarkable work provides details on Protestant martyrs of the Reformation that are not available elsewhere. Its publication in German was a major event. Rare. $ 900.00

THE COMPLETE PAINTER / ARTIST IN GERMAN

273. Crostern, Johann Melchior. **DER WOHL ANFUHRENDE MAHLER...** Jena: 1753. 536p. + Register + Frontis & Woodcut Illustrations + 7 pages of *Extensive German (American?) manuscript written in a tight hand, of secret formulas, color recipes, & directions.* Rare 18th century guide to the tools, techniques, and formulas necessary to all kinds of crafts and fine arts. Superlative example of the kind of guide that might have been used by the Pennsylvania German fraktur and decorative artist. $ 400.00

274. Crostern. **DER WOHL ANFUHRENDE MAHLER...** Jena: 1778. pp. 12, 536, 8 + Frontis and woodcut illustrations. *American manuscript ownerships of Abraham Beam, clearly demonstrating that these guides were used by German-American artisans.* $ 300.00

TRIAL & DYING CONFESSION OF A 19 YEAR OLD MURDERER

275. Cunningham, Carl/Charles. **(CARL CUNNINGHAM'S VERHOR UND DAS LESSTE BEKENTNISS)**. York? 1805? 24p. Lacks Tp? Plain wraps. 24mo. Cunningham was drinking with Joseph Rothrock in Yorktown. Convinced that he had been cheated in a game of "hustlecap", Cunningham resolved to kill his companion. On the road home he strangled Rothrock with a piece of twine. He was hung for the crime. *Apparently Not in GLP/USA, AI, McDade, nor Seidensticker.* Rare. $ 200.00

IMPORTANT VETERINARY GUIDE PRINTED BY CHRISTOPHER SAUR

276. Deigendesch, Johanes. **NACHRICHTERS: Oder Nützliches und aufrichtiges Ross = Artzney = Buchlein...** Christoph Saur, Germantown: 1770. pp. 209, 7. Ink stain on one leaf. 24mo. Worn leather backed boards. *GLP/USA* 378, Evans 11627, Hild. 2517, Austin 641, Seid. p. 81. First American Edition. Scarce little guide, that was usually read to tatters on the rural homestead. In Colonial America. the horse was of surpassing importance. $ 220.00

277. Deigendesch. **NACHRICHTERS: Nützliches und aufrichtiges Ross = Artzney = Buchlein...** Basel: 1770. pp. 223, 18. + Early German manuscript formulas. 24mo. Disbd. The prototype for guides printed by Christopher Saur in 1770-1. $ 125.00

278. (Deigendesch). **NACHRICHTER'S: Nützliches und Aufrichtiges Ross = Artzneibuch...** Edited by Johannes Hornberger. Allentown: 1838. 256p. Worn printed paper boards. 24mo. *Apparently Not in AI.* Shoemaker/L p. 60 *[Recording this copy only]. WST.* $ 140.00

279. Deknatel, Johannes. **ACHT PREDIGTEN, uber Wichtige Materien...** Bound With / **Morgen und Abend Gebete in sangen.** By J. H. W. Witschel. Blumer, Allentown: 1835. pp. 288, 107. Shoemaker/L p. 53. *Not in AI. WST.* $ 45.00

280. Denner, Jacob [1659-1746]. **CHRISTLICH UND ERBAULICHE BETRACHTUNGEN Uber die Sonn und Festtags Evangelia des Ganzen Jahrs...** (Konigsburg): 1751. pp. 1502, 64. Full leather Germanic styled (probably American) binding with head and tail bands present as are the small corner bosses. *Early Manuscript Fraktur Ownership of Christian Meier.* Denner's writings exerted a tremendous influence in & beyond the Mennonite church, and did much to promote pietistic tendencies among the Mennonites. These sermons were read verbatim at home and from the Sunday pulpit. *HSH.* $ 375.00

281. **DER DEUTSCH FARMER, im Busch und auf der Prairie...** Milwaukee. Ca: 1888. 335p. Gilt decorated cloth. Fine copy. Designed for new American immigrants & settlers. $ 40.00

282. **DIE DEUTSCHE THEOLOGIE, ein edles Büchlein vom rechten Verstande... mit D. Luther's und Arnd's Vorreden...** Edited by J. A. Desser. Villee, Lancaster: 1829. pp. 16, 16, 159 + Printer's ad. First American Edition. *GLP/USA* 3024, AI 38373, Seid. p. 242. $ 50.00

283. **DEUTSCHER VOLKSLIEDER = SCHATZ...** NY. Ca: 1890. 189p. Oblong Pa. German Song Book. Not shaped note. $ 20.00

284. Diefenbach, Daniel. **DER SIEG JESU...** Miller, New Berlin: 1840. 360p. 16mo. Disbound. Printed booklabel from "Isaac F. Christ's Cheap Bookstore & Printing Office, Kutztown, PA". $ 40.00

REFORMATION BIBLE HISTORY FOR YOUNG FOLKS

285. Dieterich, M. Veit. **SUMMARIA OBER DAS ALTE TESTAMENT...** Nickel Schirlentz, Wittemburg: 1545. 376p. Attractive woodcut title page in red and black. Small 4to. Fine contemporary full alum tawed vellum, nicely tooled in blind. Both decorated brass clasps present. Very scarce and curious Reformation era bible paraphrase.
$ 750.00

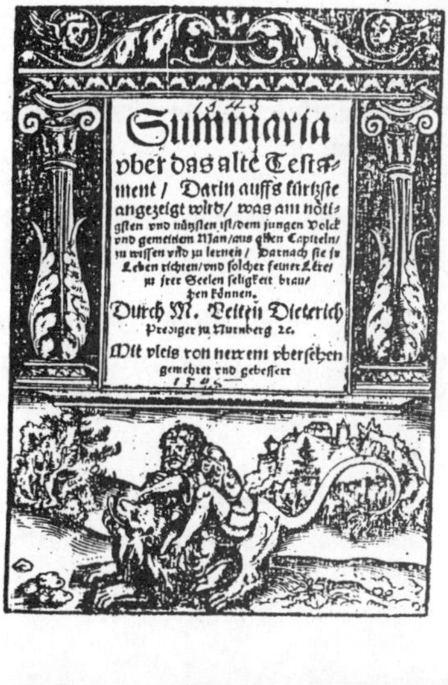
Summaria
vber das alte Testa=
ment / Darin auffs kürtzste
angezeigt wird / was am nötis
gsten vnd nützsten ist / dem jungen Volck
vnd gemeinen Man / aus allen Capiteln /
zu wissen vnd zu lernen / Darnach sie jr
Leben richten / vnd solcher seiner Lere /
zu jrer Seelen seligkeit brau=
chen können.
Durch M. Veltin Dieterich
Prediger zu Nurnberg zc.
Mit vleis von newem vbersehen
gemehret vnd gebessert

286. (Dilworth, W. H.). **DAS LEBEN UND HEROISCHE THAFEN DES KONIGS VON PREUSSEN, FRIEDERICHS DES II(I)...** Christoph Saur, Germantown: 1761. 288p. Worn. XLib. Frederick the Great is mistakenly called Frederick III throughout, but our copy has this corrected in manuscript (by Saur?) to Frederick II. The first 165 pages translate and reprint Dilworth's book, the rest is a compilation (probably by Saur) of later accounts. *GLP/USA* 233, Evans 8841, Seid. p. 55. Scarce. *HSH.* $ 400.00

"WINE MAKETH GLAD THE HEART OF MAN" = Psalms CIV

287. Distiller's Guide. **DIE WAHRE BRANTEWEIN = BRENNEREN; oder Brantwein Gin und Cordialmacher Kunst...** Salomon Mäyer, York: 1802. 44p. Leather backed boards. The title also promises a Cloth Dyer's Companion that was apparently never issued. *The only known copy*. See: *GLP/USA* 1329 ["No copy known", but this is the same unique copy mentioned by Oda his List of Early Books on Dyeing, 3]. Rare and most interesting wine maker's and distiller's formulary. Manuscript ownership of "P. Eberts". *WST.* $ 400.00

288. Doddridge, Dr. Philip. **ANFANG UND FORTGANG DES GEISTLICHEN LEBENS IN DER MENSCHLICHEN SEELE**. American Tract Society, NY. Circa: 1860. 360p. Cloth. Doddridge's "*Rise & Progress of the Soul*". $ 8.00

289. (Dodsley, Robert) [1703-64]. **OECONOMY ODER HAUSHALTUNGSKUNST DES MENCHLICHEN LEBENS...** (Jacob Meyer) for Johnson & Warner, Phila: 1809. 78p. Illustrated by numerous (30) curious woodcuts, probably engraved by Alexander Anderson. Foxed. The first German American edition of this influential work. *GLP/USA* 1689, AI 17399, Seid. p. 176. $ 125.00

290. (Dodsley). **THE ECONOMY OF HUMAN LIFE / Haushaltungskunst des Menchlichen Lebens...** Ehrenfried, Allentown: 1813. pp. 7, 515, 2. Pretty leather backed marbled boards. Unusual version of this popular work, with the **text in both English & German.** One of the first German books printed in Allentown. This text may have been written by the Earl of Chesterfield. *GLP/USA* 1942, Shoemaker/L p. 26, AI 28347, Seid. p. 187. *WST.* $ 60.00

291. (Dodsley). **THE ECONOMY OF HUMAN LIFE / Haushaltungskunst des Menchlichen Lebens...** Ehrenfried, Allentown: 1814. Leather backed marbled boards. Text in both English & German. *GLP/USA* 2008, Shoemaker/L p. 26, AI 31347. *Not in Seid. WST.* $ 60.00

292A. Doll, Joseph. **DER LEICHTE UNTERRICHT VON DER VOCAL MUSIK... Kirchen Melodien...** Wyeth, Harrisburg: 1810. 108p. Oblong leather backed marbled boards. *Manuscript ownership of Adam Heilman.* XLib. *GLP/USA* 1736, AI 19986, *Not in Seid. The earliest German shape-note tunebook in which type was used to print the notes.* Scarce. *HSH.* $ 225.00

292B. Doll. **LEICHTER UNTERRICHT VON IN DER VOCAL MUSIK... Kirchen Melodien...** Wyeth, Harrisburg: 1814. pp. x, 110. Oblong leather backed marbled boards. *Shaped Note Songbook. Manuscript ownership and poem of "Susan Metzger, 1819".* XLib. *GLP/USA* 2018, AI 31348, Seid. p. 193. *HSH.* $ 200.00

293. **DIE DREI BLUMENTOPFE. No. 6**. Chambersburg, Ca: 1840. 16p. Yellow printed wraps. 32mo. Scarce liitle children's book. *WST.* $ 26.00

294. (Dreisbach, J. S.). **DIE KIRCHEN = ORDNUNG DER ZIONS KIRCHE, in Allen Taunschip, Northampton Caunty, Pennsylvania**. Easton? 1847. 18p. 32mo. Pretty wraps. Title page with nice decorative printer's ornaments. *WST.* $ 40.00

295. **DREISTIMMIGE KINDER - LIEDER...** Brobst, Allentown: 1862. 22p. Words & music. Plain wraps. Ds. Shoemaker/L p. 106 *[Recording this copy only]*. *WST.* $ 40.00

296. Drommers, Wilhelm Adam. ... **CASUAL PREDIGTEN**... Tubingen: 1740. 1104p. + Manuscript Index. 4to. Worn leather backed paper boards. *The Manuscript inscriptions show that this book was given to Johann Hoff in 1751 by his schoolmaster, and was bought by Conrad Berlet, Phila., 1754 + Attractive calligraphic manuscript fraktur ownership of Christian Beichtel, Tulpehocken Twp., Berks County, 1796.* $ 160.00

CIVIL WAR HISTORY IN THE ORIGINAL PARTS

297. Duyckinck, E. A. **GESCHICHTE DES KRIEGS FÜR DIE UNION**. Translated into German by Friedrich Kapp. Johnson, Fry & Co. NY. Ca: 1865. Numerous Engraved Plates. *In 50 Parts as issued.* Some wraps chipped, torn, or missing = but a remarkable survival of this 19th Century publishing form. Classic German American history of the Civil War. $ 150.00

298. Eaton & Reid. **LEBEN DES GENERAL MAJORS ANDREAS JACKSON**... Ritter, Reading: 1831. 419p. + Stipple engraved portrait of Jackson + Colored folding map of the U.S. (which is rarely present). Nice leather backed boards. Biography of Jackson, translated into German by Prof. Jager, Greenwich, Berks Cty. Howes R 171, AI 6928. $ 75.00

299. **EINFÄLTIGE UNTERHALTUNGEN MIT GOTT**. Conrad Zentler. Phila: 1817. 180p. + Powerful woodcut frontis by Gilbert + Woodcut vignette on title. Full leather. *GLP/USA* 2228, AI 40736, Seid. p. 201. Manuscript ownership of "Adam Shaal, 1830". $ 40.00

300. (Engel, J. J.). **DER PHILOSOPH FÜR DIE WELT**. Carlsruhe: 1783. 152p. Contemporary marbled wraps. One volume from a large German Sammlung. *Owned by the Pennsylvania printer Michael Billmeyer, and signed by him on the title.* $ 100.00

301. **ERBAULISCHE AUFSATZE. Herausgegben von einer zu diesem Zweck in Philadelphia errichteten Gesellschaft**. Zentler, Phila: 1816. 24p. Later wraps. Very scarce first publication of the "Society for the Distribution of Useful and Edifying Essays". *GLP/USA* 2171 (Note), AI 37525. *WST.* $ 50.00

302. **ERBAULISCHES GEBAT=BUCH**... Ebner, Allentown: 1822. Two volumes in one. 612p. Full leather with clasps. *GLP/USA* 2524, Shoemaker/L p. 35, AI 8630. Valuable collection of songs and prayers. *WST.* $ 60.00

303. **EIN ERBAULISCHES UNPARTHENISCHES KLEINES HAND = BUCHLEIN**... Bär & Sohn, Lancaster: 1854. 83p. Apparently a Mennonite work. $ 40.00

304. **DER ERSTE MORGENSCHIMMER... Fur Kleine Kinder**. American Tract Society, NY. Ca: 1840. 184p. Cloth. Children's book = "Peep of Day". $ 16.00

305. **DIE ERNSTHAFFTE CHRISTEN-PFLICHT... Bruderschafft**, Ephrata: 1770. Two vols. in one. pp. 100, 248. Ds. Full leather Ephrata binding. Important Amish / Mennonite prayer book. Classic Cloister printing. *GLP/USA* 376A, Evans 11648, Hild. 2526, Seid. p. 81. $ 275.00

306. **DIE ERNSTHAFFTE CHRISTEN-PFLICHT**... Baumann, Ephrata: 1808. 198p. Full leather. Worn. Primarily for Amish use. *GLP/USA* 1596, Seid. p. 172. AI 14952. $ 140.00

307. **DIE ERNSTHAFTE CHRISTENPFLICHT**... Bär, Lancaster: 1841. 214p. Ds. $ 50.00

308. **DIE ERNSTHAFTE CHRISTENPFLICHT**... Bär, Lancaster: 1868. 212p. $ 35.00

309. **ERNSTHAFTE BETRACHTUNGEN UBER DIE EWIGKEIT**. American Tract Society, NY. Ca: 1840. 10p. Wraps. Woodcut illus. $ 20.00

310. Ettiinger, Adam [Warrington Twp., York County]. **DER KONIG SAUL**... Jacob Baab, Harrisburg: 1828. 76p. Ds. *GLP/USA* 2932, Seid. p. 237, AI 33086. Bizarre collection of Bible stories & prophetic visions. $ 40.00

SONGBOOKS OF THE EVANGELICAL ASSOCIATION OF NORTH AMERICA

311. Evangelical Association of North America. **EVANGELISCHES LIEDERBUCHLEIN für Sonntagsschulen**... New Berlin: 1843. 104p. 32mo. Rare little children's song book. $ 60.00

312. Evangelical Assoc. **EVANGELISCHES GESANGBUCH**... Bound with / **Die Geistliche Viole**... Heinrich Fischer, New Berlin: 1850. pp. 600, 226. Disbound. $ 40.00

313. Evangelical Assoc. **DIE GEISTLICHE VIOLE, Eine Kleine Sammlung alter und neuer Geistricher Lieder**. New Berlin: 1846. 236p. 32mo. Full leather. $ 45.00

314. Evangelical Assoc. **DER KLEINE GEISTLICHE VIOLE**. Geo. Miller, New Berlin: 1830. 240p. 32mo. Full leather. *GLP/USA* 3113. *Not in AI, nor Seidensticker.* $ 60.00

315. Evangelical Assoc. **GLAUBENSLEHRE UND KIRCHEN = ZUCHT=ORDNUNG**... George Miller, New Berlin, Pa: 1831. 135p. 24mo. Leather backed marbled boards. *Manuscript ownership of "Jacob Hertzler, 1832".* AI 6971. $ 50.00

316. Evangelical Assoc. **GLAUBENSLEHRE UND KIRCHEN = ZUCHT=ORDNUNG**... Reissner, New Berlin: 1845. 146p. 24mo. Leather backed marbled paper boards. $ 40.00

317. Evangelical Assoc. **GLAUBENSLEHRE UND KIRCHENZUCHTORDNUNG**... Bound With / **CONSTITUTION DER MISSIONGESELLSCHAFT**. Bound With / **THE DOCTRINES OF DISCIPLINE (English)**... Hammer, for the Assoc. Cleveland: 1860. pp. 176, 13, 169. 32mo. Full leather. $ 32.00

318. Evangelical Assoc. **LEBEN... JACOB ALBRECHT UND GEORGE MILLER**. Miller, New Berlin: 1834. 176p. Ds. Full leather. XLib. AI 24332. Important biographies of the earliest founders of the Evangelical Association. Scarce. $ 60.00

SONG BOOKS OF THE AMERICAN EVANGELICAL LUTHERAN CHURCH

319. Evangelical Lutheran Church in North America. **DEUTSCHES GESANGBUCH**... Phila: 1849. 524p. *HSH.* XLib. Full morocco. $ 32.00

320. Evang. Luth. Church, N.A. **DEUTSCHES GESANGBUCH**... Phila: 1862. 408p. 32mo. Full embossed morocco $ 28.00

321. Evang. Luth. Church, N.A. **DEUTSCHES GESANGBUCH**... Phila. Ca: 1880. 428p. 32mo. Beautiful full gilt tooled morocco in slip case. Dorothea Hillemann's book. $ 30.00

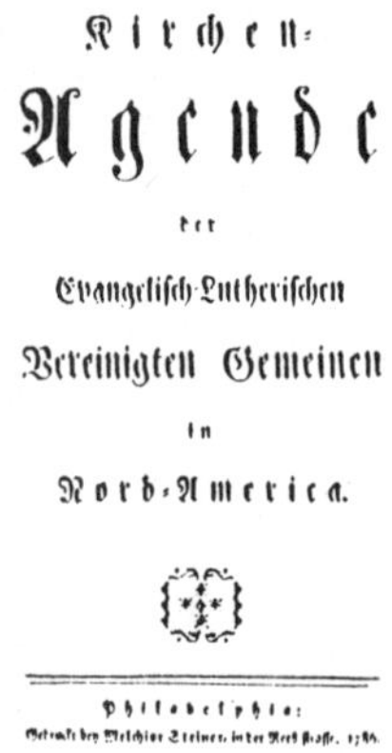
Kirchen-
Agende
der
Evangelisch-Lutherischen
Vereinigten Gemeinen
in
Nord-America.
Philadelphia:
Gedruckt bey Melchior Steiner, in der Rees-Strasse, 1786.

THE FIRST PRINTED EDITION OF THE LUTHERAN LITURGY IN NORTH AMERICA

322. Evangelical Lutheran Church, N. A. **KIRCHEN = AGENDE**... Melchior Steiner, Phila: 1786. pp. 3, 58. Worn full leather. The preface is signed by the most prominent American Lutheran ministers, including H. M. Muhlenberg, who was most responsible for the project. This "liturgy essentially harmonizes with the 1786 hymn book, and even more purely expresses the creed of genuine Lutheranism. The object of both publications was to strengthen the bond of union of German American Lutheran congregations" = Seid. p. 119, *GLP/USA* 667, Evans 19629. $ 220.00

323.. Evang. Luth. Church, N.A. **SONNTAGSCHULBUCH.** Philadelphia & Allentown: 1876. 351p. With printed music. $ 15.00

324. Evangelical Lutheran Church, in Pa. **ERBAULISCHE LIEDER=SAMMLUNG.** Billmeyer, Germantown: 1795. Three volumes in one. 710+p. Worn. Second Edition. *GLP/USA* 978, Evans 28641, Seid. p. 140. $ 80.00

325. Evang. Luth. Church, Pa. **ERBAULISCHE LIEDER=SAMMLUNG...** Billmeyer, Germantown: 1803. 3 Vols. in 1. pp. (12), 602 + Reg. Etc. + Woodcut Frontis engraved by Reiche. Worn with some loss. 3rd Edition. *GLP/USA* 1334/1337-8, AI 4171-2/4360. $ 50.00

326. Evang. Luth. Church, Pa. **ERBAULISCHE LIEDER=SAMMLUNG...** Billmeyer, Germantown: 1805. pp. (12), 327 + Reg. Etc. + Woodcut Frontis engraved by Reiche. Small print version. *Contemporary binding of full red morocco. AEG. Boards with gilt roll and stamped initials of Catherine Foering.* Needs rebacking. 4th Ed. *GLP/USA* 1426, AI 8405. $ 44.00

327. Evang. Luth. Church, Pa. **ERBAULISCHE LIEDER=SAMMLUNG.** Billmeyer, Germantown: 1811. pp. (12), 607 + 10p. + Register & 26p. Kurze Andachten [1812] + Frontis. Nice full leather w/ original Clasps. *HSH*. XLib. *Early manuscript ownership of Catherine Snively (Grottinger). GLP/USA* 1810/1887, Seid. 181, AI 22785/25625. $ 42.00

328. Evang. Luth. Church, Pa. **ERBAULISCHE LIEDER = SAMMLUNG.** Billmeyer, Germantown: 1812. 356p. + Frontis. Small print edition. *GLP/USA* 1884, AI 25351, Seid. p. 185. Needs rebinding. $ 26.00

329. Evang. Luth. Church, Pa. **ERBAULISCHE LIEDER = SAMMLUNG.** Billmeyer, Phila: 1814. pp. 20, 626p. + Reg. & Andachten. Full leather. *Nice Manuscript Ownership of "David Fischer, Lebanon, 1816". GLP/USA* 2032/2034, Seid. p. 192, AI 31426. $ 60.00

330. Evang. Luth. Church, Pa. **ERBAULISCHE LIEDER = SAMMLUNG.** Billmeyer, Phila: 1814. *Extensive (Mennonite) Manuscript Clemens Family Record.* $ 100.00

331. Evang. Luth. Church, Pa. **ERBAULISCHE LIEDER = SAMMLUNG.** Billmeyer, Phila: 1818. 489p. Small Print Version. Bound with Helmuth's "Kurze Andachten". *GLP/USA* 2286, AI 43969/44299. *Not in Seidensticker.* $ 36.00

332. Evang. Luth. Church, Pa. **ERBAULISCHE LIEDER = SAMMLUNG.** Billmeyer, Germantown: 1826. 489p. Small Print. Full leather. *Pretty 1829 German Manuscript fraktur ownership of Magdelena Schuy = "God give me wisdom & understanding that I prepare myself in this time of grace for eternity". GLP/USA* 2802/4, AI 24446, Seid. p. 229. $ 100.00

333. Evang. Luth. Church, Pa. **ERBAULISCHE LIEDER = SAMMLUNG.** Billmeyer, Germantown: 1829. Full leather. *GLP/USA* 3007-8, Seid. p. 241, *Not in AI.* $ 32.00

334. Evang. Luth. Church, Pa. **ERBAULISCHE LIEDER = SAMMLUNG.** Billmeyer, Germantown: 1830. 489p. Small Print. Full leather. *GLP/USA* 3078-9, AI 1284/1812. $ 30.00

335. Evang. Luth. Church, Pa. **ERBAULISCHE LIEDER = SAMMLUNG.** Mentz & Son, Phila: 1832. 489p. Small Print. Full leather. AI 12317 *[2 Copies only].* $ 30.00

336. Evang. Luth. Church, Pa. **ERBAULISCHE LIEDER = SAMMLUNG.** Mentz & Son, Phila: 1834. 489p. Small Print. Full leather. *Apparently Not in AI.* $ 32.00

337. Evang. Luth. Church, Pa. **ERBAULISCHE LIEDER = SAMMLUNG.** Mentz & Son, Phila: 1840. 489p. Small Print. Pretty full leather gilt. *HSH.* $ 30.00

338. Evang. Luth. Church, Pa. **LITURGIE UND KIRCHEN=AGENDE...** (Hartman) for Diezel, Lebanon: 1838. 115p. Leather backed marbled boards. *Colored ownership of "Mary M. Weigley, 1847."* AI 50237. $ 60.00

339. Evang. Luth. Church, Pa. **LITURGIE UND KIRCHEN=AGENDE...** (Hartman) for Diezel, Lebanon: 1838. 115p. Leather backed marbled boards. AI 50237. $ 38.00

340. **EVANGELISCHES LIEDERBUCHLEIN FUR SONNTAG-SCHULEN**. Cleveland. Ca: 1880. 239p. 32mo. Cloth. *WST.* $ 12.00

341. **EVANGELISCHES MAGAZIN...** Zentler, Phila: 1813. 243p. + Stipple Engraved Frontis of Johann Frederick Schmidt. Boards Detached. Second Volume of an extremely scarce periodical published by the German Evangelical Lutheran Church. $ 80.00

342. **ES EVANGELIUM VUM MATTHEUS. Aus der griechische Schprooch ins Pennsilvenideitsch iwwersetzt vum Ralph Charles Wood**. Stuttgart & Allentown: 1955. 56p. Wraps. $ 16.00

THE GOSPEL OF NICODEMUS

343. **EVANGELIUM NICODEMI, Oder Historicher Bericht Von derm Leben Jesu Christi, Welches Nicodemus, Ein Rabbi und Oberster der Jūden...** Jacob Bailey, Lancaster: 1784. 247p. *GLP/USA* 603, Evans 18362, Seid. 113. *WST.* $ 160.00

344. **EVANGELIUM NICODEMI...** Bound With / **TESTAMENT UND ABSCHRIFT DER ZWOLF PATRIARCHEN DER SOHNEN JACOBS...** Jacob Bailey, Lancaster: 1791. pp. 95, 113. XLib. *GLP/USA* 809, Evans 23203, Seid. p. 129. *HSH.* $ 120.00

345. **DAS EVANGELIUM NICODEMI...** Bruckman for Stocker & others, Reading, 1819. 225p. Nice leather backed paper bds. *GLP/USA* 2385, AI 47209. *Not in Seid.* Curious Pennsylvania German versions of the mystical gospels. $ 80.00

346. **DAS EVANGELIUM NICODEMUS...** Bound With / **Genoveva un Helena**, Etc. Bruckman, Reading: 1819. 302p. Lacks the second title page. Worn paste paper binding. *GLP/USA* 2386, AI 47208/48256-8. $ 85.00

347. **DAS EVANGELIUM NICODEMUS...** Bär, Lancaster: 1843. 219p. Leather backed marbled boards. Scarce edition. $ 50.00

OWNED AND DECORATED BY A KNOWN FRAKTUR ARTIST

348. Eyer, J. F. & Gerhart, Isaac. **CHORAL HARMONIE... Kirchen = Melodien...** Wyeth, Harrisburg: 1818. pp. 11, 100. Some leaves with slight loss. Oblong Pa. German Shaped Note Song Book. ***This is the copy of Philip Mumbauer, a Lehigh County Schoolmaster and Fraktur Artist sometimes called "The P. M. Artist". There are four pages of manuscript songs and verses written in 1827 and 1833, and signed by Mumbauer. In addition, there is an outlined, unfinished fraktur dedication page with the classic design of two hearts sprouting decorative tulips on opposite sides of the page, within a geometric border.*** Possibly the artist's own song book. $ 400.00

349. Eyer & Gerhart. **CHORAL HARMONIE...** Wyeth, Harrisburg: 1818. pp. 11, 100. Last 2 leaves repaired with some loss. Ds. Worn oblong leather backed marbled boards. *GLP/USA* 22574, AI 44154. *Not in Seid.* Oblong Pa. German Song Book. Shaped Notes. $ 125.00

350. Eyer & Gerhart. **CHORAL HARMONIE...** Wyeth, Harrisburg: 1822. 132p. Oblong leather backed marbled board. XLib. Oblong Pa. German Song Book. Shaped Notes. *Manuscript ownership of John Rothermel. GLP/USA* 2545, AI 8821, *Not in Seid.* $ 155.00

351. Eyer, Henry C. **UNION CHORAL HARMONIE...** With Text in English & German. Phila. Ca: 1840. 192p. Oblong leather backed printed bds. XLib. Shaped Notes. $ 65.00

352. Eyer. **UNION CHORAL HARMONIE...** With Text in English & German. Schaefer & Koradi, Phila. Ca: 1860. 192p. Oblong yellow printed bds. XLib. Shaped Notes. $ 65.00

353. **DIE FACKEL...** Samuel Ludvigh, Baltimore: 1852. 384p. Sm. folio. Contains: "Die Geheimnisse der Inquisition" by Fereal & Meher. + Other articles & comments. Scarce German-American magazine. $ 30.00

354. **DIE FAMILIEN=MUTTER...** Fanshaw for the American Tract Society. NY. Circa: 1850. 163p. + Frontis. Lovely copy. $ 22.00

355. (Fegley, Sylvester). **NEUJAHR-WUENSCHE.** (Topton, Pa: 1907). 16p. Plain wraps. New Years wishes in Pennsylvania German dialect. $ 30.00

READY RECKONERS FOR FARMERS & TRADESMEN

356. Fenning, Daniel. **DER GESCHWINDE RECHNER...** Jacob Johnson, Phila: 1794. 195p. Full leather. Worn. Manuscript ownership of Jon Dubs, Lebanon. *Not in Seid. GLP/USA* 949, Evans 26969. Karpinski p. 56. $ 100.00

357. (Fenning). **DER GESCHWINDE RECHNER...** Blumer, Allentown: 1834. 130p. 32mo. AI 24601, Shoemaker/L p. 50. $ 20.00

358. (Fenning). **DER GESCHWINDE RECHNER...** Allentown: 1836. 134p. Ds. 32mo. *Not in AI.* Shoemaker/L p. 56 *[Recording this copy only]. WST.* $ 45.00

359. (Fenning). **DER GESCHWINDE RECHNER...** Harrisburg: 1854. $ 15.00

360. (Fenning). **DER FERTIGE RECHNER...** Zentler & Mentz, Phila: 1817. 144p. 24mo. Full leather. *GLP/USA* 2231, AI 40824, Karpinski p. 211. *Not in Seid.* $ 22.00

361. **DIE FESTZEITEN DES CHRISTLICHEN KIRCHENJAHRS.** Reading & Allentown. Ca: 1878. Illustrated book for children. $ 10.00

THE ASTRONOMER OF LEHIGH COUNTY

362. Fingado, Johann. **FORSCHUNGEN IM WELTGEBANDE.** Allentown: 1857. pp. 6, 104, 1. Very scarce work on Astronomy by John Findago [1796-1884], who came to Macungie, Pa. in 1830. Shoemaker/L p. 17 & p. 93. *WST.* $ 120.00

363. Fischer (Fisher), Henry Lee [1822-1909]. **'S ALT MARIK-HAUS MITTES IN D'R SCHTADT, Un Die Alte' Zeite' E'n Centennial Poem in Pennsylfanisch Deutsch.** York: 1879. 275p. Charming illustrations. Includes an English introduction. Great York cultural and historical work. A classic of Pennsylvania German dialect poetry. *WST.* $ 50.00

364. Fischer, H. L. **KURZWEIL UN ZEITFERTREIB, odder Pennsylfaanisch Deutsche Folks-Lieder...** York: 1882. 187p. Illus. Original adaptations and translations into Pennsylvania German dialect, with glossary. *WST.* $ 50.00

365. Fischer, H. L. **KURZWEIL UN ZEITFERTREIB. Ruhrende un' Launige Gedichte in Pennsylfanisch Deutscher Mundart...** York: 1896. 266p. + Illus. This 2nd Edition includes additional poems, photos, and a glossary. *WST.* $ 40.00

366. Fischer. **"POE'S RAVEN". A Pennsylvania German Version.** York: (1891). 7p. Self wraps. Rare translation into the dialect, printed at Fisher's home - "Mapleshade". $ 40.00

367. Försch, J. A. **LEBEN THATEN MEINUNGEN DES ULRICH ZWINGLI...** Scriba, Chambersburg: 1837. 162p. + Frontis portrait beautifully engraved by W. Wagner, York, Pa. Leather backed marbled boards. AI 44329. Biography of the Swiss Reformer. $ 50.00

41
Bewährte
Recepte;
für
Handwerker und Hausväter.
Erste Auflage.
Millgrove, gedruckt von
Samuel und Salomon Siegfrieds; 1834.

RARE PENNSYLVANIA GERMAN FORMULA BOOK

368. **41 BEWAHRTE RECEPTE; FÜR HANDWERKER UND HAUSVATER.** Siegfried, Millgrove, Pa: 1834. 32p. Woodcut on titlepage. 32mo. Plain wraps. *Apparently Not in AI.* Really unusual little formulary. $ 150.00

369. Fox, J. B. **DER INHALT VON LUTHERS KLEINEM KATECHISMUS...** Allentown. Ca: 1870. 85p. Printed corrections tipped in. Wraps. 24mo. Shoemaker/L p. 182. $ 15.00

370. Fox, John. **ALLGEMEINE GESCHICHTE DES CHRISTLICHEN MARTERTHUMS...** Phila: 1833. 934p. Woodcut illustrations. Ds. Full leather. Sm. 4to. $ 40.00

371. (Fox). **ALLGEMEINE GESCHICHTE DES CHRISTLICHEN MARTERTHUMS...** Phila. Ca: 1860. 934p. Woodcut illustrations from the 1831 edition. Binding worn. $ 20.00

372. Franke, August H. **DER SICHERE HIMMELS = WEG...** Wheit, Harrisburg: 1823. 36p. Original Marbled wraps. Franke [1663-1727], was the intellectual and political leader of Pietism in central and northern Germany. *GLP/USA* 2591, AI 12576. *HSH.* $ 75.00

373. Franke. **DER SICHERE HIMMELS = WEG oder Anleitung zum Christenthm...** Bauman, Ephrata: 1828. 36p. Later wraps. *GLP/USA* 2918, Seid. p. 237, AI p. 236. $ 175.00

FRANKLIN'S "THE WAY TO WEALTH"

374. (Franklin, Benjamin). **DER WEG ZUM GLUCK, Oder: Das Leben und Meynungeng des Dr. Benjamin Franklin...** Sage, Reading: 1820. 128p. Ds. Square 24mo. Early printed bookseller's label of Blumer, Allentown. *GLP/USA* 2465, Seid. p. 212, AI 1278. $ 140.00

375. Franz, Helene Andre. **POESIE UND PROSA.** Pittsburgh: (1895). 87p. $ 24.00

376. Freitag, Doctor Eberhard [of Bethlehem]. **DER DEUTSCHE PFERD = ARZT.** Hütter, Easton: 1809. 98p. Leather backed boards. 16mo. One of the scarcest 19th Century German "Horse Doctor" books. *GLP/USA* 1656, AI 17575, Austin 796. *WST.* $ 150.00

377. (Frey, August Emil). **MISSIONS BIBLIOTHEK für Jung und Alt. I = "Vier Jahre in Asante"...** Allentown: 1886. 161p. + Illus. Missionary travels in Africa. Shoemaker/L p. 162 *[Recording this copy only]*. *WST.* $ 40.00

378. (Frey). **MISSIONS BIBLIOTHEK für Jung und Alt. II = "Bartholomäus Ziegenbalg... Mission unter den Tamulen in Ostindien".** Allentown: 1883. 111p. + Illus. Missionary travels in India & Ceylon. Shoemaker/L p. 155-6. *WST.* $ 32.00

379. Frey, J. William. **JAKE UN JOHNNY 'n Buweg'schicht in siwwe Schtreech**. Clinton, SC: 1943. 53p. Illus. Printed wraps. "Max & Moritz" in Pa. "Dutch" dialect. *WST*. $ 20.00

380. Frey, J. W. **DER PENNSYLVAANISCH DEITSCH EILESCHPIGGEL**... F & M, Lancaster: 1945-6. Four Issues (All published?). Unusual little dialect periodical. $ 30.00

381. (Friedel, H. A.). **ERZÄHLUNGEN FÜR DIE JUGEND**. Mit Schönen Bildern. NY. Ca: 1860. 16p. Charming woodcut illus. 32mo. Printed wraps. Five different issues, each with two stories. Unusual children's publications. $ 54.00

382. (Friedel). **DIE KINDER FREUDE. Erzählungen für die Jugend**. NY. Ca: 1860. 32p. Great woodcut illus. 32mo. Eight different stories. Embossed black boards. *WST*. $ 32.00

383. (Friedel). **LÄMMERWEIDE**... NY. Ca: 1860. 32p. Woodcut illus. 32mo. Eight stories, including one about India. Embossed black boards. *WST*. $ 22.00

384. (Friedel). **MANNA FÜR DIE KLEINEN**... NY. Ca: 1860. 32p. Woodcut illus. 32mo. Eight stories. Embossed black boards. *WST*. $ 20.00

385. (Friedel). **WAS DER WEIHNACHTSBAUM SAGT**... NY. Ca: 1860. 16p. Stiff wraps. 32mo. Christmas gift book. All of Friedel's children's books are rather scarce. $ 22.00

386. Fries Rebellion. **DAS ERSTE UND ZWEITE VERHOR VON JOHN FRIES... In den Caunties Bucks, Northampton und Montgomery, In den Jahren 1799 und 1800**. Including a German translation of both the Pennsylvania & U. S. Constitutions. Allentown: 1839. 324p. Fries' insurrection raised several hundred Pennsylvanians in opposition to the "Window Tax" on houses. Once captured, he was convicted of treason and sentenced to death, but was pardoned by President Adams. This Pennsylvania German printing was issued to capitalize on the "Buckshot War" agitation. "Among the most interesting German imprints from the Allentown presses" = Shoemaker/L p. 17, 61-2. $ 125.00

387. **DIE FROMME ISABELLA**. Chambersburg. Ca: 1840. 16p. Ill. Printed wraps. 32mo. Scarce little childrens book. $ 20.00

388. Fuchs, Leonhart. **NEW KREÜTERBUCH** ...

Please See the Following Page for a Brief Description of this Rare German Medicinal Herbal

389. Funk, Ralph S. (Feldy Grumberkeffer). **DIE LICHTER SHTECK, En Gedicht in der Pennsilfanisch Deitscher Mundart**. (Allentown: 1935). 6p. Warm dialect inscription to *WST*. $ 22.00

390. Gardner, G. F. **GESCHICHTE DER EV. LUTH. ST. PETERS GEMEINDE, 1867-92**. Allentown: 1892. 12p. Illus. + Inserted memorial for Dr. Gardner (1908). Wraps. $ 12.00

THE DANGERS OF THE STREET

391. **DIE GEFAHR IN DEN STRASSEN. Nebst Einigen andern Erzählungen**. Jacob Meyer for Johnson & Warner, Phila: 1810. 36p. Woodcut on title by Alexander Anderson. Contemporary stiff wraps. *GLP/USA* 1770, AI 20192, Welch 431 (256), Rosenbach 418. German language version of a scarce 1808 juvenile. $ 125.00

392. (Gehring, P. J.). **HAUS = OECONOMIE = RECHNUNGS = TABELLEN**... Reutlingen. Ca: 1800. 72p. + Special Erasable Leaves (Made of horn?) + *Interleaved with the manuscript notes and accounts of David Buhl (Beal/Biel) born in 1773; Emigrant to America (Ohio) in 1816.* Tooled pigskin wallet bound reckoner used on his 1816 journey, and in America. $ 100.00

RARE GERMAN HERBAL

388. Fuchs, Leonhart. **NEW KREÜTERBUCH, in welchem nit allein die gantz histori, das ist, namen, gestalt, statt und zeit der wachsung der Kreüter**. Michael Isingrin, Basel: 1543. First Edition in German. Approximately 1000p. Illustrated by over 500 incredible full page floral and herbal cuts + portraits of the artists engaged on the work. Folio. Contemporary embossed leather over oak boards. Later leather back. First and last leaves repaired with slight loss. Few old stains. Early manuscript marginal notes and herbal cures. For the most part, a very clean copy of an extraordinary book. The illustrations "are most carefully drawn in outline with very little shading, and are as carefully cut; all are rendered with the greatest fidelity to Nature (with only one other Herbal on a par in this respect). These cuts, naturally, were often copied and imitated." = Fairfax-Murray German #175. It was also a new departure to show the artists at work. Before this time, illustrators and woodcutters were very rarely mentioned; and as to a portrait, we know of no other instance. As a medical reference it was very highly prized. A copy of this same elaborate Herbal was used by Rev. Lucas Raus, as the basis for his medical practice at Goshenhoppen and York, in the 1760's. "It is said to be one of the rarest books in the country" - Schmauk, *The Lutheran Church in Pa.* p. 374-5. Our copy came from Lehigh County, and was certainly used by "doctors" there. Adams F 1107, BMC STC German p. 326. Not in the National Library of Medicine, Etc. Altogether, an attractive, significant and intriguing book.

$6600.00

393. Gell, Robert. **REMAINS, oder Uberbliebene Brocken... Schrift = Texten das Neuen Testaments**... Berleburg: 1724. 900+p. Contemporary full vellum. Gell [1595-1665] was an eminent English preacher, whose collected sermons, or "*Remaines*", were edited by R. Bacon. Rare First German Edition. $ 120.00

394. **GEMÄHLDE VON JOHANN UND GEORG**. ASSU, Phila: 1833. 16p. Nice woodcut illus. Printed wraps. German American manuscript. Translation = "*Judith Susana O. Mester - I love what is fine but not mine*". Scarce Sunday School Union publication. $ 35.00

395. **DAS GEMEINSCHAFTLICHE GESANGBUCH**... Schaffer & Maund, Balt: 1817. 399p. Full leather. Prepared for use in Lutheran and Reformed Churches. *GLP/USA* 2196, AI 40896, Seid. p. 200. $ 30.00

396. **DAS GEMEINSCHAFTLICHE GESANGBUCH**... Schaffer & Maund, Balt: 1818. 399p. Full leather. Boards broken. *GLP/USA* 2260, AI 44136. *Not in Seid.* $ 30.00

397. **DAS GEMEINSCHAFTLICHE GESANGBUCH**... Mentz & Son, Phila: 1835. 384p. 24mo. AI 31809 *[2 Copies only]*. $ 26.00

398. **DAS GEMEINSCHAFTLICHE GESANGBUCH**... Mentz & Son, Phila: 1838. 384p. 24mo. Full leather. AI 50473. $ 18.00

399. **DAS GEMEINSCHAFTLICHE GESANGBUCH**... NY: 1862. Includes music. 420p. Heavily gilt tooled morocco, stamped "Kate Staub, 1863". Nice brass clasp. $ 22.00

THE PREVIOUSLY UNKNOWN FIRST AMERICAN EDITION OF GENOVESA

400. Genovesa. **EINE SCHONE ANM(UTHIGE) UND LESENS WU(RDIGE) HIS(TOR)Y VON DER UNSCHULDIG = (BEDRA)NGTEN HEILIGEN PFALTZ (GRA)FIN GENOVESA...** Armbruster & Hasselbach, in Moravian Alley, Phila: 1762. 72p. Lacks last leaf (?). Title page with an unrecorded woodcut, but defective - with loss of words as indicated above. Browned and worn. The popular medieval German legend of Genevieve of Barbant had special appeal for the emigrants to Pennsylvania. Her wrongful exile, wondrous survival (with the help of a deer), and eventual triumph made thrilling and encouraging reading. It was a tale that could be enjoyed by all ages and classes. Into the 1860's copies were eagerly read to tatters. Very rare. Even the later 1774 Lancaster edition is known in only one imperfect copy; and no copy of the 1790 edition can be found. Little is known of the printer N. Hasselbach. He seems to have been associated with Armbruster for only one year. ***Not located or noticed by the new GLP/USA bibliography, nor by Evans, Seidensticker, Hildeburn, Etc.*** $ 650.00

401. Genovesa. **DIE LEIDENS - GESCHICHTE DER UNSCHLDIGEN GENOVESA**... Scheffer, Harrisburg. Ca: 1850. 38p. Fine copy. Scarce in such well preserved original printed wraps. This is the version of the tale most familiar to American readers in the 19th Century. See Illustration. $ 135.00

402. Genovesa. **DIE UNSCHULDIGE GENOVESA, Wie sie durch Berläumdung zum Tode verurtheilt, und nach-dem sie 7 Jahre von Kräutern und Hirschmilch gelebt hatte, wunderbar errettetworden war**... Kneule, Pennsburg: 1865. 31p. Yellow printed wraps. One of the scarcest Genovesa imprints. See also Part II #'s 1293 & 1294. $ 125.00

403. German Reformed Church, U. S. **EINE SAMMLUNG EVANGELISCHER LIEDER...** Chambersburg: 1842. 480p. Full leather. First Edition. $ 40.00

404. German Reformed Church. **EINE SAMMLUNG EVANGELISCHER LIEDER...** Chambersburg: 1843. 738p. Full leather. XLib. $ 30.00

405. German Reformed Church. **EINE SAMMLUNG EVANGELISCHER LIEDER...** Chambersburg: 1851. 744p. Worn full leather. XLib. *Ownership of "L. S. Worman, Saddlier / Boyertown, Berks Co. PA."* $ 30.00

406. German Reformed Church. **EINE SAMMLUNG EVANGELISCHER LIEDER...** Chambersburg: 1863. 744p. XLib. $ 14.00

407. (Germann, W.). **HEINRICH MELCHIOR MUHLENBERG, Patriarch der Lutherischen Kirche Nordamerika's...** Allentown: 1881. 256p. Ill. Mainly composed from Muhlenberg's autobiography. Shoemaker/L p. 151-2 *[Recording this copy only]*. *WST.* $ 50.00

408. Gerok, Karl. **ALBUM FÜR SONNTAGSCHILER - Vierundsechzig Denkspruche...** Kohler, Phila. Ca: 1875. Oblong 24mo. Very pretty initials, etc. $ 8.00

409. Gerok. **BLUMEN & STERNE.** Phila: 1884. 461p. 24mo. $ 8.00

410. Gerok. **PALMBLÄTTER.** Phila: 1894. 388p. Illus. 24mo. $ 8.00

411. **GESANGBUCH FUR DIE SONNTAGS=SCHULEN.** Brobst, Allentown: 1853. 271p. 32mo. Publisher's cloth. Evang. Lutheran & Ger. Reformed Songster. $ 20.00

412. **GESANGBUCH FUR DIE SONNTAGSCHULEN.** Kohler for Brobst, Allentown: 1860. 271p. 32mo. Black cloth. Spine taped. $ 12.00

413. **GESÄNGE BEI DER CONFIRMATION am Palm-Sonntage 1849, in der Deutschen Evangelisch - Lutherischen Zions - Kirche.** (Wollenweber, Phila: 1849). 4p. Worn. Self wraps. These little song sheets are ephemeral and rather rare. $ 22.00

414. **DIE GESCHICHTE DER TAGE DES MENSCHEN = SOHNES Von der Marter = Woche an zu Seiner Himmelfahrt.** Henrich Miller, Phila: 1769. 88p. Leather backed boards. *Mary A. Wiser's copy.* *GLP/USA* 370, Evans 11273, Bristol B2989, Hild. 2444, Seid. p. 80. $ 200.00

415. **GESCHICHTE DES AMERICANISCHEN KRIEGS... 1812-1815...** Ritter, Reading: 1817. 273p. + Frontis of the explorer Zebulon Pike + 6 other unusual engraved plates. Full leather. XLib. *GLP/USA* 2249, AI 40910, Seid. p. 202. Important. $ 60.00

416. **GESCHICHTE DES WAISENHAUSES IN PHILADELPHIA...** ASSU, Phila: 1833. 61p. + Woodcuts and a frontis showing the famous fire at a Philadelphia ophanage. 24mo. Leather backed marbled boards. AI 17376. $ 36.00

PETERS COLOR PRINTED HISTORY OF JOSEPH & HIS BROTHERS

417. **DIE GESCHICHTE JOSEPH'S UND SEINER BRÜDER...** G. S. Peters, Harrisburg. Ca: 1840. 18p. Color Printed Woodcut Illustrations. Original printed orange wraps. One of the most popular of Peter's chapbooks for children. $ 220.00

418. **GESPRACH DES HERZENS MOT GOTT in Andächtigem Gebet...** Andreas Billmeyer, York: 1803. 144p. 18mo. Quite stained. Disbound. Scarce little prayer book that was first published in Onolzbach in 1729. *GLP/USA* 1365 *[4 copies only]*, AI 4273. $ 100.00

AN UNFORTUNATE MARRIAGE AND MURDER

419. Getter, Carl/Charles. **(EINZIG RICHTIGER BERICHT) GERICHTLICHES VERHOR VON CARL GETTER, wegen Ermordung seines Weibes...** Allentown: 1833. 58p. [of 59]. Lacks last leaf. Outer wrap with woodcut. Chipped. Ds. Getter, held in the Easton jail as a fornicator; was freed when he married his "mistress", Rebecca Lawall. Within two months, he strangled the "wife" he had not wanted. Not in McDade, though see: 335-6. Shoemaker/L p. 49, AI 18986 *[Locating only one copy]*. $ 100.00

420. Gilpin. **JOHN GILPIN'S POSSIERLICHE REISE NACH WEHR**. G.S. Peters, Harrisburg, Ca: 1845. 17p. Color printed illustrations. Ds. Lacks wraps. Title page repaired. See Part II # 1305 for the important Peters Gilpin in English. $ 100.00

421. **DIE GLEICHNISSE DES HERRN Fur Schule und Haus**. Kohler, Phila: 1869. 30p. *30 Color Printed Woodcut Illustrations in the style of Peters*. Stiff printed wraps. $ 50.00

422. Gock, Carl. **DIE VERTHEIDIGUND DER FREYEN KIRCHE VON NORD = AMERIKA**. Gedruct auf Kosten des Versassers (Sage), Reading: 1822. 120p. 24mo. Original plain paper wraps. *GLP/USA* 2571, AI 8842, Seid. p. 218. Arguments against the establishment of theological seminaries. See # 425 for Gossler's reply. Unusual. $ 40.00

423. (Gock, Carl). **CARL GOCKS'S NEUESTES SELBSTLEHRENDEDS RECHENBUCH...** Sage, Reading: 1823. 348p. (Including an unusual Subscribers List). Full leather. XLib. Scarce Pa. German arithmetic text. *GLP/USA* 2615, AI 12691, Karpinski 253. *Not in Seid.* $ 40.00

424. Göhring, W. H. **ZWENTES BUCH DES VERKUNDIGERS DER LESSTEN ZEIT, LICHT UND WAHRHEIT...** Lancaster: 1839. pp. 282, 10. 24mo. Full leather. XLib. *Apparently Not in AI*. Presumably a Mennonite work. *HSH*. $ 45.00

425. (Gossler, Johann Carl). **CARL GOCKS'S VERLAUMDUNGEN, oder Die Rechtfertigung der Hochdeutschen Lutherischen und Reformirten Synoden von Nord-America**. Bruckman, Reading: 1823. 160p. Leather backed paste paper decorated boards. Gossler's reply to # 422. *GLP/USA* 2608, AI 12709, Seid. p. 220. $ 40.00

426. (Gossler). **LEBENSGESCHICHTE NAPOLEON BONAPARTE'S...** Bruckman, Reading: 1822. 4 vols in 1. 443p. + Woodcut illus. Rather worn. Early Hartzel Family Ownerships. *GLP/USA* 2564, AI 8864, Seid. p. 217. $ 45.00

PENNSYLVANIA GERMAN MYSTICAL & RELIGIOUS SYMBOLISM

427. (Gossner, Johannes E.) [1773-1858]. **DAS HERZ DES MENSCHEN EIN TEMPEL GOTTES ODER EINE WEKSTATTE DES SATANS**. Heinrich B. Sage, Reading: 1822. 48p. + 10 Unusual engraved plates. First German American edition. See: Mennonite Encyclopedia II, 551-2, *GLP/USA* 2572, AI 9006, Seid. p. 217. *WST*. $ 75.00

428. (Gossner). **DAS HERZ DES MENSCHEN EIN TEMPEL GOTTES ODER EINE WEKSTATTE DES SATANS**. Gustav S. Peters, Harrisburg: 1828. 58p. + 10 Emblematical engravings. Text worn. Pretty leather backed paste paper boards. *GLP/USA* 2936. *Not in AI, nor Seidensticker*. Scarce. $ 100.00

429. (Gossner). **DAS HERZ DES MENSCHEN ENTWEDER EIN TEMPEL GOTTES; Oder, Die Werkstätte des Teufels**. Scheffer, Harrisburg. Ca: 1840. 72p. Emblematic illus. Worn printed boards. *HSH*. $ 40.00

430. (Gossner). **DAS HERZ DES MENSCHEN EIN TEMPEL GOTTES ODER EINE WEKSTATTE DES SATANS**. Radde, NY: 1876. 68p. + Plates + Bookseller's ad. $ 22.00

431. (Gossner, Johannes). **DAS HERZ DES MENSCHEN EIN TEMPEL GOTTES ODER EINE WEKSTATTE DES SATANS.** NY: 1881. 68p. + Plates. Printed wraps. The symbolism of the plates is especially clear in this edition. $ 22.00

432. (Gossner). **DAS HERZ DES MENSCHEN EIN TEMPEL GOTTES ODER EINE WEKSTATTE DES SATANS.** Reprint ed. Baltic, OH: 1979. 48p. + Illus. Wraps. $ 9.00

433. Gossner. **SCHATZKASTCHEN, Bibliches Betrachtungen auf alle Tage in Jahre...** Amer. Tract. Soc. NY. Ca: 1850. 474p. Disbound. $ 16.00

434. Gossner. **WEG ZUR SELIGKEIT...** Allentown: 1837. 72p. 32mo. Printed wraps. Shoemaker/L p. 58. Questions & answers on the "Way to Salvation". $ 22.00

435. Gossner. **WEG ZUR SELIGKEIT...** Amer. Tract. Soc. NY. Ca: 1850. 64p. Nice Embossed cloth binding. $ 16.00

436. Gottschall, Abraham. **EINE VERSCHREIBUNG DER NEUEN CREATUR...** Jung, Doylestown: 1838. 100p. Leather backed bds. The author of the "New Creature" was a Doylestown Mennonite pastor. AI 50597. $ 40.00

437. (Grosch, David). **DER LEBENSLAUF VON T. JEFFERSON UND J. ADAMS, Zwey ausgezichnete Patrioten und Helden von 1776...** Jacob Myers, Lancaster: 1839. 52p. Wraps. Grosch [from Earl Twp., Lancaster Cty.], wrote this in 1827. *Apparently Not in AI.* $ 75.00

THE MURDERER'S TRUE DYING CONFESSION

438. (Gross, William). **LETZTE WORTE UND STERBE=BEKENNTNISS VON WILHELM GROSS...** (Zentler), Phila: (1823). 16p. Impressive woodcut of a gallows on Tp. Last leaf with slight loss. Ds. Plain wraps. Ever-jealous, Gross brutally killed his mistress, Kesiah Stow, who kept a bawdyhouse in Philadelphia. McDade 397n *[Locates NHi only, GLP/USA* 2605 *[2 Copies only]*, Seid. p. 220 [Cited from an ad only]. *Not in AI.* Rare. *WST.* $ 190.00

439. Grumbine, Ezra (Wendell Kitzmiller). **DIE INSHURANCE BUSINESS. A Serio-Comic Drama in the Pennsylvania German Vernacular, "As She is Spoke" in the German Districts of Pa.** Lebanon, Ca: 1905. 16p. Printed wraps. First Edition of this extremely popular dialect melodrama. *WST.* $ 40.00

440. Grumbine. **DER PRAHL - HANS, THE GHOST, & Other Rhymes in the Pennsylvania German, the Teuton, & the American English.** Lebanon: 1917. 113p. + Short typescript by *WST.* Signed by the author. $ 40.00

THE EARLIEST DATED BOOK FROM THE EPHRATA PRESS THE = "GOLDEN APPLE"

441. **GULDENE AEPFFEL IN SILBERN SCHALEN, Oder: Schöne und nützliche Worte und Warheiten zur Gottseligkeit...** Ephrata, im Jahr des Heyls: 1745. pp. 8, 519 [i.e. 534], 14. Several unusual printer's ornaments. Ds. Original Ephrata binding of polished leather. One clasp. One of the most important devotional books of the Swiss-Mennonite Brethren, and among the earliest produced at Ephrata. *GLP/USA* 76, Evans 5603, Seid. p. 26, Hild. 932. $1250.00

442. Guldin, Johannes C. [1799-1863]. **BETRACHTUNGEN U. GEBETE, Gedanken und Unterhaltungen des Frommen mit Gott.** Ritter, Reading: 1826. pp. 10, 94, 323. + Blank printed family register. Worn. XLib. *GLP/USA* 2829, Seid. p. 231, AI 24763. $ 30.00

443. Günther, Friedrich August. **HOMÖOPATISCHER THIERARTZ. Ein Hülfsbuch für Landwirthe, Pferdebesitzer und Hausväter...** (John Hrelffrich), Weisenburg: 1849. pp. X, 430. Woodcut on Tp. Contemporary half leather. Ds. First American edition of this remarkable homoeopathic work. Rare. Shoemaker/L p. 77 *[Recording this copy only]*. *WST*. $ 150.00

THE JOVIAL PENNSYLVANIA GERMAN'S SONGBOOK

444. (Gutesmuths, Johann Friedrich). **DER LUSTIGE SANGER, Eine Auswahl der besten Lieder und Neujahrsprüche. Mit einem Anhang von Spatzigen Anecdoten, und Humorische Bilder...** Allentown: 1841. 205p. Unusual woodcut illustrations. Ds. "Copies are extremely scarce" = Shoemaker/L pp. 17 & 65 *[Recording this copy only]*. Remarkable collection of merry songs, light verse, and satire. *WST*. $ 150.00

445. (Gutesmuths). **DER LUSTIGE SANGER, Eine Auswahl der besten Lieder und Neujahrsprüche. Mit einem Anhang von Spatzigen Anecdoten, und Humorische Bilder...** Allentown: 1843. 205p. Unusual woodcut illustrations. Ds. Shoemaker/L p. 68 *[Again, recording this copy only]*. *WST*. $ 150.00

446. (Gutesmuths?). **DER LUSTIGE SANGER, Ein Volks=Liederbuch...** Allentown: 1856. 159p. Obviously based on the earlier editions... but the text is different. Shoemaker/L p. 89. *WST*. All of these song books are quite remarkable. $ 75.00

447. Habermann, Johann. **CHRISTLICHE MORGEN = UND ABEND = GEBETER...** Cist, Phila: 1794. pp. 2, 63, 63, 2. Woodcut portrait. Later binding and later *Manuscript (Amish?) inscription of Christian Kauffmann, 1802*. The calligraphic ownership has been somewhat washed out but is still legible. *GLP/USA* 939, S&M 47068, Bristol B8687. Rather scarce. Habermann [1516-90], who was also called Avenarius, was an important Lutheran theologian and linguist in Jena & Wittenberg. He was best known to German Americans through the many, eagerly read, editions of this little prayer book. $ 200.00

448. Habermann. **CHRISTLICHE MORGEN = UND ABEND = GEBETER...** Leibert, Germantown: 1795. 220p. Three outstanding woodcut illus. 24mo. Worn full leather. *Extensive Manuscript (Mennonite?) ownerships of the Eby and Schnäbelin (Snavely) families*. *GLP/USA* 984, Evans 28783, Seid. p. 141. Most known copies of this edition are incomplete. $ 200.00

449. Habermann. **CHRISTLICHE MORGEN=UND ABEND = GEBETTER...** Reutlingen, Ca: 1790. 216p. 32mo. *HSH*. $ 32.00

450. Habermann. **CHRISTLICHE MORGEN=UND ABEND = GEBETER...** Merklein, Chambersburg: 1815. 144p. 24mo. *GLP/USA* 2070 *[4 Copies only]*, AI 34837. $ 50.00

451. Habermann. **CHRISTLICHES GEBET = BUCHLEIN...** Sage, Reading: 1820. 168p. + Curious frontis woodcut in relief. 24mo. Leather backed diamond paper boards. XLib. *GLP/USA* 2467, Seid. p. 212, AI 1481. *HSH*. $ 40.00

452. Habermann. **CHRISTLICHES GEBET = BUCHLEIN...** Ebner, Allentown: 1821. 160p. + Frontis. 24mo. *GLP/USA* 2472, Shoemaker/L p. 33, Seid. p. 213, AI 5512. $ 24.00

453. Habermann. **CHRISTLICHES GEBET=BUCHLEIN...** Jacob Steck, Greensburg: 1829. 168p, + Curious woodcut frontis. 24mo. Handsome paste paper boards, leather backed. *GLP/USA* 3011, AI 38876. Scarce Grünsburg imprint. $ 75.00

454. Habermann, Johann. **CHRISTLICHES GEBET = BUCHLEIN...** Baab, Harrisburg: 1829. 153p. + Frontis. 24mo. Marbled boards. *GLP/USA* 3015, Seid. p. 242, AI 38876. $ 22.00

455. Habermann. **CHRISTLICHES GEBET = BUCHLEIN...** Peters, Harrisburg: 1833. 144 + Typical Peters version of the frontis. 24mo. Leather backed boards. AI 19158. $ 50.00

456. Habermann. **CHRISTLICHES GEBET = BUCHLEIN...** Peters, Harrisburg: 1844. 144 + Frontis. 24mo. Leather backed marbled boards. XL. *Nice Manuscript ownership of John Fox, Bern Township, Berks County.* $ 60.00

457. Habermann. **DAS KLEINE GEBET=BUCH.** Blumer, Allentown: 1833. 144p. 24mo. AI 19159, Shoemaker/L p. 49. Nice early manuscript ownership. *WST.* $ 22.00

458. Habermann. **DAS KLEINE GEBET=BUCH.** Blumer, Allentown: 1834. 144p. 24mo. *Not in AI.* Shoemaker/L p. 50. *WST.* $ 18.00

459. Habermann. **DAS KLEINE GEBET=BUCH.** Grater, Allentown: 1835. 144p. Unusual woodcut illustration. Leather backed marbled boards. *Isaac Kuntz ownership.* Probably printed in Germany for Grater. Shoemaker/L p. 54. $ 20.00

460. Habermann. **DAS KLEINE GEBET=BUCH.** Jung, Doylestown: 1839. $ 24.00

461. Hachenberg, P. **KURZE UBERSICHT VON DER HAUPT = LEHREN DER CHRISTLICHEN RELIGION.** Miller, New Berlin: 1838. 280p. 18mo. Ds. AI 50662. $ 50.00

RARE INDIAN CAPTIVITY IN THE "WILD WEST" = 1832

462. (Hall). **GESCHICHTE DER GEFANGENNEHMUNG UND DER FRANCES UND ELMIRA HALL...** Joseph Miller, Harrisburg: 1833. 16p. Small old ink stain. Plain wraps. When the settlement at Indian Creek was attacked in 1832, fifteen people were killed, and two young sisters (ages 16 & 18) were taken prisoner. They later escaped. Also included in this pamphlet is an account of Philip Brigdon, a Kentuckian, who later fell into the hands of the same Indians. Uncommon Pennsylvania German version of the rare St. Louis edition. *Apparently Not in AI.* $ 175.00

463. Hall, Newman. **KOMM ZU JESU!.** Amer. Tract. Soc. NY. Ca: 1850. 95p. $ 12.00

464. Halle Reports. **NACHRICHTEN VON DEN VEREINGTEN DEUTSCHEN EVANGELISCH - LUTHERISCHEN GEMEINEN IN NORD-AMERICA...** Introduced and Edited by Schulze, Mann, Schmucker, & Germann. Allentown: 1886. 2 Vols. 1600p. 1/2 Morocco. One of the best historical source records on the early church in Pa. $ 75.00

465. **HANDBUCH FÜR DEUTSCHE; Formen zu Handschriften...** Bound with / Caesar's **Interesten=Rechner** [1816]. Ritter, Reading: 1819. pp. 112, 42. Leather backed boards. Form book showing how to write letters, legal forms, & accounts in both English & German. First edition. *GLP/USA* 2391, AI 48147/37790. $ 50.00

466. **HANDBUCH FÜR DEUTSCHE...** Bound with / Caesar's *The Ready Calculator of Interest [in English]* [1816]. Ritter, Reading: 1819. pp. 112, 42. Leather backed marbled boards. XLib. *GLP/USA* 2391, AI 48147. *HSH.* $ 40.00

467. **HANDBUCH FÜR DEUTSCHE...** Ritter, Reading: 1828. pp. 8, 108, 18, + Folding Chart. Leather backed marbled boards. *GLP/USA* 2980, AI 33471, Karpinski p. 239. $ 32.00

468. Harbaugh, Henry. **HARBAUGH'S HARFE. Gedichte in Pennsylvanisch Deutscher Mundart**... Edited by Benj. Bausman. Phila: 1870. 121p. + Illus. The most popular work of Pennsylvania German dialect poetry, with English translations & a glossary. 1st Ed. $ 26.00

469. Hassel, Carl. **DER NEU-ERFAHRNE PFERDE=ARTZ, Enthaltend 100 Curen und Recepte**... Miller, New Berlin: 1843. 48p. Later wraps. First Edition. Rare & ephemeral horse - doctor guide written in Franklin County. $ 125.00

470. Haury, Samuel S. **BRIEFE UBER DIE AUSBREITUNG DES EVANGELIUMS IN DER HEIDENWELT. Allen Mennoniten in Nord Amerika**. Halstead, Kansas: 1877. 109p. Plain wraps. 24mo. Haury [1847-1929] was an important Mennonite (GMC) missionary. $ 40.00

471. Hechler, Samuel. **BIBLISCHES FRAGEN = BUCHLEIN, für Kinder**... Puwelle, Reading: 1859. 48p. Yellow printed wraps. $ 30.00

472. Hechler, Samuel. **BIBLISCHES FRAGEN = BUCHLEIN, für Kinder**... Reading: 1868. 48p. Printed wraps. $ 20.00

473. Heerbrandt, G. **HUMORISTISCHE PERLEN. Eine Sammlung Heiterer Geschichten.** NY. Ca: 1880. 64p. Later wraps. Acidic. *WST.* $ 16.00

474. **DAS HEILIGE VATERUNSER, Illustrirt und Ausgelegt Gottes Lieben Kindern zu Nutz und Frommen.** Allentown: 1878. 30p. Charming woodcut illustrations. 4to. Scarce children's book. Shoemaker/L p. 146. *WST.* $ 30.00

475. Heinen, Dr. Henry. **GESUNDHEITS-SCHATZKAMMER**... Baer, Lancaster: 1831. 118p. Full leather. Prominent and popular Pennsylvania German medical handbook and formulary. AI 7494. $ 75.00

476. Heinen. **GESUNDHEITS-SCHATZKAMMER**... Phila: 1840. 118p. Disbound. This medical handbook has a curious publishing history that adds to its mystique. $ 55.00

477. Helffenstein, J. C. Albert. **EINE SAMMLUNG AUSERLESENER PREDIGTEN**. Victor Scriba, Chambersburg: 1835. 298p. XLib. AI 32109. $ 27.50

478. Helffenstein. **EINE SAMMLUNG AUSERLESENER PREDIGTEN**. Weinbrenner, Harrisburg: 1839. 292p. Ds. AI 56248. *WST.* $ 28.00

479. (Helffrich, J.). **CHRISTLICHER UNTERRICHT DER RELIGION. In Fragen und Antworten**. Allentown: 1826. 52p. (Lacks Foreword leaf?). 18mo. Marbled wraps. Ds. Early Schwartz / Linibach ownerships. *GLP/USA* 2780, Shoemaker/L p. 41 *[Recording this copy only]*, AI 24828. *WST.* $ 50.00

480. (Helffrich). **CHRISTLICHER UNTERRICHT DER RELIGION**... Allentown: 1839. 63p. 18mo. Shoemaker/L p. 63. *Apparently not in AI. WST.* $ 36.00

481. (Helffrich). **CHRISTLICHER UNTERICHT DER RELIGION**... Allentown: 1839. 61p. 18mo. Shoemaker/L p. 62. Third edition. *WST. Apparently not in AI.* $ 36.00

482. (Helffrich). **CHRISTLICHER UNTERICHT DER RELIGION**... Weisenburg: 1847. 80p. Pretty leather backed marbled boards. 4th Ed. Shoemaker/L p. 73. *WST.* $ 34.00

483. (Helffrich). **CHRISTLICHER UNTERICHT DER RELIGION**... Weisenburg: 1852. 71p. 5th Ed. Provincial "job" printing. Shoemaker/L p. 82. *WST.* $ 30.00

484. Helffrich, Wm. A. **LEBENSBILD AUS DEM PENNSYLVANISCH = DEUTSCHEN PREDIGIGERSTAND**... Allentown: 1906. 592p. + Illus. 1/2 leather. 4to. Fine history of a family of ministers & their churches. Excellent content. *WST.* $ 40.00

485. Helmuth, Justus Henry Christian [1745 - 1825]. **BETRACHTUNG DER EVANGELISCHEN LEHRE VON DER HEILGEN SCHRIFT...** Billmeyer, Germantown: 1793. 346p. Leather backed paper boards. Includes several charming woodcut vignettes. *GLP/USA* 884, Evans 25594, Seid. p. 135. $ 60.00

1793 YELLOW FEVER EPIDEMIC PAMPHLET

486. (Helmuth, J. H. C.). **"KURZE NACHRICHT VON DEM SOGENANNTEN GELBEN FIEBER IN PHILADELPHIA..."** Bound with / **TODTEN LISTE VON DER MONATEN AUGUST, SEPTEMBER & OCTOBER IN PHILADELPHIA 1793.** Steiner & Kammerer, Phila: 1793. pp. 4, 100 (of 104), 21, 4. ***Woodcut figure of death and a woodcut of a Phila. home.*** Sewn as issued. Worn. Scarce & important record of the devastating Yellow Fever epidemic. Includes: a history of the disease; a list of the dead; weather observations by David Rittenhouse; & a poem by J. H. Winkhauses. *GLP/USA* 908, Evans 25595/46777, Seid. p. 136. $ 240.00

RARE GERMAN AMERICAN VELLUM BINDING

487. (Henderson, David). **DES LANDMANN'S ADVOCAT...** Henrich Miller, Phila: 1761. pp. 4, 8, 170, 4 + 1 of the 2 rare folding charts. Small 4to. ***Really unusual full contemporary American vellum binding. Manuscript ownership of Jacob Wolf (York County?).*** *GLP/USA* 235, Evans 8897, Seid. p. 56. $ 400.00

488. (Herman, J. C.). **GEBET FÜR KINDER, Für alle Begebenheiten im Leben.** (Kutztown): 1856. 63p. 24mo. Children's prayer book. $ 30.00

489. (Herr, J. Friedrich). **ETWAS UBER DIE METHODISTEN, und die Unschicklichkeit ihrer Lager-Versammlungen.** Allentown: 1837. 32p. Printed wraps. Shoemaker/L p. 58. *Apparently Not in AI. WST.* $ 40.00

490. Herr, Johannes [1782-1850]. **ERLAUTERUNGS=SPIEGEL, Oder Eine Gründliche Erklärung Von der Bergpredigt Unsers Herrn Jesu Christi.** Bär, Lancaster: 1827. 395p. 16mo. Full leather. *GLP/USA* 2873, Seid. p. 234, AI 29205. Scarce First Edition. Vital work by the founder of the Reformed Mennonite Church. $ 100.00

491. Herr. **ERLAUTERUNGS=SPIEGEL...** Bär & Sohne, Lancaster: 1854. 395p. 16mo. Xlib. Almost disbound. Reformed Mennonite Church. $ 24.00

492. (Herrman, C. G.). **KOMMUNIONBUCH. Abendmahls=Feier und Religiose Unterhaltungen für Abendmahls=Gäste.** "Geist der Zeit" Druckerei, Kutztown: 1850. 203p. Leather backed boards. 18mo. Ds. *WST.* $ 24.00

493. (Hertz, Daniel). **POETISCHER HIMMELS-WEG, Kleine Geistliche Lieder-Sammlung...** Hartman, Lebanon: 1830. pp. 11, 286, 8. 24mo. Full leather. *GLP/USA* 3109, AI 1826, Seid. p. 246. $ 24.00

494. Hess, Samuel. **KURZGEFASSTER UNTERRICHT DER CHRISTLICHEN RELIGION, in Fragen und Antworten zum Gebrauch der Jungend.** Held, Easton: 1843. 47p. Ds. $ 30.00

495. Hess. **KURZGEFASSTER UNTERRICHT DER CHRISTLICHEN RELIGION...** Allentown: 1850. 72p. Shoemaker/L p. 79. *WST.* $ 30.00

496. (Himmelbergern, Catharina). **WEISSAGUNG Von der Zukunst unsers Herrn Jesum Christum und taufendjährrigen Reich...** Reading: 1845. 60p. Unusual woodcut illus. Marbled wraps. Rare mystical / prophetic work. *WST.* $ 100.00

497. **DAS HIMMLISCHE VERGNUGEN IN GOTT, Oder Vollstandiges Gebet = Buch.** Brobst & Blumer, Allentown: 1839. 824p. Attractive full leather, with clasps. Shoemaker/L p. 62-3, AI 56295. Very scarce. $ 60.00

498. **DAS HIMMLISCHE VERGNUGEN IN GOTT, Oder Vollstandiges Gebet = Buch.** *Gedruct fur John Kraus in Pennsylvanien, Stuttgart*: 1854. 827p. + Illus. Full leather. No clasps. Small 4to. These imports are most interesting and intriguing. $ 24.00

499. **DAS HIMMLISCHE VERGNUGEN IN GOTT...** NY & Phila: 1865. 827p. + Illus. Full embossed morocco. Brass clasps. Small 4to. $ 22.00

"THE AMERICAN GOLD MINE"

500. (Hirte, Tobias). **DER AMERICANISCHE GOLDGRUBE; das ist die Kunst des Landmanns, seine zeitlichen Güter fünfzig = bis hunderfältig zu vermehren... Ein Lehrreichs Lese= und Rechenbuch für alle wahre Patrioten...** Sage, Lebanon: 1810. pp. 8, 192. Ds. Worn. Plain wraps. Curious instructional piece, full of political, economic, and social theory. *GLP/USA* 1750, AI 19359, Seid. p. 179, Karpinski p. 181, Rink/Tech 1159. *WST.* $ 150.00

501. (Hochstetler, J. D.). **EIN ALTER BRIEF...** Gordonville, Pa: (1974). 31p. Wraps. An important Mennonite document from 1781. Reprint of the 1916 edition. $ 10.00

502. Hoffman, Franz. **EHRE VATER UND MUTTER...** Kohler, Phila: 1866. 68p. Ill. Ds. Cloth. Moral tale for children. $ 14.00

HOHMAN'S "POW WOW"
= ADVICE FOR MAN, BEAST, AND MYSTIC =

The works of Hohman, "Aristotle", and "Albertus Magnus" have been consulted by the German American community, and their "Pow Wow" doctors for over two centuries. Their zesty mix of folklore, science, and superstition provided a handy preventative and cure for the ills of life. They are especially important as authentic modern survivors of the medieval folk medicine and alchemical traditions.

503. (Hohman, Johann George). **DER FROMME ZU GOTT. in der Andacht, oder Merkwüdige Begebenheiten unsers Herrn Jesu...** (For Hohman, Reading): 1846. 160p. Scarce and unusual collection of songs and mystical text. *WST.* $ 100.00

504. Hohman. **DIE LAND= UND HAUS=APOTHEKE... Nebst einem Grossen Anhang von der Aechten Färberen...** Bruckman, Reading: 1818. pp. 11, 169 + a valuable 11p. Subscriber's List. Ds. First "American" edition of Hohman's first book. The appendix of recipes for dyes and color mixing is especially important to historians of fraktur and textiles. *GLP/USA* 2312, Seid. p. 205, AI 44367, Austin 921. $ 165.00

505. Hohman. **DER LANGE VERBORGENE FREUND, oder: Getreuer und Christlicher Unterricht für Jedermann, enthaltend: Wunderbare und Probmässige Mittel und Künste, Sowohl für Menschen als das Vieh...** (Bruckman), Reading: 1820. 100p. Very stained and well used. First dated edition of the great Pow Wow Book = "The Long Lost Friend". *GLP/USA* 2462, AI 1642. Scarce. *WST.* $ 250.00

506. Hohman. **DER LANGE VERBORGENE FREUND...** Harrisburg: 1840. 84p. Leather backed paste paper boards. Early ownership of Joseph L. Heisey. Fine copy of the "standard" German text of the great "Long Lost Friend" = Pow Wow book. *WST.* $ 150.00

507. Hohman, J. G. **DER LANGE VERBORGENE FREUND...** New Berlin, Pa: 1843. 80p. Leather backed paper boards. Crisp copy. Highly prized edition. *WST.* $ 200.00

508. Hohman. **DER LANGE VERBORGENE FREUND...** Harrisburg: 1846. 71p. Leather backed boards. *WST.* $ 125.00

509. Hohman. **DER LANGE VERBORGENE FREUND...** Bound with / Helfenstein's influential Homoeopathic work: **HAUSSCHATZ DER SYMPATHIE.** Scheffer & Beck, Harrisburg: 1853. 108p. Ds. Another "classic" edition of the text. $ 140.00

510. Hohman. **DER LANGE VERBORGENE FREUND...** Kutztown: 1872. 86p. 16mo. Leather backed boards. *WST.* $ 100.00

511. Hohman. **DER LANGE VERBORGENE FREUND...** Harrisburg. Ca: 1875. 110p. 18mo. *WST.* An unusual little pocket edition. $ 100.00

512. (Hohman). **DER LANGE VERBORGENE SCHATZ UND HAUS = FREUND...** Puwelle, Skippacksville, Pa: 1837. 123p. Leather backed marbled boards. Certainly by Hohman , or pirated from his works. AI 45115 ***[One copy only].*** *WST.* $ 180.00

513. (Hohman). **DER LANGE VERBORGENE SCHATZ UND HAUS = FREUND...** (Harrisburg?): 1847. 127p. Leather backed boards. *WST.* $ 135.00

514. (Hohman?). **DER SYMPATHETISCHER HAUS = FREUND, oder die Wunder der Sympathie und des Magnetismus. Enthaltend erprobte Mittel für Gebrechen bei Menschen und Vieh...** Dreisbach, Bath, Pa: 1857. 24p. Marbled wraps. Very Scarce. *WST.* $ 140.00

= END HOHMAN =

FOLK ARTIST JACOB WHISLER'S COPY

515. Hollaz(ens), David. **...EVANGELISCHE GNADEN=ORDNUNG...** Bound with / Thomas Wilcocks' **KÖSTLICHE HONIGTROPFEN AUS DEM FELSEN CHRISTO...** Johann Herschberger, Chambersburg: 1810. pp. 6, 167, 38. Leather backed boards. First American editions. *The copy of the now famous Folk Artist - Jacob Whisler. GLP/USA* 1716/1720, AI 20360/22055, fSeid. p. 178 [2nd title]. $ 140.00

516. Hollaz(ens), David. **GEBAHNTE PILGER=STRASSE Nach dem Berge Zion...** Zessener for Scholler, Baltimore: 1844. 144p. 16mo. XLib. Marbled bds. *HSH.* $ 25.00

517. Homoeopathy. **ALLGEMEIN VERSTANDLISCHE BELEHRUNG UBER HOMÖOPATHISCHE.** Allentown: 1834. 24p. Self wraps. Ds. 24mo. Rare. *Apparently Not in AI or Shoemaker/L.* Throughout this catalog are many homoeopathic works. $ 140.00

518. (Horlacher, Jacob). **IST SCLAVEREI VERDAMMT IN DER BIBEL? Oder in der Constitution verboten?.** Reading? (1868). 19p. Ills. Self wraps. Ds. 24mo. *Scarce political campaign pamphlet = "Is Slavery forbidden by the Bible or the Constitution?"* $ 50.00

519. (Horne, A. R.). **DAS LEBEN UND WIRKEN VON VATER JOSUA JÄGER...** Allentown: 1889. 230p. + Illus. Biography of Rev. Joshua Yeager [1802-88], in German & English. Includes marriages & confirmations performed by Yeager. Shoemaker/L p. 166. *WST.* $ 40.00

520. Horton, R. G. **VOLKS GESCHICHTE DES GROSEN BURGERKRIEGES IN DEN VEREINIGTEN STAATEN, 1861-5.** NY: 1867. 234p. + Illus. Worn cloth. German - American Youth's History of the Civil War. $ 22.00

RARE STUDY OF RELIGIOUS CEREMONIES PRINTED BY FROSCHAUER

521. Hospiniano, Rodolpho. **DE ORIGINE, PROGRESSU, CEREMONIIS ET RITIBUS FESTORUM DIERUM JUDAEORUM, GRAECORUM, ROMANORUM & TURCARUM LIBRITRES...** Bound With / **FESTA CHRISTIANORUM...** Froschouer, Tiguri (Zurich): 1592-3. Two volumes in one. pp. 28, 308, 18, 230. First titlepage with some loss. Original vellum binding. ***Contemporary Manuscript ownership of the Heidelberg Professor Jacob Kimedoncius*** (See: Mennonite Encyclopedia). Adams 1039 & 1041. $ 750.00

522. Hübner, Johann. **...BIBLISCHE HISTORIEN...** Basel. Ca: 1714. pp. 27, 408, 8 + Fifty Three unusual Engraved Plates. Full leather American(?) binding with clasps. $ 120.00

523. Hübner. **...BIBLISCHE HISTORIEN...** Wheit & Boyer, Harrisburg: 1826. pp. 335, 24 + *104 Engraved Copper Plates*. Includes Subscribers List. ***Handsome full leather German American binding with a gilt border on the boards & gilt floral florets on the spine.*** No clasps. XLib. The most profusely illustrated of all German - American imprints. *GLP/USA* 2809, Seid. p. 229, AI 24908. $ 140.00

524. Hübner. **...BIBLISCHE HISTORIEN...** Wheit & Boyer, H'burg: 1826. *Some of the Engraved Plates are Printed in Sanguine.* Full leather binding is a worn version of the above. No clasps. XLib. *GLP/USA* 2809, Seid. p. 229, AI 24908. $ 120.00

525. Hübner. **...BIBLISCHE HISTORIEN...** Wheit & Boyer, H'burg: 1826. 104 Engraved plates. More common full leather binding. XLib. $ 40.00

526. Hübner. **...BIBLISCHE HISTORIEN...** Grater & Blumer, Allentown: 1833. 576p. + Numerous Engraved Plates. This was probably printed in Germany; the imprint cut out & replaced in the form of a paster. *WST.* $ 50.00

527. Hübner. **...BIBLISCHE HISTORIEN...** Mentz & Sohn, Phila: 1840. 490p. Includes a very different series of woodcut plates. Nice mottled full leather w/clasps. XLib. $ 50.00

528. Hübner. **...BIBLISCHE HISTORIEN...** Mentz & Rovoudt, Phila: 1846. 490p. Woodcut Illustrations. $ 20.00

529. Hulsbuck, Solly (Harvey M. Miller). **G'SHBOS UND ARNSHT. A Volume of Pennsylvania German Poetry & Prose.** (Elithabethville, Pa: 1939). 384p. + Illustrations by LeRoy Gensler. 1/2 Morocco. Preston A. Barba's copy. Charming collection of dialect pieces. For other dialect pieces by Solly Hulsbuck, please see also Part II # 1423-5. $ 50.00

530. Humbolt, Alexander von. **KOSMOS. Entwurf einer Physischen Welt-beschreibung.** Thomas, Phila: 1855. 637p. Binding worn. $ 75.00

THE FAMED HUNDRED YEAR CALENDAR OF PREDICTIONS

531. **DER HUNDERTJÄHRIGE CALENDER, auf das Gegenwärtige Jarhr=hundert nach Christi Geburt von 1799 bis 1899...** Hanzsche, Baltimore: 1830. 80p. Woodcut Illustrations. Includes the very rare folding chart. 16mo. Marvelous book of prophesy that was popular among the "Pow Wows" in York County and Maryland. Rarely found complete. *Not in Seid.* AI 1951. *GLP/USA* 3070 *[2 Copies only].* $ 180.00

532. Hunzinger, Abraham. **DAS RELIGIONS, KIRCHEN, UND SCHUL = WESEN DER MENNONITEN ODER TAUFGEFINNTEN...** Milford Square, Pa: 1862. 192p. Old newspaper wraps. First American edition. Full of proposals to "reform" Mennonite practice. $ 60.00

GERMAN VINICULTURE IN MISSOURI

533. Husmann, Georg. **WEINBAU IN AMERIKA. Im Speziellen Die Cultur der Rebe in Missouri.** Allentown: 1857. 15p. + Frontis. Ds. Printed Wraps. Important. *The only copy known?* = See Shoemaker/L p. 92. $ 150.00

534. **INDIANER = ZEIT...** Cleveland. Ca: 1880. 127p. + Illustrations, including a Mormon Temple). 16mo. Cloth. Mostly about the earliest German / Moravian missions to the American Indians. $ 24.00

535. **DIE INSEL...** Amer. Tract Soc. NY. Ca: 1860. 32p. Illustrations, including a nice woodcut of a whaling scene. Printed wraps. *WST.* $ 28.00

536. Insurance Companies. **INCORPORATIONS - AKTE und Neben = Gefetze der Lecha County Gegenseitigen Feuer = Versicherungs = Gesellschaft.** Keck, Guth & Helfrich, Allentown: 1856. 18p. 32mo. Plain wraps. *Apparently Not in Shoemaker/L. WST.* $ 50.00

537. Insurance Companies. **INKORPORATIONS - AKTE und Bei = Gefetze der Bauern Feuer - Versicherungs Compagnie von Berks und Lecha Counties.** Allentown: 1857. 16p. Plain wraps. *Not in Shoemaker/L. WST.* $ 50.00

INSURANCE AGAINST HORSE THIEVES

538. Insurance Companies. **INCORPORATIONS - AKTE und Neben = Gefetze der Lecha County gegenseitigen Pferde = Versicherungs = Gesellschaft.** Allentown: 1857. 16p. 32mo. Plain wraps. *Apparently Not in Shoemaker/L. WST.* $ 75.00

539. Insurance Companies. **INCORPORATIONS - AKTE und Neben = Gefetze der Lecha County gegenseitigen Pferde = Versicherungs = Gesellschaft.** Allentown: 1858. 16p. 32mo. Plain wraps. *Apparently Not in Shoemaker/L. WST.* $ 55.00

540. Jacoby, Daniel. **AMERIKANISCHER RECHNUNGS=SCHLUSSEL, Oder Anfangs-Grunde der Rechenkunst...** Bär, Lancaster: 1818. 120p. Nice leather backed marbled bds. *GLP/USA* 2277, AI 44451, Seid. p. 204, Karpinski p. 218. $ 34.00

541. Jobst, Johann G. **KURZER INNBEGRIFF DES EWIGEN EVANGELIUMS...** Samuel Siegfried, Bath, Pa: 1838. 420p. Binding worn. Unusual Northampton Cty. imprint. $ 45.00

542. Johnson, Willis Fletcher. **SCHILBERUNG DER JOHNSTOWN UEBER-SCHWEMMUNG.** Edgwood: 1889. 458p. + Illus. Scarce German edition of the standard account of the Johnstown Flood. $ 22.00

543. Jörres, Ludwig. **DIE FREYMAUREREY, oder Offenbarung aller Geheimnisse, Cereminien, Eides=Formeln, Handgriffe und Sinnbilder der drey ersten Grade... Nebst einer genauen Beschreibung von der Entführung des William Morgan...** Pennsylvanien (Harrisburg): 1829. 164p. Masonic woodcuts. Original leather backed marbled boards. Joseph Reinhard's copy. *GLP/USA* 3054, AI 39140. Seid. p. 243. Important Anti-Masonic work. $ 100.00

544. **JUBELTONE...** Cleveland: (1871). 176p. Small oblong song book. $ 20.00

545. **DES JUGENDFREUNDES CHRISTTAGS-GESPRACHE.** (Allentown, Ca: 1860). 16p. Self wraps. A Christmas play. *WST.* $ 20.00

546. Jung-Stilling, Johann Henrich [1740-1817]. **ANTWORT DURCH WAHRHEIT IN LIEBE. Auf die an Mich Gerichteten Briefe des Herrn Prof. Sulzers in Konstanz, uber Katholicismus und Protestantismus.** Nurnberg: 1811. 319p. 1/2 Leather. $ 50.00

547. Jung-Stilling, J. H. **DER CHRISTLICHE MENSCHENFREUND...** Gruber, Hagerstown, Md: 1807. 2 volumes in 1. pp. 102, 94 + an unusual ad from Gruber to subscribers. Leather backed boards. *Heinrich Luther's copy. GLP/USA* 1543, AI 12850, Seid. p. 169. $ 100.00

548. Jung-Stilling. **DER CHRISTLICHE MENSCHENFREUND...** Friedrich Sanno, Carlisle, Pa: 1809. 119p. First Amer. Ed. of vol. III. Worn. *GLP/USA* 1651, AI 17855. $ 60.00

549. Jung-Stilling. **DAS HEIMWEH...** Marburg & Cassel: 1817-18. 4 Volumes. Contemporary full leather. *HSH.* $ 125.00

550. Jung-Stilling. **HEINRICH STILLING'S ALTER, Von Ihn Selbst Geschreiben...** Ebner, Allentown: 1821. 94p. Leather backed marbled boards. Includes an account of the author's last days by his Uncle, Wilhelm Schwarz. *GLP/USA* 2473, Shoemaker/L p. 34, AI 5737. $ 60.00

551. Jung-Stilling. **LEBENSBESCHREIBUNG VON HEINRICH STILLING (Sonst Heinrich Jung genannt).** Sage, Reading: 1811. 408p. + Printer's advertisement. First American Edition. Leather backed marbled boards. XLib. *GLP/USA* 1870, AI 23135, Seid. 184. $ 75.00

552. Jung-Stilling. **DIE SIEBENLEZTEN POSAUNEN ODER WEHEN.** Printed by Bruckman for Charles M'Williams, Reading: 1820. 142p. + Powerful emblematic woodcut frontis of the "Antichrist" (a seven headed dragon with 10 horns). Leather backed paste paper boards. Authorship of this work has been attributed to Christian Armbrüster: cf. Cazden, p. 672-3. *GLP/USA* 2461, AI 1815, Seid. p. 212. Important mystical treatise. $ 100.00

553. Jung-Stilling. **THEOBALD, Oder Die Schwärmer...** Jacob Stöver for Schnee, Lebanon: 1811. 2 vols in 1. pp. 272, 192. Leather backed boards. *GLP/USA* 1831, AI 23136. $ 60.00

554. Jung-Stilling. **THEORIE DER GEISTER = KUNDE...** Bound with the / **APOLOGIE...** Sage, Reading: 1816. pp. 384, 72 + Engraved frontis. Worn. One of the most important works of Jung-Stilling; recognized as significant in the worlds of both Science and Mysticism. *GLP/USA* 2187/8, AI 37979-80, Seid. p. 199. *WST.* $ 75.00

555. Kapp, Friedrich. **GESCHICHTE DER DEUTSCHEN IM STAATE NEW YORK...** NY: 1869. 414p. Half Leather. Ds. Praiseworthy history of the Germans in NY. $ 55.00

556. Kaufmann, Peter [Bucks Cty.]. **BETRACHTUNG ÜBER DEN MENSCHEN.** Conrad Zentler, Phila: 1825. 244p. *GLP/USA* 2743, AI 21088. *Not in Seid.* Curious philosophical study. Quotation on title-page = "The proper study of man is man - Pope". $ 22.00

557. Kaul, Anton F. **GESANGBUCH FÜR DIE KATHOLISCHE JUNGEND...** Lancaster. Ca: 1865. 160p. 24mo. Printed paper boards. Scarce Catholic hymnal. $ 30.00

558. Kelz, Heinrich. **PHONOLOGISCHE ANALYSE DES PENNSYLVANIA-DEUTSCHEN.** Bonn: 1969. 154p. Wraps. XLib. $ 15.00

559. Kempis, Thomas 'a. **DER KLEINE KEMPIS... Kurtze Sprüchche und Gebätlein...** Solingen: 1758. 215p. 32mo. Titlepage stained. $ 60.00

560. Kempis, Thomas 'a. **DER KLEINE KEMPIS... Kurtze Sprüchche und Gebätlein...** Leibert, Germantown: 1795. 180p. + Frontis woodcut (mounted). Worn. Ds. Foreword by Gerhard Tersteegen. *GLP/USA* 986, Evans 28920, Seid. p. 141, Brethren Bibliography 957. $ 45.00

562. Kempis. **DER KLEINE KEMPIS...** Altdorf: 1832. 283p. + Frontis. 24mo. $ 22.00

563. Kempis. **VIER BUCHER VON DER RACHFOLGUNG CHRISTI...** William Hamilton, Lancaster: 1810. pp. 295, 16. Ill. Contemporary full leather. XLib. *GLP/USA* 1742, Seid. p. 179, AI 20425, Parsons 386. The earliest German-American Edition of this particular version that we've been able to locate. Scarce. *HSH.* $ 150.00

EARLY AMERICAN SILK FARMER'S GUIDE

564. Kenrick, William. **DES AMERICANISCHEN SEIDEBAUERS ANWEISUNG, Oder Die Kunst den Maulbeer-Baum & Die Seide zu Ziehen. System von Mehreren Auseinander Folgenden Ernten Wahrend Einer Jeden Jahrszeit...** Edited & Translated from the English by Joel Schelly. Edmund Y. Schelly, Phila: 1838. 103p. Leather backed boards, printed with an illus. of a Silk Spinning machine. Contains material not in the English edition. Mulberry trees & silk culture promoted in Berks County, Pa. AI 51116. $ 125.00

565. Kessler, C. R. **EINE PREDIGT UBER DIE KINDER - TAUFE...** Allentown: (1848). 36p. Original orange wraps. Shoemaker/L p. 75. *WST.* $ 28.00

566. (Kessler, Charles). **ANFANGSGRUNDE DE RECHENKUNST...** Ritter, Reading: 1807. 176p. Leather backed boards. XLib. *GLP/USA* 1578, Seid. p. 171, AI 12865, Karpinski 170. Early school mathematics text. *HSH.* $ 40.00

Kleine
Biblische Historien,
aus dem
Alten und Neuen Testament.
Mit vielen bunten Bildern geziert.
Harrisburg, Pa.
Gedruckt und zu haben bey G. S. Peters.

PETERS' COLOR ILLUSTRATED BIBLE HISTORY

567. **KLEINE BIBLISCHE HISTORIEN, aus dem Alten und Neuen Testament**. G. S. Peters, Harrisburg, Ca: 1845. 18p. Each with a colored woodcut illustration. Fine original printed orange wraps. Another of Peters' popular color printed children's books. $ 300.00

"LITTLE PRATTLE OVER A BOOK OF PRINTS"

568. **KLEINE ERZAEHLUNGEN UBER EIN BUCH MIT KUPFERN, Oder Leichte Geschite Fur Kinder**. Jacob Meyer, for Johnson & Warner, Phila: 1809. 44p. Illustrated by 19 fine line woodcuts. Very fine copy in contemporary stiff marbled wraps. *GLP/USA* 1690, Seid. p. 176, AI 17875, Welch 739 (777), Rosenbach 395. Important Pa. German Juvenile. $ 150.00

569. Klotz, Johann (Joseph H. Warner). **AMERIKANISCHE HISTORIE.** Annville, Pa: 1905. 100p. Illus. Very scarce work in the Pennsylvania German dialect. *WST.* $ 45.00

570. Knecht, Leonhard. **EINE AUSWAHL REIM=GEBATE...** Siegfried, Millgrove, Buschkill Twp. Northampton Cty: 1835. 95p. Decorated wraps. 32mo. *Apparently Not in AI.* $ 75.00

571. (Knerr, Sylvester). **EIN SCHONES BILD FÜR DIE JUGEND...** Hereford Twp., Berks County. Ca: 1870. 24p. 32mo. Printed wraps. $ 28.00

572. Knights of Pythias. **CONSTITUTION... Emaus Loge No. 378.** Allentown: 1874. 64p. 24mo. W / List of Members. Shoemaker/L p. 139 *[Recording this copy only]*. *WST.* $ 34.00

573. Krahn, Cornelius. **MENNO SIMONS; Ein Beitrag zur Geschichte und Theologie der Taufgesinnten**. Scottdale: 1984. 194p. Illus. Wraps. Mennonite biography. $ 14.00

574. Krauss, Johann. **OECONOMISCHES HAUS = UND KUNST = BUCH** ... Ebner, Allentown: 1819. pp. 16, 452. Krauss [1770-1819] was a teacher, surveyor, organ builder, etc. Important folk craft formulary and household recipe book, which includes essential coloring information for practitioners of fraktur illumination. *GLP/USA* 2322, Seid. p. 206, AI 48443, Shoemaker/L p. 30, Rink 186. $ 120.00

GERMAN AMERICAN GUIDE FOR DYEING WOOL, LINEN, SILK, ETC.

575. Kuder, Solomon. **DER PRAKTISCHE FAMILIEN=FARBER**... Allentown: 1858. 64p. + 6p. *Seventeen actual mounted samples of Dyed Fabric.* Shoemaker/L p. 17-18 & p. 96. A rare and significant Pennsylvania German dyer's formula book. *WST.* $ 300.00

576. Kunst, P. J. **EIN AMERIKANISCHES WORTERBUCH**... Harrisburg: 1852. 2 vols in 1. pp. 416, 397. Morocco backed boards. Foxed. Originally issued by Peters. $ 38.00

SAUR CHILDREN'S BOOK

577. **KURTZE UNTERWEISUNG VOR KLEINE KINDER**... Saur, Germantown: 1767. 48p. 24mo. Paste paper boards. *Early ownership of Christian Martin (Lancaster County Mennonite?). GLP/USA* 344, Evans 10661, Seid. p. 76, Hild. 2332. Scarce little Saur Juvenile. $ 400.00

578. **KURZER BIBLISCHER UNTERRICHT**... Blumer, Allentown: 1837. 94p. Issued by the Allentown German Sunday School Union. Unusual. Shoemaker/L p. 58, Not in AI? $ 32.00

IMPORTANT PENNSYLVANIA GERMAN GUIDES FOR MAN, BEASTS, AND MID=WIVES

579. **KURZGEFASSTES ARZNEY = BUCHLEIN, Für Menschen und Vieh, Darinnen CXXVII. Auserlesene Recepten, nebst einer Prognostischen Tafel**. Wien gedruckt, Ephrata nachgedruckt: 1791. 24p. Wraps. *GLP/USA* 794, Bristol B7739, S&M 46202, Austin 1101. One of a popular group of German American medical manuals for "Man and Beast". These consist mainly of recipes for medicines that could be concocted in the rural home; and ancient precepts conjured from "Aristotle", "Alburtus Magnus", the "Pharaohs", etc. Like the "Long Lost Friend", they are genuine survivors of the medieval folk medicine tradition. $ 275.00

580. **KURZGEFASSTES WEIBER = BUCHLEIN. Enthalt Aristotels und Alberti Magni Hebammen = Kunst, mit den Darzu gehorigen Recepten**. Die zehente Auflage. (Benjamin Mayer, Harrisburg): 1799. 64p. 32mo. Crisp copy. Original leather backed boards. *GLP/USA* 1173, Bristol B10844, Austin 1109. Scarce little Pa. German handbook of midwifery, medicine, and mysticism. The imprint is usaually attributed to Baumann in Ephrata. $ 340.00

Kurzgefaßtes
Weiber=Büchlein.
Enthält
Aristotels und Alberti Magni
Hebammen=Kunst,
mit den Darzu gehörigen
Recepten.
Die zehente Auflage.
Im Jahr, 1799.

582. **KURZGEFASSTES WEIBER = BUCHLEIN. Enthält Aristoteli und A. Magni Hebammen=Kunst, mit endarzu gehörigen Recepten.** For Jacob Sala, Canton, Ohio: 1831. 64p. 32mo. Original leather backed boards. AI 7878 *[Only the NY Public Library copy].* $ 275.00

583. Lampe, F. C. H. **GEDICHTE...** Altoona & Williamsport: 1881. 280p. 24mo. Red cloth gilt. AEG. Secular and religious poetry & songs. $ 14.00

584. Lavater, J. C. **ANDACHTSUBUNGEN UN GEBETE ZUM GEBRAUCHE, FÜR NACHDENKENDE UND GUTGESINNTE CHRISTEN.** Frank, Lancaster: 1834. 139p. AI 25280. *WST.* $ 34.00

585. Leib, Isaac. **WOHLERFAHRNER PFERDE=ARTZ...** Hartman, Lebanon: 1842. pp. 12, 184. With the rare woodcut before the title. Ds. One of the best original Pennsylvania German works on the care & handling of horses and other livestock. $ 120.00

586. **LIED EINES LEHRERS, an Seine Confirmanten...** Ritter, Reading: 1821. 12p. Sewn. Inspirational confirmation song of 98 verses set to "Ringet Recht wenn Gottes Gnade". *GLP/USA* 2518, AI 5824. $ 30.00

587. **LIEDERBUCH FÜR DIE JUNGEND...** Amer. Tract Soc. NY. Ca: 1850. 240p. + Frontis. 24mo. Cloth. Includes music. $ 14.00

LINCOLN AS A PENNSYLVANIAN !

588. (Lincoln). **DAS LEBEN VON ABRAHAM LINCOLN.** Young Men's Republican Union, NY: 1860. 16p. Woodcut illus. Self wraps. Monaghan 3738. Curious political campaign biography that claims (perhaps correctly) that Lincoln's ancestors were from Pa. $ 100.00

589. Lindl, Ignaz [1774-1834]. **DER KERN CHRISTENTHUMS, Nebst einer Abhandlung über die Snde wider den heiligen Geist, in Predigten vorgetragen.** Peters, Harrisburg: 1830. Two volumes in one. pp. 108, 58. 16mo. Disbd. *GLP/USA* 3095, Seid. p. 246, AI 2245. $ 40.00

590. Lisberger, Robert. **GRAB UND EWIGKEIT, und der Traum.** Reading: (1859). 14p. Ills. Printed wraps. 16mo. $ 20.00

591. **LOBEGESÄNGE ZU EHREN DEM HEILGEN UND GERECHTEN IN ISRAEL...** Gruber, Hagerstown: 1808. 212p. 24mo. Full leather. The foreword of this unusual little hymnal is signed by George A. Güthing for "Vereinigten Brüderschaft in Christo" = the group known as the "River Brethren"? *GLP/USA* 1603, AI 15643/15179, Seid. p. 172. $ 140.00

592. (Lochman, Johann Georg) [1773-1826]. **HAUPT=INHALT DER CHRISTLICHEN LEHRE...** Jacob Schnee, Phila: 1810. 47p. Nice paste paper boards. Written and probably printed in Lebanon. What's the story behind the Philadelphia imprint? *GLP/USA* 1776, AI 20297, Repp p. 226. $ 60.00

593. (Lochman). **HAUPT=INHALT DER CHRISTLICHEN LEHRE...** Sage, Reading: 1821. 51p. 24mo. Ds. *GLP/USA* 2521, Seid. p. 215, AI 5559, Repp p. 229. *WST.* $ 40.00

594. Lochman. **HINTERLASSENE PREDIGTEN...** G. S. Peters, Harrisburg: 1828. 334p. Worn. *GLP/USA* 2939, Seid. p. 238, AI 33890. $ 40.00

595. (Lochman). **KURZER INBEGRIFF DER CHRISTLICHEN LEHRE Nebst einer Kurzgefassten Kirchengeschichte des Alten u. Neuen Testaments.** Albrecht, Lancaster: 1804. 56p. 24mo. XL. *GLP/USA* 1392, AI 6608, Seid. p. 162. Lochman, while a pastor in Lebanon [1794-1815], prepared this German catechism for the children of his parish. *HSH.* $ 50.00

596. (Löfflerin, F. L.). **OEKONOMISCHES HANDBUCH FÜR FRAUENZIMMER... NEUES KOCHBUCH...** Stuttgart: 1833. 612p. Uncut. Original paper wraps. Wonderful German cookbook issued as the first volume in a series. Popular in America. $ 60.00

597. Loos, Isaak. **TISCHGEBETE...** Phila: 1872. 32p. Cloth wraps. Text in German, English, and phonetic Hebrew. Unusual children's prayerbook. $ 30.00

FIRST EDITION OF LOSKIEL'S "HISTORY OF THE MISSION OF THE UNITED BRETHREN AMONG THE INDIANS OF NORTH AMERICA"

598. Loskiel, George Henry. **GESCHICHTE DER MISSION DER EVANGELISCHEN BRUDER UNTER DEN INDIANERN IN NORDAMERIKA...** Zu finden den Brüdergemeinen, und in Leipzig in Commission bey Paul Gotthelf Kummer. Gedruckt bey Lorem Friedrich Spellenberg, Barby: 1789. pp. (14), 784p. Lovely copy in contemporary half leather. The best authority on the early Moravian missions among the Delawares, Nantikokes, Shawnees, & other Indian tribes in Pennsylvania & New York. Based largely upon the letters and journals of Zeisberger and Spangenberg, this important edition contains much that was omitted from the English translation. See: Sabin 42109, Vail 795, Howes L 474 aa. Rare. $ 600.00

RARE SWEDISH EDITION OF LOSKIEL

599. Loskiel. **HISTORISKE BESKRIFNING OFWER EVANGELISKA BRODERNES MISSIONS=ARBETE IBLAND INDIANERNE UTI NORRA AMERICA...** Stockholm: 1792. pp. 21, 872. Contemporary half leather. Very rare Swedish translation of Loskiel's account of the Moravian Missions among the American Indians. $ 600.00

600. Lohr, Otto. **DAS DEUTSCHAMERIKANERTUM VON HUNDERT JAHREN UND DER KRIEG VON 1812=1815**. German-Amer. Hist. Soc. of Ill: 1914. 59p. Printed wraps. XL. German-Americans & the war of 1812. Scarce. $ 28.00

601. **LUST UND FREUDE. Gedichte und Geschichten mit Bildern für die Kinderwelt.** Diehl, Allentown. Ca: 1880. 96p. + Chromolithographed plates. Woodcut illus. Chromo cover. Shoemaker/L p. 185 *[Recording this copy only]*. *WST.* $ 28.00

602. **DER LUSTIGE WAHRSAGER, in Freud=und Lach=Stunden. Ober Antwortendes Trillerbuch für die Jungend**. Siegfried, Millgrove, (Northampton County): 1835. 64p. Self wraps. 32mo. See also # 444-6. *Apparently Not in AI. WST.* $ 130.00

RARE 1598 EDITION OF LUTHER'S BOOK OF FAMILY DEVOTION

603. Luther, Martin. **HAUSS POSTILLA. Ober die Sontags und der Fürnemesten Feste Evangelien / Durchs Ganze Jar**. Laurent Sueberlich, Wittemberg: 1598. pp. 26, 336, 312, 204. ***Illustrated throughout by a really wonderful series of bibical woodcuts.*** Worn contemporary binding with clasps. Not in Adams, BMC STC, Etc. Rare edition. $1500.00

604. Luther. **WIDER DIE HIMLISCHEN PROPHETEN, Von den Bildern unnd Sacrament &c.** Bound with / Luther. **VON ABENDMAL Christi / Bekändtniss**. Bound with / Luther. **DAS DISE WORT CHRISTI, Das ist mein Leib &c. noch fest stehn / wider die Schwermegeister**. Laugingen: 1589. Three volumes in one. Over 600p. 4to. Title pages in red and black, with portrait of Luther. The title page portraits in two of the works are facsimiles, but these early Reformation texts are otherwise clean and tight. Not in Adams. $ 600.00

605. **LUTHERS BIBEL=ERKLARUNGEN...** By Heinrich Ginal. May & Flory, York, Pa: 1831. 372p. AI 8031. Unusual York imprint. $ 40.00

606. **LUTHERS VOLLSTANDIGE AUSLEGUNG DER EPISTEL ST. PAULI AN DIE GALATER...** Salmon S. Miles, (Phila?): 1842. 738p. Worn full leather gilt. Scarce. $ 40.00

ALBERTUS MAGNUS' LONG LOST FRIEND AND "POW WOW" BOOK

607. Magnus, Albertus. **ALBERTUS MAGNUS, ODER DER LANGE VERBORGENE SCHATZ UND HAUS FREUND...** Pennsylvanien: 1839. 100p. Printed "For the Purchaser", probably in Lancaster. *Important Pa. German "Pow=Wow hex" book & health guide, that bears remarkable similarity to the works of Hohman. Apparently not in AI.* $ 140.00

608. Magnus, Albertus. **...EGYPTISCHE GEHEIMNISSE, Fur Menschen un Vieh...** Braband: (1832-33). 3 Volumes in one. 230p. Printed in Germany for the American market. The source of this important collection of herbal cures and formulae was ascribed to the wisdom of Ancient Egypt. It was long considered a necessary companion to Hohman. *WST.* $ 100.00

609. Magnus, Albertus. **...EGYPTISCHE GEHEIMNISSE...** Brabant, For Wilhelm Radde, NY: 1848. 3 Volumes in one. 225p. + Ads. *WST.* $ 80.00

610. Magnus, Albertus. **EGYPTISCHE GEHEIMNISSE...** Allentown: 1869. 4 Vols. in 1. 284p. The only "Pow Wow" book printed in Lehigh County. Shoemaker/L p. 125. $ 100.00

611. Mahnenschmidt, Peter. **CHARFREYTAGS GEBANKEN...** Ritter, Reading: 1821. 12p. Self wraps. Scarce poem of 51 stanzas on a Good Friday theme, with admonitions to both children and parents. *GLP/USA* 2519, AI 5904, Seid. p. 217. $ 35.00

612. Mann, W. J. **DIE "GUTE ALTE ZEIT" IN PENNSYLVANIEN.** Phila: 1880. 106p. Cloth. 16mo. Little known history of the Germans in Pennsylvania German. *WST.* $ 32.00

613. **MARK. Sei E'Fagelylium in Pa. Deitsh.** Sugarcreek, Ohio & Waxhaw, NC: 1975. 58p. + Explanatory Folder. Wraps. The Gospel of St. Mark in the dialect. $ 12.00

614. (Martens, B.). **VORSCHLAG ZU EINER HEILIGEN ALLIANZ, oder Fromme Brüderliche Vereinigung für Wahre Freiheit und Gleichheit...** Martens, Allentown: 1861. 104p. 24mo. Shoemaker/L p. 104. Scarce polemic. *WST.* $ 32.00

615. Marx, Karl T. **DEUTSCH-AMERIKANISCHE APHORISMEN...** Munchen: 1956. 59p. Collection of dialect sayings. *WST.* $ 16.00

ESSAYS AND SERMONS ON MINING AND METAL WORK

616. Mathesius, Johannes. **BERG=POSTILLA SAREPTA. Darinnen von Allerlen Berkwerk und Mettallen...** Freyberg: 1679. pp 29, 892, 170 + Manuscript additions. Thick 4to. Contemporary 1/2 leather. This astonishing text provides biblical and scientific commentary on mining, metals, minerals, gold, silver, copper, iron, steel, magnets, mirrors, and glassmaking, etc. Mathesius [1504-1565], was one of the most powerful preachers of the early Reformation. He is best known for the earliest full biography of Luther (1566), and an extraordinary tome on Noah and the deluge. Bound with this scarce edition of "Sarepta" is his Chronicle of the Reformation in Joachimsthal. The metallurgical works of Mathesius and Barba were eagerly consulted (and even reprinted) by the early German emigrants to America. A very fine copy. $ 750.00

617. Mathesius. **SAREPTA. Darinn von Allerlen Berkwerk und Mettallen...** Nürnberg: 1571. pp. 11, 474 + Chronicle of the Reformation in Joachimsthal 50p. (of 54). Heavy manuscript annotations. Folio. An extremely scarce 16th century edition of this remarkable text. Not in Adams. BMC STC German p. 600. $ 800.00

618. Mattei, Cesare. **ELECTRO HOMOEOPATHIE. Grundfätze einer Neuen Medizinischen Wissenschafte**. Chicago: 1884. 234p. Illus. XLib. $ 25.00

619. Mead, Mathew. **DER BEYNAHE EIN CHRIST ENDECKT: Oder, Der Irrige Religions=Bekenner, Gepruft & Verworfen...** Edited & Translated by Daniel Weiser. Amos Stroh, Selins=Grove: 1830. pp. 36, 192 + 5p. family register [blank]. AI 2505. $ 36.00

620. **MEIN DRITTES BUCH...** Bendel, Reading: 1877=8. 104p. Ill. $ 7.00

621. Mel, Conrad. **POSAUNEN DER EWIGKEIT, oder Predigten vom Tode, Auferstehung der Todten, jüngsten Gericht, Untergang der Welt, Hölle und Ewigkeit...** J. Estienne, Cassel: 1755. Over 900p. Full contemporary alum tawed pigskin binding, tooled in blind, with clasps. Mel [1666-1733] was an influential German Reformed Pietist author and preacher. $ 125.00

622. Mel. **POSAUNEN DER EWIGKEIT...** Leipzig & Köningsburg: 1759. 900+p. Full leather with clasps. Ds. *Early Pennsylvania (Mennonite?) manuscript ownerships of Henry Keely and John Stauffer.* $ 100.00

THE FIRST ORDERED PRESENTATION OF THE DOCTRINES OF THE REFORMATION

623. Melanchthon, Philipp. **LOCI COMMUNES, Das ist fie furnemesten Artikel Christlicher Lere...** Justum Jonam / Hans Frischmut, Wittemberg: 1538. pp. 16, 482. Old worming. Disbd. Ds. Melanchthon [1497-1560], was a friend and co-worker of Martin Luther, and one of the most important figures of the early Reformation. This is undoubtably one of his greatest and most influential works. Not in Adams, nor BMC STC German. Scarce. $ 800.00

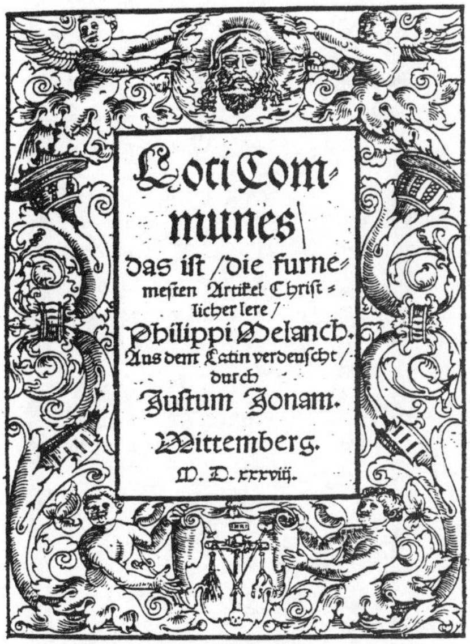

624. Melsheimer, Rev. Frederick Valentine [1749=1814]. **WARHEIT DER CHRISTLICHEN RELIGION...** C. T. Melsheimer, Frederick, Md: 1811. 328p. Paper boards. *By the father of American entomology. GLP/USA* 1807, AI 23367, Seid. p. 181. $ 75.00

THE FOUNDER OF THE MENNONITES

625. (Menno Simmons) [1496-1561]. **EIN FUNDAMENT UND KLARE ANWEISUNG, Von der Selig-machenden Lehre unsers Herrn Jesu Christ...** Gedruct in Europa im Jahr 1575. Pennsylvanien (Albrecht & Co. Lancaster: 1794). pp. 10, 675, 5. Original full leather with one clasp. *GLP/USA* 931, Evans 27310, Seid. p. 138, Sabin 81284. *First American edition of the fundamental Mennonite text.* $ 150.00

626. Menno Simmons. **EIN FUNDAMENT UND KLARE ANWEISUNG...** Baer, Lancaster: 1835. pp. 9, 698, 4. Worn full leather with tooled spine. $ 60.00

627. Menno Simmons. **EIN FUNDAMENT UND KLARE ANWEISUNG...** Allentown: 1849. pp. 22, 681. Full leather. Shoemaker/L p. 77. $ 55.00

628. Menno Simmons. **EIN FUNDAMENT UND KLARE ANWEISUNG...** Bär & Sohn, Lancaster: 1853. 710p. Full leather with clasps. $ 45.00

629. Menno Simmons. **DIE VOLLSTANDIGEN WERKE MENNO SIMON'S...** (Funk: 1876). Aylmer, Ontario: 1982. Approx. 1050p. Modern German Edition. $ 20.00

630. Mennonite. **DER CHRISTLICHE SANGER.** Schünemann for Cassel, Skippacksville, Upper Salford Township, Montgomery County, Pa: 1855. 438p. Worn binding. 24mo. *This was a private printing that was used by some Franconia Conference Mennonites. WST.* $ 40.00

631. Mennonite. **DIE KLEINE GEISTLICHE HARFE DER KINDER ZIONS...** Bound With / **SAMMLUNG ALTER UND NEUER GEISTREICHEN GESANGE...** Billmeyer, Germantown: 1811. pp. 39, 1, 412, 18, 20, 1 + Woodcut frontis signed "D". Pretty polished calf with clasps. Second Edition of the first Mennonite hymnbook compiled & published in North America. Issued by the Franconia Mennonite Conference. *GLP/USA* 1812, AI 23165. $ 100.00

632. Mennonite. **DIE KLEINE GEISTLICHE HARFE DER KINDER ZIONS.** Etc... Billmeyer, Germantown: 1820. pp. 40, 412, 42 + Frontis. Full leather. Third Edition. *GLP/USA* 2419, Seid. p. 211, AI 2239. $ 60.00

FINE MENNONITE FRAKTUR BOOKPLATE

633. Mennonite. **DIE KLEINE GEISTLICHE HARFE DER KINDER ZIONS.** Etc... Billmeyer, Germantown: 1820. pp. 40, 412, 42 + Frontis. Full leather. *Beautifully executed colored floral bookplate of Jacob Joder (Yoder). Drawn on December 15, 1821. This fine calligraphic plate (with a handsome headpiece of spiked flowers) has lettering and decorations in black, red, green, and yellow .* Yoder was probably a Bucks or Lehigh County Mennonite. See also # 139 for Yoder's fine double page bookplate. $1500.00

634. Mennonite. **DIE KLEINE GEISTLICHE HARFE DER KINDER ZIONS.** Etc... Bar, Lancaster: 1870. Over 500p. + Frontis. Full leather. Sixth Edition. $ 30.00

635. Mennonite. **DIE KLEINE GEISTLICHE HARFE DER KINDER ZIONS.** Etc... Elkhart, Ind: 1904. 500p. + Frontis. Embossed full leather. Seventh Edition. $ 25.00

636. Mennonite. **DIE KLEINE GEISTLICHE HARFE DER KINDER ZIONS.** Etc... Elkhart, Ind: 1904. 500p. + Frontis. Library binding. $ 20.00

637. Mennonite. **DAS UNPARTEIISCHE BIBLISCHE FRAGENBUCH...** Mennonite Druck = Berein, Milford Square, Bucks County, Pa: 1859. 121p. *WST.* $ 40.00

638. Mennonite. **EIN UNPARTHEYISCHES GESANG=BUCH... Enthaltend Geistreiche Lieder und Psalmen...** Albrecht, Lancaster: 1804. pp. 79, 415, 17. Old paper repairs. Binding worn. *First Edition of this important Mennonite / Amish song book.* It had a longer lifespan than any other similar hymnal. *GLP/USA* 1395, Seid. p. 162, AI 6767/6863. $ 120.00

639. Mennonite. **EIN UNPARTHEYISCHES GESANG=BUCH...** Albrecht, Lancaster: 1808. pp. 80, 448, 18. *GLP/USA* 1613, Seid. p. 173, AI 15580-1. $ 60.00

640. Mennonite. **UNPARTHEYISCHES GESANG=BUCH...** Bar, Lancaster: 1820. pp. 5, 80, 472, 18. Contemporary polished full leather. *GLP/USA* 2438, Seid. p. 211, AI 4070. $ 55.00

641. Mennonite. **UNPARTHEYISCHES GESANG=BUCH...** Bar, Lancaster: 1829. pp. 483, 19. Full leather. XLib. *GLP/USA* 3022, Seid. p. 242, AI 39557. $ 44.00

642. Mennonite. **UNPARTHEYISCHES GESANG=BUCH...** Bar, Lancaster: 1841. pp. 483, 19. Nice full leather. First edition with rounded notes. Seid. p. 242, AI 39557. $ 40.00

643. Mennonite. **UNPARTHEYISCHES GESANG=BUCH...** Bar, Lanc: 1857. $ 26.00

MURDERS MOST CRUEL AND FOUL

644. **MERKWURDIGE CRIMINAL GESCHICHTEN, oder Verhöre, Geständnisse und Hinrichtung Verschiedener Verbrecher...** Ebner, Allentown: 1818. pp. 3, 176 + ***Seven unusual plates, including an unrecorded Colored Woodcut Frontis.*** Remarkable accounts of infamous murders [Including McDade #'s 24, 255, 305, 854, Etc.]. *GLP/USA* 2257 *[2 Copies only]*, Shoemaker/L p. 29, Seid. p. 203, AI 44811. One of the scarcest and most interesting books to come from the prolific German press of Lehigh County. *WST.* $ 240.00

645. (Methodist). **EIN PAAR WORTE UBER DIE METHODISTEN...** Siegfried, Bath, Northampton County, Pa: 1839. 36p. Stiff wraps. 16mo. Early steel stamped ownership. AI 55482 *[Locating only one copy].* $ 60.00

646. Meuschen, Johann Gerhard & Prits, J. G. **POSTILLA MYSTICA EVANGELICA. Das ist: Der Geheime Geistliche Sinn Der Sonn-und Festags Evangelien.** Frankfurt am Mayn: 1755. Over 1600p. Lacks leaf of index. Frontis worn. Ds. Thick 4to. Blind stamped alum tawed pigskin binding. Mystical Protestant theology. Rare. $ 250.00

647. Michaelis, Johann David. **DEUTSCHE UEBERSETZUNG DES ALTEN TESTAMENTS...** Göttingen & Gotha: 1773. Four volumes (of 13?). Disbd. *Printed American Bookplate of Benjamin German (1808).* $ 50.00

648. Miller, George [1774-1816]. **DES EVANGELISCHEN PREDIGERS G. MILLER'S KURZE UND DEUTLICHE LEHREN Zum Wahren und Thätigen Christenthum...** Jungman (Sunbury): 1814. 225p. Full leather. XLib. 18mo. Important Evangelical Association text. *GLP/USA* 2062, Seid. p. 193, AI 32131-2. *HSH.* $ 60.00

649. Miller, Johann Peter. **ABHANDLUNG VON DEN PLICHTEN DER CHRISTEN IN DER EHE UND IM HAUSLICHEN LEBEN.** Leipzig: 1771. 396p. XLib. *HSH.* $ 40.00

Der Verborgene Arzt, oder Nützliche Hausfreund; Ein neues System der Arzeney-Kunst: Hauptsächlich auf Kräuter gegründet. Enthaltend: Erstens:—Eine kurze Beschreibung des menschlichen Körpers. Zweytens—Eine Abhandlung von den Entstehungsarten und Kennzeichen der im menschlichen Leben vorkommenden Krankheiten, mit einer unfehlbaren Heilung für sie Alle; nebst einer Anweisung und Heilmittel für Beinbruch und äusserliche Beschädigungen. Drittens—Eine Beschreibung der vornehmsten Kräuter, deren Eigenschaften, Ortsbeschaffenheit, Art und Weise dieselben zum Gebrauch zu zubereiten.

Aus den besten Schriften zusammengetragen, nach dem berühmten Thompsonien System organisirt, mit vielen Verbesserungen, von einem in diesem System erfahrnen Arzt, für den Eigenthümer, Joseph Miller.

Neu-Berlin, Penn. Gedruckt und zu haben bey Joseph Miller. 1830.

GERMAN AMERICAN HOUSEHOLDERS' GUIDE TO HEALTH AND WEALTH

650. (Miller, Joseph). **DER VERBORGENE ARTZ, ODER NUTZLICHE HAUSEFREUND. Ein Neues System der Arzeney = Kunst...** Joseph Miller, New Berlin, Pa: 1830. 180p. Original leather backed boards. Manuscript formulae. Possibly written by H. A. Zellers. *GLP/USA* 3114, Seid. p. 247. *Not in AI. WST.* $ 160.00

651. Miller, Samuel. **DAS KERNWESEN IN DER ERLOSUNG SO DURCH JESUM CHRISTUM GESCHEHEN; Oder, Der Ansang und Wachsthum im' Wahren Christenthum...** Erste Auflage. Lebanon: 1836. 144p. Disbound. $ 20.00

652. Milton, J. & F. Schwalbe. **NEUE ENGLISCHE SPRACHLEHRE...** Ebner, Allentown: 1823. 188p. Ds. Course of instruction in English for American Germans. *GLP/USA* 2580, Shoemaker/L p. 36, Seid. p. 218, AI 13347. *WST.* $ 45.00

653. Mininger, David. **DAS CHRISTLICHE GEBET=BUCH...** John G. Dreisbach, Zion's Church, Northampton Cty: 1846. 32p. Sm. 16mo. Printed wraps. Worn. Ad for Dreisbach as a printer, etc. on back cover. Rare. $ 50.00

654. Moravian. **GESANGBUCH, zum Gebrauch der Evangelischen Brudergemeinen.** Spellenberg, Barby: 1783. pp. 836, 100 + *A remarkable 2 page printed poem apparently inserted by the bookbinder = C. F. Autenrieth, Stuttgart.* Contemporary full leather. $ 175.00

655. Moravian. **GESANGBUCH...** Barby: 1802. pp. 836, 100. Full leather. Boards loose. *Owned by Eliza Kapp, Lititz. Probably from the Moravian Linden Hall Girls School.* $ 100.00

656. Moravian. **GESANGBUCH...** Gnadau: 1824. pp. 836, 100. Full leather. American ownership. $ 60.00

657. Moravian. **GESANGBUCH...** Phila: 1848. pp. 38, 289. 16mo. Nice full leather binding, handsomely tooled in gilt. $ 40.00

658. Moravian. **DIE GESCHICHTE DER TAGE DES MENSCHENSHONES von der Marterwoche an bis zu Seiner Himmelfahrt.** Barby: 1808. 88p. $ 60.00

659. Moravian. **DIE GESCHICHTE UNSERS HERRN UND HEILANDES JESU CHRISTI aus der vier Evangelisten zusammen gezogen.** Barby: 1800. 272p. Ds. Worn. $ 60.00

660. Moravian. **ORTS = STATUT DER GEMEINE ZU HERRNHUT...** (Bethlehem?: 1845). 15p. Original plain wraps. *WST.* $ 30.00

=== FOR SOME RARE AMERICAN MORAVIAN SONG SHEETS SEE: #921-936 ===

661. More, Hannah. **DER SCHAFER DER EBENE VON SALISBURY.** Amer. Tract. Soc. NY. Ca: 1870. 32p. Woodcut illustrations. Self wraps. $ 18.00

662. Morrah, Dave. **FRAULEIN BO-PEEPEN & More Tales Mein Grossfader Told.** NY: 1953. 79p. Pidgin dialect humor. $ 14.00

663. Mosheim, J. L. von. **INSTITUTIONES HISTORIAE CHRISTIANAE...** Lipsiae: 1783. 504p. Mosheim [1694-1755] is called the "father of modern church historiography". This Compendium by J. P. Miller includes an interesting section on the Anabaptists, etc. $ 60.00

664. Mucke, Albert. **GELCHICHTE DER DEUTCHEN EVANGELISCHEN SYNODE VON NORD-AMERIKA...** St. Louis & Chi: 1915. 330p. Illus. Valuable contribution to the history of German-Americans in the Mid-West and South West. $ 28.00

665. Mueller, Heinrich. **EVANGELISCHER HERTZENS = SPIEGEL... Passion=Predigten...** Frankfurt: 1725. 1100+p. Thick 4to. Disbound. Some page repairs. Müller [1631-71] was a German Lutheran Pietist, who anticipated the mystical flowering of erotic pietism. $ 100.00

666. Mühlenberg. **HEINRICH MELCHIOR MUHLENBERG. Selbstbiographie, 1711-43.** Allentown: 1881. 256p. Cloth. Important and scarce auto-biography. Shoemaker/L p. 152 *[Locating this copy only]*. *WST.* $ 50.00

THE FIRST GERMAN DICTIONARY PUBLISHED IN AMERICA

667. (Muhlenberg, Dr. Henry & J. B. Schipper). **ENGLISH = GERMAN DICTIONARY / ENGLISH = DEUTSCHES WORTERBUCH.** William Hamilton, Lancaster: 1812. Two Vols. Disbound. *GLP/USA* 1898, Seid. p. 185, AI 26151. Very comprehensive. $ 160.00

THE STANDARD HYMNBOOK OF THE REFORMED CHURCH

668. **DAS NEUE UND VERBESSERTE GESANGBUCH...** With / **Sammlung Alter & Neuer Geistreicher Lieder...** Billmeyer, Germantown: 1799. 779p. + Frontis (Signed D). Leather binding. *GLP/USA* 1162, Evans 36193, Seid. p. 152. Early ownerships. $ 75.00

669. **DAS NEUE UND VERBESSERTE GESANGBUCH...** Bound with / **Sammlung Alter & Neuer Geistreicher Lieder (1806)...** Billmeyer, Germantown: 1807. pp. 148, 585 + Register & Catechismus. Full leather. *Nice Early Ownership of Henrich Licht. GLP/USA* 1542, AI 13177/13473, Seid. p. 169. $ 40.00

SPLENDID FRAKTUR BOOKPLATE

670. **DAS NEUE UND VERBESSERTE GESANG - BUCH...** Small type edition. Billmeyer, Phila: 1813. pp. 72, 300, 8. *GLP/USA* 1954, AI 29632, Seid. p. 188. *Finely decorated and lustrously colored Fraktur Bookplate of Elizabeth Groff, Maiden Creek Township, Berks County, 1819. Embellished with a bird, flowers, and geometric designs - in red, yellow, green, brown, and black.* The strong colors have eaten through the paper a bit, but the fraktur is still very handsome, and easily conserved. $2200.00

671. **DAS NEUE UND VERBESSERTE GESANG - BUCH...** Billmeyer, Phila: 1814. Frontis. (Unsigned). Full leather. Manuscript ownerships. *GLP/USA* 2037, AI 32226/32708. $ 40.00

672. **DAS NEUE UND VERBESSERTE GESANG - BUCH...** Billmeyer, Germantown: 1828. pp. 95, 422. 24mo. Small type edition. Worn full morocco gilt. *GLP/USA* 2923, AI 34421. $ 38.00

673. **DAS NEUE UND VERBESSERTE GESANG-BUCH...** Benner, Sumnytaun: 1838. 650+p. *Lovely crimson morocco binding, beautifully gilt. Yellow painted edges. One of prettiest German American bindings of this era that we've ever seen.* $ 140.00

674. **DAS NEUE UND VERBESSERTE GESANGBUCH...** Benner, Sumneytown: 1850. 612p. These are unusual Montgomery County imprints. $ 20.00

675. **NEUES BUCHSTABIERBUCH, Enthaltend Regeln der Orthographie und Materialien zum Dictiren, Für Schulen und zum Selbstunterricht.** Allentown: 1837. 168p. One leaf with slight loss. Later wraps. Not in AI? Shoemaker/L p. 58. *WST*. Scarce and curious. $ 50.00

676. **EIN NEUES ENGLISCH = DEUTSCHES & DEUTSCHES = ENGLISCH WORTER-BUCH.** Mentz, Phila: 1849. Two Vols. 1175p. Modern cloth. $ 50.00

677. **NEUES FORMULAR-BUCH...** Bound With / **Neuer Deutscher Briefsteller...** Bound With / **Tabelle zur Ausrechnung von Interessen...** Blumer & Busch, Allentown: 1838. 3 Volumes in 1. 145p. Publisher's embossed cloth. Popular legal form book and guide to business and social letter writing. In English & German. First Edition. Shoemaker/L p. 60. Not in AI? *WST*. $ 50.00

678. **NEUES FORMULAR-BUCH...** Blumer & Busch, Allentown: 1838-41. 3 Volumes in 1. 145p. Andrew Yeakle's copy. Shoemaker/L p. 65. *WST*. $ 40.00

679. **NEUES FORMULAR - BUCH...** Blumer & Busch, Allentown: 1846. 170p. Leather backed marbled boards. Shoemaker/L p. 72. $ 32.00

680. **NEUSTES GEMEINSCHAFTLICHE GESANGBUCH...** NY: 1856. Prepared for use in Lutheran & Reformed Churches. $ 16.00

681. **NEUSTES GEMEINSCHAFTLICHE GESANGBUCH...** NY: 1863. Nice leather gilt, with clasps. $ 14.00

682. **NEU - VERMEHRT UND VOLLSTANDIGES GESANG - BUCH...** Christoph Saur, Germantown: 1763. pp. 210, 536, 10, 24, 79 (of 83). No frontis. Very worn and stained. *GLP/USA* 273, Evans 9495, Hild. 1896, Seid. p. 61. Reformed Church Hymnbook. $ 200.00

683. **NEU - VERMEHRT UND VOLLSTANDIGES GESANG - BUCH...** Christoph Saur, Germantown: 1772. 688p. No frontis. Ds. *GLP/USA* 410, Seid. p. 84, Evans 12534. $ 220.00

GERMAN FOLK ART BINDINGS

684. **NEU - VERMEHRT UND VOLLSTANDIGES GESANG - BUCH...** Brönner, Marburg & Frankfurt: 1771. pp. 216, 424, 20, 96 + Frontis. Later spine. Boards with slight loss. Clasps present. ***Original vellum boards, embossed and colored in a very decorative style extremely reminiscent of typical Pennsylvania German folk art motifs: stylized & folksy foliage, roses, hearts, tulips, vases, poetic religious sentiments, etc. + Gauffred gilt edges with tulips and roses.*** See: Goff. *German Folk Bindings on "Philadelphia" books of 1774.* Guttenberg Jahrbuch (1968). Both the text and the bindings were very popular in early America. The Philadelphia printer, Ernst Ludwig Baisch probably imported these, as well as some bibles and other songbooks. These wonderful bindings influenced, or at least reflected, the fashionable decorative tastes of the German American market. Painted vellum bindings in any era are scarce, but these are especially significant to collectors of German American folk art. ***Manuscript (American?) fraktur ownership of Maria Sophia Schnederin (Snyder), 1780.*** $ 325.00

685. **NEU - VERMEHRT UND VOLLSTANDIGES GESANG - BUCH...** Brönner, Marburg & Frankfurt: 1775. pp. 216, 424, 20, 96 + Frontis. No spine nor clasps. ***Full vellum. Embossed as above. Colored in red, green, yellow, and gilt.*** The decorative style is very similar to the copy described above. ***Manuscript (American) family record of Cristina Weiss, who married Adam Weidner in 1787.*** $ 300.00

686. **NEU - VERMEHRT UND VOLLSTANDIGES GESANG - BUCH...** Brönner, Marburg & Frankfurt: 1782. ***Full vellum. Embossed as above. Colored in red, green, yellow, and white.*** The decorative style is again similar to the copy described above. ***Manuscript (American?) fraktur ownership of Susanna Hendrickin (Hendrickson), May 4, 1788.*** $ 350.00

687. **NEU - VERMEHRT UND VOLLSTANDIGES GESANG - BUCH...** Brönner, Marburg & Frankfurt: 1794 - 5. ***Full blue vellum. Embossed in a slightly more subdued style. Colored in red and yellow.*** Partial spine. One clasp. This example, while attractive, is not as gay as those from twenty years earlier. The fashion for these decorative bindings was fading in America. Very few were imported after 1800, and none were apparently ever produced here. These bindings are all quite rare and deserve more extended study and analysis. ***Tipped in manuscript birth record of Anna Marie Ochs.*** $ 270.00

688. Nevin, J. W. **DIE ANGST - BANK...** Chambersburg: 1844. 154p. 18mo. Leather backed marbled boards. XLib. $ 25.00

689. New Bethel Church. **GESCHICHTLICHE EINLEITUNG UND KIRCHEN = ORDNUNG der Neu Bethel Zionskirche in Grimsville, Berks County, Pa.** Kutztown: 1890. 16p. 32mo. Printed wraps. $ 20.00

690. Northampton Coal Co. **BERICHT DER DIREKTOREN DER NOTHAMPTON KOHLEN GESELLSCHAFT.** Allentown: 1855. 15p. Printed yellow wraps. Shoemaker/L p. 87 *[Recording this copy only].* $ 45.00

GUIDE FOR MID-WIVES AND FAMILY DYERS

691. **NUTZLICHES UND SEHR BEWAHRT BEFUNDENES WEIBER = BUCHLEIN...** Ephrata: 1806. 32p. Ds. Sm. 16mo. Contemporary paste paper wraps. Traditional medicine, advice, and formulary - mixed with a healthy dose of "Pow-Wow". *GLP/USA* 1481, AI 50702, Austin 1426. *WST.* $ 200.00

692. (Oberholtzer, J. H.). **AUFSCHLUSS DER VERFOLGUNGEN GEGEN DANIEL HOCH, Prediger der Mennonitten Gemeinschaft in Ober Canada.** Bound With / **Eine Erleiterung Geschrieben von Samuel B. Bauman an Benjamin Eby.** Oberholtzer, Pennsylvanien (Lancaster?): 1853. pp. 68, 108. Original printed blue wraps. Scarce and significant artifact in the history of the Mennonite / Amish congregations in Ontario, Canada. $ 80.00

693. Oehlschläger, J. C. **ENGLISCH - DEUTSCHES UND DEUTSCH - ENGLISCHES TASCHEN = WORTERBUCH...** Phila: 1856. 700+p. Thick 24mo. Half leather. $ 22.00

694. **ORDNUG DER GEMEINSCHAFTLICHEN KIRCHE IN HEIDELBERG, Lecha Caunty...** Allentown: 1897. 30p. 32mo. Printed wraps. Apparently a reprint of the 1848 edition. *Not in Shoemaker/L.* $ 30.00

695. (Orwig, Seybert, & Rank). **EINE BERSUNG AUF THATSACHEN UND GESUNDEN MENSCHENVERSTAND...** Miller, New Berlin, Pa: 1839. 248p. Original publisher's embossed cloth binding. AI 57737. $ 85.00

696. Orwig, Wilhelm W. **EVANGELISCHES LIEDERBUCHLEIN FUR SONNTAGS - SCHULEN.** Miller, New Berlin, Pa: 1843. 104p. 32mo. Ds. Scarce little songbook for the Evangelical Association. $ 40.00

697. (Ott, George). **JOSEPHI=BUCH: Die Macht der Fürbitte des Heiligen Patriarchen Joseph...** Regensburg, NY & Cincinnati: 1887. 462p. + Chromolithographed frontis. $ 20.00

698. Otterbein, Georg Gottfried [1731-1800]. **LESEBUCH FÜR DEUTSCHE SCHUL - KINDER...** Zentler & Mentz, Phila: 1813. 228p. *GLP/USA* 1989, AI 29425. $ 40.00

699. (Otterbein, Johann D.) [1736-1804]. **JESUS UND DIE KRAFT SEINES BLUTS GANZ BESONDERS VERHERRLICHET.** Neuen Buchdruckerey (Albrecht), Lancaster: 1790. 230p. 16mo. Worn contemporary half leather. Dedicated to Johann Jost Weygand, a murderer who was executed in 1785. *GLP/USA* 768, Evans 22752, Seid. p. 126. $ 120.00

700. ("Owlglass" Practical Joker). **DER WIEDERERSTANDENE EULENSPIEGEL. Volksbücher.** NY? Ca: 1850? 96p. Later cloth. Great collection of Tom-Foolery. $ 65.00

701. Palm, H. W. **HEYLSAME WORTE DES GLAUBENS UND DER GOTTSEELIGKEIT. Oder Kurtzer Entwurff der im Jahre 1733=4.** London: 1734. 258p. Curious history of the Evangelical Lutheran Church. From the library of J. F. Sachse. Has there ever been a census of German printing in England? $ 50.00

702. Pastorius, F. D. **BESCHREIBUNG VON PENNSYLVANIEN...** Crefeld: 1884. 139p. XLib. Very worn and fragile. Scarce. $ 30.00

703. **PENNSYLFAWNISCH DEITSCH FERSOMMLING.** Collection of Attractive Pamphlets, Programs, Etc. from the foundation of the Pennsylvania German Folk Festival movement, 1936 - 1956. 17 Pieces. *WST.* $ 55.00

704. Pennsylvania Constitution. **VERHANDLUNGEN UND DEBATTEN DER CONVENTION DER REPUBLIK PENNSYLVANIEN UM VERBESSERUNGEN ZU DER CONSTITUTION...** Band I. Guyer, Harrisburg: 1837. 728p. Full roan. $ 25.00

705. **PENNSYLVANISH DEITSH. DE CAMPAIN BREFFA FUM PIR SCHWEFFLE - BRENNER UN DE BEVVY, SI ALTY. Gepublished Olly Woch im "Father Abraham".** Rauch & Cochran, Lancaster: 1868. 44p. + Ads. Humorous dialect letters on Grant's Presidential Campaign. $ 50.00

THE FOUNDATION OF GERMAN PHILADELPHIANISM

706. (Petersen, Johann W.) [1649-1727]. [Greek Title]... **DAS GEHEIMNISS DER WIEDERBRINGUNG ALLER DINGE...** "Gedruckt in Pamphilia / und daselbst bey dem Authore zu finden: 1701. 600+p. + Allegorical plate. Illus. Folio. Disbound. Probably printed at Schwarzenau. This became a cornerstone text for disaffected Protestants throughout Germany. Petersen, and his wife Elenora, were the leaders of the, Boehme inspired, German Philadelphic movement. According to Stoeffler, this philosophy can "hardly be separated from the general phenomenon of radical Pietism." For a more thorough discussion of Philadelphianism please see: Stoeffler. *German Pietism During the 18th Century*. Scarce & important. $ 600.00

707. (Petri, Albert). **AUS MEINEN KNABENJAHREN IN CHINA VON YAN PHOU LEE.** Allentown: 1889. 80p. Vignettes. 16mo. Cloth. *Apparently not in Shoemaker/L.* $ 45.00

708. Petri, F. E. **GEDRANGTES DEUTSCHUNGS = WORTERBUCH...** Dresden: 1817. 497p. Nice full leather American binding. *HSH.* $ 25.00

709. Pfautz, J. E. **DER KLEINE PERLEN=SAMLUNG. Oder Auswahl Geistreicher Lieder...** Pfautz, Ephrata: 1858. pp. 115, 41. Worn full leather. 32mo. Printed in English & German. First edition of this curious little hymnal. $ 38.00

710. (Pfenning, Michael A.). **DAS UNSCHATZBARE SCHLOSS IN DER AFRIKANISCHEN HOLE XAXA...** Allentown: 1845. 116p. 24mo. Later wraps. Ds. Shoemaker/L p. 70 *[Recording this copy only]. WST.* $ 45.00

711. Philip, Dietrich. **ENCHIRIDION. Oder Handbuchlein von der Christlichen Lehre und Religion...** Ehrenfried, Lancaster: 1811. 568p. Original full leather. The first American edition of the most important work of Dirk Philips [1504-68]. Highly valued by the early Mennonites and other Pietists. *GLP/USA* 1824, AI 23679, Seid. p. 182. $ 60.00

712. (Probst, Johann August). **DIE WIEDERVEREINIGUNG DER LUTHERANER UND REFORMIRTEN...** Ebner & Co. Allentown: 1826. pp. 19, 172. Includes a Foreword by J. C. Jaeger. *GLP/USA* 2782, Shoemaker/L p. 41, Seid. p. 227, AI 25838. *WST.* $ 40.00

PSALTERS

713. **DER KLEINE DAVIDISCHE PSALTERSPIEL DER KINDER ZIONS...** Sauer, Germantown: 1764. pp. 5, 570, 24. Disbound. Enlarged from the first edition of 1744. The first Brethren hymnal to include musical notation. *GLP/USA* 296B, Evans 9602, Seid. p. 66, Hild. 2045, Brethren Bibibliography 20. $ 260.00

714. **DER KLEINE DAVIDISCHE PSALTERSPIEL...** Samuel Saur, Chestnut Hill: 1791. pp. (6), 572, (20). No Kleine Harfe. Badly stained. Some loss on a few leaves. Original full leather. *GLP/USA* 792C, Evans 23917, Seid. p. 128, Brethren Bib. 41. $ 100.00

715. **DER KLEINE DAVIDISCHE PSALTERSPIEL...** Billmeyer, Germantown: 1797. pp. 572, 24, 22. Pretty full leather with clasps. *GLP/USA* 1069, Evans 31816, Seid. p 146, Brethren Bibliography 51-2. $ 95.00

716. **DER KLEINE DAVIDISCHE PSALTERSPIEL...** Bound with / **DIE KLEINE HARFE.** Samuel Saur, Balt: 1797. pp. (6), 572, (22), 55, (1). Original polished calf with clasps. 18th Century plain leather back. *GLP/USA* 1058, Evans 31815, Brethren Bib. 49. ***Bound in the front is a rare little broadside song sheet: "Ein Bittend Lied, an den Schöpfer"... with another unusual mourning song broadsheet used as a paste-down.*** Unusual. $ 240.00

717. **DER KLEINE DAVIDISCHE PSALTERSPIEL...** Billmeyer, Phila: 1817. Pretty copy with clasps. *GLP/USA* 2223/4, Seid. p. 201, AI 40207/8, Brethren Bib. 72/3. $ 50.00

718. **DER KLEINE DAVIDISCHE PSALTERSPIEL...** Mentz & Son, Phila: 1833. 504p. Worn full leather w/clasps. *Extensive Manuscript ownership of Johannes Moonschein.* The first of four editions printed by Mentz. AI 17791. $ 40.00

719. **DER PSALTER DES KONIGS UND PROPHETEN DAVIDS...** Samuel Saur, Balt: 1796. 280p. Text worn. Nice calf binding. *GLP/USA* 10006, Evans 30074, Seid. p. 142. $ 85.00

720. **DER PSALTER...** Billmeyer, Germantown: 1802. 252p. Worn. 24mo. *GLP/USA* 1290, AI 50276. See: Luthy, Amish Usage of the Psalms. $ 50.00

721. **DER PSALTER...** Billmeyer, Germantown: 1804. 252p. Full leather. 24mo. *GLP/USA* 1374. *Apparently not in either AI nor Seidensticker.* $ 40.00

722. **DER PSALTER...** Billmeyer, Germantown: 1815. 252p. Full leather. 24mo. XLib. *Early Sherk (Shirk) family ownership.* *GLP/USA* 2099, AI 34101, Seid. p. 195. $ 40.00

723. **DER PSALTER...** Jacob Meyer, Phila: 1812. 216p. 24mo. *Manuscript ownership of Jacob Weaver.* *GLP/USA* 1911, Variant of AI 24852, Seid. p. 186. $ 40.00

724. **DER PSALTER...** Zentler for Mentz, Phila: 1816. 252p. 24mo. Full leather. XLib. *GLP/USA* 2164, Seid. p. 198, AI 36988. *HSH.* $ 24.00

725. **DER PSALTER...** Hütter, Easton: 1821. 266p. Pretty terminal device. Edges decorated by binder. *GLP/USA* 2481, AI 4698. Scarce. $ 38.00

726. **DER PSALTER...** Bär, Lancaster: 1826. Worn. *GLP/USA* 2813, AI 23815. $ 15.00

727. **DER PSALTER...** Ritter, Reading: 1827. 252p. Very pretty mottled calf binding. XL. *GLP/USA* 2889, AI 28170. *Not in Seid.* $ 39.00

728. **DER PSALTER...** Howe for Mentz, Phila: 1828. 252p. 32mo. Small type and small format edition. Full leather. XLib. *Not in Seid.* *GLP/USA* 2967, AI 32360. $ 26.00

729. **DER PSALTER...** Bär, Lancaster: 1834. 219p. 24mo. Full leather. AI 23410. These small Psalters were probably meant for use by children and in Sunday schools. $ 35.00

730. **DER PSALTER...** Howe for Mentz, Phila: 1839. 252p. + Frontis. 18mo. $ 15.00

731. **DER PSALTER...** Zentler, Phila: 1844. Unusual manuscript ownerships. $ 34.00

732. **DER PSALTER...** Mentz & Rovoudt, Phila: 1848. 252p. Full leather. $ 14.00

GERMAN AMERICAN FORMULARY

733. (Puwelle, Arnold). **DER PRAKTISCHE UND ERFAHRENE RATHGEBER FÜR KUNSTLER UND PROFESSIONISTEN... REZEPTBUCH.** Puwell, Reading: 1840. 303p. Leather backed marbled boards. Great collection of formulae. $ 120.00

RARE PROTESTANT MARTYROLOGY AND REFORMATION HISTORY

734. Rabus, Ludovicus. **HISTORIEN [DER MARTYRER] ... DER HEILIGEN AUSSERWOHLTEN GOTTES ZEUGEN / Bekennern und Martyren.** B.Beck Erben & S. Emmel, Strassburg: 1552-1556. Four volumes in three. Approximately 175 woodcut illustrations + extra portraits. Contemporary vellum / alum tawed (non-uniform) bindings. Entirely complete but some restoration is needed. Extremely scarce. We have located only one other copy (Royal Library, Munich) identical to our Vol. 1. Ludwig Rabe [1514-92] has left us one of the most remarkable documents in the history of German iconography and Reformation history, biography, & folklore. Not only does he relate the tales of those who suffered and died for their faith (including a few Anabaptists), but he also paints an extensive and reliable *contemporary* picture of the prime movers of the Reformation. The discussion of Luther alone occupies 488 pages in Volume IV. A fuller description will be provided upon request. $1250.00

735. Rambach, Johann Jacob [1693-1735]. **BERTRACHTUNGEN UBER DAS LEIDEN CHRISTI...** Schelly, Phila: 1837. 1000+p. Illus. Pretty full mottled calf. Ds. $ 34.00

736. (Rauch, Edward Henry). **PENNSYLVANISH DEITSCH. DE CAMPAIGN BREFFA FUM PIT SCHWEFFLEBRENNER ... Fum "Father Abraham"... Grant Campaign, 1868.** (Lancaster: 1868). 46p. Outer wraps and ad leaf from a reprint edition. New cloth. Vivid political commentary written in the dialect. See also, Part II #1697-99. *WST.* $ 45.00

GERMAN ACCOUNT OF TRAVELS THROUGH AMERICA

737. Raumer, Friedrich von. **DIE VEREININGTEN STAATEN VON NORDAMERIKA.** Schwacke, Phila: 1846. 223p. + Folding chart. Taped spine. First American Edition. See: Sabin 67973. Insightful observations on the U. S. *Preston A. Barba's copy.* $ 75.00

738. (Reich, Johann C. F.). **BESCHÄFTIGUNGEN DES HERZENS MIT GOTT...** Held, Easton: 1826. 251p. Full leather. *GLP/USA* 2795, AI 25914, Seid. p. 228. *WST.* $ 32.00

739. Rieger, George Conrad. **HERZENS = POSTILLE, Oder zur Fortpflanzung des Wahren Christenthums...** Zuellichau: 1748. 1800+p. Thick 4to. Handsome contemporary polished calf binding, with clasps. *Extensive Manuscript Embich Family Record (Lebanon, Pa: 1790's).* The most popular work of Rieger [1687-1743], who contributed much to the Pietist movement in Swabia & Württemberg. $ 175.00

740. Reinhold, Werner. **PHILOSOPHIE DER DEUTSCHEN SPRACHE...** Trexler, Allentown: 1869. 55p. Shoemaker/L p. 125. *WST.* $ 40.00

741. Reitz(en), Johann Heinrich. **DAS FÜRBILDE DER HEILSAMEN WORTEN, Vom Glauben und Liebe...** Steimer, Albrecht, & Lahn, Lancaster: 1788. pp. 12, 167. 24mo. Leather backed boards. Reitz [1655-1720] was one of the Wittgenstein Separatists. Early manuscript ownership. *GLP/USA* 716, Evans 21422, Seid. p. 122. $ 125.00

ILLUSTRATED GERMAN AMERICAN NATURAL HISTORY

742. Reubelt, J. A. **KURZGEFASSTES HANDBUCH DER NATURGESCHICHTE...** Reubelt & Gunther, Pottsville, Pa; 1848. 392p. Numerous intriguing woodcut illustrations of men and a wide variety of animals. Attractive 1/2 leather binding. $ 80.00

743. **DER RICHTIGE WEG Zum Ewigen Leben...** Zentler, Phila: 1814. 144p. 16mo. XL. Worn. First American edition. *GLP/USA* 2046, Seid. p. 192, AI 32657. $ 20.00

744. Roberts, Wuchter, & More. **LEWENDICHE SCHTIMME AUS PENNSILVENI.** Stuttgart & NY: 1929. 153p. Printed wraps. German study of the dialect literature. $ 22.00

745. Roemeling, C. A. **...NACHRICHT SEINER VON GOTT GESCHEHENEN VOLLIGEN HERAUSFUHRUNG AUS BABEL...** With tracts by Arnold and Tersteegen. Ephrata (Cloisters): 1792. Five works in one. pp. 12, 466, 21-96. Contemporary full leather. Christian Anton Römeling was a Lutheran minister at Harburg who was excommunicated and banished for his pietist / mystical theology. He found refuge in Holland and joined the Mennonites. This publication has "a mystical drift quite in accord with the religious temper of Ephrata" - Seidensticker p. 132, *GLP/USA* 840, Evans 24755. $ 500.00

THE IRREPLACEABLE GERMAN HORSE AND STOCK DOCTOR

746. (Rohlwes, Johann Nicolaus). **ALLGEGMEINES VIEHARZNEIBUCH, oder Unterrich, wie der Landmann, seine Pferde, Rindvieh, Schafe, Schweine und Hunde...** Goeb, Schellsburg, Pa: 1823. pp. 12, 291. Illus. *GLP/USA* 2619, AI 13982. *Not in Seid.* $ 150.00

747. (Rohlwes). **DER VOLLSTANDIGE PFERDE=ARZT (GAULS DOCTOR BUCH)...** Sage, Reading: 1817. pp. 10, 108. Woodcut Horse Illustration. Original printed paper boards with Sage's ad for his printings of Jung-Stilling, etc. *GLP/USA* 2252, AI 42008, Austin 1618. These veterinary manuals become especially significant as one considers the crucial role of stock and horses in the 18th & 19th century; and even among many peoples today. $ 160.00

748. (Romer, Ignaz) [of Dauphin County, PA]. **DAS GEHEIMNISS DER BOSHEIT...** Grimler, Lancaster: 1809. 240p. Full leather. XLib. Arcane mystical text that includes in the foreword a grand poem about America. *GLP/USA* 1671, AI 18534, Seid. p. 175. $ 50.00

749. (Roosen, Gerhard) [1612=1711]. **CHRISTLICHES GEMUTHS = GESPRACH...** Billmeyer, Germantown: 1790. 241p. 24mo. Leather w/clasps. Spine taped. *GLP/USA* 762, Evans 22858/22493, Seid. p. 126 = "Presents the Mennonite view of Christian doctrine & life, & contains some edifying songs by Christopher Dock, the schoolmaster of the Wisahickon". *Nice red and black manuscript (Mennonite) bookplate of Henrich Jansen (1791)* + Manuscript genealogical information for the Miller & Jensen families. $ 220.00

750. (Roosen). **CHRISTLICHES GEMUTHS = GESPRACH...** Grimler, Lanc: 1811. 241p. Nice full leather. XLib. *GLP/USA* 1825, AI 22527, Seid. p. 182. $ 50.00

751. (Roosen). **CHRISTLICHES GEMUTHS = GESPRACH...** Baer, Lancaster: 1836. 256p. 32mo. Extremely popular pietist text. $ 20.00

752. (Ross, James). **EIN ERNSTLICHER RUF AN DIE DEUTSCHEN IN PENNSYLVANIEN.** Albrecht, Lancaster: 1799. 15p. Uncut. Sewn as issued. Federalist appeal to the Pennsylvania Germans to support James Ross for Governor. *GLP/USA* 1174, Evans 35450, Seid. p. 152. Classic political pamphlet. $ 60.00

753. Rothbaust, Johannes. **DIE FRANKLIN HARMONIE....** Wyeth, Harrisburg 1821. pp. 12, 144p. First 2 leaves repaired with some loss. Lacks front bd. Oblong Pa. German Song Book. Shaped Notes. *GLP/USA* 2494, Seid. p. 214, AI 6671. Some text in English. $ 125.00

754. Rothbaust. **THE FRANKLIN HARMONY...English & German Church Tunes.** Ruby, Chambersburg: 1830. pp. 12, 195. Text in English & German. Oblong Pa. German Song Book. Shaped Notes. *Not in GLP/USA*, AI 3350. $ 150.00

755. Rupp, I. D. **GESCHITE DER MARTYRER...** Robinson & Fairbank, Cincinnati: 1830. Two volumes in one. Woodcut illus. Lovely full leather binding. Translation of Foxe's Book of Martyrs by the "Father of Pennsylvania Local History". One of the earliest surviving Cincinnati German imprints. Seid. p. 245, AI 1429. $ 80.00

756. St. Johns Church. **JUBILAUMS BUCHLEIN...** Pastor Kündig's 50 Years, 1860-1910. (Reading: 1910). 207p. Illus. Cloth. Gilt. $ 16.00

757. St. Paul's Church. **KIRCHEN=ORDNUNG der Evangelisch - Lutherischen Gemeinde...** (New Goshenhoppen, Montgomery Co.) Kneule, Pennsburg, Pa: 1873. 20p. $ 22.00

758. St. Peter's Church. **CONSTITUTION DES FRAUEN = VEREINS der Deutschen Ev. Luth. Kirche**. Allentown: 1905. 8p. Printed wraps. *WST*. Ladies' Association. $ 14.00

759. (Salem, Pa. Sunday School Union). **SONNTAGSCHUL = GESANGBUCHLEIN...** Christlichen Zeitschrift, Chambersburg: 1840. pp. 228, 9. 32mo. Leather backed. $ 38.00

760. (Salem, Pa. Sunday School Union). **SONNTAGSCHUL = GESANGBUCHLEIN...** Phila: 1845. pp. 284, 11. Sm. 32mo. *WST*. $ 28.00

761. **EINE SAMMLUNG VON GEISTLICHEN, LIEBLICHEN LIEDERN...** Baab, Harrisburg: 1830. 389p. 24mo. Worn. By a Committee from the General Conference of "Vereinigten Brüder". First Edition. *GLP/USA* 3091, AI 3393, Seid. 245. $ 38.00

762. **EINE SAMMLUNG VON CHRISTLICHEN, LIEBLICHEN LIEDERN...** Wm. Raine, Balt: 1840. 389p. 24mo. Worn. *Ownership of Rudolf Sherk (Shirk).* $ 24.00

BEAUTIFUL AND RARE EIGHTEENTH CENTURY METAMORPHOSIS

763. (Sands, Benjamin & Poupard, James). **(METAMORPHOSIS, oder eine Verwandlung von Bildern)**. (Philadelphia, Ca: 1792). Four woodcut illustrated panels, each with two colored, folded segments. *The most famed of American puzzle books, these Metamorphosis' were sometimes called "changing books" or "turn-ups". Reading the rhymed German text, and turning the components up or down in sequence; a curious youngster would be entertainingly lead beyond the ABC's and the story of Adam and Eve - to the inevitability of death, and moral truth & salvation.* See: Welsh 1163.4 and Evans 46570, but probably not identical to either of these. $ 950.00

764. **DER SANGER AM GRABE. Eine Auswahl Lieder zum Gebrauch bei Leichen = Begangnissen, wie auch Trost=Lieder fur Solche die um Geliebte Todte Trauren.** Edited by C. G. Herrman. Hawrecht & Wink, Kutztown: 1842. 180p. Full leather. The first edition of this important and popular song book. *WST.* $ 50.00

765. **DER SANGER AM GRABE...** Hawrecht & Wink, Kutztown: 1845. 212p. Leather backed boards. *J. S. Dreisbach's copy. WST.* $ 40.00

766. **DER SANGER AM GRABE...** Blumer & Busch, Allentown: 1847. 223p. Very stained. 24mo. Shoemaker/L p. 74. *WST.* $ 32.00

767. **DER SANGER AM GRABE...** "Geist der Zeit" Office, Kutztown, Pa: 1848. 212p. Pretty leather backed marbled boards. *WST.* $ 36.00

768. **DER SANGER AM GRABE...** Blumer & Busch, Allentown: 1849. 223p. Stained. 24mo. Shoemaker/L p. 76. *WST.* $ 26.00

769. **DER SANGER AM GRABE...** Blumer & Busch, Allentown: 1852. 223p. Very pretty full leather gilt. Shoemaker/L p. 82. *WST.* $ 38.00

770. **DER SANGER AM GRABE...** "Geist der Zeit" Druckerei, Kutztown, Pa: 1852. 220p. With a Family "death" register. 18mo. $ 30.00

771. **DER SANGER AM GRABE...** Phila: 1854. 240p. *WST.* $ 20.00

772. **DER SANGER AM GRABE...** "Geist der Zeit" Druckerei, Kutztown, Pa: 1856. 214p. With the "Death" register. 24mo. Attractive embossed cloth. *WST.* $ 28.00

773. **DER SANGER AM GRABE...** Blumer, Busch & Co. Allentown: 1857. 223p. Cloth. Shoemaker/L p. 93. *WST.* $ 26.00

774. **DER SANGER AM GRABE.** Herrman, Kutztown: 1873. 211p. *WST.* $ 20.00

775. **DER SANGER AM GRABE...** Kohler, Phila. Ca: 1873. 240p. + Ads. $ 12.00

776. **DER SANGER AM GRABE...** Kohler, Phila. Ca: 1890. 240p. *WST.* $ 10.00

777. Sangmeister, Ezechiel (Heinrich). **MYSTISCHE THEOLOGIE...** Bauman, Ephrata: 1819-20. Two volumes in one. 168p. + ***The Remarkable Mystical Irrgarten Broadside printed by Bauman and missing from most copies.*** Lovely contemporary checker board binding. *GLP/USA* 2415 (Not mentioning the broadside), Seid. p. 207, AI 49359. Copies of this impressive broadside, have often been separated from the complete publication, to be sold alone at a very high price. $ 250.00

Mystische Theologie,
oder
Wahrer Wegweisser
nach unserm
Ursprung und Vaterland!
Bestehend in 3 Theilen,
1. Theil, von den Irr- und Abwegen gutmeinender Frommen.
2. Theil, ist eine Erklärung über Mathäi 24,
3. Theil, ist eine Erklärung der Sechstägigen Schöpfung und den Zeitläuften dieser Welt.
Gestellt nach dem hohen Licht und Erkenntniß durch
Ezechiel Sangmeister.
Erster Theil.
Erste Auflage.
Ephrata, Gedruckt und zu haben bey Joseph Bauman, im Jahr 1819 und 20.

778. Sangmeister. **MYSTISCHE THEOLOGIE...** Bauman, Ephrata: 1819-20. Without the Broadside. Worn checker board binding. *GLP/USA* 2415, Seid. p. 207, AI 49359. $ 100.00

779. Sauder, Ben. **DER NACHBAR AN DE SCHTROAS.** Ontario, Canada: 1955. 35p. Wraps. Pennsylvania German dialect verse. $ 12.00

SAUR'S ANSWER TO FRANKLIN'S "PLAIN TRUTH"

780. (Saur, Christopher). **VERSCHIEDENE CHRISTLICHE WAHRHEITEN, Und Kurtze Betrachtung Uber das kurtzlich herausgegebene Buchlein, Genandt: Lautere Wahrheit...** Christoph Saur, Germantown: 1748. 32p. Slight loss on Tp. Browned. Plain wraps. In 1747 Franklin issued a pamphlet called "Plain Truth", where he advocated vigorous measures for the defense of Pennsylvania's frontiers against the Indians. The Quakers, Mennonites, and other non-resistant sects deplored the call to arms, and there arose among the Pennsylvania Germans an animated controversy. Saur strongly opposed warfare of any kind, and was severely censured for his stand. This is one of the most eloquent of the several pamphlets that Saur published on the subject. *GLP/USA* 110 *[4 copies only]*, Evans 6233, Seid. p. 32, Hild. 1100. $ 545.00

SAUR'S "WANDERING SOUL"

781A. Schabalje, Johann Philip. **DIE WANDLENDE SEEL...** Christoph Saur, Germantown: 1768. pp. 8, 463, 25. Ds. Contemporary full leather with early home-made spine. *GLP/USA* 358, Evans 11067, Seid. p. 78, Hild. 2394. An important pietist / Mennonite work, by Jan Philpsz Schabaelje [1585-1656], that had special appeal for the sectarians in America. $ 500.00

781B. Schabalje. **DIE WANDLENDE SEEL...** Christoph Saur, Germantown: 1771. pp. 8, 463, 23. Ds. Contemporary full leather. Evans 12221, Seid. p. 83. $ 225.00

782. Schabalje. **DIE WANDLENDE SEEL...** Liebert, Germantown: 1794. pp. 8, 463, 22. Contemporary full leather. Ds. *GLP/USA* 929, Evans 27674, Seid. p. 137. See also Part II # 1768, for the scarce Winchester, Va., English edition. $ 125.00

783. Schaf(f), Philipp. **DER ANGLOGERMANISMUS EINE REDE Gehalten den 10ten Marz, 1846, von der Schillers = Gesellschaft des Marschall Collegiums zu Mercersburg.** Chambersburg: 1846. 22p. Plain wraps. $ 38.00

784. Schaff, Philipp. **DEUTSCHES GESANGBUCH...** Phila. & Chambersburg: 1860. 672p. + Ads. Presentation copy from Schaff in a fine embossed morocco binding. $ 40.00

785. Scheffmacher & Stoltz. **PRAMIE ZUM STEBENTEN JAHRGANG DER KATHOLISCHEN VOLKSZEITUNG Diamant oder Glas; und Controversie uber den Vosprung des Protestantismus.** Baltimore: 1866. pp. 47, 144. Ds. Worn. $ 15.00

786. Schmauk, J. G. **DEUTSCHE HARMONIE, oder Mehrstimmige Gesange fur Deutsche Singerschulen und Kirchen...** Mentz, Phila. Ca: 1847. 264p. Oblong Pa. German Song Book. Not shaped notes. Lacks front board. XLib. $ 22.00

787. Schmolk(ens), Benjamin. **...MORGEN UND ABEND ANDACHTEN...** Nürnberg: 1773. pp. 14, 384 + Plates. Ds. Contemporary full leather, handsomely tooled in blind, with clasps. Schmolk [1672-1737] was a German Lutheran, whose hymns are still sung today. $ 75.00

788. (Schmolkens). **DAS HIMMLISCHE VERGNUGEN IN GOTT. Vollstandiges Gebat=Buch.** Aarau: 1836. 816p. + Frontis. Prayers & songs. $ 24.00

789. Schmucker, J. Geo. [York,PA]. **DIE PROPHETISCHE GESCHICHTE VON DEN SIEGEN CHRISTI UND SEINER KIRCHE... Erklärung der Offenbarung Johannis...** Zessener for Weyl, Balt: 1843. 347p. + Litho portrait. Full leather. $ 24.00

790. Schmucker, S. S. **KURZGEFASSTE GESCHICHTE DER CHRISTLICHEN KIRCHE...** Neinstadt, Gettysburg: 1834. 352p. Damp stained. Most interesting for its history of the Lutheran Church in America. AI 26654. $ 24.00

791. Schneck, Benjamin S. **ABENTHEUERLICHE EREIGNISSE AUS DEN LEBEN DER ERSTEN ANSIEDLER...** Hills, Lancaster: 1842. 537p. Folding Lithographs & woodcut illustrations. Famous book on the early pioneers & Indian Wars. Disbd. Probably co-written by Joseph Pritts, and first published by Ruby of Chambersburg in 1839. $ 75.00

792. Schnorr, Julius of Carolsfeld. **DAS NEUE TESTAMENT IN ACHTZIG BILDERN...** English & German Text. Phila. Ca: 1870. Eighty N.T. pictures. $ 30.00

793. Schnorr. **DAS NEUE TESTAMENT IN ACHTZIG BILDERN...** English & German Text. Ontario: 1981. Reprint of the above. $ 10.00

794. **EIN SCHÖNER UND WOHL APPROBIRTER HEIL. SEEGEN Zu Wasser und Land, Wider Alle seine Feinde, so ihm begegnen auf allen Wegen und Stegen.** Cum. Licent. 1705. Gedruct zu Wien, in Oesterreich. (Vienna? 1705). 127p. 48mo. *Contemporary morocco gilt binding. Calligraphic ownership of Owen Allen (1833).* This little prayer book was often given to travellers; among them emigrants to America. It is even possible that some of these editions, were printed in Pennsylvania. $ 100.00

795. **EIN SCHÖNER UND WOL APPROBIRTER H. SEGEN ZU WASSER UND LAND...** Prague: (1705). 3 vols in 1. Illustrated by 24 unusual woodcuts of Saints, etc. 48mo. Another very scarce edition of this popular devotional book. $ 100.00

796. **EIN SCHÖNER UND WHOL APPROBIRTER HEIL. SEEGEN ZU WASSER UND LAND, Wider Alle Seine Feinde, so ihm begegnen auf allen Wegen und Stegen.** Reading, Pa: 1842. 125p. 48mo. The only edition we know of that is *clearly* American. $ 85.00

797. (Schröckh, J. M.). **KURZER BEGRIFF DER BIBLISCHEN GESCHICHTE. Ein Schulbuch für die Americanische Jungend und zum Gebrauch für Jedermann...** Hütter, Easton: 1819. 116p. + Folding Table. Unusual marbled boards. *GLP/USA* 2338, AI 49373, Seid. p. 207. Scarce book for instruction of children. *WST.* $ 50.00

SCHWENKFELDERIANA

Organized by Kaspar Schwenkfeld von Ossig [1489-1561], in the 16th century, the entire sect emigrated to America in 1734. They settled outside Philadelphia, along the Perkiomen Creek, from Pennsburg to Skippack. They exerted an influence that went beyond their small numbers. Please note the important Schwenkfelder manuscripts that we offer in Part III, # 2203 & 2204.

SCHWENKFELDER PIONEER DAVID SHULTZE'S COPY

798. Schwenkfeld. (Schultz, Christoph). **CATECHISMUS, ODER ANFAENGLICHER CHRIST - LICHER GLAUBENS-LEHRER...** Henrich Miller, Phila: 1763. pp. 4, 146 (1/2 of the rare folding chart is present). Contemporary full leather. *Manuscript ownership of David Shultze (1765), an important Schwenkfelder pioneer. Nice pen & ink tulip on rear pastdown.* See also # 806. *GLP/USA* 282, Evans 9512, Seid. p. 63, Hild. 1882. $ 225.00

799. Schwenkfeld. (Schultz, Christoph). **CATECHISMUS...** Henrich Miller, Phila: 1763. Some loss of text. Contemporary full leather. *Early Manuscript ownership of Rosina Andersin, with a two tone drawing of a large tulip blossom pasted on the flyleaf.* Rosina [1757-1781] was the eldest daughter of George & Barbara (Diehl) Anders. She married George Schneider (Snyder) in 1780. $ 180.00

800. Schwenkfeld. (Schultz, Christoph). **KURZE FRAGEN UBER DIE CHRISTLICHE GLAUBENS=LEHRE.** Cist, Phila: 1784. 140p. *Unusual full leather binding with an uncommon & significant decorative roll on the boards. A rare binding that can be ascribed to Christopher Hoffmann, the Schwenkfelder minister and binder. GLP/USA* 610, Seid. p. 114, Hild 4503, Evans 18779. Essentially a reprint of the 1763 Catechism. $ 300.00

801. Schwenkfeld. (Schultz, Christoph). **KURZE FRAGEN...** Cist, Phila: 1784. 140p. Nicely printed. Original full leather. Front board broken. $ 100.00

802. Schwenkfeld. **EIN CHRISTLICHER SEND=BRIEF...** Blumer, Allentown: 1835. 96p. Leather backed marbled boards. First American Ed. *Not in AI.* Shoemaker/L p. 53. $ 40.00

803. Schwenkfeld. **EINIGE CHRISTLICHE UND LEHREICHE SEND=BRIEFE...** Bound with /**VON DER HIMMLISCHEN ARZENEY. Oder dass Jesus Christus der Wahre Artz, und der Arme Sund=hafte Mensch der Patient, Verwundete oder Kranke Sey**. Bound w / **VON DREYERLEY LEBEN DER MENSCHEN...** Ebner, Allentown: 1819=20. 3 volumes in 1. 337p. Nice contemporary full leather. An attractive copy of a very popular book. *GLP/USA* 2324/2400-1, AI 49374/3123-4, Seid. p. 206/210, Shoemaker/L p. 32. $ 75.00

804. (Schwenkfeld Church). **GEBET=BUCHLEIN...** Billmeyer, Germantown: 1806. 271p. Crisp copy. Original full leather. *Light fraktur ownership of Lydia Jackel. GLP/USA* 1486, AI 10468, Seid. p. 167. $ 50.00

805A. (Schwenkfeld Church). **LEHR TRACTATE...** Blumer & Busch, Allentown: 1846. pp. 14, 206, 1. Pretty mottled full leather. Shoemaker/L p. 72. $ 24.00

THE FIRST SCHWENKFELDER HYMNBOOK PRINTED IN AMERICA

805B. (Schwenkfeld Church). **NEU EINGERICHTETES GESANG = BUCH...** Christoph Saur, Germantown: 1762. pp. 34, 760, 40. Last leaf w/ slight loss. Contemporary full leather. Rebacking needed. See: Seipt. *Schwenkfelder Hymnology, GLP/USA* 250, Evans 9266, Seid. p. 57, Hild. 1834. At a general conference held in 1762 the Schwenkfelders adopted this standard hymnal augmented with borrowings from Moravian, Lutheran, and Reformed Gesangbuchs. Compiled by Christopher Schultz. $ 360.00

Neu-Eingerichtetes
Gesang-Buch
in sich haltend
eine
Sammlung
(mehrentheils alter)
schöner lehr-reicher und erbaulicher
Lieder,
Welche von langer Zeit her bey den Bekennern
und Liebhabern der Glorien und Wahrheit
Jesu Christi bis anjetzo in Uebung
gewesen.
Nach den Haupt-Stücken der Christlichen
Lehr und Glaubens eingetheilet,
und
Mit einem Verzeichniß der Titel
und dreyen Nützlichen Registern
versehen
Anjetzo also zusammen getragen,
und
Zum Lobe GOttes und heilsamen
Erbauung im Christenthum,
ans Licht gegeben.
Germantown, gedruckt bey Christoph Saur,
auf Kosten vertrauter Freunde, 1762.

SCHWENKFELDER PIONEER DAVID SCHULTZ'S COPY OF THE 1762 HYMNBOOK

806. (Schwenkfeld Church). **NEU EINGERICHTETES GESANG = BUCH...** Christoph Saur, Germantown: 1762. Some leaves with old repairs and slight loss. Worn full leather binding by Christopher Hoffman, with six [of 8] original iron(?) corner bosses. *The copy of David Schultz (Shultz) [1717-97], Schwenkfelder pioneer, scrivener, surveyor, conveyencer, and diarist/historian.* Signed three times by David Schultz; and once by Kregorius Schöltz (Gregory Schultz). *Of special importance is a carefully written, six page, manuscript biographical guide to the composers of the hymns. Throughout the text the author of almost every hymn is identified by initials in manuscript, correlating directly to the biographies.* It is possible that this index is in the hand of Christopher Hoffman. Unique. See also # 798, and the manuscripts in Part. III. $ 600.00

807. (Schwenkfeld Church). **NEUEINGERICHTETES GESANG=BUCH...** Conrad Zentler, Phila: 1813. pp. (8), 538, 24. Pretty original full leather. *Nice manuscript ownership of Jacob Schultz. GLP/USA* 1988, AI 29737, Seid. p. 189. $ 70.00

808. **SEELEN=MEDICIN...** Bound With / **Die Herrlichkeit des Eingebohrnen Fürgestellt in den Namen...** Mayer & Atkinson, Harrisburg: 1804. 350+p. Three vols in one. Contemporary full leather. XLib. *GLP/USA* 1390, Seid. p. 162, AI 6471/7237/7676. $ 85.00

809. Seidensticker, Oswald. **FESTGRUSS ZU DR. CONSTANTIN HERINGS'S ACHTZIGSTEN GEBURTSTAGE, Jan. 1, 1880.** (Phila: 1890). 101p. English & German text. Spine taped. Issued to celebrate the famous Homoeopath's 80th (& 90th) birthdays. $ 45.00

810. Seward, Senator Wm. H. **REDE... Uber den Vorgeschlagenen Protest der Vereinigten Staaten, gegen die Bewassnete Intervention von Russland in der Ungarischen Revolution...** DC: 1852. 15p. Wraps. $ 20.00

811. Sheppard, Thomas. **SCHALMER WEG ZUM LEBEN...** "Pennsylvanien": 1838. 544p. Full leather w/ clasps. XLib. First American Edition. *Apparently Not in AI.* $ 30.00

812. Siegfried, Samuel. **DEUTSCHE GEOGRAPHIE, oder Welt=Beschreibung...** Siegfried, Millgrove, Buschkill Twp. Northampton County, Pa: 1834. 360p. Curious woodcut on tp. Ds. 1/2 leather. AI 26774. $ 80.00

813. (Singmaster, J. A.). **"GOSPEL HYMNS," verdeutschet zum Gebrauch der Bestunde.** Knauss, Macungie, Pa: 1884. 12p. 32mo. Printed wraps. Shoemaker/L p. 159 = *"The only Lehigh County German imprint not printed in Allentown, or by Helfrich in Weissenberg."* $ 38.00

814. Sinking Spring Fire Co. **INCORPORATIONS AKTE DER GEGENSEITIGEN FEUERVERSICHERUNGS COMPANIE VON DER SINKING SPRING, BERKS COUNTY.** Ritter, Reading: 1846. 12p. Plain paper wraps. Rare. $ 85.00

815. (Smith, Caroline). **EINE ERZAHLUNG VON DEM SELIGEN TODE DER CAROLINE HANNA SMITH...** Miller, New Berlin: 1840. 32p. Wraps. 32mo. Kindig ownership. $ 40.00

816. **DER SONNTAGSSCHUL=SANGER.** Brobst, Allentown: 1865. 32p. Music & Words. Printed wraps. Oblong 24mo. Scarce. Shoemaker/L p. 114. $ 30.00

817. Späth, A. **BROSAMEN VON DES HERRN TISCHE...** Phila: 1871. 117p. + 17p. German Bookseller's ad (Kohler). 24mo. Original cloth. $ 15.00

818. **SPRUCHBUCH... Sammlung von Biblischen Sprüchen, Psalmen und Gebeten...** Stuttgart: 1806. 143p. Ds. *Manuscript American ownership of Frederick Aldinger.* $ 34.00

819. Stangl, Chrysostomus. **SPAZIERGANG NACH NORDAMERIKA...** Freiburg im Breisgan & St. Louis: 1880. 362p. Walking tour of the U. S. $ 48.00

820. Stark, Johann Friedrich. **GEBÄT, ODER TÄGLICHES HAND=BUCH...** Herschberger, Chambersburg: 1812. 475p. Contemporary full leather. XLib. *GLP/USA* 1880, AI 26796. In German American homes, the handbook of Stark [1680-1756] was undoubtedly one of the most popular and avidly read of all devotional books. $ 42.00

821. Stark. **GEBÄT, ODER TÄGLICHES HAND=BUCH...** Zentler & Mentz, Phila: 1812. pp. 566, 134. Worn full leather. XLib. *GLP/USA* 1927, AI 26797. $ 36.00

822. Stark. **TÄGLICHES HAND = BUCH...** Bound with / **TAGLISCHES GEBET = BUCHLEIN...** Stuttgart: 1766. pp. 660, 132. *Owned (and repaired) by Jacob Harpel, 1829 (Lebanon County?).* $ 65.00

823. Stark. **TÄGLICHES HAND=BUCH...** Moser & Peters, Carlisle: 1825. 472p. + Several woodcut illus. Text worn & Ds. *Remarkable full mottled calf binding with the boards lined and framed in blind; and the spine decorated in gilt using at least six different tools. GLP/USA* 2728, Seid. p. 224, AI 22362. $ 145.00

824. Stark. **TÄGLICHES HAND=BUCH...** Mentz & Son, Phila: 1834. 644p. Full leather. *Partially colored Manuscript ownership of "Susanna Disinger, 1841".* AI 26913. $ 40.00

825. Stark, Johann. **TÄGLICHES HAND=BUCH...** Mentz & Son, Phila: 1839. 644p. Full leather w/ clasps. XLib. *Apparently not in AI.* $ 34.00

826. Stark. **TÄGLICHES HAND=BUCH...** Stuttgart: 1839. 568p. Very unusual embossed full leather binding with clasps. Ds. Printed for the American market. $ 40.00

827. Stark. **TÄGLICHES HAND=BUCH...** Kohler, Phila: 1857. 700+p. + Illus. Attractive embossed full leather with brass clasps. Decorated edges. $ 22.00

828. Stark. **TÄGLICHES HAND=BUCH...** Kohler, Phila. Ca: 1868. Attractive full morocco. Offered with a really handsome copy of the same edition in English. $ 32.00

829. (Stauffer, Jacob). **EINE CHRONIK ODER GESCHICHT=BUCHLEIN Von Der Sogenannten Mennonisten Gemeinde...** Lancaster: 1855. 439p. Spine taped. Important historic and controversial work on the Mennonite and Amish doctrine of shunning, the ban, and the doctrine of separation. $ 52.00

830. (Steckel, A. D.). **DUMHETE = EN GLEH BUCH MIT TSEEH SHTORIES IN PENNSYLVANIA DEUTSCH.** Fullerton, Pa: 1930. 36p. Illus. Leather wraps. Dialect stories. Very scarce. *WST.* $ 24.00

831A. (Stein, Kurt M.). **DIE SCHONSTE LENGEVITCH. By K. M. S.** Introduction by Richard Atwater. Chicago: 1927. 103p. *WST.* $ 22.00

831B. Steiner, J. C. **DIE HERRLICHE ERSCHEINUNG DES HERRN JESU SUM ALLGEMEINEN WELT=GERICHT...** Henrich Miller, Phila: 1763. pp. (8), 478p. Ds. Worn. Steiner [1707-62] was an important Reformed pastor in Pa. & Maryland. This work, which contains a biographical sketch by H. M. Muhlenberg, was published by his widow as a fund raiser and memorial. *GLP/USA* 283, Evans 1518, Seid. p. 64, Hild. 1922. $ 220.00

832. Stetzel, E. Henry. **EIN GESCHICHTLICHER WEGWEISER...** Allentown: 1878. 273p. 16mo. Scarce mystical work on the Prophecies of Daniel and John. *WST.* $ 25.00

833. Stetzel, E. Henry. **KURZE LEBENSGESCHICHTE VON MOSES DISSINGER...** Allentown: 1892. 27p. Wraps. Dissinger was an Evangelical Assoc. preacher, known as "The Pennsylvania German Billy Sunday". *Not in Shoemaker/L. WST.* $ 30.00

834. Stewart, Robert. **DAS PFERDEBUCH DES AMERIKANISCHEN FARMERS...** Cincinnati: 1879. 594p. Illus. German American Horse Doctor. $ 36.00

835. (Stoll [St-ll], Jacob). **GEISTLICHES GEWÜRZ=GARTLEIN Heilsuchender Seelen...** Bauman, Ephrata: 1806. 191p. Contemporary full leather. *Catherine Rinehart's book, 1809. Not in Seidensticker. GLP/USA* 1481, AI 11414, Hinks p. 135. Scarce Brethren hymnal. $ 80.00

836. Strüf, Marrianne. **VOLLSTANDIGES KOCHBUCH, für alle Stände**. Stuttgart: 1842. pp. 16, 386 + Engraved title & plate. *American Manuscript ownership of Maria Streler, 1842. Original printed & decorated paper binding is present, and preserved in a contemporary slip case.* Rare thus. This must have benn a treasured cook book. $ 95.00

837. Stuers, Heinrich. **KURZGEFASSTE GESCHICHTE DEUTSCH = FRANZOFISCHEN FELDZUGES, 1870-1871.** Reinbeck, Iowa: 1890. 37p. Printed wraps. German American view of the Franco-Prussian War. $ 20.00

838. Sumner, Charles. **DAS VERBRECHEN GEGEN KANSAS. Die Entschuldigungen wegen des Verbrechens. Das Richtige Gegenmittel...** DC: 1856. 32p. Uncut & unopened. Kansas/Nebraska speech. $ 20.00

AMERICA'S 1783 TREATY WITH SWEDEN IN THE ORIGINAL SHEETS

Wänskaps och Handels Tractat
Emellan
Hans Maj:t Konungen af Swerige
Och
The Förente Staterne i Norra America,
Afslutten i Paris then 3 April 1783,
Ratificerad Stockholms Slott then 23 Maji 1783,
Och uti Congressen af Förente Staterne i America
then 29 Julii samma år.

Traite d'Amitie et de Commerce
Entre
SA MAJESTÉ LE ROI DE SUÈDE
Et
LES ETATS UNIS DE L'AMÉRIQUE SEPTENTRIONALE,
Conclu à Paris le 3 d'Avril 1783.
Ratifié à Stockholm le 23 Mai 1783.
Et au Congrés des Etats Unis de l'Amérique le 29 Juillet la même année.

Cum Gratia & Privilegio S:æ R:æ Maj:tis.

STOCKHOLM, Tryckt i Kongl. Tryckeriet, 1785.

839. Sweden. **WAENSKAPS OCH HANDELS TRACTAT... Traite d'Amitie et de Commerce**... Stockholm: 1785. 48p. 4to. ***In the original uncut and unfolded sheets.*** Sweden was among the first to recognize the newly independent United States. This, the first Swedish printing of this important treaty of friendship & commerce, is all the more remarkable for its survival in original unfolded sheets. A rare and outstanding artifact of early Americana. Sabin 100931. $ 500.00

840. (Tauler, Johann). **EINIGE ÜBRIGE STÜKE AUS TAULERO.** (Lancaster? 1835?). 185p. 24mo. Marbled wraps. Tauler was a noted mystic of the Middle Ages, whose authentic and apocryphal works were eagerly read by Mennonites in Europe and America. Scarce. $ 60.00

841. Taylor, C. B. **ALLGEMEINE GESCHICHTE DER VEREINIGTEN STAATEN VON AMERIKA...** Johnson, Phila. for Ezra Strong, NY: 1838. 612p. Numerous wood engraved illus. Lovely full leather binding. XLib. AI 53210. $ 55.00

842. Tersteegen, Gerhard [1697-1769]. **GEISTLICHE BROSAMEN, von des Herrn Tisch...** Ritter, Reading: 1807-8. Two volumes in one. pp. 16 [Subscriber's List], 295, 334. Ds. First American Edition. Important Pietist work. *GLP/USA* 1580, Seid. p. 171, AI 13678. $ 65.00

843. Tersteegen. **KLEINE PERLEN=SCHNUR, Für die Kleinen Nur...** Hartman for Schmidt & Licht, Lebanon: 1830. 324p. Ds. Spine taped. First Amer. Ed. Seid. p. 247. $ 75.00

844. (Tersteegen). **MERKWURDIGE LEBENSBESCHREIBUNG DES SEELIGEN GERHARD TERSTEEGEN...** Sage, Reading: 1811. 96p. Woodcut of an angel with horn on tp. *GLP/USA* 1871, AI 24022, Seid. p. 184. Includes an printer's ad. $ 65.00

845. **THIRZA, oder die Anziehungskraft des Kreuzes.** Amer. Tract. Soc. NY. Ca: 1850. 72p. Cloth. 24mo. Bookseller's label = "S. Hechler's Cheap Book Store, Reading, Pa." $ 16.00

846. (Tischler, J. F. W.) [1767-1842]. **LEBEN, THATEN UND MEYNUNGEN, D. MARTIN LUTHERS. Ein Lesebuch für den Bürger und Landmann...** Ritter, Reading: 1811. pp. 6, 162. Ds. ***Manuscript ownership of Jacob Soder (Sauder).*** *GLP/USA* 1868, AI 23251/24040. $ 50.00

847. (Trexler, B. F.). **SKIZZEN AUS DEM LECHA=THALE. Eine Sammlung von Nachrichten über die Ersten Ansiedlungen der Weissen in Dieser Gegend** By "Ben". Allentown: 1880-86. 260p. Printed paper boards. Pasted in publisher's and bookbinder's ad. Shoemaker/L p. 162, One of the most important contributions to Lehigh County history. $ 80.00

848. Troxel, William S. ("Pumpernickle Bill"). **ALTA NEIYOHRS - WINSCHA...** Allentown: 1933. 16p. Printed wraps. 32mo. Pa. "Dutch" dialect New Years Wishes. $ 14.00

849. Troxel. **BILDERBUCH...** (Allentown: 1941). 8p. Troxel Family Album / Christmas Gift. *WST.* $ 24.00

850. Union Cemetery. **REGELN IN BEZUG AUF DAS UNION CEMETERY...** Allentown: 1866. 8p. Plain wraps. *Not in Shoemaker/L. WST.* $ 45.00

851. **UNSER VATER. Das Gebet des Herrn. In Bildern. Für gute und Fromme Kinder gezeichnet.** NY. Ca: 1870. 16p. Chromo. illus. Charming Christmas gift book. $ 30.00

852. **UNSERS HERRN JESU CHRISTI KINDER=BUCH... Historische Beschreibung von Joachim und Anna... von ihrer Tochter, der Jungfrau Maria...** (Ehrenfried, Lancaster): 1818. 46p. XLib. Fine condition. *GLP/USA* 2278 *[3 Copies only]*, AI 46624, Parsons 597. $ 145.00

853. **UNSERS HERRN JESU CHRISTI KINDER=BUCH...** Hamburg (Berks County, Pa.): 1818. 48p. Title page and last ten leaves with some loss. Browned. Plain wraps. Seid. p. 203. *Not in GLP/USA or AI.* Rare. *WST.* $ 150.00

854. **VERHANDLUNGEN DER DEUTSCH=EVANGELISCH=LUTHERISCHEN SYNODE VON PENNSYLVANIEN...** Ebner, Allentown: 1820. 28p. Original marbled wraps. Synod meeting at Lancaster's Trinity Church. *GLP/USA* 2397, Shoemaker/L p. 32, AI 1133. $ 40.00

855. Villee, H. W. (Spang's Iron Works, Oley, Berks Cty.). **DER BAUER ALS LANDMESSER, Oder die Practische Feldmesskunst.** Ritter, Reading: 1824. pp. 12, 154 + *Folding surveying & geometrical plates Engraved by Egelmann.* Pretty leather backed paste paper boards. Includes a curious & most interesting subscribers' list. *GLP/USA* 2707, AI 19146, Seid. p. 223, Karpinski p. 261, Rink 2429. $ 120.00

856. Vogelbach, J. **DAS LEBEN DR. MARTIN LUTHERS...** Brobst, Allentown: (1859). 104p. 24mo. Shoemaker/L p. 98. *WST.* $ 12.00

857. **VOLLSTANDIGES EVANGELISCHES GESANG = BUCH...** (Marburg? Ca: 1770). 324p. + Woodcut Titlepage & Frontis. *Fraktur Manuscript ownership of Wilhelm Hüber drawn by an anonymous Lancaster County Artist, Ca: 1811.* Very browned. $ 150.00

858. **VOLLSTANDIGES GEBAT BUCH...** Sage, Reading: 1813. 512p. Ds. Full leather. *GLP/USA* 2000, AI 29707/30432, Seid. p. 190. $ 40.00

859. **VOLLSTANDIGES MARBURGER GESANG = BUCH...** Bound with / **Evangelia und Epistelin** [1760]. Saur, Germantown: 1759. pp. 12, 527, 16, 14, 94 + Frontis. Ds. Worn full leather. *GLP/USA* 218/222, Seid. p. 51, Hild. 1633/1670, Evans 8390/8594. $ 650.00

860. **VOLLSTANDIGES MARBURGER GESANG = BUCH...** Saur, Germantown: 1762. pp. 12, 527, 16, 14, 84 (of 94) + Frontis. Quite worn. *HSH.* XLib. *GLP/USA* 249, Hild. 1829, Seid. p. 58, Evans 9166. Scarce. $ 200.00

861. **VOLLSTANDIGES MARBURGER GESANG = BUCH...** Marburg & Frankfurt: 1766. pp. 492, 96. Woodcut title & frontis. Full leather. $ 50.00

862. **VOLLSTANDIGES MARBURGER GESANG = BUCH...** Marburg & Frankfurt: 1768. Full leather [American?] binding w/ clasps. Borneman family copy. $ 50.00

SAUR'S MARBURGER GESANG = BUCH

863. **VOLLSTANDIGES MARBURGER GESANG = BUCH...** Saur, Germantown: 1770. pp. 10, 470, 13, 82 + Woodcut frontis. *1774 Manuscript ownership of Catherine Franciscus, Lancaster (Upper Leacock?) + Family records.* Seid. p. 82, *GLP/USA* 384, Evans 11714. $ 200.00

864. **VOLLSTANDIGES MARBURGER GESANG = BUCH...** Marburg & Frankfurt: 1774. pp. 492, 96. Woodcut title & frontis. (American?) full leather binding. $ 60.00

865. **VOLLSTANDIGES MARBURGER GESANG = BUCH...** Saur, Germantown: 1777. pp. 14, 522, 16, 14, 50 (of 56). No frontis. *GLP/USA* 491, Seid. p. 97, Evans 15387. $ 145.00

866. **VOLLSTANDIGES MARBURGER GESANG = BUCH...** Marburg & Frankfurt: 1784. Very worn full leather. *American manuscript ownership of Elizabeth Melsinger, 1790.* $ 45.00

867. **VOLLSTANDIGES MARBURGER GESANG = BUCH...** Cist, Phila: 1799. 262p. + Frontis. Full leather. Board detached. Small type edition. *HSH*. XLib. *GLP/USA* 1184, Evans 3660, Seid. p. 153. The first printing after the five Saur editions. $ 75.00

868. (Voss, Carl A.). **JUBILAUMS SOUVENIR DER DEUTSCHEN EV. PROT. SMITHFIELD GEMEINDE 1782-1907. Gedenkschrift zur Einhundertfuenfund - zwanzig - Jaehrigen Jubel - Feier...** Pittsburgh: 1907. 157p. + Illus. $ 22.00

869. Wackerhagen, August. **KURZER INBEGRIFF DER CHRISTLICHEN GLAUBENS = UND SITTENLEHRE...** Gedruckt auf Kosten des Verfassers, Bey Heinrich Schweitzer, Phila: 1804. pp. 288, 12 (Contents & Subscribers List) + Errata slip. Full leather. Nicely printed. *GLP/USA* 1414, Seid. p. 162, AI 7677-80. $ 70.00

870. (Waltersdorf, Ernst Gottlieb) [1725=61]. **FLIEGENDER BRIEF EVANGELISCHER WORTE AN DIE JUNGEND...** Albrecht & Co., Lancaster: 1794. pp. 20, 218. Ds. 1/2 leather. Contains a poignant foreword addressed to children by Peter Blässer, of Manheim Twp., Lancaster County. Blässer probably also wrote the initial 4p. poem, and sponsored this edition. *GLP/USA* 934, Evans 26981, Seid. p. 138. $ 75.00

871. (Waltersdorf). ... **NEUE LIEDER ODER EVANGELISCHE PSALMEN...** Greiz: 1773. 376p. 1/2 leather. $ 30.00

872. Walz, E. L. [of Hamburg, Berks County]. **ALLGEMEINE BESCHREIBUNG FER WELT** (GEOGRAPHIE). Edited for America by Heinrich Diezel u. Co., Lebanon Cty. Wesselhoeft, Phila: 1835. 428p. Numerous woodcut illustrations. Full leather. AI 35352. *HSH*. $ 60.00

IMPORTANT SCIENTIFIC PLATES BY ENGELMAN

873. Walz. **VOLLSTANDIGE ERKLARUNG DES CALENDARS, MIT EINEM FASTLICHEN UNTERRICHT UBER DIE HIMMELS = STZORPER, Insbesondere uber die Sonne und der Sich um sie bewegenden Planeten**. Ritter, Reading: 1830. 315p. + *Six engraved scientific / astronomical plates by Engelman*. Ds. AI 5328, Seid. p. 248. $ 100.00

874. **WASCHINGTON'S ABSCHIEDS=ADDRESSE... 1796.** (Gettysburg? Ca: 1850?). 13p. Rare in printed blue wraps. Washington's Farewell Address. $ 24.00

875. (Watson, Thomas). **DAS EIFRIGE CHRISTENTHUM...** Albrecht, Lancaster: 1802. pp. 3, 269, 6. Foxed. Ds. Full leather. Worn. *GLP/USA* 1306, Seid. p. 158, AI 3500. $ 30.00

876. (Webb, Elizabeth). **EINIGE GLAUBENS=BEKENTNISSE und Gottliche Erfahrungs=Proben, in einem Send=schreiben von Elisabetha Webb an Anton Wilhelm Boehm...** Cist, Phila: 1783. pp. 55. + *Fascinating 22p. annex by Anthony Benezet on the benefits of Brandy, etc. = "Branntwein und Vererben."* Later wraps. Ds. *Early Schwenkfelder ownership of M. Schultz*. *GLP/USA* 586, Evans 18296, Seid. p. 111. $ 160.00

877. (Webb). **EINIGE GLAUBENS=BEKENTNISSE...** Cist, Phila: 1783. pp. 55, 22 *["Branntwein"]*. Fine in original wraps. *GLP/USA* 586, Evans 18296. $ 140.00

878. (Weber, L. W.) [of Cumberland Cty. Pa.]. **DER KLUGE LAND - MEDICUS UND HAUS - APOTHEKE...** Chabersburg: 1846. 259p. Orginal cloth. XLib. First American Edition of this important medical guide. *HSH*. $ 100.00

879. Weber, Thomas R. **DIE NEUE CHORAL HARMONIE...** (Hellertown): 1850. 96p. Shaped notes. Small oblong song book. Church music in German and English. $ 40.00

880. Weber. **DIE PENNSYLVANISCHE CHORAL HARMONIE...** Allentown: 1844. 204p. Printed paper boards, with publisher's promotional ad on rear cover. Oblong Song Book. Shaped notes. Words in English & German. Shoemaker/L p. 69. First Edition. $ 150.00

881. Weber. **DIE PENNSYLVANISCHE CHORAL HARMONIE...** (Allentown?): 1854. 376p. Unusual decorated boards, with printed label. Oblong. Shaped notes. Words in English & German. *WST.* $ 135.00

882. Weber. **DIE PENNSYLVANISCHE CHORAL HARMONIE...** Hellertown: 1870. 488p. Printed paper boards, with publisher's promotional ad on rear cover. Oblong Song Book. Shaped notes. Words in English & German. Probably the most extensive collection of shaped note tunes. *WST.* $ 125.00

883. Wecken, Dr. Friedrich. **FAMILIENGESCHICHTLICHE BIBLIOGRAPHIE, Jahrgang 1921, 1922, 1926...** Leipzig: 1925=8. Three vols. Printed wraps. Bibliographies of Germanic genealogies, etc. $ 23.00

884. Weems, M. L. **DAS LEBEN DES GEORG WASCHINGTON...** Schaeffer & Maund, Baltimore for Carey & Son, Phila: 1817. 240p. + 5 Engraved plates. Full leather. Some copies have more plates. *GLP/USA* 2201, AI 42863, Seid. p. 200. *WST.* $ 45.00

885. Weems. **LEBENSBESCHREIBUNG DES GEORG WASCHINGTON...** Schelly, Phila: 1838. 300p. + 7 Woodcut Illus. AI 53558. $ 38.00

THE ONLY KNOWN COPY

886. **WEIBLICHE STANDHAFTIGKEIT, oder die Geschichte einer Italiänischen Herzogin...** Hütter, Easton: 1809. 80p. + 2 Engraved plates. Slight loss to one leaf. A sensational tale, that appealed to all ages, and was voraciously read to extinction. This is the same unique copy seen by Oda (p. 6) & Shoemaker/L (p. 27). *GLP/USA* 1658, AI 19198. *WST.* $ 240.00

BINDING BY CHRISTOPHER HOFFMANN

887. Weichenhan, Erasmus. **CHRISTLISCHE BETRACHTUNGEN UBER DIE EVANGELISCHEN TEXTE...** Billmeyer, Germantown: 1791. pp. 8, 785, 3. 4to. ***Very unusual full leather binding (w/loss at head & foot) decoratively tooled in blind. No clasps. This binding can certainly be ascribed to Christopher Hoffmann, the Schwenkfelder scribe, teacher, minister and binder. His tools and high style are unlike most of his German contemporaries, and apparently were reserved only for Schwenkfelder works.*** The author was a minister from Silesia and a close associate of Schwenkfeld. "This work, which was first, posthumously printed in 1672, reflects the religious views of the Schwenkfelders. In typography, paper, and binding, this reprint 'at the expense of the United Friends' is a very creditable piece of bookmaking" - Evans 23975, Sabin 102503, *GLP/USA* 803. The preface is dated, "Montgomery Co. Feb. 12, 1791." $ 550.00

888. **WEIHNACHTS = ANDACHT...** By Pastor J. N. Allentown. Ca: 1879. 16p. Wraps. 24mo. Christmas songs. Shoemaker/L p. 149/186. $ 20.00

889. **WEIHNACHTS GESCHICHTEN...** Cleveland, Ohio. Ca: 1880. 32p. Printed wraps with color appliques. Christmas gift book. $ 15.00

890. (Weik, John). **VEREINIGTEN STAATEN DRIESSTELLER... The U.S. Letter Writer...** Phila: 1882. pp. 264, 264. Cloth. English & German. $ 20.00

891. (Weiser, Daniel). **LICHTSCHNAUTZE, oder Hülfe zur Wahrheit. Ein Erwiderung auf "Das Licht aus dem dunkeln Eck."** Phila: 1839. 88p. Wraps. Scarce artifact of a bitter political/theological dispute between Weiser and Frederick Waage. Not in AI?. $ 75.00

892. (Weiser & Schultz). **OEFFENTLICHE CORRESPONDENZEN ZWISCHEN JOSUA SCHULTZ (Schwekfeldter, Berks Cty.) UND DANIEL WEISER (Reformirter, Montgomery Cty.) IM 1858.** Shupe, Lansdale, Pa: 1861. 128p. Cloth. *Unusual small circular hand-drawn mystical[?] bookplate of Samuel Musselman.* $ 75.00

IMPORTANT MYSTICAL / SCIENTIFIC BOOK

893. Welling, George von. **OPUS MAGO-CABBALISTICUM ET THEOSOPHICUM...** Homburg: 1735. pp. 7, 582, 21 + Folding Mystical Plates. Ds. Disbd. 4to. + *Alchemical / Mystical manuscript notes in the hand of Peter Ensminger, a German-Amemerican Revolutionary War patriot.* Early American ownership of a rare mystical & alchemical work. $ 600.00

894. (Weninger, Franz). **HERZ JESU MISSIONSBUCH...** NY & Cinn: 1872. 480p. Full embossed morocco. Inscribed by the author. $ 12.00

895. (Wesley, John). **DAS CHRISTEN HANDBUCH...** Bobbs, Harrisburg: 1830. 216p. 32mo, XLib. *Not in Seid.* AI 5405. *HSH.* $ 36.00

896. **WESTENTASCHEN=VOLKS=LIEDERBUCH.** King & Baird for Weik, Phila: 1850. 192p. Small 48mo. Printed wraps. *WST.* $ 36.00

897. **WESTENTASCHEN=VOLKS=LIEDERBUCH.** Weik, Phila: 1854. 256p. Small 48mo. Embossed cloth. All edges gilt. *HSH.* XLib. Scarce. $ 38.00

898. Wiegand, C. H. **SPRUCHE, GEDICHTE UND ERZAHLUNGEN Zur Nährung Allgemeiner Kindertugenden...** Baltimore: 1874. 118p. Scarce $ 20.00

899. Wierman & Warfel. **PENNSYLFAWNY-DEITSCHE KALLENNAR.** Lebanon High School: 1949. 7p. Quaint, colored, woodblock illustrations of "Pa. Dutch" and Amish scenes, with little poems. *WST.* $ 30.00

THE ILLUSTRATED GERMAN AMERICAN HORSE DOCTOR

900. Winter, Geo. Simon. ... **PFERDE=ARTZ...** Schelly, Phila: 1840. 839p. + *40 remarkable folding woodcut plates.* Contemporary full calf with clasps. A very nice copy. $ 130.00

901. Winter. ... **PFERDE=ARTZ...** Kleckner, Rolf & Williams, (Bethlehem?) Northampton County, Pa: 1841. 839p. + *40 remarkable folding woodcut plates (by Valentin Trichter?).* Contemporary full calf with clasps. We've never seen a copy with all the plates present in such fine state. The grandest of the Pennsylvania German "Horse Doctor" books. $ 175.00

902. (Witschel, J. H. W.) [1769-1847]. **GOTT IST DIE REINSTE LIEBE...** Bruckman for M'Williams, Reading: 1822. 300p. Contemporary full leather with clasps. XLib. The authorship is also ascribed to Karl von Erckartshausen. *GLP/USA* 2565, AI 8591, Seid p. 217. Curious prayer book highly recommended by Muhlenberg, Melsheimer, et. al. $ 40.00

903. **WOHLGEMUTHS LIEDERBUCH, Eine Sammlung der besten Deutschen Lieder für Freunde des Scherzes und der unschuldigen Frende.** Hütter, Easton: 1811. 100p. Browned. 24mo. Later wraps. *GLP/USA* 1804 *[2 Copies only]. Not in AI, nor Seid.* $ 125.00

904. **DIE WOLKE UBER DEM HEILIGTHUM...** Mentz, Phila: 1841. 112p. 24mo. Brilliant blue paper boards. Uncommon. *WST.* $ 38.00

905. Wollenweber, L. U. **DIE BEIDEN ERSTEN DEUTSCHEN ANSIEDLER IN PENNSYLVANIEN**... Kohler, Phila: 1880. 72p. + Illus. German pioneers in Pa. $ 38.00

906. Wollenweber. **DIE BERG = MARIA, oder Wer nur den lieben Gott lässt walten. Eine Geschichtliche Erzählung aus Pennsylvanien**. Kohler, Phila: 1880. 68p. Woodcut illus. Printed wraps. 24mo. $ 24.00

907. Wollenweber. **GEMALDE AUS DEM PENNSYLVANISCHEN VOLKSLEBEN**... Phila. & Leipzig: 1869. 143p. Poems & stories about the Pa. Germans. Cloth. 16mo. $ 40.00

908. Wollenweber. **GEMALDE AUS DEM PENNSYLVANISCHEN VOLKSLEBEN**... Phila. & Leipzig. Ca: 1880. 143p. Cloth. 16mo. *WST.* $ 20.00

909. Worman, James H. **ERSTES (ZWEITES) DEUTSCHES BUCH**... NY & Chi: 1880. 147p. Illus. Home / school instruction in the Natural or Pestalozzian Method. $ 22.00

910. Woyt, Dr. Johann Jacob. **GAZOPHYLACIUM MEDICO-PHYSICUM, oder Schatz = Kammer Medicinisch und Natürlicher Dinge**... Edited by Dr. Johann Ernst Hebenstreit. Leipzig: 1784. Over 1200p. + Plates. Ds. Disbd. 4to. *Early American (Mennonite?) ownership of Abraham Good.* Compendious medical encyclopedia / dictionary. Scarce. $ 320.00

911. Wuchter, A. C. **ON DER LUMPA PARTY**. Lititz: 1912. 36p. Printed wraps. 32mo. Dialect poem & vocabulary. *WST.* $ 28.00

912. Yoder, Joseph W. **AMISCHE LIEDER**. Huntingdon, Pa: 1942. 141p. Illus. Signed by Yoder for *WST.* Scarce collection of Amish songs. $ 45.00

913. Ziegler, Charles Calvin (of Brushvalley, Pa.). **DRAUSS UN DEHEEM. Gedichte in Pennsylvänisch Deitsch**. Leipzig: 1891. 51p. Decorative cloth. Rare example of the dialect printed in Germany. *WST.* $ 50.00

THE FIRST FULL-LENGTH BOOK PRINTED IN GERMAN TYPE IN AMERICA

914. **ZIONITISCHER WEYRAUCHS-HUGEL**... Christoph Sauer, Germantown: 1739. pp. 12, 792, 14 [Lacks 2 leaves at the end of the text & some of the register]. Stained. Contemporary full leather. One of the scarcest and most famous of all German-American imprints, the Weyrauchs Hügel was printed by Saur for the Ephrata Brethren, and is the largest & most important collection of hymns sung at the Ephrata Cloister. The publication of this book led to the establishment of the press at Ephrata. Complete copies are rarely encountered, especially since Biessel apparently ordered the "Zionitischen" to be burnt as a result of his intense dispute with Israel Eckerlin. See: *GLP/USA* 17, Evans 4466, Seid. p. 11, Hild. 617, et. al. $ 900.00

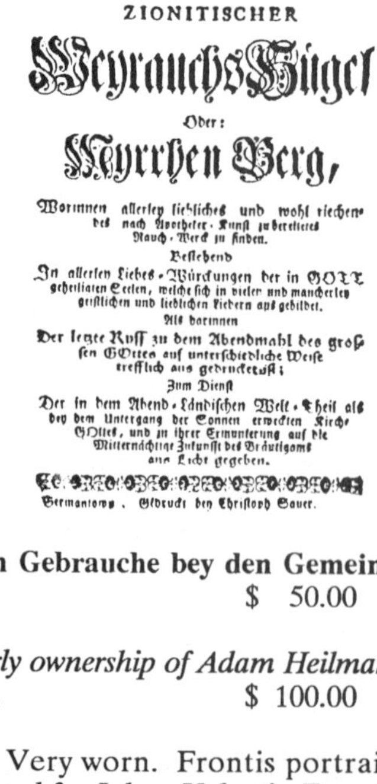
ZIONITISCHER
Weyrauchs Hügel
Oder:
Myrrhen Berg,
Worinnen allerley liebliches und wohl riechendes nach Apotheker-Kunst zubereitetes Rauch-Werck zu finden.
Bestehend
In allerley Liebes-Würckungen der in GOTT geheiligten Seelen, welche sich in vieler und mancherley geistlichen und lieblichen Liedern aus gebildet.
Als darinnen
Der letzte Ruff zu dem Abendmahl des grossen GOttes auf unterschiedliche Weise trefflich aus gedrucket ist;
Zum Dienst
Der in dem Abend-Ländischen Welt-Theil als bey dem Untergang der Sonnen erweckten Kirche GOttes, und zu ihrer Ermunterung auf die Mitternächtige Zukunfft des Bräutigams ans Licht gegeben.
Germantown, Gedruckt bey Christoph Sauer.

915. Zollikoffer, G. Joachim. **ANREDEN UND GEBETE, zum Gebrauche bey den Gemeinschaftlichen**... Leipzig: 1777. 415p. Nicely printed. $ 50.00

916. Zollikoffer. ...**GEBATT=BUCH**... Basel: 1766. 768p. *Early ownership of Adam Heilman [Lebanon, Pa].* Full leather [American?] binding with clasps. *HSH.* $ 100.00

917. Zollikoffer. ...**GEBATT=BUCH**... Basel: 1784. 768p. Very worn. Frontis portrait defective. ***Extensive 18th century American manuscript family record for Johan Valentin Franck and Chatariena Frank(in).*** $ 90.00

918. Zollikoffer. ...**GEBATT=BUCH...** Basel: 1787. 768p. *Early ownership of George Müller, Lebanon, Pa.* Full leather [American?] binding. *HSH.* $ 70.00

919. Zollikoffer. ...**HIMMLISCHER WEIHRAUCHSCHATZ, Oder Vollstandiges Gebet = Buch...** Ashmead, Phila: 1838. 688p. + Illus. Handsome straight grained full leather. Elaborately gilt tooled spine. First Edition of Zollikoffer as enlarged by the Reading, Pennsylvania minister - A. L. Herman. AI 53803. $ 50.00

920. Zollikoffer. ...**HIMMLISCHER WEIHRAUCHSCHATZ...** Phila: 1859. 688p. + Illus. & Family Register. Beautiful embossed full leather gilt. $ 40.00

RARE PENNSYLVANIA GERMAN (MORAVIAN) CHORAL = FEST PAMPHLETS

921. **ZUM 4TEN MAY, 1775.** Chorus. Seyd inniglich gesrüzt... (Henrich Miller, Phila: 1775). 4p. Self wraps. *Not in Evans, Seid. Etc. GLP/USA* 473 *[Two Locations Only].* $ 175.00

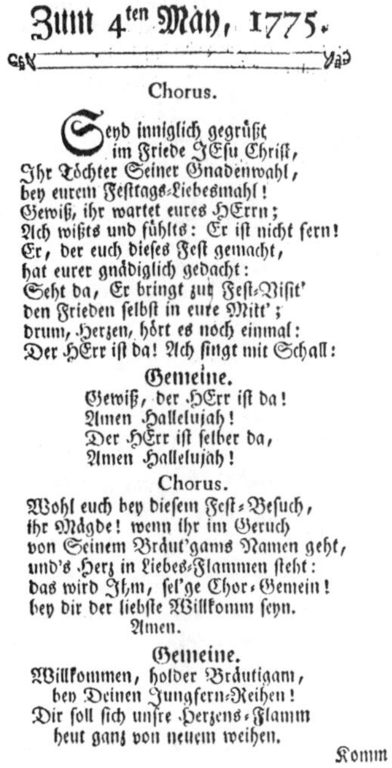

Zum 4ten May, 1775.

Chorus.

Seyd inniglich gegrüßt
im Friede JEsu Christ,
Ihr Töchter Seiner Gnadenwahl,
bey eurem Festtags-Liebesmahl!
Gewiß, ihr wartet eures HErrn;
Ach wißts und fühlts: Er ist nicht fern!
Er, der euch dieses Fest gemacht,
hat eurer gnädiglich gedacht:
Seht da, Er bringt zur Fest-Visit'
den Frieden selbst in eure Mitt';
drum, Herzen, hört es noch einmal:
Der HErr ist da! Ach singt mit Schall:

Gemeine.

Gewiß, der HErr ist da!
Amen Hallelujah!
Der HErr ist selber da,
Amen Hallelujah!

Chorus.

Wohl euch bey diesem Fest-Besuch,
ihr Mägde! wenn ihr im Geruch
von Seinem Bräut'gams Namen geht,
und's Herz in Liebes-Flammen steht:
das wird Ihm, sel'ge Chor-Gemein!
bey dir der liebste Willkomm seyn.
Amen.

Gemeine.

Willkommen, holder Bräutigam,
bey Deinen Jungfern-Reihen!
Dir soll sich unsre Herzens-Flamm
heut ganz von neuem weihen.

Komm

922. **ZUM 7TEN SEPTEMBER, 1775.** Chorus. Du solt anbeten vor dem Herrn deinem Gott... (Henrich Miller, Phila: 1775). 8p. Self wraps. S&M 42989, Bristol B4175, *GLP/USA* 474 *[Two Locations Only].* $ 160.00

923. **ZUM 4TEN MAY, 1780.** Lit. und Gäste. Gnad und Fried und Heil den Jungfern-Chören! ... (Steiner & Cist, Phila: 1780). 8p. Self wraps. *Not in Evans, Seid. Etc. GLP/USA* 542 *[Two Locations Only].* $ 140.00

924. **ZUM 4TEN MAY, 1781.** Lit. und Chor. Jesu Menschheit Morgenroth... (Steiner, Phila: 1781). 8p. Self wraps. *Not in Evans, Seid. Etc. GLP/USA* 560 *[Two Locations Only].* $ 120.00

925. **ZUM 4TEN MAY, 1782.** Chor. Lasset uns lobsingen, und mit süssen Weisen... (Steiner, Phila: 1782). 8p. Self wraps. *Not in Evans, Seid. Etc. GLP/USA* 578 *[2 Copies Only].* $ 120.00

926. **ZUM 4TEN MAY, 1785.** Liturgus. Viel Gnade zuvor... (Steiner, Phila: 1785). 8p. Self wraps. *Not in Evans, Seid. Etc. GLP/USA* 644 *[One Copy Only].* $ 150.00

927. **ZUM 7TEN SEPTEMBER, 1785. in Litiz.** Liturgus. Chor des Herrn:,: dessen Eigenthum du Bist! ... (Ephrata, Typis Societatis: 1785). 4p. Self wraps. *Not in Evans, Seid. Etc. GLP/USA* 625 *[Two Locations Only].* $ 160.00

928. **ZUM 4TEN MAY, 1787.** Chor. Gott sey uns gnädig, und segne uns... (Steiner, Phila: 1787). 8p. Self wraps. *Not in Evans, Seid. Etc. GLP/USA* 691 *[One Location Only].* $ 170.00

929. **ZUM 13TEN AUGUST, 1788.** Chorus. Wie lieblich sind Deine Wohnungen Herr Zebaoth! ... (Albrecht & Lahn, Lancaster: 1788). 4p. Self wraps. *Not in Evans, Seid. Etc. GLP/USA* 712 *[Two Locations Only].* $ 120.00

930. **ZUM CHRISTNACHT 1788 IN LITIZ.** Chorus. Freuet euch und seyd frölich, die ihr Seinen Tag sehet... (Albrecht & Lahn, Lancaster: 1788). 4p. Self wraps. *Not in Evans, Seid. Etc. GLP/USA* 714 *[One Location Only].* $ 150.00

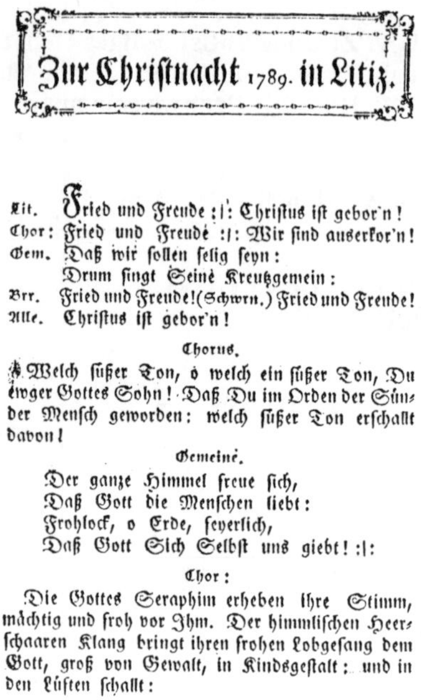

Zur Christnacht 1789. in Litiz.

Lit. Fried und Freude :|: Christus ist gebor'n!
Chor: Fried und Freude :|: Wir sind auserkor'n!
Gem. Daß wir sollen selig seyn:
Drum singt Seine Kreutzgemein:
Brr. Fried und Freude!(Schwrn.) Fried und Freude!
Alle. Christus ist gebor'n!

Chorus.

Welch süßer Ton, o welch ein süßer Ton, Du ewger Gottes Sohn! Daß Du im Orden der Sünder Mensch geworden: welch süßer Ton erschallt davon!

Gemeine.

Der ganze Himmel freue sich,
Daß Gott die Menschen liebt:
Frohlock, o Erde, feyerlich,
Daß Gott Sich Selbst uns giebt! :|:

Chor:

Die Gottes Seraphim erheben ihre Stimm, mächtig und froh vor Ihm. Der himmlischen Heerschaaren Klang bringt ihren frohen Lobgesang dem Gott, groß von Gewalt, in Kindsgestalt: und in den Lüften schallt:

931. **ZUM CHRISTNACHT 1789 IN LITIZ.** Lit. Fried und Frede :°: Christus ist gebor'n! ... (Albrecht & Lahn, Lancaster: 1789). 4p. Self wraps. Not in Evans, Seid. Etc. *GLP/USA* 736 *[One Location Only].* $ 150.00

932. **ZUM 4TEN MAY, 1789.** Liturgus und Gäste. Im Namen des Herrn der sich heut so gern Mit Friede umschliezt... (Cist, Phila: 1789). 4p. Self wraps. *Not in Evans, Seid. Etc. GLP/USA 745 [Two Locations Only].* $ 120.00

933. **ZUM GEDÄCHTNISS... Selig entschlafenen Bruders Ludwig David von Schweiniz.** (Bethlehem: 1834). 4p. Self wraps. *Apparently not in AI nor Shoemaker/N.* $ 65.00

934. **ZUM GEDÄCHTNISS... Selig entschlafenen Bruders William Henry Van Vleck...** (Bethlehem: 1853). 4p. Self wraps. Shoemaker/N p. 74. $ 40.00

935. **ZUR FEIER DER FUNFZIGJÄRIGEN GESEGNETEN AMTS - THÄTIGKEIT unserer verehrten und geliebten Schwester Charlotte Gräfin von Einfiedel...** (Easton? 1847). 4p. Self wraps. *Not in Shoemaker/N.* $ 35.00

936. **ZUR FEYER DES HUNDERTJÄRIGEN JUBELFESTES DER GEMEINE IN BETHLEHEM den 25sten Juny, 1842.** Held, Easton: 1842. 7p. Self wraps. Some text in English. Shoemaker/N p. 59. $ 40.00

937. Zünd, Johann Joseph. **HANDBUCH DER PFERDE UND VIEHARZEN=KUND... Fur den Landmann und Pferdebesitzen.** Heinrich Horn, Phila: 1832. 384p. Leather backed marbled boards. Early Manuscript formulae. AI 17203. First edition of this important medical guide for both man & beast. $ 80.00

938. Zünd. **HANDBUCH DER PFERDE UND VIEHARZEN=KUND...** Gräter, Northampton, Lehigh Cty. & Phila: 1834. 376p. + English / German pharmaceutical lexicon & Index. Worn leather. *Apparently Not in AI nor Shoemaker/L.* $ 75.00

939. **ZUSAMMENHANG DER CHRISTLICHEN LEHRE, Nach Anleitung des Heidelbergischen Catechismi.** Hartman, Lebanon: 1818. 50p. Pretty paste paper boards. *GLP/USA* 2280, AI 46912. *Not in Seid.* $ 75.00

THE ONLY KNOWN COPY ?

940. **ZWEEN BETTELKNABEN. Eine Lehrreiche Geschichte für Unsere Deutschen Kinder. Nebst Zwen Todes (G)eschichten.** Schnee, Lebanon: 1807. 24p. Small woodcut on title page. Original sprinkled wraps. 32mo. First published in 1806 by Schweitzer, in Philadelphia. *Previously unrecorded. Not in GLP/USA, nor any other reference consulted. WST.* $ 200.00

PART TWO

KEYSTONE TEN

= "*Die Alte Zeite*" =

PART II

GERMAN AMERICANA AND CLASSICS OF THE "PENNSYLVANIA DUTCH".

Plus Some Continental Americana.

Device Used By Der Brüderschaft, Ephrata: 1748

KEYSTONE TEN = "Die Alte Zeite"
PART II

GERMAN AMERICANA AND CLASSICS OF THE "PENNSYLVANIA DUTCH"

1001. Acrelius, Israel. **A HISTORY OF NEW SWEDEN...** Reprint 1874 1st English Edition. NY: 1966. 468p. + Map. See Pt. I # 23 for the rare First Edition (in Swedish). $ 20.00

PRINTED BY HALL AND SELLERS = 1775

1002. **ACTS OF ASSEMBLY OF THE PROVINCE OF PENNSYLVANIA.** Hall & Sellers, Phila: 1775. pp. (21), 536, 22 [Appendix], 12, 3. Old page repairs. Ds. Contemporary full leather binding with decorative tooling. *Early ownership of Ambrose Schmidt (Hanover, Pa?).* Evans 14364. Very important collection of Pennsylvania Laws, printed on the eve of the American Revolution. $ 800.00

1003. Adams, Charles Francis. **LEEDLE YAWCOB STRAUS, & Other Poems**. Boston: 1878. 147p. + Ads. With Sixty-five Illustrations by "Boz". "Dutch" humor & pidgin dialect. $ 40.00

1004. Adams, Hannah. **A VIEW OF RELIGIONS...** Boston: 1801. 504p. Full leather cover. The German - American pietists and sectarians were not overlooked in this very curious and fascinating work. Adams really attempted a compendious overview of religion, with special attention to the United States. AI 12. $ 100.00

1005. Adams, Ruth. **PA. DUTCH ART**. NY: 1950. 64p. Illus. $ 14.00

1006. Adler, G. J. **A DICTIONARY OF THE GERMAN & ENGLISH LANGUAGES**. NY: 1860. 820+p. Attractive school edition. *WST.* $ 25.00

1007. Alderfer, E. G. **THE EPHRATA COMMUNE. An Early American Counterculture**. Pitt: 1985. 273p. Important study. Wraps. $ 12.00

1008. Allan, Morton. **DIRECTORY OF EUROPEAN PASSENGER STEAMSHIP ARRIVALS 1890 = 1930 at the Ports of N.Y., Phila., Boston, & Baltimore**. Baltimore: 1980. Reprint of the 1931 edition. 268p. All of these directories are valuable for genealogical research. $ 16.00

1009. Allegheny County. **HISTORY OF ALLEGHENY COUNTY, PENNSYLVANIA...** Chicago: 1889. Two volumes in one + Many Plates. Thick 4to. $ 200.00

1010. (Allenbach, H. G.). **THE GOTTSCHALL FAMILY. 5th Reunion**. Sanatoga Park, Pa: 1909. 16p. Illus. Printed wraps. Useful family history. $ 12.00

1011. Allentown. **PAST, PRESENT & FUTURE OF THE CITY OF ALLENTOWN...** Allentown: 1886. 168p. + Illus. Wraps. *WST.* $ 50.00

1012. **THE AMERICAN HOMOEOPATHIC PHARMACOPOEIA...** Phila: 1906. 549p. One of the best Homoeopathic references available. $ 45.00

1013. **THE AMERICAN TUTOR'S ASSISTANT REVISED; A Compendious System of Practical Arithmetic...** Crukshank, Phila: 1813. 180p. + "A Course in Book-Keeping". Nice leather backed marbled boards. AI 27718. See Also # 1443-6. $ 26.00

1014. **AMISH COOKING.** Aylmer, Ontario: 1987. 331p. 800 Great Recipes. $ 12.00

1015. Anstadt, P. **LIFE & TIMES OF REV. S. S. SCHMUCKER.** York, Pa: 1896. 392p. + Illus. XLib. Signed by Anstadt. Pivotal figure in American Lutheranism. $ 22.00

WITH A FOLD-OUT ANATOMICAL BROADSIDE

1016. Aristotle. **THE WORKS OF ARISTOTLE IN FOUR PARTS...** Printed for & Sold by All the Booksellers, London: 1792. 491p. + Fold-out Anatomical poetic broadside/plate. Several curious cuts. 24mo. Contemporary full leather (American binding?). These manuals of medicine and midwifery were especially popular among the Pennsylvania Germans. $ 150.00

1017. Arndt, John Stover. **THE STORY OF THE ARNDTS. The Life, Antecedents & Descendants of Bernhard Arndt, Who Emigrated to Pennsylvania in 1731.** Phila: 1922. 427p. + Plates. Cover spotted. Outstanding historical genealogy. $ 38.00

CRITICAL TREATISE FOR THE SEAMAN

1018. Atkinson, James. **EPITOME OF THE ART OF NAVIGATION...** London: 1765. 448p. + Ten Plates & a Voulvelle. Full leather (American/Philadelphia?) binding. *"James Craig's Book, 24 Dec. 1768"*. Used by Captains of trading and Emigrant ships. $ 200.00

1019. **ATLAS OF BOROUGHS & TOWNS in Philadelphia, Bucks, and Montgomery Counties on the Line of the North Pennsylvania R. R. & Branches...** From Surveys by C. M. Hunter. Scott, Phila: 1886. 26 Colored Property Maps + Business Ads. Folio. Crisp copy of this important and scarce property owner atlas. *WST.* $ 175.00

1020. **ATLAS OF THE AMERICAN REVOLUTION.** Edited by Ken Nebenzahl and Don Higginbotham. Chicago: 1974. 280p. Beautifully illustrated. Wonderful maps. Folio. DJ. The action around Philadelphia is well depicted. $ 50.00

1021. Aurand, Charles Monroe. **RAYS OF LIGHT; Lectures on Great Subjects.** Phila: 1890. 302p. XLib. Signed by the author. $ 22.00

1022. Aurand, A. Monroe, Jr. **AURAND'S COLLECTION OF PENNSYLVANIA GERMAN STORIES & POEMS.** Beaver Springs: 1916. 128p. 24mo. Printed wraps. Fine dialect collection that is too little known. *WST.* $ 25.00

1023. Aurand. **BUNDLING.** By Henry Reed Stiles. With / **More About Bundling**. By Aurand. Harrisburg: 1928. 98p. Signed Limited Edition. The classic monographs on the curious custom of courting in bed. $ 40.00

1024. Aurand. **CHILD LIFE OF THE PENNSYLVANIA GERMANS.** Harrisburg: 1947. 32p. Illus. Printed wraps. *WST.* $ 12.00

1025. Aurand. **COOKING WITH THE PENNSYLVANIA "DUTCH".** Harrisburg: 1946. 32p. Illus. Printed wraps. *WST.* $ 10.00

1026. Aurand. **EARLY LIFE OF THE PENNSYLVANIA GERMANS.** Harrisburg: 1946. 32p. Illus. Printed wraps. *WST.* $ 12.00

1027. Aurand. **HOME LIFE OF THE PENNSYLVANIA GERMANS.** Harrisburg: 1947. 32p. Illus. Printed wraps. *WST.* $ 12.00

1028. Aurand. **HOME LIFE, Or, Good Old Times With the Pennsylvania "Dutch". Illustrated & Told in Verse.** Harrisburg: 1945. 32p. Printed wraps. 32mo. *WST.* $ 16.00

1029. Aurand, A. Monroe, Jr. **LITTLE KNOWN FACTS ABOUT THE AMISH, and the Mennonites...** Harrisburg: 1938. 30p. Printed wraps. Review Copy. *WST.* $ 15.00

1030. Aurand. **LITTLE KNOWN FACTS ABOUT BUNDLING IN THE NEW WORLD...** Harrisburg: 1938. 32p. Printed wraps. *WST.* $ 15.00

1031. Aurand. **PENNSYLVANIA = GERMAN DIALECT STORIES & POEMS..** Harrisburg: 1939. 24p. Printed wraps. *WST.* $ 14.00

1032. Aurand. **A PENNSYLVANIA - GERMAN LIBRARY.** Harrisburg: 1930. 62p. + Promotional letter from Aurand. Signed Limited Edition. The first bookseller's catalog / bibliography of Pennsylvania German materials. *WST.* $ 40.00

1033. Aurand. **THE "POW WOW" BOOK!** Harrisburg: 1929. 3 Vols. in 1. 180+p. Limited Edition. Includes a fine study of Pow Wow healing; an account of the "Witch Trial" in York, Pa.; and a reprint of Hohman's "Long Lost Friend". Rare in the original Dust Jacket. $ 75.00

1034. Aurand. **SOCIAL LIFE OF THE PENNSYLVANIA GERMANS.** Harrisburg: 1947. 32p. Illus. Printed wraps. *WST.* $ 12.00

1035. Aurand. **SOCIAL LIFE, Or, Good Old Times With the Pennsylvania "Dutch". Illustrated & Told in Verse.** Harrisburg: 1945. 32p. Printed wraps. 32mo. *WST.* $ 15.00

1036. Aurand. **WIT & HUMOR OF THE PENNSYLVANIA GERMANS.** Harrisburg: 1947. 32p. Illus. Printed wraps. *WST.* $ 12.00

1037. Bachmair, John James. **A GERMAN GRAMMAR, Containing the Theory of the Language through All the Parts of Speech.** Charles Cist, Phila: 1788. 100p. Ds. Disbound. ***"William Vance's Book".*** "The German Language is much used in this State..." = From the Preface. Evans 20937. $ 150.00

1038. Bachman, J. Fred. **CHARLES MOSER. A Pennsylvania German Boy.** Reading: 1916. 348p. + Illus. *WST.* $ 22.00

1039. Baer, G. F. **"GERMANS IN PENNSYLVANIA"...** (Reading: 1895). 15p. $ 20.00

1040. Bahn, Rachel. **POEMS.** York, Pa: 1869. 199p. First Edition. Includes some wonderful poems in the Pa. "Dutch" dialect. Bahn [1830-1902], was a remarkable, disabled, poetess from the Kreutz Creek Valley, York County, Pa. See PGS Vol. III (1970) for details on the rarity and significance of this little volume. *WST.* $ 75.00

1041. Barba, Preston A. **EDWARD HERMANY. A PENNSYLVANIA GERMAN POET.** Lehigh Cty. Hist. Soc. Vol. 22, Allentown: 1958. pp. 37-76. Wraps. $ 12.50

1042. (Barba). **'S PENNSYLFAWNISCH DEITSCH ECK. Devoted to the Literature, Lore, and History of the Pennsylvania Germans.** The Editor's Offprints from the Morning Call, Allentown: 1935-38. Two Volumes. Oblong Folio. Contains some of the most important historical and dialect materials ever published. Very rare in this form. $ 150.00

1043. Barba. **THEY CAME TO EMMAUS.** (Emmaus: 1960). 378p. Illus. DJ. First Edition. Excellent Local and Moravian history. $ 30.00

1044. Barbaroux, C. O. **L'HISTOIRE DES ETATS-UNIS D'AMERIQUE.** Hogan & Thompson, Phila: 1836. 304p. 16mo. Original paper boards backed in straight grained crimson morocco. Sabin 3298, AI 35997. $ 40.00

1045. Barber, Edwin Atlee. **LEAD GLAZED POTTERY, Part First (Common Clays). Plain Glazed, Sgraffito, & Slip-Decorated Wares.** Phila: 1907. 32p. + Many illus. Printed wraps. Very scarce and influential early monograph. *WST.* $ 85.00

1046. Barber. **TULIP WARE OF THE PENNSYLVANIA = GERMAN POTTERS. An Historical Sketch of the Art of Slip-Decoration in the U.S.** Phila: 1926. 235p. Illus. Printed wraps. The best edition of this classic text on Pennsylvania Dutch pottery. *WST.* $ 125.00

1047. Barber. **TULIP WARE OF THE PENNSYLVANIA GERMAN POTTERS**... NY: 1970. 233p. Illus. Wraps. $ 14.00

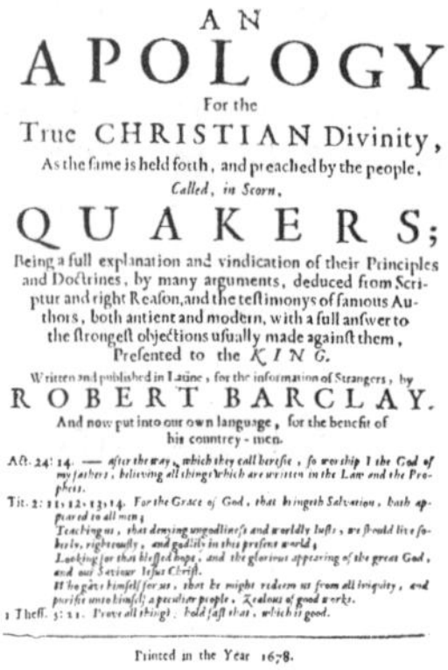

AN
APOLOGY
For the
True CHRISTIAN Divinity,
As the same is held forth, and preached by the people,
Called, in Scorn,
QUAKERS;
Being a full explanation and vindication of their Principles and Doctrines, by many arguments, deduced from Scriptur and right Reason, and the testimonys of famous Authors, both antient and modern, with a full answer to the strongest objections usually made against them, Presented to the *KING.*
Written and published in Latine, for the information of Strangers, by
ROBERT BARCLAY.
And now put into our own language, for the benefit of his countrey-men.
Act. 24: 14. — *after the way, which they call heresie, so worship I the God of my fathers, believing all things which are written in the Law and the Prophets.*
Tit. 2: 11, 12, 13, 14. *For the Grace of God, that bringeth Salvation, hath appeared to all men;*
Teaching us, that denying ungodliness and worldly lusts, we should live soberly, righteously, and godlily in this present world;
Looking for that blessed hope, and the glorious appearing of the great God, and our Saviour Jesus Christ.
Who gave himself for us, that he might redeem us from all iniquity, and purifie unto himself a peculiar people, Zealous of good works.
1 Thess. 5: 21. *Prove all things; hold fast that, which is good.*
Printed in the Year 1678.

1048.Barclay, Robert [1648-90]. **AN APOLOGY FOR TRUE CHRISTIAN DIVINITY, As the same is held forth and preached by the People, Called, in Scorn, Quakers**... (Aberdeen): 1678. pp. 20, 392, 21. Disbound. First Edition in English. An exceptional early Quaker treatise, which was first issued in Latin at Amsterdam. "Barclay's great book, is remarkable as the standard exposition of the principles of the sect ... but in many respects it is one of the most impressive theological writings of the century" - DNB. New Wing B720. $ 300.00

1049.Barclay. **AN APOLOGY FOR TRUE CHRISTIAN DIVINITY: Being an explanation & Vindication of the Principles and Doctrines of the people called Quakers.** Baskerville, Birmingham, England: 1765. 520p. Large 4to. XLib. Many leaves very damaged in the Library Company fire of 1860's. $ 75.00

1050. (Barclay). **A CATECHISM & CONFESSION OF FAITH**... Bound With / **THE ANCIENT TESTIMONY OF THE PEOPLE CALLED QUAKERS**... Crukshank, Phila: 1773. 2 vols in 1. pp. 150, 64, + 3p. Bookseller's catalog. Disbd. Evans 12661. $ 75.00

1051. (Barclay). **A CATECHISM & CONFESSION OF FAITH**... Bound With / **THE ANCIENT TESTIMONY OF QUAKERS**... Joseph James, Phila: 1788. Two volumes in one. pp. 150, 34. Spine taped. Evans 20950. $ 75.00

1052. Barnum, H. L. **THE AMERICAN FARRIER**... Uriah Hunt, Phila: 1845. 286p. + Ads. Ill. Full leather. Boards detached. Once again, the horse's importance in early America (and even today) cannot be overestimated. $ 32.00

1053. Bartram, William. **BOTANICAL AND ZOOLOGICAL DRAWINGS, 1756-1788.** Edited by Joseph Ewan. APS, Phila: 1967. 180p. Beautifully illustrated. Folio. $ 75.00

1054. Bates, Bess Royer. **LIFE OF D. L. MILLER.** Elgin, IL: 1921. 340p. + Illus. Extremely influential Brethren author. $ 20.00

1055. Bates, Samuel P. **MARTIAL DEEDS OF PENNSYLVANIA.** Phila: 1875. 1116p. + Fine Illustrations. Thick 4to. AEG. Disbound. Scarce Civil War Record. $ 100.00

1056. Bayard, Samuel P. **HILL COUNTRY TUNES. Instrumental Folk Music of Southwestern Pa.** AFS, Phila: 1944. Dances & songs with Music. $ 24.00

1057. Baxter, Angus. **IN SEARCH OF YOUR GERMAN ROOTS. Complete Guide to Tracing Your Ancestors in the Germanic Areas of Europe.** Balt: 1987. 122p. Wraps. $ 12.00

1058. Baxter, Richard & Wesley, John. **THE SAINT'S EVERLASTING REST**... Phila: 1791. pp. 391, (1). 16mo. Contemporary full leather. Evans 23161. *Extracted from the works of Baxter [1615-91] by John Wesley [1703-91], the founder of Methodism.* Scarce edition. $ 80.00

1059. Baxter, Richard. **THE SAINT'S EVERLASTING REST...** Abridged by Benjamin Fawcett. Woodward for Wm. Young, Phila: 1796. pp. 24, 383. Contemporary full leather. Evans 30040. Baxter's book was phenomenally popular for household devotions. $ 70.00

1060. Beal Rebecca J. **JACOB EICHHOLTZ, 1776 - 1842. Portrait Painter of Pennsylvania.** HSP: 1969. 402p. Well illustrated. A splendid catalog of all the portraits Eichholtz painted, and excellent biographies of his subjects. $ 35.00

1061. Bean, Theodore W. **HISTORY OF MONTGOMERY COUNTY, PA.** Phila: 1884. Over 1200p. + Illus. Last leaf in photo copy. 4to. Modern cloth. $ 150.00

1062. Bechtel, Ernest Waldo. **PENNA. DUTCH POEMS.** Ca: 1940. 8p. Wraps. $ 14.00

1063. Beidelman, William. **THE STORY OF THE PENNSYLVANIA GERMANS. Embracing an Account of Their Origin, History, & Dialect.** Easton: 1898. 254p. + Map. *WST.* $ 50.00

1064. Belcher, Joseph. **THE RELIGIOUS DENOMINATIONS IN THE U.S.** Phila: 1855. 1024p. + Illus. Thick 4to. Extensive accounts of Mennonites, Moravians, Schwenkfelders, Jews, Mormons, Etc. $ 50.00

1065. Bell, James B. **THE HOMOEOPATHIC THERAPEUTICS OF DIARRHOEA, DYSENTERY, CHOLERA, Etc...** NY: 1870. 168p. Taped Spine. $ 25.00

1066. Bender, Harold. **THE MENNONITE ENCYCLOPEDIA.** Scottsdale: 1969. Four Volumes. Valuable, but still under - utilized reference. $ 160.00

BENEZET'S NOTES ON THE SLAVE TRADE

1067. Benezet, Anthony. **THE PLAINESS AND INNOCENT SIMPLICITY OF THE CHRISTIAN RELIGION... Compared to the Corrupting Nature & Dreadful Effects of War...** Crukshank, Phila: 1782. pp. 48, 12 = "*Notes on the Slave Trade*", Etc. 16mo. Wraps. Evans 17472 & 17095/17838 {Neither with the correct date?}. Scarce & important. $ 200.00

1068. Bentley, Eliz. P. **INDEX TO THE 1850 CENSUS OF PA. Bucks and Lancaster Counties.** Balt: 1975. 2 Vols. Wraps. $ 28.00

1069. Berger, Daniel. **HISTORY OF THE CHURCH OF THE UNITED BRETHREN IN CHRIST.** Dayton OH: 1914. 682p. + Illus. $ 35.00

1070. Berks County. **ILLUSTRATED HISTORICAL ATLAS OF BERKS COUNTY, PA...** Davis, Reading: 1876. pp. 106, 32, 11. Folio. Property owner atlas with colored maps, numerous monochrome lithograph views, & ads. *WST.* $ 275.00

1071. Berky, Andrew S. **PRACTITIONER IN PHYSICK. A Biography of Abraham Wagner, 1717-1763.** PGS, (Pennsburg: 1954). 175p. + Illus. 4to. This includes a superb collection of early remedies. Same as Vol. 55 of the Pa. Ger. Soc. publications. $ 40.00

1072. Berky. **THE SCHOOLHOUSE NEAR THE OLD SPRING.** PGS, Norristown: 1955. 173p. Same as PGS Volume 56. $ 35.00

1073. Bezanson, Gray, & Hussey. **WHOLESALE PRICES IN PHILADELPHIA, 1784-1861.** Phila: 1936. 2 vols. Over 700p. Quite useful reference. $ 50.00

1074. Bible. **THE HOLY BIBLE...** Carey, Phila: 1811. 1100+p. + Maps & Plates. Ds. Thick 4to. Front board detached. ***Extensive manuscript Strickler family genealogy in English and German.*** AI 22355. $ 50.00

1075. Bible. **HOLY BIBLE**... W/Hitchcock's New & Complete Analysis... NY: 1873. Excellent Illustrated bible. *With a colored [red, green, yellow & purple] manuscript Grove/Musselman Family Record [4p.]. Executed in a style similar to the dwarf Amish artist = Barbara Ebersol, with each letter varnished in a glossy "glare".* Quite extraordinary. $ 400.00

1076. Bible. **NEW TESTAMENT**... Desilver, Phila: 1816. 335p. Full leather. *English & German manuscript ownerships of John & Christian Gibbel.* One of the first American stereotyped Testaments. AI 36969. $ 35.00

1077. Bickersteth, E. **A HARMONY OF THE FOUR GOSPELS**... Phila: 1833. 420p. Publisher's cloth, worn. AI 17775 (Bible). $ 45.00

1078. (Biddle, Henry D.). **EXTRACTS FROM THE JOURNAL OF ELIZABETH DRINKER, 1759 to 1807**. Phila: 1889. 423p. Howes B-427, Mathews p. 73. Scarce & important Quaker journal. Intimate Revolutionary War details. $ 60.00

1079. Bird, Michael S. **ONTARIO FRAKTUR. A Pa. German Folk Tradition in Early Canada**. Ontario: 1977. 144p. Well illustrated. $ 50.00

1080. Birkbeck, Morris. **LETTERS FROM ILLINOIS**. Dublin: 1818. 112p. Uncut. Original paper boards. *James Morton's copy* (See DAB). Howes B 467. Economics and realities of life in the American settlements West of Philadelphia. $ 120.00

1081. **BIRTHDAY & AUTOGRAPH ALBUM**. Bethlehem: 1874. Blank pages for each day of the year with a nicely printed heading. Handsome morocco gilt binding. Extensively used by Moravians in the U. S. & Germany. *From Benson J. Lossing's library.* $ 40.00

1082. Bitner, J. W. **GENEALOGICAL RECORD & HISTORY OF THE BITTNER-WERLEY FAMILIES, 1753-1930**. Kutztown: (1930). 239p. + Illus. *WST.* $ 50.00

1083. Bittinger, L. F. **THE GERMANS IN COLONIAL TIMES**. Phila: 1901. 314p. $ 24.00

1084. Bivins, John Jr. **THE MORAVIAN POTTERS IN NORTH CAROLINA**. Winston-Salem, NC: 1972. 300p. Well illustrated reference. $ 50.00

1085. Blake, John L. ... **A BIOGRAPHICAL DICTIONARY**... Phila: 1856. 1366p. Thick 4to. Full roan. Useful biographical reference. $ 50.00

1086. Blanchard, Amos. **A BOOK OF MARTYRS**... Cincinnati: 1831. 516p. + Woodcut illustrations. Disbd. XLib. AI 6176. $ 32.00

1087. Bogatzky, C. H. von. **A GOLDEN TREASURY For the Children of God**... Phila: 1821. 396p. + Frontis. 24mo. Nice contemporary full leather. Spine tooled in gilt with musical symbols. English version of the famed *Guldens Schatz=Kastlein.* AI 4753-4. $ 34.00

1088. Bogatzky. **A GOLDEN TREASURY For the Children of God**... NY: 1831. 387p. 24mo. Spine taped. AI 6190. Prayers for each day. $ 24.00

1089. Bomberger, C. M. **TWELFTH COLONY PLUS. The Formative Years of Pennsylvania**... Jeannette, Pa: 1934. 210p. + Illus. Fine article of the Pa. Germans = "An Influential One-Third, Too Seldom Emphasized". $ 24.00

1090. Bonninghausen, C. Von. **THERAPEUTIC POCKET - BOOK FOR HOMOEOPATHIC PHYSICIANS**... Edited by Dr. Charles J. Hempel. NY & Lond: 1847. 504p. Pretty half leather gilt. Excellent homoeopathic guide. $ 75.00

1091. Bonnycastle, John. **INTRODUCTION TO MENSURATION AND PRACTICAL GEOMETRY.** With/ A Treatise on Gauging & Mechanics by James Ryan. Kimber & Sharpless, Phila: 1839. 288p. Worn full leather. AI 54552. $ 20.00

1092. Borneman, J. H. **THE HISTORY OF THE BORNEMAN FAMILY IN AMERICA, Since the First Settlers, 1721=1878.** Boyertown: 1881. 114p. *Henry S. Borneman's copy.* $ 50.00

1093. Borneman. **PENNSYLVANIA GERMAN BOOKPLATES.** PGS [Vol. 54], Phila: 1953. 169p. + 24 Plates in Color. Decorated Cloth. Classic study that is now uncommon and avidly sought after. See also # 2053. $ 125.00

1094. Borneman. **PENNSYLVANIA GERMAN BOOKPLATES.** PGS, Phila: 1953. Same as the above, but *a unique copy, handsomely bound in full leather.* $ 160.00

1095. Borneman. **PENNSYLVANIA GERMAN BOOKPLATES.** In "The Colophon" Vol. 2, #3. NY: 1937. pp. 432-442. Color Illus. Signed by Borneman. *WST.* The earliest adventure into this subject. $ 40.00

1096. Borneman, Henry S. **PA. GERMAN ILLUMINATED MANUSCRIPTS. A Classification of Fraktur-Schriften & An Inquiry into their History & Art.** NY: 1973. 58p. + 38 Color Plates. Wraps. Useful reprint of the great classic. For the first edition, see #2045. $ 30.00

1097. Bouquet. **THE PAPERS OF HENRY BOUQUET. 1755-1760.** Harrisburg: 1951-78. Four Vols. Over 2500p. + Illus. Detailed record of the French & Indian War era. Invaluable for Western Pennsylvania research. $ 100.00

1098. Boyd, S. G. **INDIAN LOCAL NAMES, With Their Interpretation.** Boyd, York, Pa: 1885. 70p. Cloth. Signed presentation from Boyd to Dr. A. R. Horne. *WST.* $ 75.00

1099. Boyer. **AMERICAN BOYERS.** (Allentown: 1940). 663p. Useful Pennsylvania German family genealogy. *WST.* $ 60.00

1100. Boyer, Buffington, & Yoder. **SONGS ALONG THE MAHANTONGO. PA. Dutch Folk Songs.** Hatboro: 1964. 231p. XLib. Classic. $ 16.00

1101. Braght, Thielman J. van. **THE BLOODY THEATER, OR MARTYRS MIRROR... Translated into English by I. Daniel Rupp.** David Miller, Near Lampeter Square, Lancaster: 1837. 1048p. + Manuscript Notes. Worn original full roan binding. Rupp's English version of the great work may, in reality, be scarcer than that issued at Ephrata. $ 140.00

1102. (Braght). **THE DRAMA OF THE MARTYRS... Drawn and Engraved on Copper by the Renowned Engraver Jan Luyken [1649-1712].** W/ Notes by Jan Gleysteen. Lancaster: 1975. 141p. Wraps. Reproduces the complete series of plates issued in the 2nd (1685) (Dutch) edition of the Martyr's Mirror. $ 12.50

1103. Braght. **MARTYRS MIRROR.** Scottdale: 1982. 1157p. The best English version of the eminent Anabaptist work. $ 35.00

1104. (Branagan, Thomas). **RIGHTS OF GOD, Written for the Benefit of Man...** Phila: 1812. 360p. + Frontis. 1/2 Leather. AI 24927 *[Locating only one copy]. HSH.* $ 32.00

1105. Brand, Millen. **LOCAL LIVES: Poems About the Pennsylvania Dutch.** NY: 1975. 526p. DJ. $ 10.00

1106. Brandt, H. A. **CHRISTOPHER SOWER & SON. The Story of Two Pioneers in American Printing...** Elgin, Il: 1938. 135p. Illus. DJ. $ 40.00

1107. Brazer, Esther Stevens. **EARLY AMERICAN DECORATION. A Comprehensive Treatise...** Springfield, MA: 1950. 265p. + Illus. DJ. Folio. Complete course in the techniques of hand painted decoration for: tinware, furniture, and interiors. $ 50.00

1108. Brechbill, L. T. **A PEDIGREE OF THE SIEGRIST'S**. Lancaster: 1972. 76p. Mimeo. Wraps. Genealogies of the Tobias Siegrist family, 1812 - 1971. $ 22.00

1109. Brecht, Samuel Kriebel. **THE GENEALOGICAL RECORD OF THE SCHWENKFELDER FAMILIES...** Pennsburg & NY: 1923. 1752p. + Illus. 4to. Massive genealogical / reference. *WST.* $ 150.00

1110. Breidenbaugh, E. S. **THE PENNSYLVANIA COLLEGE BOOK, 1832=1882**. Phila: 1882. 475p. + ***Fifty Original Mounted Photographs of Buildings & Personalities, by Tipton.*** Founded as a Lutheran College. Great photos of this Gettysburg landmark. $ 100.00

1111. (Bremer, Fredrika). **THE HOMES OF THE NEW WORLD; Impressions of America**. NY: 1853. Two volumes. XLib. Worn cloth. "Detailed and amiable record of an extensive tour" = Howes B745, Sabin 7713. $ 50.00

1112. Brenckman, Fred. **HISTORY OF CARBON COUNTY, PA.** Harrisburg: 1913. 626p. + Illus. Half leather. *WST.* $ 120.00

1113. Brendle, Thomas R. & Troxell, Wm. S. (Pumpernickle Bill). **PENNSYLVANIA GERMAN FOLK TALES, LEGENDS, ONCE-UPON-A-TIME STORIES, MAXIMS & SAYINGS. Spoken in the Dialect Popularly Known as Pennsylvania Dutch**. PGS, Norristown: 1944. 238p. Cloth backed printed paper boards. The author's copies of this famous monograph also printed by the Pennsylvania German Society as Vol. 50. (Pt. II # 2049). *WST.* $ 60.00

1114. Brendle & Troxell. **PENNSYLVANIA GERMAN SONGS.** (Allentown: 1936-7). Five Mimeographed Music Sheets, with Words in the Dialect. *WST.* $ 4.00

1115. **BRETHREN ENCYCLOPEDIA.** Oak Brook & Phila: 1984. Three volumes. The biographical name index is especially useful. $ 150.00

SAUR'S MOST POPULAR ENGLISH IMPRINT

1116. Bromley, Thomas. **THE WAY TO THE SABBATH OF REST, Or the Soul's Progress in the Work of New=Birth**. Bound with / **A DISCOURSE ON MISTAKES CONCERNING RELIGION, ENTHUSIASM, EXPERIENCES, ETC**. By Thomas Hartley. Christopher Sower, Germantown (Also sold by Solomon Fussell & Jonathan Zane in Phila): 1759. Two volumes in one. pp. 280, 168. Should be rebound. ***Manuscript ownership of Sam Emlen, Jr.*** Evans 8309 & 8364, Sabin 8192, Hild. 1621/1628, Seid. p. 51=2. Bromley [1629-91], was one of the most prominent English followers of Jacob Boehme. $ 200.00

1117. Bromley. **THE WAY TO THE SABBATH OF REST, Or the Soul's Progress in the Work of New=Birth**. Christopher Sower, Germantown: 1759. 280p. 19th Cent. 1/2 leather. Evans 8309, Hild. 1621, Seid. p. 51. $ 120.00

1118. Brotherhead, William. **FORTY YEARS AMONG THE OLD BOOKSELLERS OF PHILADELPHIA.** A. P. Brotherhead, Philadelphia: 1891. Cloth Boards with paper label. Scarce First Edition. Fascinating reading for any Bibliophile. $ 75.00

1119. Brumbaugh, Martin G. **THE LIFE & WORKS OF CHRISTOPHER DOCK, America's Pioneer Writer on Education. With a Translation of His Works into the English Language. With an Introduction by Hon. Samuel W. Pennypacker**. Lippincott, Phila: 1908. 272p. + Illus. & Facsimiles. Cloth. No. 286 of an Edition Limited to only 1000 copies. $ 120.00

1120. Brunner, D. B. **THE INDIANS OF BERKS COUNTY, PA. A Summary of All Tangible Records of the Aborigines of Berks County**. Reading: 1881. 177p. Spine taped. First Edition. *WST*. Wonderful monograph with many details about Conrad Weiser, et. al. $ 100.00

1121. Brunner. **THE INDIANS OF BERKS COUNTY, PA.** Reading: 1897. 257p. Crisp copy of the expanded 2nd Ed. Signed presentation from Brunner to the Pennsylvania German scholar - Dr. A. R. Horne. *WST*. $ 75.00

1122. Brunner. **THE INDIANS OF BERKS COUNTY, PA...** Reprint of the Reading 1897 Edition. 214p. Illus. $ 30.00

1123. Brunner, Edmund D. **COOPERATION IN COOPERSBURG.** NY: 1916. 111p. + Illus. A Pennsylvania German town near Bethlehem. *WST*. $ 20.00

1124. Buck, Charles. **A THEOLOGICAL DICTIONARY...** Phila: 1826. 615p. + Frontis. Worn full leather. AI 23959. Includes Mennonites, Moravians, etc. $ 28.00

1125. Buck, William J. **HISTORY OF MONTGOMERY COUNTY, Within the Schuylkill Valley...** Acker, Norristown: 1859. 128p. Spine taped. Scarce early county history with good information on early Pennsylvania Germans. $ 130.00

1126. Buell, Augustus C. **WILLIAM PENN, As the Founder of Two Commonwealths.** NY: 1904. 368p. + Illus. $ 16.00

1127. Buffington & Barba. **A PENNSYLVANIA GERMAN GRAMMAR.** Allentown: 1954. 167p. DJ. Signed by Dr. Buffington. $ 30.00

1128. Bunyan, John. **THE HOLY WAR...** Phila. & Pittsburgh: 1830. 252p. + Folding frontis. Contemporary full leather. AI 697. *HSH*. $ 18.00

1129. Burkhardt, Frank A. **PIONEER DAYS OF GEORGE H. A. BURKHARDT.** Los Angeles: 1935. 32p. Illus. Printed wraps. $ 20.00

1130. Burrowes, J. F. **THE PIANO-FORTE PRIMER...** Printed by Robinson (Baltimore) for G. E. Blake, Phila: 1820. 56p. + 3p. Ad for Blake, Musical Instrument Maker & Music Publisher. 24mo. Original leather backed marbled boards. AI 631 *[One Copy Only*]. $ 100.00

1131. Byrn, Dr. M. La Fayette. **THE COMPLETE PRACTICAL DISTILLER...** Baird, Phila: 1867. 198p. + 26p. Ads. Illus. Cloth. XLib. Important American work on the making of whiskeys and spirits. See also the similar works that we offer in German. $ 75.00

1132. **THE CALENDAR, Civil & Ecclesiastical.** By a Layman of the German Reformed Church. Chambersburg: 1858. 41p. Lovely copy in blue printed wraps. *WST*. $ 22.00

1133. Carbon County. **COUNTY ATLAS OF CARBON, PA...** Beers, NY: 1875. 82p. Colored property owner maps, lithographed views, & ads + Original Subscriber's Invoice. $ 200.00

1134. Carey, Mathew [1760-1839]. **A SHORT ACCOUNT OF THE MALIGNANT FEVER LATELY PREVALENT IN PHILADELPHIA... With Accounts of the Plague in London & Marseilles; and a List of the Dead [1793]...** Phila: 1794. 164p. Library binding. "In this little book Carey left a graphic account of the epidemic, and gave a good clinical description of the disease, mentioning the efficacy & the failure of many forms of treatment" = GM 5451, Evans 26736, Sabin 10885. For the German editions see Part I # 216 & 486. $ 150.00

1135. Carey. **ACCOUNT OF THE PLAGUE, or Malignant Fever Lately Prevalent in Philadelphia.** Darton & Harvey, London: 1794. 92p. + Folding Chart. *Uncut and sewn as issued.* First English Edition of this great medical classic. Rare in this condition. $ 250.00

1136. Carpenter. **GENEALOGICAL NOTES OF THE CARPENTER FAMILY...** Edited by Edwin Sayer Walker. Springfield, Ill: 1907. 242p. + Photo illus. Limited to 500 copies. The family was very influential in early Lancaster, Pa. Includes the autobiography of Dr. Seymour D. Carpenter who served as a Colonel in the Civil War. $ 70.00

1137. Carpenter's Company of Philadelphia. **THE ACT TO INCORPORATE THE CARPENTER'S COMPANY OF PHILADELPHIA.** Phila: 1866. 153p. Original printed boards. Includes: The Act to Incorporate; Historic reminiscences of the Hall; Extracts of the Ancient Minutes; & an interesting Catalog of the Books in the Library. $ 50.00

THE CARPENTER'S COMPANY "RULES OF WORK"

1138. Carpenter's Company. **ARTICLES OF THE CARPENTER'S COMPANY OF THE CITY AND COUNTY OF PHILADELPHIA; And Their Rules for Measuring and Valuing House Carpenters Work, As Revised and Agreed on in the Year 1805.** Humphreys, Phila: 1805. pp. 16, 84 + *Wonderful Etched Architectural Plates.* Later wraps. AI 8140. There is no mystery about the scarcity of these Rule Books; They were highly restricted in their own time as "trade secrets", and were heavily used by artisans over a long period of years. Generally recognized as one of the most significant and valuable of original American Architecture books. $1800.00

1139. Carpenter's Co. **THE CELEBRATION OF THE 200TH ANNIVERSARY OF THE CARPENTER'S COMPANY OF PHILADELPHIA, 1724-1924.** Phila: 1925. 114p. + Illus. Limited Edition. Crisp blue cloth gilt. $ 20.00

1140. Carpenter's Co. **THE RULES OF WORK OF THE CARPENTER'S COMPANY OF THE CITY & COUNTY OF PHILADELPHIA, 1786.** Annotated with an Introduction by Charles F. Peterson. Princeton: 1971. Wraps. Guide to all editions of the "Rules". $ 14.00

1141. Carter, Jane Levis. **THE PAPER MAKERS. Early Pennsylvanians & Their Water Mills.** Gradyville: 1982. 104p. Illus. Limited Edition. $ 32.00

1142. Cassel, Daniel K. **HISTORY OF THE MENNONITES...** Phila: 1888. 450p. + Illus. Still useful as a historical reference. *WST.* $ 80.00

1143. (Cerny, Johni). **A GUIDE TO GERMAN PARRISH RECORDS in the Family History Library, LDS.** Vol. I = Baden, Bavaria, & Wuerttemburg. Balt: 1988. 430p. $ 30.00

1144. Chalkley, Thomas [1675=1741]. **THE JOURNAL, Or Historical Account of the Life, Travels... of Thomas Chalkley.** James Chattin, Phila: 1754. pp. viii, 325. 24mo. Contemporary Leather. A separate issue of the "Works" with the "Journal" only. Evans 7166, Hild. 1351, Vail 450-1, Sabin 11749. Scarce. $ 140.00

1145. **CHAMBER'S INFORMATION FOR THE PEOPLE...** Smith, Phila: 1858. Two Vols. Numerous woodcut illus. Publisher's cloth. Popular encyclopedia, with long articles on such things as; the Whale Fishery, Phrenology, Cookery, Farming, Steam Engines, Canals, Etc. Etc. *Hamilton Spangler's copy.* $ 50.00

1146. Chambers, Theo. F. **THE EARLY GERMANS OF NEW JERSEY. Their History, Churches, & Genealogies.** Balt: 1982. Reprint of 1895 edition. 667p. Illus. $ 40.00

1147. Chambers, Corwin, & Anderson, et.al. **CENTENNIAL DISCOURSES... REFORMED (DUTCH) CHURCH IN AMERICA.** NY: 1877. Pretty cloth gilt. $ 34.00

1148. **CHRISTIAN ADVICES: Published by the Yearly Meeting of Friends.** Kimber & Conrad, Phila: 1808. 116p. Contemporary full leather. Nice marbled endpapers. AI 15075. Good record of Pennsylvania Quaker attitudes and practices. $ 24.00

1149. **CHRONICON EPHRATENSE; A History of the Community of Seventh Day Baptists at Ephrata, Lancaster County, Penn'a**. By "Lamech and Agrippa" (Jacob Gass & J. P. Miller). Translated from the German by J. Max Hark. Lancaster: 1889. 288p. Worn original cloth. XLib. Limited Edition. Howes G 76. The chief source for any Cloister history. $ 120.00

1150. (Churchman). **AN ACCOUNT OF THE GOSPEL LABOURS OF JOHN CHURCHMAN** [1705-1775]. With a Short Memorial of Joseph White, Late of Bucks County. Crukshank, Phila: 1779. pp. 7, 256. Final leaf with some loss. Evans 16223. $ 50.00

1151. Claude, Jean. **AN HISTORICAL DEFENSE OF THE REFORMATION...** London: 1686. 535p. 4to. Ds. Wing 4593. Claude [1619-87] was an influential and controversial French Protestant divine. He was forced to flee to Holland, and received a pension from William of Orange. Several of his works were burnt in both England and France. *WST.* $ 200.00

1152. Clewell & Seyfried. **HISTORY OF THE CLEWELL FAMILY IN THE U.S.A. 1737-1907.** Bethlehem: 1907. 391p. Illus. *WST.* $ 60.00

1153. Coale, Josiah. **THE BOOKS AND DIVERSE EPISTLES OF JOSIAH COALE...** (London): 1671. pp. 102 [of 104], 343. Disbound. Smith I p. 435. Important Quaker record, that includes many letters to Friends in America. $ 225.00

CELEBRATED HISTORY OF THE IROQUOIS CONFEDERATION AND PENNSYLVANIA'S DEALINGS WITH THE INDIANS

1154. Colden, Cadwallader. **THE HISTORY OF THE FIVE INDIAN NATIONS OF CANADA, Which are Dependent on the Province of New York in America, and Are the Barrier between the English & the French in That Part of the World.** Third Edition. London: 1755. Two Volumes + the rare folding Map in excellent state + Manuscript Notes. Contemporary full leather. Early bookplates of Robert John Verney, Lord Willoughby de Broke. The outstanding early history of the Iroquois Indians and conditions on the "frontier". Almost all of Volume II is devoted to Penn's Treaties with the Indians, and the political foundations of Pennsylvania. See: Vail 479, Sabin 14275, Howes C 560. $ 750.00

A UNIQUE MUSIC BOOK

1155. **A COLLECTION OF CHURCH MUSIC. 1787. Number II.** Printed Typographically by Young and M'Culloch, Phila. (1787). 40p. + *17p. Manuscript Music* (Secular). Oblong 32mo. Manuscript ownership (1853) of Mary Elizabeth Rosenberger, Hatfield, Pa. Rare. *Apparently not in Evans, S&M, Etc.* $ 360.00

1156. (Collin, Bernadine T.) **SURNAME INDEX TO GENEALOGY & IMMIGRATION ARTICLES IN PENNSYLVANIA FOLKLIFE, THE PENNSYLVANIA DUTCHMAN, & THE DUTCHMAN.** Ursinus College, Collegeville, Pa: 1980. 182p. Photocopy. Wraps. $ 36.00

1157. Colonial Dames. **FORGES & FURNACES IN THE PROVINCE OF PENNSYLVANIA.** Phila: 1914. 204p. + Numerous Illus. Invaluable study. $ 80.00

1158. Comfort, Wm. Wistar. **WILLIAM PENN & OUR LIBERTIES.** Phila: 1947. $ 10.00

1159. **THE COMPLETE PAPERS OF WILLIAM PENN.** Univ. of Pa., Phila: 1981-6. Five volumes. Essential historical source record. $ 250.00

1160. Comstock, Helen. **AMERICAN FURNITURE. 17th, 18th, & 19th Century Styles.** West Chester. 336p. Illus. Classic reference. $ 30.00

1161. Condit, Uzal W. **THE HISTORY OF EASTON, PA. 1739-1885.** (Easton: 1885). 500p. + Illus. 4to. Cloth. Excellent illustrated history. *WST.* $ 120.00

1162. Connor, P. S. P. **SIR WILLIAM PENN, KNIGHT. Admiral, and General At Sea...** Phila: 1876. 70p. Bound with / **THE PENN FAMILY.** By John Jay Smith. + Manuscript and Photo inserts. *Connor's own copy, bound by Pawson and Nicholson.* Unique. $ 75.00

1163. Cope, Gilbert & Ashmead, H. G. **CHESTER & DELAWARE COUNTIES, PA. Historic Homes & Institutions, & Genealogical & Personal Memoirs.** NY: 1904. 2 Vols. 1200p. + Illus. Lovely set in 1/2 morocco gilt. AEG. Excellent biographical & genealogical record. $ 150.00

1164. (Corp, Harriet). **AN ANTIDOTE TO THE MISERIES OF HUMAN LIFE...** Young, Phila: 1831. 126p. Taped spine. 24mo. AI6698. An answer to Beresford's pessimistic work *Miseries of Human Life*, in a stagecoach conversation with the Quaker Widow Placid & her daughter. $ 24.00

1165. **CORRESPONDENCE BETWEEN WILLIAM PENN & JAMES LOGAN, 1700-50.** With Notes by Deborah Logan & Edward Armstrong. HSP, Philadelphia: 1870. Two volumes. Extraordinary documentary source record. $ 50.00

1166. Cottin, Marie. **ELIZABETH; or, The Exiles of Siberia: A Tale Founded Upon Facts.** Printed by Ann Cochran for Matthew Carey, Phila: 1811. 166p. + Osborn Stipple Portrait. Ds. Leather backed boards. AI 22628. $ 40.00

1167. Cox, Samuel Hanson. **QUAKERISM NOT CHRISTIANITY: Or, Reasons for Renouncing the Doctrine of Friends.** Fanshaw, Boston: 1833. 686p. XLib. $ 22.00

1168. Coxe, Trench. **A VIEW OF THE UNITED STATES OF AMERICA.** For William Hall and Wrigley & Berriman, Philadelphia: 1794. pp. 513. With Folding charts. Original boards and label binding. Front board detached, spine split. *Owned by Joshua Humphrey [1751-1838], famed ship builder and naval architect = With his drawing of a ship on the rear board.* XLib. A truly important text with a wonderful provenance. Evans 26829. $ 600.00

1169. Cramer, Edith. **HANDBOOK OF EARLY AMERICAN DECORATION.** Boston: 1968. 90p. Illus. 4to. How-to-do-it Folk Art Decoration. $ 12.00

THE FIRST AND ONLY EDITION

1170. (Crevecoeur, Michel-Guillaume Jean de). **VOYAGE DANS LA HAUTE PENNSYLVANIE ET DANS L'ETAT DE NEW YORK, 1785-1798.** Paris: 1801. Three Volumes. Illustrated by fine plates and wonderful maps engraved by Tardieu. Unusual contemporary paper binding with morocco label and spine modestly filleted in gilt. See: Howes C884, Sabin 17501, K300 #643. Written during the difficult years of the French Revolution, this was intended to be merely a fourth volume of "*Letters From an American Farmer*", but Crevecoeur eventually created an entirely new work. In its pages, one discovers the final evolution of his ideas, intimate observations, and dreams about America. It's filled with details on the gradual disappearance of the aboriginal tribes, and the great Indian Councils. It is finely printed and illustrated. Of special note are: the portrait of Washington engraved from a cameo done in NY (1789), the powerful pictures of Indian Chiefs; and the fine maps and plans. A complete edition in English was apparently never published. Rare. $1200.00

1171. Crist, R. G. **TRAILS OF FAITH. Histories of Religious Groups in Cumberland & Dauphin Counties.** Harrisburg: 1976. 122p. Double Column. Illus. Printed wraps. $ 8.00

1172. Croll, P. C. **ANCIENT HISTORIC LANDMARKS IN THE LEBANON VALLEY.** Phila: 1895. 334p. Illus. Noteworthy history. *WST.* $ 40.00

1173. Croll. **ANNALS OF THE OLEY VALLEY, In Berks County, Pa.** Reading: 1926, 148p. Double Column. Illus. Printed wraps. *WST.* $ 40.00

1174. Croll. **THE CROLL FAMILY. The Golden Wedding Ring. A Souvenir of the 50th Wedding Anniversary of John & Catherine Croll**... Lancaster: 1887. 106p. Wraps. $ 25.00

1175. Cronau, Rudolf. **THE ARMY OF THE AMERICAN REVOLUTION & ITS ORGANIZER (Maj. Gen. Baron von Steuben)**. NY: 1923. 153p. Signed by Cronau. $ 22.00

1176. **CUMBERLAND COUNTY BIOGRAPHICAL ANNALS**. Chi: 1905. 850p. Illus. 4to. Needs rebinding. Excellent biographical record. $ 50.00

1177. (Damrell, Wm. S.). **THREE EXPERIMENTS OF LIVING: Within the Means, Up to the Means, Beyond the Means**. Phila: 1846. 143p. Nice cloth binding. $ 30.00

1178. Danner, Edwin R. **PENNSYLVANIA DUTCH COLLOQUIALISMS**. (York: 1961). 20p. Printed wraps. Companion to the Dictionary. Signed by Danner. *WST*. $ 18.00

1179. Danner. **PENNSYLVANIA DUTCH DICTIONARY**. York: 1951. 178p. + Errata. Printed Wraps. First Edition. Presented by Danner to *WST*. Very helpful. $ 30.00

1180. D'Aubigne, J. H. M. **HISTORY OF THE GREAT REFORMATION OF THE 16TH CENTURY IN GERMANY, SWITZERLAND, ETC**. Phila: 1843. 426p. Full leather. $ 20.00

1181. Davidson, Jane. **CHRISTIAN SCHMUCKER. A Colonial Pennsylvania (German) Farmer**. Downingtown: 1976. 106p. Ills. Wraps. $ 10.00

1182. Davies, Richard. **ACCOUNT OF HIS CONVINCEMENT, EXERCISES, SERVICES & TRAVELS**... James Chattin, Phila: 1752. pp. (18), 223 + 1p. Printer's Advertisement that includes "Women's Plat Bonnets". Contemporary full leather (Philadelphia) binding, curiously tooled with frames formed by double/triple line fillets. *Attractive early ownerships of Ann Cooper 1753 - 1762*. Evans 6833. Fine copy of this scarce Quaker journal. $ 225.00

1183. Davis, Ed. Ziegler. **TRANSLATIONS OF GERMAN POETRY IN AMERICAN MAGAZINES, 1741-1810**. Printed by New Era in Lancaster for the Americana Germanica Press, Phila: 1905. 229p. Crisp copy. $ 34.00

1184. Day, J. C. **EARLY AMERICAN CUT & USE STENCILS**. NY: 1975. 64p. $ 5.00

1185. Day. **PENNSYLVANIA DUTCH CUT & USE STENCILS**. NY: 1975. 64p. $ 5.00

1186. DeChant, Alliene Saeger. **IT ALL BEGAN WITH A BAYONET. The Story of Pastor S. Neitz Dissinger's 52 Years in 13 Evangelical Congregational Appointments**. (Mauch Chunk: 1950?). 95p. + Ill. Cloth. $ 12.00

1187. Deibert, Joseph P. **HISTORY OF UNION CHURCH**. Unionville, Pa: 1930. 91p. + Inserts. Printed wraps. *WST*. $ 12.00

1188. Deibert, Joseph P. **SHINING LIGHTS OF SCHNECKSVILLE, PA. 1840-1940**. New Tripoli, Pa: (1940). 85p. Illus. Printed wraps. *WST*. $ 24.00

1189. Deiler, J. H. **THE SETTLEMENT OF THE GERMAN COAST OF LOUISIANA**. Balt: 1989. 170p. Illus. $ 20.00

1190. DeLong, G. K. **DIALECT DICH-TOONG**. Pennsburg, Pa: 1912. 16p. Printed wraps. Scarce little Pennsylvania German dialect piece. *WST*. $ 22.00

1191. DeLong, Dr. Irwin Hoch. **PIONEER PALATINE PILGRIMS** Lancaster: 1928. 36p. Printed wraps. Genealogical records from Hill Church, Berks Co. About the De Long, Geist, Hoch and other Pennsylvania Families. $ 20.00

1192. De Schweintz, Edmund. **THE LIFE AND TIMES OF DAVID ZEISBERGER, Western Pioneer and Apostle to the Indians.** Phila: 1870. 747p. Later cloth. The best study of one of the leading figures in the pioneer Moravian missions. *WST.* $ 75.00

1193. De Schweintz. **THE MORAVIAN MANUAL.** Phila: 1859. 178p. Embossed cloth. First edition. *C. F. Kluge's copy. WST.* $ 40.00

1194. De Schweintz. **THE MORAVIAN MANUAL.** 2nd Ed. Bethlehem: 1869. 207p. With / Historical Tables from A.D. 836=1869. + *11p. Manuscript in English & German on the "External Regulations of the Moravian Brethren's Congregation, Lebanon".* $ 60.00

1195. Dewees, W. W. & Sarah. **CENTENNIAL HISTORY OF WESTTOWN (QUAKER) BOARDING SCHOOL, 1799=1899.** Phila: 1899. 204p. + Illus. XL. $ 19.00

1196. Dickert, Thomas W. **THE LIFE OF REV. CALVIN S. GERHARD.** Phila: 1904. 256p. Influential minister in the Reformed Church. $ 12.00

1197. Diffenderffer, F. R. **THE GERMAN IMMIGRATION INTO PENNSYLVANIA THROUGH THE PORT OF PHILADELPHIA, 1700-75, and the Redemptioners.** Balt: 1988. 328p. Indexed reprint of the fine 1900 PGS edition. $ 20.00

1198. Dillin, John G. W. **THE KENTUCKY RIFLE...** York & Wilmington: 1959. 154p. + Illus. Slipcased. Scarce First Edition. Essential reference. $ 80.00

1199. Dilworth, Thomas. **THE SCHOOLMASTER'S ASSISTANT. A Compendium of Arithmetic...** NY: 1804. 272p. + Ads. Full leather. *Attractive calligraphic fraktur manuscript ownership of Henry Feeman (Fieman), (Northampton County), 1807*. AI 6167 *[Locating the NNC copy only]*. $ 50.00

1200. **THE DOAN OUTLAWS; Bucks County's Cowboys in the Revolution.** Doylestown: 1897. 176p. Double column. *WST.* $ 100.00

1201. Dobree, Bonamy. **WILLIAM PENN, QUAKER & PIONEER.** Bost: 1932. 346p. + Illus. + Folding Penn genealogical chart. First Edition. $ 14.00

1202. Doherty, R. W. **THE HICKSITE SEPARATION...** Rutgers: 1967. 157p. DJ. Fine analysis of the Quaker schism of 1827. $ 8.00

1203. Doll, Eugene E. **THE EPHRATA CLOISTER: An Introduction.** Ephrata: 1958. 32p. Wraps. Historic and interesting site. $ 6.00

1204. Dolson, Hildegarde. **WILLIAM PENN. Quaker Hero.** NY: 1961. 186p. Illus. $ 8.00

1205. Dufief, N. G. **NATURE DISPLAYED IN HER MODE OF TEACHING LANGUAGE TO MAN: Or, A New & Infallible Method of Acquiring A Language...** Phila: 1810. Vol. I (433p.) + "Le Lecteur Francais" (96p.) + Stipple engraved Frontis. Worn contemporary full leather. *Manuscript ownerships of Edward Hand & Sarah Bethel.* AI 20001. Dufief was a great friend of Jefferson, and a remarkable character. $ 100.00

1206. Durnbaugh, Donald F. **THE BRETHREN IN COLONIAL AMERICA.** Elgin, IL. 660p. Illus. Cloth. $ 22.00

1207. Durnbaugh. **EUROPEAN ORIGINS OF THE BRETHREN.** Elgin, IL: 1986. 463p. Illus. Cloth. Excellent study of primary sources. $ 22.00

1208. Durnbaugh, Hedwig T. **THE GERMAN HYMNODY OF THE BRETHREN, 1720-1903.** Phila: 1986. 322p. 4to. $ 30.00

E

1209. Earnest, Adele. **FOLK ART IN AMERICA.** West Chester: 1984. 256p. Numerous color plates. An interesting history of the practice of folk art collecting. $ 35.00

1210. Earnest, Corinne & Russell. **PAPERS FOR BIRTH DAYES. Guide to the Fraktur Artists and Scriveners**. Albuquerque, NM: 1989. 496p. Illus. 4to. Wraps. An absolute "must" for anyone interested in Pennsylvania German fraktur, manuscripts, and art. $ 50.00

1211. Eckhardt, Geo. H. **PENNSYLVANIA CLOCKS & CLOCKMAKERS. An Epic of Early American Science, Industry, & Craftsmanship**. NY: 1955. 229p. Illus. 4to. DJ. 1st Ed. Includes a useful directory of Clockmakers. $ 40.00

1212. Edmundson, William. **A JOURNAL OF THE LIFE, TRAVELS, & SUFFERINGS, ETC.** Mary Hinde, London: 1774. pp. 75, 371, 32. Quaker Edmundson [1627=1712] three times visited America before 1700. Contemporary full leather binding that is very possibly American made. Sabin 21873. *Early American ownership of Isaac Parrish.* $ 125.00

THE APOSTLE TO THE INDIANS

1213. Edwards, Jonathan. **AN ACCOUNT OF THE LIFE... OF DAVID BRAINERD... MISSIONARY TO THE INDIANS... AND PASTOR OF A CHURCH OF CHRISTIAN INDIANS IN NEW JERSEY**... Boston: 1749. pp. (2), 12, 316 + 18p. List of Subscribers. Contemporary calf. Worn and aged. Brainerd had remarkable success with numerous Indian tribes, and left us a diary account that is unequaled. First Edition. Prime Americana classic. See: Sabin 21927, Howes E 56, Evans 6311, et. al. $ 220.00

1214. Edwards, Peter. **CANDID REASONS FOR RENOUNCING THE PRINCIPLES OF ANTI-PAEDOBAPTISM.** Nahum Mower, Windsor, Vt: 1802. 199p. Bound with / **Critical Remarks on Dr. Jenkins' Defense of the Baptists**. Carlisle, Boston: 1803. 72p. Worn full leather. Ownership of Ph. Gloninger. AI 2177 & 4142-3. $ 50.00

1215. Egle. **DAUPHIN COUNTY CENTENARY MEMORIAL, 1785-1885.** Harrisburg: 1886. 397p. + Inserts. Good contribution to local history. $ 25.00

1216. Egle. **AN ILLUSTRATED HISTORY OF THE COMMONWEALTH OF PENNSYLVANIA**... Harrisburg: 1876. 1186p. Illus. Original full embossed morocco. Thick 4to. Foundation work in Pennsylvania history. $ 50.00

1217. **EGYPT REFORMED CHURCH (LEHIGH COUNTY) RECORDS, 1734-1834.** Translated by Charles R. Roberts. Pa. Archives, Harrisburg: 1906. 310p. Spine taped. $ 22.00

1218. Eisenhart, Willis Wolf. **ANCESTRY OF THE JOHN FRANKLIN EISENHART FAMILY.** Abbottstown: 1951. 150p. + Supplement. York historical genealogy. $ 30.00

1219. Elliott, Ella Zerby. **OLD SCHUYLKILL TALES.** Pottsville: 1906. 344p. Precious collection of historical anecdote. *WST.* $ 45.00

1220. (Ellwood). **THE HISTORY OF THE LIFE OF THOMAS ELLWOOD.** Crukshank, Phila: 1775. 360p. Full leather. *Manuscript ownership = "Griffith Mendenhall, 1779. His Book Bought at Philadelphia for Six Shillings."* Evans 14020. Popular Quaker journal that's Especially useful for study of the Keithian controversy. $ 100.00

1221. (Emerick, Albert G.). **SONGS FOR THE PEOPLE; National, Patriotic, Sentimental, Comic, and Naval Songs**. Zieber, Phila: 1848. 288p. Wonderful woodcut illustrations and embellishments. Publisher's embossed gilt cloth. The first volume of what was intended to be a "periodical" collection. $ 60.00

1222. Emmert, David. **REMINISCENCES OF JUNIATA COLLEGE, 1876-1901**. Huntingdon, Pa: 1901. 183p. Illus. Cloth. Brethren history. $ 18.00

1223. Erb, Paul. **SOUTH CENTRAL FRONTIERS. A History of the South Central Mennonite Conference**. Scottdale: 1974. 520p. $ 14.00

1224. Ermentrout, Dan. **OUR PEOPLE IN AMERICAN HISTORY.** An Oration at the German Centennial Jubilee. Miller, Reading: 1876. 34p. Printed wraps. A crisp copy of this scarce historical address. Important. $ 30.00

1225. Eshleman, H. Frank. **HISTORIC BACKGROUND & ANNALS OF THE SWISS & GERMAN PIONEER SETTLERS OF SOUTH-EASTERN PENNSYLVANIA, And of Their Remote Ancestors, From the Middle of the Dark Ages, Down to the Revolutionary War...** Lancaster: 1917. 386p. Double Column. *WST.* $ 75.00

1226. Eshleman. **HISTORIC BACKGROUND & ANNALS OF THE SWISS & GERMAN PIONEER SETTLERS** ... *In the original signatures. Never bound, cut, or opened.* $ 85.00

1227. Eshleman, et. al. **REPORT OF THE TRUE CHARACTER, TIME & PLACE OF THE FIRST REGULAR SETTLEMENT IN LANCASTER COUNTY.** Lancaster Historical Soc: 1910. 71p. Printed wraps. $ 20.00

1228. Eshleman, Milton B. **REGISTER OF CONSANGUINITY**... (Paradise, Lanc. County. Ca: 1875). 203p. Oblong 4to. Bound volume of unused printed forms for genealogical use. Quite remarkable and very rarely encountered. These forms could still be happily used by genealogists today. $ 50.00

1229. Eshleman, M. M. **A MODEL LIFE, Or, Uncle John Metzger on Earth**. Mount Morris, Ill: 1898. 64p. Illus. 16mo. Cloth. Interesting Brethren memoir. $ 16.00

1230. Espenshade, A. H. **PENNSYLVANIA PLACE NAMES.** State College: 1925. 375p. + Colored folding map of Pa. Limited to 1500 copies. 1st ed. Entertaining reference. $ 35.00

1231. Evangelical Association. **HYMN-BOOK**... Cleveland: 1882. 568p. Embossed morocco gilt. 32mo. *Ownerships of the Herbst Family.* $ 20.00

1232. Evans, Oliver. **THE YOUNG MILL=WRIGHT & MILLER'S GUIDE**... 10th Edition, W/Additions by Thomas P. Jones. Phila: 1840. 392p. + 28 Engraved Plates. Very foxed. Worn full leather. Classic of American technology, emphasizing advances in Flour milling. $ 80.00

1233. Everard, John. **SOME GOSPEL TREASURES**... Christopher Sower, Germantown: 1757. pp. xi, 268, 280. 4to. Contemporary Saur binding. *"Isaac Whitelock's Book, 1758"* + Extensive manuscript Henderson family genealogical records. Evans 7889, Hild. 1525. $ 200.00

1234. Everard, John. **SOME GOSPEL TREASURES**... Second Part. Sower, Germantown: 1757. *Very rare grouping of original signatures (Mm - Yyy), never bound or cut.* Important artifact of Saur's printing history. $ 150.00

1235. Fackenthal, B. F. **WILLIAM PENN & HIS HOME LIFE, At Pennsbury...** (Doylestown): 1932. 33p. + Genealogical Chart. Illus. Wraps. $ 10.00

1236. Fahlman, Betsy. **PENNSYLVANIA MODERN, CHARLES DEMUTH OF LANCASTER.** Phila. Museum of Art: 1983. 74p. Illus. Wraps. Small folio. $ 14.00

1237. Falconer, Wm. **THE SHIPWRECK, & Other Poems.** Walker, Phila: 1836. 142p. + Unusual frontis. Pretty publisher's (?) binding of gilt stamped calf spine with cloth covered boards. 24mo. AI 37373. $ 50.00

1238. Fantel, Hans. **WILLIAM PENN, APOSTLE OF DISSENT.** Morrow, NY: 1974. 298p. + Illus. Cloth. DJ. $ 8.00

1239. Faust, A. B. **THE GERMAN ELEMENT IN THE U.S. With Special Reference to Its Political, Moral, Social, & Educational Influence.** Cambridge, MA: 1909. Two Vols. 1196p. + Illus. Cloth. *WST.* $ 50.00

1240. Farnham, Emily. **CHARLES DEMUTH, BEHIND A LAUGHING MASK.** Univ. of Oklahoma, Norman: 1971. 238p. + Illus. Cloth. DJ. This Lancaster, Pa. artist / personality is finally getting the attention he deserves. $ 40.00

1241. Felldin & Inman. **INDEX TO THE 1800 CENSUS OF PA.** Balt: 1984. 453p. $ 32.00

1242. **THE FEMALE MENTOR; or, Select Conversations.** John Hoff, Phila: 1802. Two volumes in one. pp. 162, 154. Presented a "*Reward of Merit*" to Rebecca Clifford. 18th Century morals & manners. AI 2220. $ 75.00

1243. (Fenelon, Francois de Salignac de la Mothe). **THE ARCHBISHOP OF CAMBRAY'S DISSERTATION ON PURE LOVE... With an Apologetic Preface...** Christophor Sowr, Germantown: 1750. pp. 97, 120. Worn contemporary binding. ***"James Boone's Book, 1751"*** (Related to Daniel Boone?). Evans 6498, Hild. 1174, Seid. p. 36. $ 175.00

1244. (Fessenden, Thomas Green). **THE MODERN PHILOSOPHER; or, Terrible Tractoration!** By Christopher Caustick. Lorenzo Press of E. Bronson, Phila: 1806. 271p. + Engraved frontis. Front board detached. Curious work by Fessenden [1771-1837], an important early American journalist & inventor. Annotated scientific poem. AI 10410. $ 95.00

1245. (Fetterhoff). **THE LIFE OF REV. JOHN FETTERHOFF, One of the Early Fathers of the United Brethren in Christ.** Written by Himself. With an Introduction by W. O. Tobey. Chambersburg: 1883. 284p. + Frontis. $ 35.00

1246. (Files). **SOLWELL FILES (Elwood D. Fisher). DIALECT SELECTIONS AND TRANSLATIONS by Melville J. Boyer.** Lehigh Cty. Hist. Soc. Allentown: 1970. 200p. Warm, humorous, and nostalgic Pennsylvania German stories. $ 24.00

1247. Findley, William. **OBSERVATIONS ON "THE TWO SONS OF OIL", Containing a Vindication of the American Constitutions, & Defending the Blessing of Religious Liberty & Toleration against the Illiberal Strictures of Rev. Samuel B. Wylie.** Pittsburgh: 1812. 366p. Full calf. AI 25424, Howes F 134. The early American fight for true "liberty". $ 75.00

1248. Fisher (Fischer), Henry Lee [1822-1909]. **OLDEN TIMES: Or, Pennsylvania Rural Life, Some Fifty Years Ago, & Other Poems.** York: 1888. 473p. + Numerous woodcut Illustrations of great interest. Crisp copy of Fisher's own translation and enlargement of his most important dialect work. See also Part I, #363-366. *WST.* $ 40.00

1249. Fiske, John. **THE DUTCH & QUAKER COLONIES IN AMERICA.** Bost. & NY: 1899. Two volumes. 694p. + Illus. TEG. Handsome little set. $ 20.00

1250. Fogel, Edwin Miller. **BELIEFS AND SUPERSTITIONS OF THE PENNSYLVANIA GERMANS.** Phila: 1915. 387p. Compilation of folklore & Pow Wow medicine, etc. $ 125.00

1251. Fogel. **SUPPLEMENT TO = Beliefs and Superstitions of the Pa. Germans.** Phila: 1915. pp. 345-357. Printed wraps. Signed by Fogel. Proverbs relating to Sex. Rare. *WST.* $ 40.00

1252. Fothergill, Samuel. **DISCOURSES DELIVERED EXTEMPORE AT SEVERAL MEETING HOUSES OF THE PEOPLE CALLED QUAKERS.** Johnson, Phila: 1800. 275p. Ad leaf torn. Worn full leather. 12mo. Evans 47349. $ 25.00

1253. Fox, John. **BOOK OF MARTYRS.** Edited by Charles A. Goodrich. NY: 1832. 597p. Numerous woodcut plates. Full leather. Ds. $ 25.00

1254. Francis, Rev. J. G. **GENEALOGICAL RECORDS OF THE ROYER FAMILY IN AMERICA... Based on the Original Records of Michael Zug.** Lebanon: 1928. 654p. Very detailed genealogy. *WST.* $ 60.00

BENJAMIN FRANKLIN

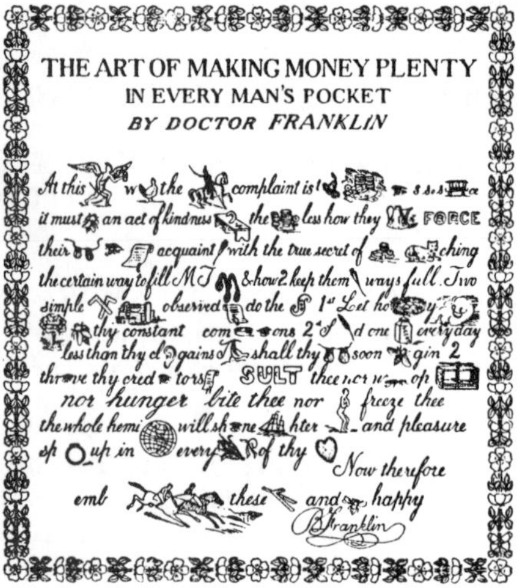

FRANKLIN'S REBUS

1255. Franklin. **ACCOUNT BOOKS Kept by Benjamin Franklin. Ledger "D" 1739-47.** Notes by Geo. Simpson Eddy. NY: 1929. 126p. $ 34.00

1256. Franklin. **APOLOGY FOR A PRINTER.** APS, Phila: 1953. 16p. Limited to only 100 copies. Good humored argument for freedom of the press. $ 22.00

1257. Franklin. **BENJAMIN FRANKLIN, A Biography in His Own Words.** Founding Fathers Series, NY: 1972. Two Vols. Illus. DJ. $ 15.00

1258. Franklin. **BENJAMIN FRANKLIN AND CATHERINE RAY GREENE, 1755-1790. Their Correspondence,** . Wm. Greene Roelker, Editor. APS, Phila: 1949. 147p. DJ. Valuable collection of very personal letters. $ 22.00

1259. Franklin. **BENJAMIN FRANKLIN: His Autobiography; With a Narrative of His Public Life & Services by H. H. Weld.** NY: (1848). 549p. Fine woodcut vignettes by J. G. Chapman. Attractive half-morocco. Owned by J. P. Evans (Lebanon). $ 30.00

1260. Franklin. **CALENDAR OF THE PAPERS OF BENJAMIN FRANKLIN. In the Library of the American Philosophical Society.** Phila: 1908. Five Volumes. Superb Franklin reference, edited by I. Minis Hays. $ 200.00

1261. Franklin. **M. T. CICERO'S CATO MAJOR, or Discourse on Old Age. Addressed to Titus Pomponius Atticus. With Explanatory Notes by Benj. Franklin.** Phila. Printed by B. Franklin. Re-Printed for Fielding & Walker, London: 1778. 163p. + Engraved Frontis of Franklin. The credit for this edition must really go to James Logan. $ 350.00

1262. Franklin. **DR. BENJAMIN FRANKLIN & THE LADIES.** Collected for the Public Delight, Peter Pauper Press, Mt. Vernon, NY: 1939. 69p. Slipcase. Limited to 1450 copies. Letters, Essays, Satires, Etc. on the Fair Sex. $ 24.00

1263. Franklin. **AN HISTORICAL REVIEW OF THE CONSTITUTION AND GOVERNMENT OF PENNSYLVANIA...** London: 1759. 444p. Worn contemporary full leather (American?) binding. An important contribution to the history of Pennsylvania, and a shining document in the tale of Colonial American freedom & liberty. Sabin 25512, Howes P 204aa. $ 250.00

THE INDIAN TREATIES

1264. Franklin. **INDIAN TREATIES PRINTED BY BENJAMIN FRANKLIN, 1736-1762.** With an Introduction by Carl Van Doren & Historical & Bibliographical Notes by Julian P. Boyd. HSP, Phila: 1938. pp. 88, 341 + Ill. Folio. XLib. This important classic was limited to only 500 copies. Very scarce & desirable. $ 250.00

1265. Franklin. **LEDGER OF DR. FRANKLIN AS POSTMASTER GENERAL, 1776.** Facsimile of the original manuscript. Modern reprint of the 1865 edition. Wraps. $ 10.00

1266. Franklin. **LETTER TO A FRIEND ON MARRIAGE.** np. nd. 5p. Wraps. Franklin's advice on the choice of a mistress. $ 10.00

1267. Franklin. **THE LIFE OF DR. BENJAMIN FRANKLIN...** Montpelier, Vt: 1809. 202p. Contemporary full leather. AI 17530. $ 40.00

1268. Franklin. **MEMOIRES DE LA VIE PRIVEE DE BENJAMIN FRANKLIN...** Buisson, Paris: 1791. pp. 156, 360 (of 363) [Lacks last two leaves]. *Uncut. With the Original front wrap present.* Rare First Edition of the greatest American autobiography. $ 225.00

1269. Franklin. **THE OLD MISTRESSES' APOLOGUE.** Rosenbach Foundation, Phila: 1956. 10p. Marbled wraps. Limited to 2000 Copies. $ 20.00

1270. Franklin. **ON THE ART OF EATING; With the Rules of Health, Long Life, Etc....** APS, Phila: 1958. 70p. Wraps. $ 14.00

1271. Franklin. **THE PAPERS OF BENJAMIN FRANKLIN, 1706-1772.** Edited by Labaree, **Bell, Willcox, et. al.** Yale, New Haven: 1959-75. 19 Volumes. Illus. Cloth. DJ. The set is in print at: $ 950.00. We can provide single Vols. 1-23 (1706-1777) at $ 55.00 /vol. A remarkable scholarly undertaking, providing a wealth of information for the student of Franklin as well as Pennsylvania-American Colonial development. $ 400.00

1272. Franklin. **PROPOSALS RELATING TO THE EDUCATION OF YOUTH IN PENNSYLVANIA.** Facsimile Reprint with an Introduction by Wm. Pepper. Phila; 1931. pp. 17, 32. Limited to only 500 copies. $ 25.00

1273. Franklin. **TWO PARABLES ON TOLERANCE & ON BROTHERLY LOVE.** Rose Valley Press, Moylan, Pa: 1951. 18p. Illus. 24mo. Limited to 50 copies. $ 25.00

1274. Franklin. **THE WILL OF BENJAMIN FRANKLIN, 1757.** Introduction by Carl Van Doren. Franklin Institute, Phila: 1949. 16p. + Folding facsimile. Wraps. $ 15.00

"THE BEST HISTORY IN THE WORLD OF A SELF-MADE MAN".

1275. Franklin. **WORKS OF THE LATE DR. BENJAMIN FRANKLIN...** For Robinson, London: 1793. 2 vols. Engraved titles show Franklin in spectacles and coon-skin cap. Worn 1/2 leather bindings. *First Issue of the First Edition in English.* Ford 437. $ 400.00

1276. Franklin. **WORKS OF DR. BENJAMIN FRANKLIN...** NY: 1825. 290p. 18mo. Spine taped. Foxed. AI 20551. $ 20.00

1277. Franklin. **WORKS (MEMOIRS) OF BENJAMIN FRANKLIN...** Continued by his Grandson and others. Phila: 1840. Two Vols. Several important engraved scientific plates. Should be rebound. $ 35.00

1278. Franklin. **VIE DE BENJAMIN FRANKLIN...** Paris: (1798). Two volumes. pp. 382, 438 + Frontis Engraving. Full leather. Rare and important edition $ 200.00

1279. Frederick, J. George. **THE PENNSYLVANIA DUTCH AND THEIR COOKERY.** NY: 1935. 275p. + Ill. DJ. *WST.* $ 22.00

1280. Freed, Theodore F. **HISTORY OF THE VIGILANT FIRE COMPANY NO. 1, YORK, PA.** York: 1955. 44p. Illustrated. Cloth. $ 24.00

1281. Freeman, Melville. **THE CONTRIBUTIONS OF THE GERMANS.** Phila: 1939. 60p. School book on German=American history. $ 10.00

1282. Frey, J. William & H. C. **THE CONESTOGA WAGON. A Pennsylvania Dutch Project.** (Lancaster: 1947). 32p. + Illus. + Promotional inserts. Printed wraps. Excellent. $ 18.00

1283. Frey, Samuel C. **AUTUMN LEAVES.** York: 1921. 212p. Poetry. $ 12.00

1284. **FRIEND'S INTELLIGENCER.** A Quaker Weekly, Edited by an Association of Friends. Phila: 1853-1875. Selected run of over 450 issues in 9 volumes. $ 100.00

1285. Frontier Forts. **REPORT OF THE COMMISSION TO LOCATE THE SITES OF THE FRONTIER FORTS OF PENNSYLVANIA...** Harrisburg: 1896. 2 vols. 1250+p. + Maps + Colored chromolithographs of the forts. Worn 1/2 morocco. AEG. Best guide to Pa. Colonial warfare & frontier defense. $ 120.00

1286. Frontier Forts. **REPORTS OF THE COMMISSION TO LOCATE THE SITES OF THE FRONTIER FORTS...** Harrisburg: 1916. 2 vols. 1250p. + Illus & Maps. Disbound. $ 70.00

1287. Fulton & Mylin. **AN INDEX TO THE WILL BOOKS AND INTESTATE RECORDS OF LANCASTER COUNTY, PA. 1729-1850.** 136p. Wraps. $ 15.00

G

1288. Galenson, David. **WHITE SERVITUDE IN COLONIAL AMERICA.** Cambridge University Press: 1981. 291p. DJ. Important cultural and economic analysis of indentured servants. $ 18.00

1289. Garvan, Beatrice B. **THE PENNSYLVANIA GERMAN COLLECTION, of the Phila. Museum of Art.** Phila: 1982. 372p. Well illustrated. 4to. Paperbound. A definitive reference guide to the Arts of the Pennsylvania Germans. $ 20.00

1290. Garvan & Hummel. **THE PENNSYLVANIA GERMANS. A CELEBRATION OF THEIR ARTS, 1683-1850.** PMA / Winterthur: 1982. 196p. + Plates. Printed wraps. 4to. Excellent catalog of this great exhibition. $ 20.00

1291. **GENEALOGIES OF PENNSYLVANIA FAMILIES.** Articles excerpted from the Pa. Genealogical Magazine. Introduction by Don Yoder. Balt: 1982. 3 Vols. 2894p. $ 150.00

1292. **GENEALOGIES OF PENNSYLVANIA FAMILIES.** Articles excerpted from the *Pennsylvania Magazine of History & Biography*, 1877-1935. Introduction by Milton Rubincam. Balt: 1983. 963p. $ 50.00

1293. Genovesa. **GENEVIEVE, God Does Not Forsake His Own...** Glandorf, OH. Ca: 1910. 64p. Printed Wraps. See Part I, # 400-402 for the German Editions. $ 20.00

1294. Genovesa. **THE THRILLING HISTORY OF GENOVEFA...** Harrisburg, Ca: 1860. 38p. Printed Wraps. This English edition is quite scarce. $ 40.00

1295. Gerberding, G. H. **LIFE & LETTERS OF W. A. PASSAVANT.** Greenville, Pa: 1906. 615p. + Illus. XLib. Pittsburgh Lutheranism in the Mid-West. $ 24.00

1296. **GERMAN = AMERICAN IMPORT CO. KATALOG.** NY: 1925. 80p. Wraps. 4to. German Goods for Germans in the U. S. Scarce but very fragile. $ 20.00

1297. Gernerd, J. M. M. **HEINRICH GERHARDT AND HIS DESCENDANTS...** Williamsport: 1904. 315p. + Illus. Excellent info on Northumberland County. Signed by author. $ 75.00

1298. Gerstell, V. S. **SILVERSMITHS OF LANCASTER COUNTY, PA. 1730=1850.** Lancaster: 1972. 145p. Illus. Excellent reference. $ 20.00

1299. (Getz). **PRECEDENTS FOR THE USE OF JUSTICES OF THE PEACE... Adapted to the Existing Laws of PA...** George Getz, Reading: 1822. 144p. AI 9996. $ 35.00

1300. Geyer, Frank P. **THE HOLMES-PITEZEL CASE. The Greatest Crime of the Century...** (Phila: 1896). 508p. + Illus. The best account of Herman W. Mudgett (Holmes), who was probably America's greatest mass murderer. Signed manuscript presentation from Geyer, the Philadelphia detective who broke the case. McDade 703. $ 50.00

1301. Gibbons, Phebe E. **"PENNSYLVANIA DUTCH" & Other Essays.** Phila: 1872. 207p. + Ads. First Edition. Classic. $ 40.00

1302. Gibbons, Phebe E. **"PENNSYLVANIA DUTCH" & Other Essays.** Phila: 1882. 427p. Cloth. 3rd Edition. *WST.* $ 24.00

1303. Giffin, James E. **WHY DO YOU WEAR IT? Or, The Fashionable Professor.** Lancaster: 1858. 128p. + Ads. 24mo. Spine taped. Important arguments against vanities in clothing = in favor of "Plain Dressing". $ 34.00

1304. Gilbert, R. W. **A PICTURE OF THE PENNSYLVANIA GERMANS.** Gettysburg: 1971. 83p. Illus. Wraps. Good introduction to the topic. $ 6.00

AN EXCEPTIONAL COPY OF PETER'S FAMOUS CHAPBOOK

1305. Gilpin. **JOHN GILPIN'S DIVERTING JOURNEY TO WARE.** G. S. Peters, Harrisburg, Ca: 1840. 18p. Original printed *blue wraps*. Exceptionally well preserved copy of one of the scarcest of Peters' chapbooks. Peters is credited with being America's first commercial color printer. ***This copy might help resolve the speculation about the process he used to color his books = for on the inside rear wrap is a partially printed color block, without the line engraved woodcut.*** We cannot solve the conundrum here, but are very pleased to present this fine evidential copy for further research. In every way, an extraordinary copy. $1200.00

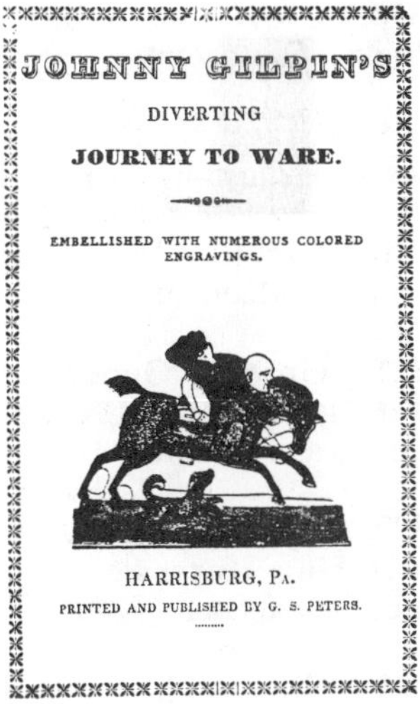

1306. Gingerich, Orland. **THE AMISH OF CANADA.** Scottdale: 1978. 248p. $ 8.00

1307. Glazier, Capt. Willard. **PECULIARITIES OF AMERICAN CITIES.** Phila: 1886. 570p. + Illus. Includes excellent accounts of: Erie, Harrisburg, Lancaster, Pittsburgh, Philadelphia & Reading. This book deserves more attention. $ 30.00

1308. Godcharles, Frederic A. **PENNSYLVANIA = POLITICAL, GOVERNMENTAL, MILITARY, CIVIL & BIOGRAPHICAL.** NY: 1933. Five volumes. 2000+ p. Illus. Special Edition in a morocco cloth gilt binding. Perhaps the most massive and under-utilized general Pennsylvania history. $ 60.00

1309. Good, James I. **THE HEIDELBERG CATECHISM IN ITS NEWEST LIGHT**. Phila: 1914. 301p. Illus. Cloth. $ 14.00

1310. Gordon, Thomas F. **A GAZETTEER OF THE STATE OF PA**. Belknap, Phila: 1832. 508p. + Map. Spine taped. XLib. Early bookseller's label. AI 12695. $ 60.00

1311. **THE GOSHENHOPEN REGISTERS, 1741-1819**. Balt: 1984. 300p. Excellent German Catholic source record. Includes nearly 15000 names in Berks, Lebanon, Lehigh, Northampton, and Montgomery Counties. Excellent genealogical reference. $ 24.00

1312. (Gossner, Johannes). **THE HEART OF MAN, Either a Temple of God, or a Habitation of Satan**... Sage, Reading: 1822. 48p. + 7 (of 10?) Emblematic Engravings. Leather backed marbled boards. AI 8988. English edition of this important German mystical text. $ 35.00

1313. (Gossner). **THE HEART OF MAN, Either a Temple of God, or a Habitation of Satan**... Scheffer, Harrisburg. Ca: 1850. 72p. + 10 Woodcut emblematic plates. Worn. $ 30.00

1314. Gotwald, F. G. **THE TEUTONIC FACTOR IN AMERICAN HISTORY**. (Springfield, Oh: 1902). 26p. Printed wraps. *WST*. $ 14.00

1315. (Gould, Marcus T. C.). **REPORT OF THE TRIAL OF FRIENDS [David Hilles & Isaac Jones] at Steubenville, Ohio**... Harding, Phila: 1829. 340p. Disbound. AI 35006, Sabin 28119. Significant contribution to the history of the Hicksite controversy. $ 35.00

1316. Gould, Mary E. **EARLY AMERICAN WOODEN WARE & Other Kitchen Utensils**. Rutland, Vt: 1962. 243p. Illus. DJ. Excellent reference to "Treenware". $ 30.00

1317. Gould Wm. L. **A LIGHT IN THE VALLEY. History of the Codorus Church of the Brethren**. Loganville, Pa: 1976. 189p. Illus. Dunkard Valley. $ 20.00

1318. **GRACE REFORMED CHURCH HISTORY**. Northampton, Pa: 1912. 66p. + Illus. + Original photograph of the congregation. *WST*. $ 20.00

1319. Graeff, A. D. **INDUSTRIAL BERKS COUNTY, 1748 - 1948**. Reading: 1948. 35p. Charming illustrations by Florence Starr Taylor. Much on the German influence. $ 12.00

1320. Graeff, A. D. **THE PENNSYLVANIA GERMANS**. Keyser, Home Craft Course, Plymouth Meeting: 1945. 32p. Illus. Wraps. Very XLib. $ 6.00

1321. Greene, George Washington. **THE GERMAN ELEMENT IN THE WAR OF AMERICAN INDEPENDENCE**. NY: 1876. 211p. Very XLib. Notable early study of German patriots as well as the "Hessian" mercenaries. $ 24.00

1322. Greenwald, D. S. **OVER SIXTY OF THE MOST VALUABLE CURES Now Known For Doctoring Horses**... Allentown: 1865. 47p. Cloth wraps. 32mo. Very scarce little veterinary manual. *WST*. $ 100.00

1323. Grier, Katherine C. **CELEBRATIONS IN WOOD. The Sculpture of John Scholl [1827-1916]**. Harrisburg: 1980. 24p. Wraps. $ 5.00

1324. Grimm Brothers. **GERMAN POPULAR TALES & HOUSEHOLD STORIES**. Phila: 1869. Two volumes in one. 886p. Illustrations by Wehnert. Worn. $ 14.00

RARE TAXIDERMY & HOME REMEDY BOOK

1325. Gross, Jacob L. **THE ORNITHON: Containing the Art of Stuffing & Preserving Birds, Beasts, Snakes, Fish, Etc. Also, A Collection of Valuable Recipes for Man & Beast...** Getz, Reading: 1859. 101p. Leather backed marbled boards. Curious "scientific" continuation of Hohman, etc. Rare. $ 145.00

THE NATIONAL PENNSYLVANIA "DUTCH" HOLIDAY

1326. Ground Hog Day. **THE "PUMPERNICKEL BILL" GRUNDSOW DAWG (GROUNDHOG DAY) AND GROUND HOG LODGE COLLECTION. 1934 - 1958.** Unique collection of over fifty programs, and related ephemera, written in the Pa. German dialect. Early and ingenious artifacts from the forefront of the wave of national interest in the Pennsylvania Germans. See: Rosenberger, "*The Pennsylvania Germans*". Mainly from Lodges #1 & #2, Lehigh County - but including many other local lodges. Brightly colored and printed, with the original wraps. With another dozen later programs included. Fascinating assembly of dialect pieces and happy imagery responsible for the popularization of "Ground Hog Day". $ 145.00

1327. (Grubb, Sarah). **SOME ACCOUNT OF THE LIFE OF...** Dublin: 1792. 435p. Spine taped. Quaker journal and biography. $ 40.00

1328. Grumbine, Dr. Ezra. **STORIES OF OLD STUMPSTOWN. History of Interesting Events, Traditions, & Anecdotes of Early Fredericksburg.** Lebanon County Historical Soc., Lebanon: 1910. 270p. + Illus. Printed wraps. Fascinating Pa. German local history. $ 25.00

1329. Grumbine, Lee Light [1858-1904]. **DER DENGELSTOCK and Other Poems & Translations in the Pennsylvania German Dialect...** Lebanon: 1903. 155p. + Illus. Crimson cloth gilt. Signed Edition Limited to 300 copies. This scarce work includes his important PGS essay on the dialect. *WST.* $ 50.00

1330. Gurney, Joseph J. **FOUR LECTURES ON THE EVIDENCES OF CHRISTIANITY...** Dorsey for Dobson, Phila: 1840. 194p. + Ad. Publisher's cloth with original paper label. First American edition of this Quaker work. $ 25.00

1331. Gurney. **MEMOIRS OF JOHN JOSEPH GURNEY...** Edited by J. B. Braithwaite. Phila: (1854). 2 Vols. in 1. Actual photo frontis of a painting of Gurney. $ 20.00

1332. Haag, Earl C. **A PENNSYLVANIA GERMAN ANTHOLOGY.** Susquehanna University Press, Selinsgrove: 1988. 352p. Wraps. A new anthology of Pennsylvania "Dutch" literature. $ 20.00

1333. Hacker, H. H. **NAZARETH HALL. Historical Sketch & Roster of Principals, Teachers, and Pupils.** Bethlehem: 1910. 190p. + Illus. $ 24.00

1334. Hain, H. H. **HISTORY OF PERRY COUNTY, PA.** Harrisburg: 1922. 1088p. Illus. Includes valuable descriptions of Indian & pioneer life. $ 130.00

1335. Haldeman, S. S. **PENNSYLVANIA DUTCH: A Dialect of South German with an Infusion of English.** Phila: 1872. 69p. + Ad. One of the more important early studies of the dialect. *WST.* $ 50.00

1336. **THE HANDBOOK OF THE LANGUAGE AND SENTIMENT OF FLOWERS...** Phila: 1847. 60p. + Hand colored frontis. Decorated cloth. 32mo. $ 32.00

1337. Harbaugh, Henry. **ANNALS OF THE HARBAUGH FAMILY IN AMERICA, 1736 - 1856.** Chambersburg: 1856. 148p. 16mo. *WST.* $ 50.00

1338. Harbaugh. **THE GOLDEN CENSOR; Devotions for Young Christians.** Phila. Ca: 1870. 419p. 32mo. Clothbound. *WST.* $ 15.00

1339. (Harbaugh). **THE GUARDIAN: A Monthly Magazine.** Vol. 8. Pearsol & Geist, Lancaster: 1857. 380p. + Sartain engraved frontis. Ds. *Bound in 1/2 leather gilt by Chr. Fried, Reading*; with his label. $ 60.00

1340. Harbaugh. **THE RELIGIOUS CHARACTER OF WASHINGTON. A Tract for the Times.** Chambersburg: 1863. 24p. Plain wraps. $ 20.00

1341. (Harbaugh). **TERCENTENARY MONUMENT. Commemoration of the 300th Anniversary of the Heidelberg Catechism.** Chambersburg: 1863. pp. 73, 574. Embossed cloth. Useful historical information. $ 30.00

1342. Harbaugh, Henry. **UNION WITH THE CHURCH...** Reading: 1908. 83p. $ 12.00

1343. Harbaugh, Linn. **LIFE OF THE REV. HENRY HARBAUGH...** Phila: 1900. 306p. Excellent guide to Harbaugh and his works. *WST.* $ 22.00

1344. Harder, Leland. **THE SOURCES OF SWISS ANABAPTISM.** Scottdale: 1985. 816p. Impressive reference. $ 75.00

1345. Hark, Ann. **BLUE HILLS & SHOOFLY PIE IN PENNSYLVANIA DUTCHLAND.** Phila: 1952. 284p. XLib. Reading copy. $ 6.00

1346. Hark. **HEX MARKS THE SPOT, In the Pa. Dutch Country.** Phila: 1938. 316p. 3rd printing of the 1st ed. Nice dust jacket. $ 20.00

1347. Hark. **THE STORY OF THE PENNSYLVANIA DUTCH.** NY: 1943. Color Lithograph Illustrations by C. H. deWitt. 4to. First Edition. *WST.* $ 24.00

1348. **THE HARMONY SOCIETY IN PENNSYLVANIA.** Federal Writer's Proj. WPA (Beaver County). Phila: 1937. 38p. Printed wraps. $ 28.00

1349. Harms. **PIONEER PUBLISHER: The Life & Times of J. F. Harms.** Scottdale: 1984. 116p. Wraps. Mennonite Brethren Church leader. $ 6.00

1350. Harringer, Russel E. **LONGRIFLES OF PENNSYLVANIA. Jefferson, Clarion, & Elk Counties.** York: 1984. Well Illustrated. $ 40.00

1351. Harry, C. P. **PROTEST AND PROGRESS IN THE SIXTEENTH CENTURY.** Phila: 1917. 162p. Illus. Reformation history for pedagogical use. $ 12.00

1352. Harter, Thomas H. **BOONASTIEL. "PENNSYLVANIA DUTCH".** Middleburgh: 1893. 240p. Illus. First Edition. Probably the first book of prose in the Pennsylvania German dialect. Full of fun and philosophy. *WST.* $ 50.00

1353. Harter. **BOONASTIEL. A VOLUME OF LEGEND, STORY & SONG IN "PENNSYLVANIA DUTCH".** (Bellefonte: 1904). 256p. Expanded Second Ed. $ 28.00

1354. Harter. **BOONASTIEL. PA. DUTCH.** Palmyra, Pa: 1928. 240p. Poor. $ 10.00

1355. Harter. **BOONASTIEL: Being the Fun & Filosophy in the Pennsylvania "Dutch" Letters...** With an Introduction and a Biographical Sketch (of Harter) by A. Monroe Aurand, Jr. Harrisburg: 1942. 253p. *WST.* $ 22.00

1356. Hartman, Peter S. **REMINISCENCES OF THE CIVIL WAR.** Lancaster: 1964. 40p. Wraps. Virginia Mennonites and the Civil War. $ 8.00

1357. Hartzler, J. S. & Kauffman, Dan. **MENNONITE CHURCH HISTORY.** Scottdale, Pa: 1905. 442p. + Illus. Original cloth. $ 28.00

1358. Hauser, James J. **A HISTORY OF LEHIGH COUNTY, PA.** Emmaus, Pa: 1901. 94p. Illus. + Ads. Cloth wraps. *WST.* $ 50.00

1359. Hausman, Ruth L. **SING AND DANCE WITH THE PENNSYLVANIA DUTCH.** Illus. by Frances Lichten. NY: 1953. 112p. 4to. Cloth. XL. $ 15.00

1360. Hawbaker, Gary. **LANCASTER COUNTY QUARTER SESSIONS ABSTRACTS, 1729 - 1742.** (Hershey: 1986). 119p. Wraps. Brief account of criminal conduct; with indexed names of judges, juries and witnesses. Fine historical and genealogical reference. $ 14.00

1361. Hawbaker. **RUNAWAYS, RASCALS, & ROGUES. Missing Spouses, Servants, & Slaves = Abstracted from the Lancaster Journal, 1794 - 1810.** (Hershey: 1987). 136p. Wraps. Very entertaining and informative reference. $ 10.00

1362. Hawbaker & Groff. **A NEW INDEX TO LANCASTER COUNTY (TAX RECORDS, ETC.) BEFORE THE FEDERAL CENSUS.** Vols. 1 - 5 = 1718 - 1780. (Hershey: 1981-89). Five volumes. Wraps. List over 30,000 names. $ 75.00

1363. (Hay, Charles A.). **HISTORY OF THE EVANGELICAL LUTHERAN SYNOD of East Pa. With Brief Sketches of Its Congregations, 1842-92.** 383p. Illus. Spine repaired. $ 30.00

1364. Hayden, A. S. **INTRODUCTION TO SACRED MUSIC...** Pittsburgh: 1838. 120p. Stained & foxed. Binding poor. Shaped note oblong song book. $ 42.00

1365. Hayes, John. **RURAL POEMS...** Press of A. Loudon (Whitehall), Carlisle: 1807. 182p. Worn full leather. AI 12734. Hayes was a professor at Dickinson College. $ 40.00

1366. Hazard, Samuel. **ANNALS OF PENNSYLVANIA, FROM THE DISCOVERY OF THE DELAWARE.** Phila: 1850. 664p. Spine taped. Probably the best single volume documentary history of Pennsylvania. $ 40.00

1367. **HEADS OF THE PEOPLE: Or, Portraits of the English. Drawn by Kenny Meadows. With Original Essays by Distinguished Writers.** Carey & Hart, Phila: 1841. 370p. + 23 Curious & humorous caricatures. Foxed. Offsetting. Original blue cloth gilt. Really unusual. $ 65.00

1368. Heckewelder. **HISTORY, MANNERS, & CUSTOMS OF THE INDIAN NATIONS WHO ONCE INHABITED PENNSYLVANIA & THE NEIGHBOURING STATES.** NY: 1971. Reprint of the HSP, Phila. 1876 edition. Great (Moravian) account of Pa. Indians, edited by William C. Reichel. 465p. Frontis portrait. Cloth. DJ. $ 25.00

1369. Heffner, Geo. B. **THE SYSTEMATIC DICTIONARY.** Siegersville (Lehigh County), Pa: 1876. 125p. 24mo. Printed boards. $ 26.00

1370. Heinecke, Samuel. **GENEALOGY FROM ADAM TO CHRIST. THE GENEALOGY OF ADAM HEINECKE & HENRY VANDERSAAL, 1747=1881...** Lancaster: 1881. 302p. Interesting genealogy, local history, and accounts of travels. $ 48.00

1371. Helman, Miss Laura. **HISTORY & GENEALOGY OF THE DREISBACH FAMILY.** Allentown: 1924. 48p. + Illus. Printed wraps. $ 18.00

1372. Hensel, W. U. **JACOB EICHHOLZ...** Lancaster: 1912. 38p. + Illus. XLib. Includes a catalog of Eichholz's works. $ 20.00

1373. Herr, John . **THE ILLUSTRATING MIRROR...** Lancaster: 1858. 360p. 16mo. Full leather. Herr [1782-1850] was the founder of the Reformed Mennonite Church. $ 32.00

1374. Herr. **JOHN HERR'S COMPLETE WORKS...** Buffalo, NY: 1890. 520p. Full leather needs repairs. Weaver family ownership. Scarce First Edition of Herr's Collected Works, and includes his autobiography. $ 55.00

1375. Herr. **THE TRUE & BLESSED WAY...** Wm. Green, Harrisburg: 1816. 315p. Worn. Disbound. Scarce Mennonite work. $ 50.00

1376. Hering, Constantin. **DOMESTIC PHYSICIAN...** The Part Relating to the Diseases of Females & Children by Walter Williamson. Phila: 1848. 415p. + Ads. Original half leather gilt. 16mo. The 4th American Edition of this Homoeopathic classic. $ 65.00

1377. Hertzler, Silas. **THE HERTZLER - HARTZLER FAMILY HISTORY.** Reprint Edition: 1989. 773p. Important Amish / Mennonite genealogy. $ 45.00

1378. Hess, Asher L. **GENEALOGICAL RECORD OF THE DESCENDANTS OF NICHOLAS HESS...** (Allentown: 1912). 332p. Illus. Historical and biographical sketches. $ 75.00

1379. Hess, Mrs. J. W. **"AS CLAY IN THE POTTER'S HANDS".** Lancaster: 1955. 71p. + Frontis. Mennonite missionary memoirs. $ 8.00

1380. Hetrick, Calvin. **THE BEDFORD COUNTY RIFLE & ITS MAKERS.** York: 1975. 41p. Well illustrated. Wraps. $ 10.00

1381. Hicks. **JOURNAL OF THE LIFE & RELIGIOUS LABOURS OF ELIAS HICKS.** NY: 1832. 451p. Disbound. Travels & controversies of a NY Quaker. $ 32.00

1382. Hildeburn, Chas. R. **A CENTURY OF PRINTING. THE ISSUES OF THE PRESS OF PENNSYLVANIA, 1685 - 1784.** NY: 1968. Two Volumes. Reprint of the rare 1st Edition. An essential reference. $ 50.00

1383. Hinke, William J. **HISTORY OF THE TOHICKON UNION CHURCH.** Meadville: 1925. 483p. + Illus. *"Autograph Edition". Limited to only 200 copies, signed twice by Hinke.* For the PGS issue, please see # 2032. Important genealogical information. $ 70.00

1384. Hinks, Don. **BRETHREN HYMN BOOKS & HYMNALS, 1720-1884.** Gettysburg: 1986. 205p. Illus. Oblong 4to. Useful bibliographical study. $ 30.00

1385. **HISTORY OF THE EVANGELICAL LUTHERAN SYNOD OF EAST PENNSYLVANIA.** Phila: (1892). 383p. Illus. Lovely decorated cloth gilt. *WST*. Excellent study of the earliest American Lutheran Congregations. $ 40.00

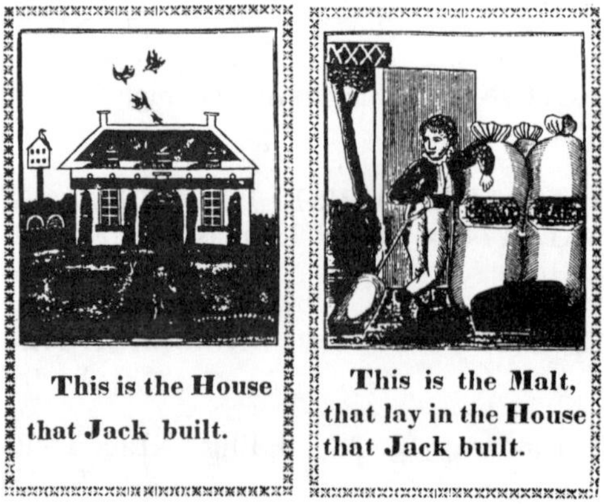

CHARMING PETERS JUVENILE

1386. **THE HISTORY OF THE HOUSE THAT JACK BUILT.** G. S. Peters, Harrisburg, Ca: 1840. 18p. Great color printed illustrations. Orange printed wraps. Ds. It is easy to see why this chapbook was so popular, even though our illustration does not do it much justice. $ 550.00

1387. **THE HISTORY OF PHILIP QUARLL, WHO LIVED THIRTY YEARS ON AN UNINHABITED ISLAND**. Bennett & Walton, Phila: 1814. 108p. Original printed paper boards, with publisher's ad. *Apparently not in AI, Welch, etc.* Rare. $ 200.00

1388. Hocker, Edward W. **GENEALOGICAL DATA RELATING TO THE GERMAN SETTLERS OF PA. & ADJACENT TERRITORY. From Ads in German Newspapers Published in Philadelphia & Germantown, 1743=1800**. Balt: 1989. 242p. Indexed. $ 22.00

1389. Hoffman, Benneville Ottomar. **SNARL OF A CYNIC: A Rhyme by a Pennsylvania Teuton**. Heitler, Ephrata: 1868. 40p. Printed yellow boards. 24mo. Remarkable. $ 32.00

1390. Hohman, John George. **THE LONG LOST FRIEND. Faithful & Christian Instructions Containing Wondrous and Well-Tried Arts & Remedies for Man as well as Animals...** Harrisburg: 1850. 72p. The standard English edition of the great "Pow Wow Book". $ 160.00

1391. Hohman. **POW - WOW'S, Or Long Lost Friend. A Collection of Mysterious & Invaluable Arts & Remedies For Man As Well As Animals...** Ca: 1965. 95p. Wraps. $ 5.00

1392. (Hohman). **THE SIXTH & SEVENTH BOOKS OF MOSES. The Mystery of All Mysteries...** Chicago: 1919. 190p. Handsomely Clothbound. $ 80.00

1393. (Hohman). **THE SIXTH & SEVENTH BOOKS OF MOSES. Moses' Magical Spirit-Art.** (Chicago: 1920)? 190p. Clothbound. Fundamental Pow-Wow text. $ 60.00

1394. Hoke, Elizabeth S. **THE PAINTED TRAY AND FREE HAND BRONZING.** Home Craft Course. (Keyser, Kutztown: 1949). 40p. Illus. Wraps. $ 9.00

1395. Hoke. **PENNSYLVANIA GERMAN PAINTED TIN (TOLE WARE).** Home Craft Course. (Keyser, Plymouth Meeting: 1945). 32p. Illus. Wraps. $ 9.00

1396. Holben, Evan. **STORIES & REMINISCENCES.** Vol. I (All Published). Allentown: 1902. 160p. Wraps. Little known humorous memoirs of the Pennsylvania Germans, and others, in Lehigh County, Pa. *WST*. $ 24.00

1397. Holdeman, John. **HISTORY OF THE CHURCH OF GOD...** Lancaster: 1876. 303p. Worn printed wraps. Holdeman [1832-1900], was the controversial founder of the Church of God in Christ, Mennonite. $ 50.00

1398. (Holford, Geo. P.) [1768-1839]. **THE DESTRUCTION OF JERUSALEM, An Absolute & Irresistible Proof of the Divine Origin of Christianity...** Rakestraw for Sharpless, Phila: 1809. 144p. Full leather. AI 17765. $ 32.00

1399. (Hollenbach, Ray E.). **CHURCH RECORD OF KEELOR'S REFORMED CHURCH & Lutheran Church Cemetery (1833-1913), Upper Frederick Twp. Montgomery County, PA.** Library bound photo-copy of this important translation. Irreplaceable record. $ 40.00

1400. Holm, Thomas Campanius. **DESCRIPTION OF THE PROVINCE OF NEW SWEDEN... Pennsylvania, in America.** With Notes by Peter S. Du Ponceau. Reprint of the scarce 1834 edition. 166p. + Illus. The best edition of this significant account. $ 18.00

1401. Hoover, Amos B. **THE JONAS MARTIN ERA, 1875=1925.** Denver, Pa: 1982. 1128p. Thick 4to. Includes a fine Amish / Mennonite bibliography. $ 50.00

1402. Hoover, Francis T. **ENEMIES IN THE REAR; Or, A Golden Circle Squared. A Story of Southeastern Pennsylvania in the Time of Our Civil War.** Boston: 1895. 604p. An extraordinary, and now very rare work. *WST.* $ 225.00

1403. Hommel, Rudolf. **ON THE TRAIL OF THE FIRST CHRISTMAS TREE.** Richlandtown, Pa: 1947. 10p. Illus. Wraps. *WST.* $ 14.00

1404. Horn, A. P. **PROCEEDINGS OF THE RE-UNION OF APPLE'S CHURCH AND OF THE BOEHM FAMILY.** Hellertown, Pa: 1902. 154p. + Illus. Printed wraps. Important historical genealogy. $ 40.00

1405. Horne, Dr. Abraham Reeser [1834 - 1902]. **HORNE'S PENNSYLVANIA GERMAN MANUAL.** Kutztown: 1875/6. 171p. + Ads. Illus. Printed paper boards. First Edition. Though intended, in some part, for the English education of children who speak the Pennsylvania German tongue; it has long been the standard text for those seeking mastery of the dialect. $ 60.00

1406. Horne. **PENNSYLVANIA GERMAN MANUAL.** Allentown: 1896. 415p. Illus. This much expanded 2nd edition of "Horne's Manual" includes a large Allentown Business Directory + Maps + Ads for books in the dialect. *WST.* $ 50.00

1407. Horne. **HORNE'S PENNSYLVANIA GERMAN MANUAL.** Allentown: 1905. 338p. + Ads. Illus. *WST.* $ 29.00

1408. Horsch, John. **THE HUTTERIAN BRETHREN, 1528-1931.** Scottdale. Reprinted from the 1931 edition. 189p. $ 14.00

1409. Horsch, John. **MENNONITES IN EUROPE.** Scottdale: (1950). 414p. Illus. $ 20.00

1410. Horst, S. L. **MENNONITES IN THE CONFEDERACY.** Scottdale: 1967. $ 12.00

1411. Horst, Irvin B. **THE RADICAL BRETHREN.** Scottdale: 1972. 216p. Definitive account of Anabaptism 1530 - 1558. $ 50.00

1412. Hostetler, B. S. **AMERICAN MENNONITES & PROTESTANT MOVEMENTS.** Scottdale: 1987. 384p. $ 30.00

1413. Hostetler, John A. **AMISH LIFE.** Scottdale: 1983. 48p. New expanded edition of this popular illustrated classic. Wraps. $ 5.00

1414. Hostetler. **AMISH SOCIETY.** Baltimore: 1981. 416p. Illus. Wraps. 3rd Ed. $ 12.00

1415. Hostetler. **ANNOTATED BIBLIOGRAPHY OF THE AMISH.** Scottdale: 1951. 100p. Wraps. Still useful. $ 16.00

1416. Hostetler. **GOD USES INK. The Heritage & Mission of the Mennonite Publishing House After Fifty Years.** Scottdale: 1958. 264p. Illus. DJ. Includes a list of all publications with their press runs. $ 22.00

1417. Hostetler. **HUTTERITE LIFE.** Scottdale: 1983. 48p. Wraps. $ 6.00

1418. Hostetler. **MENNONITE LIFE.** Scottdale: 1983. 48p. Wraps. $ 6.00

1419. Hotchkin, Samuel F. **THE YORK ROAD, OLD AND NEW.** Philadelphia: 1892. 516p. + Illus. Spine taped. Scarce and informative developmental history. $ 100.00

1420. Hottinger, J. J. **THE LIFE & TIMES OF ULRIC ZWINGLI.** Harrisburg: 1857. 421p. + Color Map. Translated from the German by F & M Professor T. C. Porter. $ 20.00

1421. Hueg, Herman. **ORNAMENTAL CONFECTIONERY & Practical Assistant to the Art of Baking... Text in English & German.** NY: 1893. 144p. + Decorative illustrations and Advertisements. The best of Continental baking skills for the American household. $ 75.00

1422. **HULL'S JAHR: A New Manual Homoeopathic Practice...** Edited by Frederick G. Snelling. NY: 1862. 804p. Disbound. $ 50.00

1423. Hulsbuck, Solly (Harvey M. Miller). **A COLLECTION OF PENNSYLVANIA DUTCH POEMS.** (Elizabethville, Pa: 1906). 96p. Illus. Satire excellently presented in dialect. *WST.* See also Part I, # 529. $ 50.00

1424. Hulsbuck. **PENNSYLVANIA GERMAN POEMS.** (Elizabethville, Pa: 1906). 116p. Nicely printed. Expanded 2nd Ed. of the above. *WST.* $ 45.00

1425. Hulsbuck. **PENNSYLVANIA GERMAN STORIES.** Elizabethville, Pa: 1907. 112p. Illus. Dialect humor at its best. *WST.* $ 50.00

1426. **HUMPHREY'S HOMOEOPATHIC MENTOR...** NY: 1886. 508p. + Illus & Ads. Blue cloth gilt. Standard, and still popular text. $ 30.00

1427. Hunt, Rachel M. **WILLIAM PENN, HORTICULTURALIST.** Pittsburgh: 1953. 38p. + Ill. Signed by author. Limited edition. $ 20.00

1428. Hunter, A. **GEORGICAL ESSAYS:.** York: 1777. 430p. + Folding engraved floral plates. Vol. I (All published?). Disbound. Botanical and Agricultural essays. *Owned and signed by William Temple Franklin (1786), the favored grandson of Benjamin Franklin.* $ 300.00

1429. Hunter, Henry. **SACRED BIOGRAPHY...** Phila: 1839. 596p. + Illus. Ds. Handsome & unusual contemporary mottled roan binding. AI 56415. $ 29.00

1430. **INDEX TO THE JOURNAL OF THE CONVENTION WHO FRAMED THE PRESENT CONSTITUTION... With a Concise Index to the Constitution Itself.** Bound With / **Indexes to the Journal(s) of the 1st -13th House of Representatives of the Commonwealth of PA.** Bioren, Phila: 1808. Fourteen volumes in one. Most not in AI, though see: 15873-4. Contemporary full leather. *Governor Snyder's Copy.* $ 120.00

1431. **THE INGLENOOK COOK BOOK.** Reprint of the 1901 1st Edition. Elgin: 1981. 212p. + Ads. Paperback. Interesting reading. Still a useful cookbook. $ 4.00

1432. **INSTRUCTION IN THE PRINCIPLES & DUTIES OF THE CHRISTIAN RELIGION, For Children & Youth...** Zentler for Daniel Braeutigam, Phila: 1821. 108p. Leather backed boards. *Apparently not in AI.* $ 30.00

1433. Irish, Donna R. **PENNSYLVANIA GERMAN MARRIAGES...** Balt: 1982. 817p. Indexed. Based on the records of about 100 churches, this work provides data on nearly 50000 persons of German descent. $ 50.00

GREAT CLASSIC OF OVERLAND TRAVEL

1434. (Irving, Washington). **ASTORIA, or Anecdotes of an Enterprise Beyond the Rock Mountains.** Phila: 1836. Two Volumes. pp. 285, 279 + Fine folding map + Ads. 1" trimmed from Tp. 1/2 Morocco. 1st Edition, 1st State. See: BAL 10148, AI 38219, Sabin 35130, Howes I81, Graff 2158, Wagner-Camp 61, Wheat (Transmississippi) 419, Bradford 2623, Streeter 3347, Etc. The earliest extended accounts of John Jacob Astor's settlement on the Columbia River (the basis for American claims to Oregon and Washington), and of Hunt's overland expedition from St. Louis to that settlement. $ 350.00

J

1435. Jahr. **G. H. G. JAHR'S MANUAL OF HOMOEOPATHIC MEDICINE.** Translated From the German. With an Introduction and Additions by C. Herring. Allentown, Pa: 1838. 600p. Some old page repairs. *Apparently Not in AI.* Scarce and important early work issued by authority of the "North American Academy of the Homoeopathic Healing Art. *WST.* $ 150.00

1436. **JAHR'S NEW MANUAL, of Homoeopathic Practice. Symptomatology**. Edited with Annotations by A. Gerald Hull. Radde, NY: 1851. 1025p. + Ad printed on yellow paper for Smith's Homoeopathic Pharmacy. Nice half leather gilt. $ 100.00

1437. James, Dr. Arthur E. **POTTERS AND POTTERIES OF CHESTER COUNTY, PA.** West Chester. 208p. 84 Illustrations. $ 20.00

1438. Janney, Samuel M. **AN ESSAY ON THE TRUE GROUNDS OF RELIGIOUS UNION, Addressed to All who Profess the Principles of Friends**. Phila: 1856. 22p. Original printed wraps in fine condition. $ 22.00

1439. Janney. **MEMOIRS OF SAMUEL M. JANNEY...** Phila: 1881. 309p. + Engraved frontis. Includes much on the Virginia Quakers. $ 22.00

1440. Janney. **THE LIFE OF WILLIAM PENN...** Phila: 1852. 576p. + Illus. Disbd. $ 20.00

1441. Jenkins, Charles Francis. **JEFFERSON'S GERMANTOWN LETTERS.** Campbell, Phila: 1906. pp. 24, 194, + Index + Frontis + excellent photogravure illus. TEG. Uncut. Limited edition of only 500 copies, initialed by Campbell. $ 40.00

1442. Jenkins. **WASHINGTON IN GERMANTOWN. An Account of the Various Visits of the Commander-in-Chief & First President to Germantown, Pa**. Phila: 1905. pp. 16, 318 + Over 20 fine photogravures. TEG. Uncut. Limited to 500 copies. $ 50.00

1443. Jess, Zachariah. **THE AMERICAN TUTOR'S ASSISTANT IMPROVED...** M'Carty & Davis, Phila: 1818. 188p. + "A Course in Book-Keeping". Leather backed marbled boards. ***This imprint not in AI***, though see: 44466. *HSH.* $ 30.00

1445. Jess. **THE AMERICAN TUTOR'S ASSISTANT IMPROVED...** M'Carty & Davis, Phila: 1819. Full Leather. AI 48375 *[1 copy only]*. *HSH.* $ 30.00

1446. Jess. **THE AMERICAN TUTOR'S ASSISTANT IMPROVED...** M'Carty & Davis, Phila: 1821. Worn full leather. $ 20.00

1447. Johnson, Amandus. **THE INSTRUCTION FOR JOHAN PRINTZ, Governor of New Sweden; "The First Constitution, or Supreme Law, of the States of Pennsylvania and Delaware.** Phila: 1930. 303p. + Illus. XLib. $ 40.00

1448. Johnson. **JOURNAL & BIOGRAPHY OF NICHOLAS COLLIN, 1746-1831**. Phila: 1936. 368p. + Illus. The last Swedish pastor of Gloria Dei (Old Swedes) Church. $ 40.00

1449. Jordan, John W. **COLONIAL & REVOLUTIONARY FAMILIES OF PENNSYLVANIA.** Balt: 1978. Three Vols. 1700+p. Reprint of the 1911 edition. $ 100.00

1450. Jordan, Mildred. **APPLE IN THE ATTIC. A Pennsylvania Legend**. NY: 1942. 200p. DJ. Decorated cloth. Signed by Miss Jordan for *WST*. Fine Pa. "Dutch" story. $ 22.00

1451. Jordan. **THE SHOO-FLY PIE**. NY: 1944. 118p. Illus. by Henry C. Pitz. DJ. $ 30.00

1452. (Jordan, Richard). **A JOURNAL OF RICHARD JORDAN...** Kite, Phila: 1829. 172p. Bound in contemporary plain cloth. AI 39164. American Quaker travel journal. $ 32.00

K

1453. (Kaminkow, Marion J.). **GENEALOGIES IN THE LIBRARY OF CONGRESS.** Bibliography, Supplements, & Complements. Balt: 1972-87. Four Volumes. Over 3800p. Lists almost 50,000 genealogies and family histories. The comprehensive genealogical bibliography. $ 400.00

1454. Kastrup, Allan. **THE SWEDISH HERITAGE IN AMERICA.** Np: 1975. 863p. + Illus. DJ. Weighty, but readable, international study. $ 25.00

1455. Kauffman, Daniel, et. al. **MENNONITE CYCLOPEDIC DICTIONARY...** Scottdale: 1937. 443p. + Space for notes. DJ. Useful for every Mennonite Library. $ 36.00

1456. Kauffman, Henry J. **EARLY AMERICAN GUNSMITHS. 1650-1850.** NY: 1952. 94p. + Illus. Cloth. DJ. $ 35.00

1457. Kauffman. **PENNSYLVANIA DUTCH AMERICAN FOLK ART.** NY: (1964). 146p. Well illus. Wraps. Sm. 4to. Revised & enlarged edition. $ 10.00

1458. Kauffman. **PENNSYLVANIA GERMAN PEWTER.** Home Craft Course. Keyser, Plymouth Meeting: 1944. 44p. Illus. Wraps. $ 10.00

1459. Kauffman. **THE PENNSYLVANIA=KENTUCKY RIFLE.** Harrisburg: (1960). 376p. Well illustrated. The best edition of this standard and popular reference. $ 40.00

1460. Keith, Charles P. **CHRONICLES OF PENNSYLVANIA, 1688-1748.** Phila: 1917. 2 Vols. 981p. Important details of the early German emigration. $ 40.00

1461. Kemmerer. **TWO CENTURIES OF KEMMERER FAMILY HISTORY, 1730-1929.** Allentown: 1929. 152p. + Illus. *WST.* $ 40.00

1462. Kemp, Alvin F. **PENNSYLVANIA DUTCH STORIES.** F&M, Lancaster: 1952. 24p. Wraps. Humorous stories in the dialect. Signed for *WST.* $ 20.00

1463. Kercheval, Samuel. **A HISTORY OF THE VALLEY OF VIRGINIA.** John Gatewood, Woodstock, VA: 1850. 347p. Contemporary full leather. Scarce account of the early Indian wars and the customs of early settlers. $ 150.00

1464. Kersey, Jesse. **A NARRATIVE OF THE EARLY LIFE AND TRAVELS OF JESSE KERSEY...** Phila: 1851. 288p. Disbd. $ 20.00

1465. Kersey. **A TREATISE ON FUNDAMENTAL DOCTRINES OF THE CHRISTIAN RELIGION, In Which Are Illustrated the Profession, Ministry, Worship, & Faith of the Society of Friends.** Joseph Painter, West Chester: 1842. 120p. 24mo. Front board detached. $ 22.00

1466. Keyser, Mrs. C. Naaman. **METHOD OF MAKING PENNSYLVANIA GERMAN DESIGN.** Home Craft Course. Plymouth Meeting: 1943. 36p. Illus. Printed wraps. $ 10.00

1467. Keyser. **POTTERY.** Home Craft Course. 1943. 40p. Illus. $ 10.00

1468. Kichline, T. J. **THE KICHLINES IN AMERICA.** Easton: 1926. 29p. Wraps. $ 14.00

1469. Kieffer, Aldine S. **THE NEW STARY CROWN // THE SHINING LIGHT // LAST WORDS...** Sabbath School Song Books. Dayton, Rockingham County, Va: 1886. 464p. Small oblong song book. A late survivor of the shaped note tradition. $ 36.00

1470. Kieffer, E. C. **HENRY HARBAUGH IN LANCASTER.** Lancaster County Historical Soc: 1941. pp. 57-83. $ 10.00

1471. Kindig, Joe Jr. **THOUGHTS ON THE KENTUCKY RIFLE IN ITS GOLDEN AGE.** York & Wilmington: 1960. 561p. Highly illustrated. DJ. Scarce First Edition of this great classic which treats the flintlock as a work of art. $ 150.00

1472. Kindig. **THOUGHTS ON THE KENTUCKY RIFLE IN ITS GOLDEN AGE.** York: 1983. 561p. Highly illus. Annotated 2nd Edition. $ 80.00

1473. Kindig, Paul E. **BUTTER PRINTS & MOLDS.** West Chester. 248p. Over 800 molds are illustrated. Folio. $ 50.00

1474. King, Wilbur L. **KNAUSS GENEALOGY. Lukas Knauss [1633-1713] & His American Descendants.** Bethlehem: 1930. 239p. + Illus. *WST.* $ 48.00

1475. Kingston, W. H. G. **TRUE HERO; The Story of William Penn.** London. Ca: 1870. 174p. Illus. Spine taped. $ 10.00

1476. Kipping, Ernst. **THE HESSIAN VIEW OF AMERICA, 1776=1783.** Monmouth Beach, NJ: 1971. 48p. Thin 4to. Attractive and informative. $ 32.00

1477. Klees, Fredric. **THE PENNSYLVANIA DUTCH.** NY: 1951. 451p. $ 25.00

1478. Kleppinger, S. J. **KLEPPINGER-CLIPPINGER FAMILY HISTORY.** Bethlehem: 1928. 209p. *WST.* $ 50.00

1479. Klinefelter, Walter. **THE GUNSMITHS OF YORK COUNTY, PA.** Author's offprint from PGS Vol. 14. 1980. 50p. Wraps. Excellent study. $ 12.00

1480. Klinefelter. **YORK'S LIBERTY BELL.** Sumac Press, La Crosse, Wisc: 1975. 13p. Illus. Wraps. Limited to only 300 copies. $ 14.00

1481. Knauss, O. P. **HISTORY OF MACUNGIE (MILLERSTOWN), PA.** Macungie: 1932. 46p. Double Column. Printed wraps. *WST.* $ 30.00

1482. Knauss. **HISTORY & GENEALOGY OF THE KNAUSS FAMILY IN AMERICA...** Emmaus, Pa: 1915. 242p. + Illus. *WST.* $ 50.00

1483. Knauss. **SOME WRITINGS & FAVORITE CLIPPINGS.** Macungie, Pa: 1939. 47p. Printed wraps. 24mo. Includes a few dialect pieces. $ 22.00

1484. Knepper, B. **SATAN BOUND, or Resurrection, Judgment and the Happiness of the Future World Considered.** Kiefer & Co's. Caloric Printing Press, Chambersburg: 1860. 72p. Leather backed cloth. Crisp copy. Very scarce Millennial text by this German Reformed pastor from Wellersburg, Pa. $ 40.00

1485. Knittle, Walter Allen. **EARLY 18TH CENTURY PALATINE EMIGRATION. A British Government Redemptioner Project to Manufacture Naval Stores.** Phila: 1937. 320p. Illus. First Edition. Signed by Knittle for *WST.* Attractive copy. $ 50.00

1486. Kohl, John Y. **CHRISTMAS COOKIES. A Controversy.** Lehigh Cty. Hist. Soc. Vol. 22, Allentown: 1958. pp. 77-96. New wraps. $ 13.00

1487. Kohler, E. Xenophon. **REAL HAPPINESS, Its Nature & Sources Described & Mistakes Concerning it Corrected.** Harlacher & Weiser, Allentown: 1873. 128p. 24mo. Kohler was from Egypt, Lehigh County, Pa. *WST.* $ 28.00

1488. Kollmorgen, Walter M. **CULTURE OF A CONTEMPORARY RURAL COMMUNITY, The Old Order Amish of Lancaster County, Pa.** Washington: 1942. 105p. + Illus. $ 24.00

1489. Koogle, J. D. **THE FARMER'S OWN BOOK...** Middletown, Md: 1858. pp. 224, 37 + Indexes. Worn. 24mo. Natural and herbal recipes for the treatment of horses, cattle, and men; as well as formulae for trades, etc. $ 30.00

1490. **KOONS' ILLUSTRATED HISTORY OF THE LEHIGH VALLEY.** Catasauqua: (1885). 80p. Illus. Many charming advertisements. Embossed cloth. 4to. *WST.* $ 75.00

1491. (Koons, U. S.) **A TALE OF THE KLOSTER. A Romance of the German Mystics of the Cocalico.** By Brother Jabez. Phila: 1904. 336p. + Ill. Decorated cloth. A very readable and detailed contribution to understanding life at the Ephrata Cloister. $ 40.00

1492. Korson, George. **BLACK ROCK. MINING FOLK LORE OF THE PENNSYLVANIA DUTCH.** PGS, (Balt: 1960). 453p. Illus. DJ. Cloth. Same as PGS Vol. 59. $ 40.00

1493. Korson. **MINSTRELS OF THE MINE PATCH. SONGS AND STORIES OF THE ANTHRACITE INDUSTRY.** Phila: 1938. 332p. DJ. Presented by Korson to *WST.* $ 45.00

1494. (Korson). **PENNSYLVANIA FOLK SONGS AND BALLADS, For School, Camp & Playground.** Pa. Folk Festival, Lewisburg: 1937. 14p. 4to. Self wraps. *WST.* $ 4.00

1495. Kriebel, H. W. **THE SCHWENKFELDERS IN PENNSYLVANIA...** Lancaster: 1904. 246p. + Illus. Author's offprint from PGS Vol. 13. *WST.* Foundation study. $ 80.00

1496. Kriebel. **SEEING LANCASTER COUNTY FROM A TROLLEY WINDOW.** Express Printing Co., Lititz, Pa: 1910. 96p. With Ads. Illus. Printed wraps. Great guide to the early history and sights of Lancaster County. $ 38.00

1497. Kriebel, Heydrick, et. al. **GENEALOGICAL RECORD OF THE SCHWENKFELDERS...** From the German of Balthasar Heebner. Manayunk: 1879. 339p. *WST.* $ 100.00

1498. Kuhns, Oscar. **THE GERMAN AND SWISS SETTLEMENTS OF COLONIAL PA. A Study of the So-Called Pennsylvania Dutch.** NY: 1914. 268p. Useful early monographs on the emigration to and settlement of Pa. XLib. $ 24.00

1499. **THE KUNTZ FAMILY.** Northampton, Pa: 1931. 12p. 24mo. $ 16.00

1500. Lambert, M. B. **A DICTIONARY OF THE NON-ENGLISH WORDS OF THE PENNSYLVANIA-GERMAN DIALECT, With an Appendix.** PGS, Lancaster: 1924. 193p. + Inserts. "Pumpernickle Bill's" own copy. Later cloth. *WST.* See also PGS Vol. 30. $ 40.00

1501. Lambert. **PENNSYLVANIA-GERMAN DICTIONARY.** Reprint of 1924 Edition, with a New Introduction by Dr. Willard Martin. Exton: 1977. pp. 34, 187. $ 20.00

1502. Landis, David Bachman. **LANCASTER LYRICS. A Cheerful Volume of Popular Poems.** Printed by Landis at the "Pluck Art Printery", Lancaster: 1914. 313p. Illustrated with fine Lancaster County photos. Lovely crimson cloth gilt. Signed by Landis. Includes some Pennsylvania German Dialect poems. *WST.* $ 40.00

1503. Landis, Ira D. **THE LANCASTER MENNONITE CONFERENCE = History & Background.** Lancaster: 1956. 114p. Illus. Wraps. Useful little history. $ 10.00

1504. Landis. **THE MISSIONARY MOVEMENT AMONG THE LANCASTER CONFERENCE MENNONITES.** Scottdale: 1937. 119p. Illus. Wraps. $ 14.00

1505. Landis Valley Assoc. **PENNSYLVANIA GERMAN FRAKTUR & COLOR DRAWINGS.** Lancaster: 1969. 72p. Well illustrated. 4to. Wraps. $ 25.00

1506. (Lapp, Henry). **A CRAFTSMAN'S HANDBOOK = Henry Lapp.** Phila: 1975. 90p. Color plates with notes by Beatrice B. Garvan. Reproduction of a 19th century Pennsylvania German furniture maker's "handbook". $ 25.00

ONE OF THE EARLIEST USES OF THE INSANITY DEFENSE

1507. (Laros). **THE LAROS MURDER. A Whole Family Poisoned by an Ungrateful Son...** Easton: 1876. 36p. + Illus. Printed wraps chipped. With some German language text. McDade #584. Allen C. Laros was a 22 year old school teacher, who put 2000 grains of arsenic in the family coffee pot - killing his parents and a hired hand. A defense of insanity did not convince the jury. $ 95.00

1508. Lasansky, Jeannette. **CENTRAL PA. REDWARE POTTERY, 1780-1904.** Phila: 1989. 60p. 82 Illus. 4to. Wraps. $ 15.00

1509. Latrobe, C. I. **CONCISE ACCOUNT OF THE PRESENT STATE OF THE MISSIONS OF THE UNITED BRETHREN / MORAVIANS.** (London: 1801). 16p. New wraps. $ 26.00

1510. Laury, Preston A. **A HISTORY OF LUTHERAN MISSIONS.** Reading: 1899. 266p. Fine historical record and cultural study. $ 25.00

1511. Laury. **THE HISTORY OF THE ALLENTOWN CONFERENCE of the Ministerium of Pa.** Kutztown: 1926. 387p. Illus. 4to. *WST.* $ 25.00

1512. Laux, James B. **COLONEL STEPHEN BALLIET. Soldier, Patriot, & Statesman of the Revolution = Ancestry, Youth & Education.** Lehigh Cty. Hist. Soc., Allentown: 1918. 24p. Wraps. *WST.* $ 12.00

THE PHRENOLOGIST'S POCKET GUIDE

1513. (Lavater). **THE POCKET LAVATER, Or the Science of Physiognomy...** John Perry, Phila: 1841. 116p. + *44 Stipple Engraved Plates.* 24mo. Cloth. Extraordinary little edition of this phrenology classic. $ 150.00

1514. **LEBANON COUNTY HISTORICAL SOCIETY, Papers and Addresses.** Vols. I - IV. Lebanon & Annville: 1898-1909. 4 Vols. Over 1600p. Augmented by the addition of several scarce pamphlets. Uniform 1/2 morocco bindings signed by local artisans. Dr. Ezra Grumbine's set. Superlative collection of historical papers and essays. Important. *WST.* $ 150.00

SENSATIONAL LANCASTER MURDER CASE

1515. (Lechler). **TRIAL OF JOHN LECHLER...** Reported by Daniel Fuller. Maxwell, Lancaster: 1822. 64p. Wraps. Cockholded by his friend Haag, Lechler strangled his unfaithful wife & shot (by accident) Mrs. Haag. McDade 593, AI 10478. $ 110.00

1516. Lehigh County. **HISTORY OF LEHIGH COUNTY, PA.** Allentown: 1914. Three volumes. Thick 4to. 1/2 Leather. AEG. Edited by Roberts, Stoudt, Krick, and Dietrich. Lehigh County's best historical / biographical guide. $ 175.00

1517. **LEHIGH COUNTY HISTORICAL SOCIETY = PROCEEDINGS.** Vol. 1 #1 to Vol. 19. Allentown: 1906-1952. Fourteen of the first 19 Volumes. $ 75.00

1518. Leland, Charles Godfrey. **HANS BREITMAN'S BALLADS.** Phila: 1897. 312p. Pretty embossed decorated cloth. Classic satire in "pidgin German/American". Fine introduction & glossary. $ 22.00

1519. Lewis, Arthur H. **HEX.** NY: 1967. 255p. DJ. Famous York County witchcraft murder trial of the late 1920's. Fascinating account. $ 20.00

1520. Lewis, Fred E. **A SUMMARY OF WIT & WISDOM.** Allentown: (1947). Printed wraps. Includes some dialect. Signed for *WST*. $ 15.00

1521. Lichten, Frances. **FOLK ART OF RURAL PENNSYLVANIA.** NY: 1946. 276p. Numerous illustrations, with some in color. Folio. First edition of this classic. Rich in historical and anecdotal lore. $ 60.00

1522. Lichten. **FOLK ART MOTIFS OF PA.** NY: (1976). Many color illus. Wraps. 4to. Invaluable record of basic designs. $ 5.00

1523. Lichten. **DECORATING THE PENNSYLVANIA GERMAN CHEST.** Home Craft Course. (Keyser, Plymouth Meeting: 1947). 32p. Illus. Wraps. $ 14.00

1524. Liechty, Daniel. **ANDREAS FISCHER & THE SABBATARIAN ANABAPTISTS...** Scottdale: 1988. 192p. $ 30.00

1525. **THE LIFE OF WILLIAM PENN...** Phila: 1849. 210p. + Ads + Wood Engraved Illus. Handsome red cloth gilt. $ 16.00

1526. (Light, Joseph H.). **PENNSYLVANIA GERMAN LETTERS, Penned Under the Nom de Plume DER ALT SCHULMESHTER.** Vol. 1 (All Published?). Lebanon: 1928. 125p. Printed paper boards. Pennsylvania "Dutch" dialect tales, first published in the Lebanon Semi-Weekly News in the late 1890's. *WST.* $ 25.00

1527. Lindsay, Merrill. **THE KENTUCKY RIFLE.** NY & York: 1972. Beautifully illustrated and documented study of a great display of guns. DJ. $ 30.00

1528. Lindsay, Thomas. **A HISTORY OF THE REFORMATION.** NY: 1914. Two Volumes. Over 1100p. + Map. Penned annotations. Useful. $ 22.00

1529. (Linn & Egle). **PENNSYLVANIA IN THE WAR OF THE REVOLUTION, Battalions & Line, 1775-83.** Harrisburg: 1880. 2 vols. pp. 794, 805 + Engraved & Color Plates. Spines repaired. An essential history. $ 100.00

1530. Linn & Egle. **PENNSYLVANIA MARRIAGES PRIOR TO 1810.** Balt: 1987. 2 Vols. 1391p. Useful reprint from the Pa. Archives, Series 2 (1880). $ 75.00

1531. Lins, James C. **COMMON SENSE PENNSYLVANIA GERMAN DICTIONARY...** Kempton, Pa: 1887. 80p. Scarce early dialect dictionary. *WST.* $ 25.00

1532. Lins. **COMMON SENSE PENNSYLVANIA GERMAN DICTIONARY...** Reading: 1895. 170p. 24mo. Printed paper boards. Revised and enlarged 2nd edition. *WST.* $ 25.00

1533. Lipman, Jean & Winchester, Alice. **THE FLOWERING OF AMERICAN FOLK ART, 1776-1876.** NY: 1974. 288p. Highly illustrated. A landmark exhibition and catalog that includes much on German American Folk Art. $ 35.00

1534. Litchfield, Carter. et. al. **THE BETHLEHEM OIL MILL, 1745-1934. German Technology in Early Pennsylvania.** Kemblesville, Pa. 128p. Illus. $ 25.00

1535. Lochman, A. H. **PRACTICAL SERMONS & ADDRESSES...** York: 1885. 360p. + Frontis. For 46 years Lochman was pastor at York's Evangelical Lutheran Church. $ 20.00

1536. Long, J. H. **SIXTY JANE... And the Strike on the Schlafe=Platz Railroad...** NY: 1903. 208p. + Frontis. Decorated cloth. $ 14.00

1537. Long, Lucile. **ANNA ELIZABETH...** Elgin, Il: 1946. 208p. Illus. DJ. 1st edition of this classic of Brethren historical fiction. $ 14.00

1538. **LONG FAMILY OF PENNSYLVANIA.** Compiled by W. G. Long. Huntington, WVa: 1930. 365p. Folio. Important record of the Pa. German-Swiss Long/Lang family. $ 100.00

1539. Longenecker, S. L. **THE CHRISTOPHER SAUERS = Courageous Printers who Defended Religious Freedom in America.** Elgin, Il: 1981. Paper bound. Best modern work on the Saur [Sower] printing clan. $ 10.00

1540. Loskiel, George Henry. **EXTEMPORE ON A WAGON; A Metrical Narrative of a Journey from Bethlehem to the Indian Town of Goshen, Ohio in 1803.** Translated with notes by J. Max Hark. Lancaster: 1887. 45p. + Ill. Limited to only 200 copies. $ 60.00

1541. (Lowe, Paul E.). **NEW DUTCH JOKE BOOK.** Baltimore, Ca: 1900. 94p. Color printed wraps. Pidgin dialect humor. *WST.* $ 22.00

1542. Ludwig, Christian. **A DICTIONARY. English, German, & French.** Revised and Augmented with 12000 Words taken out of Samuel Johnson's Dictionary, by J. B. Rogler. Leipzig: 1763. 1022p. 4to. Modern cloth. Early Virginville, Pa. ownership. *WST.* $ 145.00

1543. Ludwig & Doebler. **ST. PETER'S LUTHERAN CHURCH 1752-1952.** (Barren Hill, Pa: 1952). 192p. Illus. Cloth. $ 12.00

1544. (Luhrs, Henry). **YESTERDAY, AND TODAY, AND FOREVER. Memorial Lutheran Church, 1775-1950.** Shippensburg: 1950. 16p. Wraps. $ 2.00

1545. (Lukens, H. Clay). **LEAN' NORA: Supernatural, though Sub-Pathetic Ballad... A Good Long Way (Almost 97 Years) After the German of Gottfried August Bürger.** By Heinrich Yalc Snekul. Abel's Literary Curiosity Shop, Phila: 1870. 84p. In English & German. $ 40.00

1546. Luther. **COMMENTARY ON ST. PAUL'S EPISTLE TO THE GALATIANS...** Includes: Tischer's Life of Luther & Schmucker On the Reformation. Phila: 1840. 632p. + Front. Very attractive mottled calf. $ 30.00

1547. **LUTHER ON THE SACRAMENTS; The Distinctive Doctrines of the Evang. Lutheran Church, Respecting Baptism and the Lord's Supper...** Solomon D. Henkel & Bros., New Market, Va: 1853. 423p. Probably translated from German by Henkel. $ 60.00

1548. **LUTHERAN CHURCH ALMANAC.** Baltimore, Allentown, & Phila: 1865-1900. A Complete run of 35 issues. Bound. Especially useful for the annual Clerical Register, and numerous historical anecdotes. $ 50.00

1549. **LUTHERANS IN BERKS COUNTY, 1723-1923.** Edited by H. S. Kidd, (Reading: 1923). 503p. Excellent history. *WST.* $ 30.00

1550. Luthy, David. **AMISH IN AMERICA: Settlements that Failed, 1840-1960.** Ontario: 1986. 555p. Illus. 4to. Fascinating accounts. $ 25.00

1551. Luzerne County. **ATLAS OF LUZERNE COUNTY, PA.** By Beers. Pomeroy, Phila: 1873. 183p. Folio. Colored property owner atlas. *WST.* $ 200.00

1552. Mackenzie, Colin. **FIVE THOUSAND RECEIPTS In All the Useful & Domestic Arts...** Woodward, Phila: 1829. 546p. Full leather, worn. The great American formulary and guide to all trades & crafts. This particular edition is quite scarce. AI 39367 *[Locating one copy only].* $ 65.00

1553. MacMaster, Richard K. **LAND, PIETY & PEOPLEHOOD**. Scottdale: 1985. 344p. Wraps. Early Mennonites in America. $ 20.00

1554. MacMaster, Horst, & Ulle. **CONSCIENCE IN CRISIS. Mennonites & Other Peace Churches in America, 1739-89**. Scottdale: 1979. 528p. DJ. Great documentary record. Should be examined more thoroughly. $ 22.00

1555. MacWethy, L. D. **THE BOOK OF NAMES, Especially Relating to the Early Palatines & the First Settlers in the Mohawk Valley**. (1933). Balt: 1981. 209p. Ills. 20,000 names with much military information. $ 20.00

1556. Madden, R. R. **TRAVELS IN TURKEY, EGYPT, NUBIA, & PALESTINE, 1824-1827.** Carey & Lea, Phila: 1830. 2 Vols. pp. 250, 238 + Publisher's ads. Original cloth backed paper boards. *Printed lending library label for Levi Uhler, Lebanon, PA*. AI 2350. Early travels in the Holy Land. $ 55.00

1557. Maginness, James. **THE FAMILY CLERK & STUDENTS' ASSISTANT, Containing a Neat, Concise, & Plain Method of Book Keeping, by Single Entry**. Greer, Harrisburg: 1817. 196p. Leather backed boards. AI 41330. $ 32.00

1558. Maginness. **NEW, COPIOUS, & COMPLETE SYSTEM OF ARITHMETIC, For the Use of Schools & Counting Houses in the U.S....** Greer, Harrisburg: 1821. 372p. Full leather. AI 5903. *HSH.* $ 32.00

1559. Magnus, Albertus. **EGYPTIAN SECRETS. Or, White & Black Art for Man & Beast...** Translated from the German. (NY? Ca: 1880). 3 vols in 1. 160p. Plain wraps. Acidic paper. English edition of this important "Pow Wow" book. $ 40.00

BLOODY AXE MURDER - 1866

1560. (Mann, William B.). **OFFICIAL REPORT OF THE TRIAL OF ANTON PROBST, FOR THE MURDER OF CHRISTOPHER DEARING...** Phila: 1866. 120p. Original printed wraps. Uncut and unopened. One of the most sensational & bloody murders of the era. Probst, a German immigrant, killed eight members of the same family with an axe, & was searching for the youngest child when caught. After his execution his cadaver was used to test the theory that the eye's retina retains what was seen at the moment of death. $ 125.00

1561. Mann, William J. **LIFE & TIMES OF HENRY MELCHIOR MUHLENBERG**. Phila: 1887. 547p. + Frontis. First Edition. Outstanding biographical study and an significant contribution to German American history. *WST.* $ 65.00

MANUSCRIPT ANNOTATIONS IN GERMAN
BY THE GREATEST QUAKER HISTORIAN = WILLIAM SEWEL

1562. Marshall, Charles. **SION'S TRAVELLERS COMFORTED, and the Disobedient Warned...** London: 1704. Several vols in one. Original leather boards. Spine taped. *Apparently this was William Sewel's copy. It is most remarkable for the numerous marginal manuscript annotations he made = translating portions of this important English Quaker text into German and Dutch. Furthermore, this copy has manuscript corrections of the text, in a neat English hand, probably also by Sewel.* Further details upon request. Unique. $ 400.00

1563. Marsillac, J. **LA VIE DE GUILLAUME PENN, FONDATEUR DE LA PENSYLVANIE; Premier Legislateur connu des Etas-Unis de l'Amerique...** Paris: 1791. Two volumes in one. Disbd. Sabin 44820. Remarkable study of Penn as the originator of humane and Constitutional law in America. Rare. $ 220.00

1564. Martin, Helen R. **BARNABETTA.** NY: 1914. 340p. *WST.* $ 16.00

1565. Martin. **MARTHA OF THE MENNONITE COUNTRY.** NY: (1915). 318p. $ 22.00

1566. Martin. **SABINA. A Story of the Amish.** NY: 1905. 233p. Pretty decorated cloth covers. First Edition. *WST.* $ 22.00

1567. Martin. **THE SCHOOLMASTER OF HESSVILLE.** NY: (1920). 289p. $ 16.00

1568. Martin. **THOSE FITZENBERGERS.** NY: 1917. 363p. + Ill. *WST.* $ 18.00

1569. Martin. **TILLIE: A MENNONITE MAID. A Story of the Pennsylvania Dutch.** NY: 1906. 336p. Decorated cloth. Pretty copy. $ 16.00

1570. Martin, John Hill. **HISTORICAL SKETCH OF BETHLEHEM IN PA. With Some Account of the Moravian Church.** Phila: 1872. 190p. + Engravings + Signed photogravure portrait frontis. Double column. Very scarce and important. *WST.* $ 100.00

1571. Martindale, Joseph C. **A HISTORY OF THE TOWNSHIPS OF BYBERRY AND MORELAND...** Edited by A. W. Dudley. Phila. Ca: 1900. 416p. Essential contribution to Philadelphia Quaker history and genealogy. $ 50.00

THE MOST FAMOUS HISTORY OF THE AMISH / MENNONITE HEARTLAND

1572. Mast, C. Z. & Simpson, R. E. **ANNALS OF THE CONESTOGA VALLEY in Lancaster, Berks, and Chester Counties, Pa.** (Scottdale): 1942. 689p. Illus. Absolutely indispensable historical genealogy. *WST.* $ 400.00

1573. Mathews, Alfred & Hungerford, A. N. **HISTORY OF THE COUNTIES OF LEHIGH AND CARBON, PA.** Phila: 1884. 802p. + Illus. Handsome half leather gilt. Bursting with important information on the Pennsylvania German influence. *WST.* $ 225.00

1574. Mayer, Brantz. **MEMOIR & GENEALOGY OF THE MARYLAND & PENNSYLVANIA FAMILY OF MAYER, Which Originated in the Free Imperial City of Ulm, Wurtemberg, 1495-1878.** Baltimore: 1878. 179p. + Illus. 4to. Spine taped. Mayer was best known for his travels and historical works on Mexico, but the last years of his life were devoted to this noteworthy genealogical history. $ 75.00

1575. Mayser, E. P. **LITTLE TREASURES FOR LITTLE CHILDREN.** Lancaster: 1876. 108p. Woodcut chapter heads. 16mo. Curious binding. $ 17.00

1576. McAllister, W. J. **PENNSYLVANIA GERMAN WOOD CARVING.** Home Craft Course. Keyser, Plymouth Meeting: 1945. 24p. Illus. Wraps. $ 8.00

1577. M'Cauley, I. H. **HISTORICAL SKETCH OF FRANKLIN COUNTY, PA...** Reprint of the scarce 1878 edition. 322p. + Illus. + New Index (30p.). $ 25.00

1578. McClure, Robert. **DISEASES OF THE AMERICAN HORSE, & Cattle and Sheep.** Phila: (1870). 413p. Illus. $ 24.00

1579. McConnel, Kevin. **REDWARE, America's Folk Art Pottery.** West Chester. 96p. Well illustrated. Wraps. $ 15.00

1580. M'Henry, Dr. James. **THE ANTEDEILUVIANS...** Phila: 1840. 272p. Publishers cloth. First American Edition. Narrative poem about a Biblical Atlantis. $ 44.00

1581. McKenney, Frederic. **KEY TO THE AMERICAN TUTOR'S ASSISTANT REVISED...** Crukshank, Phila: 1809. 183p. + Publisher's ads. Pretty leather backed marbled boards. Copy of Adam Göttinger, Palmyra, PA. AI 17959. $ 28.00

1582. McKnight, Wm. J. **A PIONEER OUTLINE HISTORY OF NORTHWESTERN PENNSYLVANIA... 1780-1850**. Phila: 1905. 749p. + Fine Illus. 1/2 Leather. TEG. Very readable history with striking content. $ 125.00

1583. McMurtrie, Douglas C. **THE FIRST PRINTERS OF YORK, PENNSYLVANIA. Including the Text of Some of the Imprints of the York Press during the early days of the Revolutionary War**. Maple Press, York: 1977. 48p. Folio. Wraps. $ 16.00

1584A. Menno Simon. **A FOUNDATION AND PLAIN INSTRUCTION OF THE SAVING DOCTRINE OF OUR LORD JESUS CHRIST...** John Herr, Lancaster: 1835. 480p. Attractive full leather. The first edition in English. Fundamental Mennonite text. AI 32975. $ 60.00

1584B. (Menno Simon). **MENNO'S DEPARTURE FROM POPERY.** Translated by Ira Chase. (Lancaster?) Ca: 1830. 12p. Plain wraps. $ 18.00

1585. Mennonite. **A COLLECTION OF PSALMS & HYMNS...** Elkhart, Ind: 1884. pp. 384, 48. 32mo. Full leather. $ 30.00

1586. Mennonite. **THE COMPLETE WORKS OF MENNO SIMON**. Aylmer, Ontario: 1983. 740+p. Reprint of Funks's 1871 English edition. $ 24.00

1587. Mennonite. **THE COMPLETE WRITINGS OF MENNO SIMON.** Scottdale: 1984. Over 1000p. DJ. Compiled by J. C. Wenger, Leonard Verduin, and H. S. Bender. The best edition in English. $ 35.00

1588. **THE MENNONITE ENCYCLOPEDIA.** Scottdale: 1982. Four volumes. Over 3800p. Truly, a comprehensive and essential Anabaptist reference guide. $ 160.00

1589. Mennonite Quarterly Review. **THE PLAIN PEOPLE.** Goshen, IN: 1977. pp. 261-396. Important articles on the Anabaptists. $ 8.00

1590. Mercer, Dr. Henry C. **ANCIENT CARPENTERS' TOOLS...** Doylestown: 1975. 339p. Well Illus. DJ. Woodworkers & builder's tools. $ 14.00

1591. Mercer. **THE BIBLE IN IRON. Pictured Stoves & Stoveplates of the Pa. Germans. Notes on Colonial Firebacks, the Ten Plate Stove, Franklin's Fireplace, & the Tile Stoves of the Moravians in Pa. & N.C., with a List of Colonial Furnaces in the U.S. & Canada**. Doylestown: 1914. pp. 178p. + Illus. Wraps. 4to. Scarce First Edition. Wonderful reference to a great variety of Pennsylvania arts, symbols, industries, trades, and technologies. *WST*. $ 75.00

1592. Mercer. **THE BIBLE IN IRON...** 2nd Edition. Revised & Enlarged by Horace M. Mann. Doylestown: 1941. 217p. Illus. 4to. XLib. Spine taped. $ 40.00

1593. Mercer. **THE BIBLE IN IRON...** 3rd Edition. Revised & Enlarged by Horace M. Mann and Joseph E. Sandford. Doylestown: 1961. 256p + Numerous Illus. 4to. Cloth. The "best" edition for modern reference use. $ 30.00

1594. Mercer. **THE SURVIVAL OF THE MEDIAEVAL ART OF ILLUMINATIVE WRITING AMONG THE PENNSYLVANIA GERMANS.** APS, Phila: 1897. 11p. Illus. Xerox of the Author's offprint. The first article written on Fraktur. $ 12.00

1595. Mercer County. **HISTORY OF MERCER COUNTY, PA...** Chi: 1888. 1210p. No Map. 4to. Should be rebound. $ 55.00

1596. (Meulman, Isaac). **LUTHERS SCHRIFTEN = Catalogus van de Bibliotheek van Het Evangelisch Luthersch Seminarium**. Nieuwkoop: 1967. Wraps. Bibliography that lists 777 works by Luther. $ 25.00

1597. Meynen, Emil. **BIBLIOGRAPHY OF THE COLONIAL GERMANS OF NORTH AMERICA...** Reprint of the 1937 Edition. Balt: 1982. 636p. Basic reference work relating especially to the Germans in America, and their Descendants. $ 35.00

1598. Michel & Bees. **MORAVIAN TRAVEL GUIDE**. Bethlehem: 1952. 63p. Illus. Spiral bound. 246 Places of Moravian Interest in U.S. $ 10.00

1599. Mickley, Jos. J. **BRIEF ACCOUNT OF MURDERS BY THE INDIANS, & the Cause Thereof, in Northampton County, Pa. Oct. 8, 1763**. Phila: 1875. 37p. Wraps. $ 40.00

1600. Mickley, Minnie F. **THE GENEALOGY OF THE MICKLEY [MICHELET] FAMILY OF AMERICA...** Mickleys, Pa: 1893. 183p. *WST.* $ 85.00

1601. Miller, Adam. **EXPERIENCE OF GERMAN METHODIST PREACHERS...** Cincinnati: 1859. 430p. Pretty embossed blue cloth gilt. *WST.* $ 40.00

1602. Miller, Daniel. **EARLY HISTORY OF THE REFORMED CHURCH IN PENNSYLVANIA**. Reading: 1906. 280p. *WST.* $ 26.00

1603. Miller. **HISTORY OF THE REFORMED CHURCH, READING, PA**. Reading: 1905. 468p. + Illus. Thorough congregational history. $ 22.00

1604. Miller, Daniel. **PENNSYLVANIA GERMAN. A Collection of German Productions in Poetry & Prose**. Reading: 1903/4 & 1911. Two Volumes. Over 550p. One of the most important collections of dialect writings. *WST.* $ 75.00

1605. Miller. **RAMBLES IN EUROPE**. Reading: 1911. 399p. + Reading, Pa. ads. Grand Tour of the well-springs of the Reformed Church. $ 8.00

1606. Miller, D. L. **LETTERS FROM EUROPE & BIBLE LANDS**. Brethren's Pub., Mt. Morris, Ill: 1892. 439p. Illus. Worn cloth. $ 8.00

1607. Miller, Edwin C. **MILLER'S PROSE AND VERSE. Part English / Part Pennsylvania German**. (Allentown: 1924). 150p. Fine poems and stories in dialect. *WST.* $ 25.00

1608. Miller, Levi. **OUR PEOPLE: The Amish and Mennonites of Ohio**. Scottdale: 1983. 56p. Illus. Wraps. $ 5.00

1609. (Miller, Lewis). **LEWIS MILLER, SKETCHES AND CHRONICLES: The Reflections of a 19th Century Pennsylvania German Folk Artist**. York: 1966. 185p. 160 Watercolor illustrations of York, Pa. and her peoples, 1800=82. 4to. Slipcased. $ 25.00

1610. (Miller, M. E.). **AMISH COOKING**. Scottdale: 1981. 320p. $ 16.00

1611. Milner, Vincent L. **RELIGIOUS DENOMINATIONS OF THE WORLD**. Phila: 1872. 662p. + Plates. Includes German Sectarians & Anabaptists, Etc. $ 22.00

1612. Mohr, John W. **MEDICAL GUIDE IN TREATING ALL INTERNAL & EXTERNAL DISEASES OF HORSES, MULES, AND NEAT CATTLE**. Reading: 1866. 264p. 18mo. Leather backed boards. Text in English, with the formulas in both German and English. $ 120.00

1613. Mombert, J. I. **AN AUTHENTIC HISTORY OF LANCASTER COUNTY, PA.** Barr, Lancaster: 1869. pp. 617, 175 + Lithographed & engraved illustration + several maps. Modern buckram. Howes M 720. $ 120.00

1614. Monroe County. **COUNTY ATLAS OF MONROE, PA...** Beers, NY: 1875. 100p. Folio. Colored property owner maps, lithographed views, & ads. Very Scarce. *WST.* $ 200.00

1615. Montgomery, Morton L. **HISTORY OF BERKS COUNTY IN PA.** Phila: 1886. 1204p. + Illus. 4to. Rebound with titlepage and contents in typed facsimile. $ 180.00

1616. Montgomery, Richard S. **PENNSYLVANIA GERMAN ARCHITECTURE.** Home Craft Course, Keyser, Upper Darby: 1945. 30p. Illus. Wraps. $ 20.00

1617. Moran, James. **PRINTING PRESSES. History & Development from the 15th Century to Modern Times**. Berkeley: 1978. 265p. Illus. Wraps. 4to. Everyone interested in printing history should have a copy of this book. $ 12.00

1618. **THE MORAVIANS & THEIR FAITH.** Bethlehem: 1924. 20p. Wraps. $ 10.00

MORAVIANS TO HELP POPULATE THE AMERICAN COLONIES

1619. (Moravian - United Brethren). **ANNO REGNI GEORGII II [AN ACT FOR ENCOURAGING THE PEOPLE KNOWN BY THE NAME UNITAS FRATRUM, OR UNITED BRETHREN, TO SETTLE IN HIS MAJESTY'S COLONIES IN NORTH AMERICA]**... London: 1749. pp. 633-8. 4to. Disbound. Important and unusual artifact that demonstrates the British Crown's interest in German emigration to America. The act further provides that the Moravians may "affirm" rather than take oaths, and frees them from military service, in deference to their religious beliefs. $ 160.00

1620. (Moravian - United Brethren). **THE LITURGY & HYMNS OF THE AMERICAN PROVINCE OF THE UNITAS FRATRUM...** Bethlehem: 1890. 684p. Spine taped. $ 20.00

1621. Moss, Alf. Charles. **PENNSYLVANIA DUTCH "H. M. S. PINAFORE".** Phila: 1885. 20p. The Gilbert and Sullivan operetta in English and the Pennsylvania German Dialect. First Edition. *WST.* $ 22.00

1622. Moss & Newhard. **POLYGLOT OPERA. H. M. S. PINAFORE in Pennsylvania Dutch** . Allentown: 1901. 16p. + Ads. Text in English and Dialect. *WST.* $ 22.00

1623. Muhlenberg, William A. **SERMON PREACHED AT THE RE-OPENING OF THE CHURCH OF AUGUSTUS, Trappe, Montgomery County, Pa**. NY: 1861. 46p. New wraps. Important historical address. $ 20.00

1624A. Murtagh, Wm. J. **MORAVIAN ARCHITECTURE & TOWN PLANNING.** Chapel Hill, NC: 1967. 145p. Illus. DJ. Mainly on 18th Century Bethlehem, Pa. $ 40.00

1624B. Myers, Albert Cook. **NARRATIVES OF EARLY PENNSYLVANIA, WEST NEW JERSEY, & DELAWARE, 1630-1707**. NY: (1912). 476p. + Maps. $ 26.00

1624C. Myers, Elizabeth Lehman. **A CENTURY OF MORAVIAN SISTERS...** NY: 1918. 243p. Signed by the author. $ 24.00

1625. Nazareth. **TWO CENTURIES OF NAZARETH, PA. 1740-1920.** Nazareth: 1940. 276p. + Patron's List. Illus. *WST.* $ 22.00

1626. Nead, Dr. D. W. **THE PENNSYLVANIA GERMAN IN THE SETTLEMENT OF MARYLAND.** Author's Edition. PGS, Lancaster: 1914. 304p. + Illus. Blue cloth gilt. The Pa. German influence in Maryland is often overlooked and misunderstood. $ 60.00

1627. Nead. **THE PA. GERMAN IN THE SETTLEMENT OF MARYLAND.** Balt: 1980. 304p. Reprint of the 1914 ed. Cloth. $ 25.00

1628. Neidermyer, Dan. **JONATHAN.** Scottdale, Pa: 1973. 291p. Cloth. XLib. A novel about the Old Order Amish and their youth. $ 5.00

1629. Netherlands Society of Phila. **ADDRESSES MADE AT THE ANNUAL MEETINGS, 1913-30.** 573p. Xlib. J. Bennett Nolan's copy. Some excellent information. $ 22.00

1630. Nevin, Alfred. **MEN OF MARK OF CUMBERLAND VALLEY, PA. 1776-1876. Centennial Biography.** Phila: 1876. 452p. + Illus. $ 80.00

1631. **THE NEW AMERICAN POCKET FARRIER & Farmer's Guide.** Leary & Getz, Phila. Ca: 1850. 284p. + Ads. Illus. 24mo. Cloth. $ 25.00

1632. **NEW TOPOGRAPHICAL ATLAS OF PA. With Descriptions Historical, Scientific, & Statistical.** By Walling & Gray. Phila: 1872. 110p. Fine Colored Maps of Towns and Counties + Classified Ads. These decorative plates of the Pennsylvania Counties are favorites with print and map enthusiasts. Worthwhile. $ 125.00

1633. Newswanger, Kiehl & Christian. **AMISHLAND.** NY: 1954. 128p. Illustrated. 4to. DJ. Graphic vignettes of the Amish. Rather scarce. $ 38.00

1634. Nolan, J. Bennett. **ANNALS OF PENN SQUARE, Reading.** Phila: 1933. 106p. + Illus. Many details of Pennsylvania German history. $ 15.00

1635. Nolan. **THE FOUNDATION OF THE TOWN OF READING IN PENNSYLVANIA.** Reading: 1929. 210p. + Illus. XLib. Invaluable history. $ 20.00

1636. Nolan. **NEDDIE BURD'S READING LETTERS. An Epic of the Early Berks Bar.** 104p. + Illus. Grand series of letters. Fine copy. $ 22.00

1637. **THE NORRISTOWN NEW & MUCH IMPROVED MUSICAL TEACHER...** D. Sower, Jr. Norristown: 1832. 144p. Oblong Song Book. Leather backed marbled boards. $ 50.00

1638. Northampton County. **ATLAS OF NORTHAMPTON COUNTY, PENNSYLVANIA.** By Beers. Pomeroy, Phila: 1874. 91p. Folio. Colored property owner atlas. + Manuscript note in dialect by *WST.* $ 160.00

W. W. DENSLOW = THE ILLUSTRATOR OF "THE WIZARD OF OZ"

1639. Northampton County. **HISTORY OF NORTHAMPTON COUNTY, PA. 1752-1877...** Fritts/Davis, Reading & Phila: 1877. 293p. + Numerous Important Lithographed Views. *Includes a double page "Birds-Eye" view of Easton, which is the first published drawing executed by W. W. Denslow - the famed illustrator of the "Wizard of Oz".* $ 250.00

1640. **NORTHUMBERLAND COUNTY HISTORICAL SOCIETY PROCEEDINGS.** Vols. I to XVII. Sunbury: 1929-49. Lacks only Vol. IV. Wraps. Very readable articles, well researched. Exceptional historical content. $ 100.00

1641. **THE NOW AND THEN**. Muncy, Pa: 1888-92. Vol. 2 & 3. 444p. Presentation copies from the publisher J. M. M. Gernerd (with his photo). Bound in half leather by John D. Lingle of Sunbury. Volume One was published in 1868, and is *very* rare. Truly, a singular journal of local history and amusement. *WST*. $ 100.00

1642. Nutting, Wallace. **FURNITURE TREASURY...** NY: 1948-9. 3 vols. Highly illustrated. Best edition. Massive work. An essential reference to early American furniture. $ 125.00

1643. Nykor, L. M. & Musson, P. D. **MENNONITE FURNITURE. The Ontario Tradition in York County**. Toronto: 1977. 95p. Illus. Cloth. DJ. 4to. $ 35.00

1644. Nykor. **MENNONITE FURNITURE...** Toronto: 1977. 95p. Illus. Wraps. $ 15.00

1645. Ohl, Albert. **HISTORY OF UPPER SAUCON TOWNSHIP / and the Milfords - Upper & Lower, Lehigh County, Pa. 1732-1947...** (Allentown: 1947). 225p. Cloth. Photo reproduction of a unique Manuscript. *WST*. $ 25.00

1646. **OLD TIME MUSIC OF YORK, 1777-1927**. 56p. 32mo. Wraps. $ 10.00

1647. O'Connor, Richard. **THE GERMAN-AMERICANS...** Bost: 1968. 484p. Xlib. $ 8.00

1648. Omwake, Landis, Hargrave, & Frey. **THE CONESTOGA SIX HORSE BELL TEAMS OF EASTERN PENNSYLVANIA**. Cinn: 1930. 163p. Illus. 4to. Signed by Omwake. The most celebrated work on this famed, Pennsylvania born, early American form of cartage and transport. Howes O-85. *WST*. $ 85.00

1649. (Omwake, Henry). **THE OMWAKES OF INDIAN SPRING FARM. Pictorial, Descriptive, Biographical**. Cincinnati: 1926. 96p. Very scarce. Fine study of these Brethren descendants of Leonard Am Weg. $ 50.00

1650. Osburn, Burl N. **BOOKBINDING**. Home Craft Course. Plymouth Meeting: 1945. 28p. Illus. Handy little guide. $ 12.00

1651. **OVID'S ART OF LOVE...** Printed for the Purchaser, Phila: 1812. 214p. + 2 plates. Disbound. AI 26367 *[Recording one copy only]*. $ 55.00

1652. Packull, W. O. **MYSTICISM AND THE EARLY SOUTH GERMAN - AUSTRIAN ANABAPTIST MOVEMENT, 1525-31**. Scottdale: 1977. 296p. + Illus. $ 24.00

1653. Peissner, Elias. **A COURSE OF GERMAN LITERATURE...** Baltimore: 1861. 378p. Interesting English introduction, with the remainder of text in German. $ 14.00

1654. **PENCILINGS ABOUT EPHRATA, By A Visitor**. Phila: 1860. 40p. Chipped Printed Wraps. Historical pamphlet. Partially a promotional for Ephrata Mountain Springs. $ 75.00

WILLIAM PENN

1655. Penn, William [1644=1718]. **A BRIEF ACCOUNT OF THE RISE AND PROGRESS OF THE PEOPLE CALLED QUAKERS...** Bound With Robert Barclay's / **THE ANARCHY OF THE RANTERS, & OTHER LIBERTINES...** Bound With Joseph Pike's / **AN EPISTLE TO THE NATIONAL MEETING OF FRIENDS IN DUBLIN...** James Adams, Wilmington: 1783. Three volumes in one. pp. (8), 88, vii, (1), 111, 24. *Early Quaker ownership of Maria Mott.* Evans 18083. $ 75.00

1656. Penn. **GOOD ADVICE TO THE CHURCH OF ENGLAND, ROMAN CATHOLICK, & PROTESTANT DISSENTER... It is their Duty, Principles & Interest to Abolish the Penal Laws and Tests.** London: 1687. 61p. 4to. Marbled wraps. First Edition. Important text on "Liberty of Conscience". Rare. $ 150.00

1657. Penn. **NO CROSS, NO CROWN...** Johnson, Phila: 1796. 358p. Contemporary full leather. Ds. *Manuscript ownership of Benjamin Garrett.* Evans 30972. $ 175.00

1658. Penn. **PRIMITIVE CHRISTIANITY REVIVED, IN THE FAITH & PRACTICE OF THE PEOPLE CALLED QUAKERS...** Bound With / **Select Pieces on Religious Subjects...** by Isaac Pennington. Crukshank, Phila: 1783. pp. (2), 66, 4, 98 (2). Lacks vertical half of the first title page. Contemporary 1/4 leather. Evans 18081. Apparently overlooked by Smith in "*Friend's Books*". *Manuscript ownership of the famed Quaker, William Savery [1750-1804].* $ 100.00

1659. Penn. **PRIMITIVE CHRISTIANITY REVIVED, IN THE FAITH & PRACTICE OF THE PEOPLE CALLED QUAKERS...** With / A Memoir of Penn by James M. Brown of Va. Phila: 1857. 89p. Illus. $ 20.00

1660. Penn. **REASON AGAINST RAILING, & TRUTH AGAINST FICTION. Being an Answer to those Two late Pamphlets... by one Thomas Hicks, an Anabaptist Teacher...** Bound with/ **An Appendix... Animadversions upon certain passages in Tho. Hicks' "Dialogue"... by George Whitehead**. (London): 1673. pp. (7), 186, 50. Contemporary full leather. Worn. *Interesting early ownerships, with one mentioning George Fox.* Smith p. 289, Sabin 59728. First Edition. A powerful & important Quaker work, further enhanced by the contribution of George Whitehead [1636 - 1723]. $ 200.00

1661. Penn. **THE RISE AND PROGRESS OF THE PEOPLE CALLED QUAKERS.** Bound with / **A Key Opening the Way...** Phila: 1849. 86p. + 40p. $ 20.00

1662. Penn. **THE SANDY FOUNDATION SHAKEN...** Phila: 1825. 80p. $ 22.00

1663. Penn. **SOME FRUITS OF SOLITUDE.** NY: 1900. 170p. 24mo. $ 12.00

1664. Penn. **A TREATISE OF OATHS, Containing Several Weighty Reasons why the People Called Quakers Refuse to Swear... Presented to the King & Great Council of England, Assembled in Parliament.** (London): 1675. 166p. May lack (colophon) last leaf. Later 1/2 morocco. "*Friend's Books*" p. 293. Written by Penn & Richard Richardson. Seventeenth century Quaker texts are now quite uncommon. $ 245.00

1665. Penn. **THE TRYAL OF WILLIAM PENN & WILLIAM MEADE FOR CAUSING A TUMULT... AT THE OLD BAILEY, SEPT. 1670.** Don C. Seitz, Editor. Boston: 1919. pp. 17, 37. Fine copy. DJ. Record of Penn's remarkable defense of the rights of human liberty against the onslaughts of government. $ 34.00

THE FOUNDATION OF THE AMERICAN PHILOSOPHICAL SOCIETY

1666. **PENNSYLVANIA CHRONICLE, & Universal Advertiser**. Phila: Feb. 29 - March 7, 1768. 4p. 4to. Important and rare early newspaper, with an extensive article on the enlargement of the activities of the American Philosophical Society. There is also an interesting piece on the settlement of Indian lands. $ 150.00

1667. Pennsylvania College. **CATALOGUES OF THE OFFICERS, ALUMNI AND STUDENTS OF PENNSYLVANIA COLLEGE & MEDICAL SCHOOL; + Catalogue & Constitution of the Theological Seminary of Evangelical Lutheran Church; + Sketches of the Alumni & Linnean Associations**. Neinstedt, Gettysburg: 1859-62. Seven volumes. Disbd. Wraps. *Owned by A. R. Horne.* $ 40.00

1668. **PENNSYLVANIA DUTCH COOK BOOK OF FINE OLD RECIPES**. Reading, Pa: 1936. 48p. Illus. Printed wraps. $ 8.00

1669. **THE PENNSYLVANIA DUTCHMAN: Devoted to Pennsylvania Dutch Culture**. Vol. 1 # 1 to Vol. 8 # 4. Lancaster. 1949-57. A complete run of this remarkable journal, edited by Shoemaker, Yoder, Frey, et. al. Nicely bound in cloth [The last 3 years in Wraps]. Folio. Jammed with irreplaceable information. "Pumpernickle Bill's" copies. *WST.* $ 200.00

1670. **THE PENNSYLVANIA DUTCHMAN...** Vol. I # 1 to Vol. III # 22. Lancaster. 1949-52. A long run of over 65 issues. Folio. $ 80.00

THE PENNSYLVANIA GERMAN MAGAZINE

1671. **THE PENNSYLVANIA GERMAN & THE PENN GERMANIA**. Vol. 1 #1 to XV #3. Lebanon, East Greenville, and Cleona, Pa: 1900-14. Nicely bound with covers, ads, and promotionals in ten cloth bound volumes. Consecutive run of this magnificent journal. Invaluable articles and information. *WST.* $ 500.00

1672. **THE PENNSYLVANIA GERMAN. & THE PENN GERMANIA**. An almost complete run in original wraps. From Vol. 1 #3 to XV #3. Lebanon, East Greenville, and Cleona, Pa: 1900-14. Over 100 Issues. An unparalleled resource. *WST.* $ 275.00

1673. **PENNSYLVANIA GERMAN CHURCH RECORDS OF BIRTHS, BAPTISMS, MARRIAGES, BURIALS, ETC**. Introduction by Don Yoder. Extracted From the Proceedings and Addresses of the Pennsylvania German Society. Balt: 1983. Three volumes. 2371p. Illus. Indexed. Essential genealogical records. $ 150.00

1674. **PENNSYLVANIA VITAL RECORDS**. Balt: 1983. Three volumes. 2491p. + Indexed from the Pennsylvania Magazine of History & Biography and the Pennsylvania Genealogical Magazine. $ 150.00

1675. Pennypacker, Samuel Whitaker [1843-1916]. **ANNALS OF PHOENIXVILLE & ITS VICINITY...** Phila: 1872. 295p. + Illus. Original morocco cloth. One of the scarcest & most important of Pennypacker's books. Especially good on the military history of Chester and Montgomery Counties. $ 100.00

1676. Pennypacker. **THE AUTOBIOGRAPHY OF A PENNSYLVANIAN**. Phila: 1918. 564p. + Illus. Reform Governor of Pa. and great book collector. $ 20.00

1677. (Pennypacker). **THE DESECRATION & PROFANATION OF THE PENNSYLVANIA CAPITOL**. Phila: [1911]. 104p. Classic study of corruption and waste in building the beautiful State capitol building. H. B. Cassel's copy. $ 22.00

1678. Pennypacker. **HISTORICAL & BIOGRAPHICAL SKETCHES.** Phila: 1883. 416p. Buckram. XLib. Excellent articles on: Early Pennsylvania German Imprints, Christopher Dock, Rittenhouse, the Settlement of Germantown, Etc. $ 80.00

1679. Pennypacker. **THE PENNSYLVANIA DUTCHMAN, & Wherein he has Excelled.** Author's Offprint. HSP, Phila: 1899. 6p. Printed wraps. $ 20.00

1680. Phila. Mayor's Office. **RECORD OF INDENTURES OF INDIVIDUALS BOUND OUT AS APPRENTICES, SERVANTS, ETC... 1771=1773.** Reprinted with a new index. Balt: 1973. 364p. Includes the German Redemptioners. $ 25.00

1681. Phila. Museum of Art. **PENNSYLVANIA DUTCH FOLK ARTS.** Phila. Ca: 1956. 34p. Illus. Decorative wraps. The Geesey Collection, etc. $ 12.00

1682. Phillips, Henry. **GERMAN LYRICS.** Printed for Private Circulation, Phila: 1892. 141p. Uncut. Gilt stamped cloth. Text in English. $ 22.00

1683. Phipps, Joseph. **THE ORIGINAL & PRESENT STATE OF MAN...** William Ross, NY: 1788. 230p. Contemporary full leather. Evans 21391. Classic Quaker treatise. $ 55.00

1684. **PORTRAIT AND BIOGRAPHICAL RECORD OF LEHIGH, NORTHAMPTON, AND CARBON COUNTIES, PA...** Chicago: 1894. 999p. + Illus. 4to. Spine taped. $ 125.00

1685. Pound, Arthur. **THE PENNS OF PENNSYLVANIA & ENGLAND.** NY: 1932. 349p. + Illus. Especially useful in that it covers Penn's successors who are not included in other biographies and studies. $ 30.00

1686. Powell & Rarey. **TACHYHIPPODAMIA; or, the New Secret of Taming Horses.** Phila: 1872. 161p. + Ill. Nice cloth gilt. 24mo. The Pennsylvania Germans have long been known as skillful horse trainers. $ 40.00

1687. Prentice, Archibald. **A TOUR OF THE UNITED STATES. WITH TWO LECTURES ON EMIGRATION...** London: 1849. 217p. + Folding U. S. Map. 32mo. Original cloth, chipped. Sabin 65059. American travels & observations. $ 40.00

1688. Punkin, Jonathan (Pseud.). **DOWNFALL OF FREEMASONRY... & The Origin & Increase of Abolition...** (Phila:) 1838. pp. 48, 159 + Unusual caricature plates. Ds. One leaf torn with loss. Humorous account of Governor Ritner's adventures against the Masonic party. See Sabin 66668, AI 52553. $ 50.00

1689. Quakers. **A COLLECTION OF MEMORIALS CONCERNING DIVERS MINISTERS AND OTHERS OF THE PEOPLE CALLED QUAKERS, In Pa. NJ, Etc...** Crukshank, Phila: 1787. 439p. Disbound. Evans 20377. $ 95.00

1690. Quakers. **A COLLECTION OF TESTIMONIES CONCERNING SEVERAL MINISTERS OF THE GOSPEL AMONGST THE PEOPLE CALLED QUAKERS, Deceased...** Hinde, London: 1760. pp. 11, 372. Contemporary full leather, boards detached. $ 75.00

1691. Quakers. **MEMORIALS CONCERNING DECEASED FRIENDS: Being Selections from the Records of the Yearly Meetings of Pa. 1788=1819.** Phila: 1821. 184p. Full leather. Foxed. AI 5412. Important biographies. $ 22.00

1692. Quakers. **RULES OF DISCIPLINE OF THE YEARLY MEETING OF FRIENDS, Held in Phila.** Kimber, Conrad & Co. Phila: 1806. 135p. + *Extensive Manuscript Additions.* *"This Book belongs to the Womens Preparative Meeting at Lower Mansfield."* Full sheep. AI 10457. These books with manuscript additions make fascinating artifacts. $ 70.00

1693. Quakers. **RULES OF DISCIPLINE OF THE YEARLY MEETING OF FRIENDS, Held in Phila.** John Richards, Phila: 1831. 115p. + *Manuscript and Printed Notes and Additions. "Property of the Plumstead Preparative Meeting"* Full sheep. AI 7188. $ 50.00

1694. Quakers. **RULES OF DISCIPLINE OF THE YEARLY MEETING OF MEN & WOMEN FRIENDS.** Phila: 1877. 136p. $ 10.00

1695. Quakers. **THE TESTIMONY OF THE SOCIETY OF FRIENDS ON THE CONTINENT OF AMERICA.** Rakestraw, Philadelphia: 1830. 39p. New wraps. AI 1508, Sabin 86070. Essential statement of American Quaker philosophy and opinion on a wide variety of theological, social and political matters. $ 24.00

1696. Rank, Henry Haverstick. **THE LIFE OF THE REV. BENJAMIN BAUSMAN.** Phila: 1912. 439p. + Illus. Important contribution to Reformed Church history. *WST.* $ 24.00

1697. Rauch, Edward Henry [1820-1902]. **PENNSYLVANIA DUTCH RIP VAN WINKLE...** Mauch Chunk: (1883). 32p. Wraps. XLib. "Rip" written in the Pennsylvania German dialect - the arena of action moved from the Catskills to the Blue Mountains. $ 30.00

THE FIRST PENNSYLVANIA "DUTCH" PERIODICAL

1698. Rauch. **THE PENNSYLVANIA DUTCHMAN.** Lancaster: 1873. Vol. 1 #1 - #3 [All Published]. Clothbound with original wraps. With Prospectus and most text in both English & the Pennsylvania German Dialect. Extremely scarce and important. *WST.* $ 120.00

1699. Rauch. **RAUCH'S PENNSYLVANIA DUTCH HAND BOOK...** Mauch Chunk: 1879. 238p. + Ad. Crisp copy of this important early guide in both English & the Dialect. $ 50.00

1700. Raymond, Eleanor. **EARLY DOMESTIC ARCHITECTURE OF PENNSYLVANIA.** West Chester. 158p. Illustrated. Modern edition of a true classic. $ 25.00

1701. Reaman, G. Elmore. **THE TRAIL OF THE BLACK WALNUT.** NY: 1957. 256p. + Illus. DJ. First Edition. Pennsylvania Mennonites in Upper New York & Canada. $ 60.00

1702. Rebman, Earl F. **CONESTOGA RIVER WATERSHED. Outline of History, 1710-1973.** (Lancaster: 1973). 215p. Many illus. $ 10.00

1703. Reckitt & Gough. **SOME ACCOUNT OF THE LIFE OF WILLIAM RECKITT...** Bound With / **MEMOIRS OF THE LIFE OF JAMES GOUGH...** Crukshank, Phila: 1783. pp. 164, 184. Evans 17961 & 18146. *Manuscript ownership of William Snowden.* $ 125.00

1704. Reeder, Eastburn. **EARLY SETTLERS OF SOLEBURY, BUCKS COUNTY, PA. Compiled from Deeds, Wills, & the Records of Friend's Meetings.** Doylestown: 1971. 89p. + Excellent Appendix & Index. Cloth. $ 20.00

1705. **REFORMATION ALBUM.** Wischan, Reading: 1886. Collection of 44 Illustrations with very informative explanatory text. $ 10.00

1706. Reformed Church in America. **THE CONSTITUTION OF THE REFORMED DUTCH CHURCH IN THE U. S. A.** Durell, NY: 1793. pp. 12, 354. Full leather. *Joseph Onderdonk's copy.* Evans 26065. $ 95.00

1707. (Reichard, Harry Hess). **THE CHRISTMAS POETRY OF THE "PENNSYLVANIA DUTCH...** Allentown: 1961. 87p. Ills. Pretty printed crimson wraps. *WST.* $ 24.00

1708. Reichard. **PENNSYLVANIA - GERMAN DIALECT WRITINGS AND THEIR WRITERS.** PGS, Lancaster: 1918. 400p. Cloth. Author's edition, signed by Reichard for *WST.* Essential reference guide to the dialect literature. $ 125.00

1709. Reichard. **PENNSYLVANIA GERMAN VERSE. An Anthology of Representative Selections in the Dialect Popularly Known as Pennsylvania Dutch...** PGS, Norristown: 1940. 299p. Cloth. "Pumpernickle Bill's" copy, with his manuscript notes, inserts, etc. Thus, unique. *WST.* $ 80.00

1710. Reichel, Levin T. **A HISTORY OF NAZARETH HALL 1755 = 1855; And of the Reunions of Its Former Pupils, 1854-55.** Phila: 1855. 162p. + Engraved frontis. Historic Moravian Boarding School. *WST.* $ 26.00

1711. Reichel, William C. **THE CROWN INN, Near Bethlehem, Pa. 1745.** (Phila: 1872). 162p. + Illus & Map. Plain wraps. Limited to 499 Copies. Significant annals of the early Moravian settlements in Pennsylvania. $ 36.00

1712. Reichel. **HISTORICAL SKETCH OF NAZARETH HALL, 1755 = 1869.** Phila: 1869. 356p. + Folding map & Illus. Essential Moravian history. $ 42.00

1713. Reitz, J. J. **FAMILY HISTORY & Record Book of the Descendants of Johan Friedrich Reitz, The Pioneer Who Landed at Philadelphia, Sept. 7, 1748.** Walnutport: 1930. 289p. + Illus. $ 50.00

1714. **REMEMBER WILLIAM PENN, 1644=1944.** Penn Tercentenary Com., H'burg: 1945. 190p. + "Some Fruits of Solitude". 84p. Illus. $ 6.00

1715. Repp, Arthur C. **LUTHER'S CATECHISM COMES TO AMERICA.** NY: 1982. 323p. Theological and cultural effects of the Small Catechism prepared in, and for, America prior to 1850. $ 32.00

1716. Ressler, Martin E. **AN ANNOTATED BIBLIOGRAPHY OF MENNONITE HYMNALS & SONGBOOKS, 1742-1986.** Lancaster: 1987. 117p. Fine reference. $ 14.00

1717. Rhoads, Thomas J. **ONKEL JEFF'S REMINISCENCES OF YOUTH, And Other Poems.** (Williamsport: 1904). Two Volumes. 800p. Illus. Little known Pennsylvania German poet. Includes some pieces in the Pennsylvania "Dutch" dialect. *WST.* $ 45.00

1718. Rice, A. H. & Stoudt, John Baer. **THE SHENANDOAH POTTERY.** Strasburg, Va: 1929. 277p. + Illus. First Edition of this classic study. *WST.* $ 120.00

1719. Rice, Charles S. & Shenk, John B. **MEET THE AMISH, A Pictorial Study of the Amish People.** Rutgers: 1947. 21p. + Hundreds of great photos. Long ms. presentation. $ 60.00

1720. Rice, Charles S. & Steinmetz, Rollin C. **THE AMISH YEAR.** Rutgers: 1956. 224p. DJ. Charming text and outstanding photographs. $ 50.00

1721. Rice, Wm. H. **DAVID ZEISBERGER AND HIS BROWN BRETHREN.** Bethlehem: (1897). 57p. + Illustrations. Indians & Moravians. *WST.* $ 34.00

1722. Richards, H. M. M. **CONRAD WEISER, Early Lutheran Patriot.** Lebanon Hist. Soc: 1926. pp. 163-185. Illus. $ 10.00

1723. (Richards). **HEBRON MORAVIAN CEMETERY.** Lebanon County Hist. Soc: 1929. 63p. Illus. Wraps. Issued for the unveiling of a tablet at the cemetery. $ 12.00

1724. Richards, H. M. M. **PENNSYLVANIA'S EMERGENCY MEN AT GETTYSBURG; A Touch of Bushwhacking**. Reading: 1895. 35p. +Double column. Printed wraps. $ 26.00

1725. Richardson, Wm. H. **THE PICTURESQUE QUALITY OF THE PENNSYLVANIA GERMAN**. Author's Offprint. Lancaster: 1904. 27p. + Illus. Printed wraps. $ 28.00

1726. Richman, Irwin. **PENNSYLVANIA'S DECORATIVE ARTS IN THE AGE OF HANDCRAFT**. Harrisburg: 1978. 76p. Printed wraps. Well composed. $ 8.00

1727. Riddle, William. **NICHOLAS COMENIUS: YE PENNSYLVANIA SCHOOLMASTER OF OLDEN TIME**. Lancaster: 1897. 469p. Crimson cloth gilt. Controversial tale of early education & the powerful influence of the old schoolmasters. $ 16.00

1728. Riddle. **150 YEARS OF SCHOOL HISTORY IN LANCASTER, PENNSYLVANIA.** Lancaster: 1905. 442p. + Illus. Cloth. XLib. Biographical & historical reference. $ 16.00

1729. Riedesel, Madame de. **LETTERS & MEMOIRS RELATING TO THE WAR OF AMERICAN INDEPENDENCE, & THE CAPTURE OF GERMAN TROOPS AT SARATOGA.** NY: 1827. 323p. Uncut. Disbd. First English Edition. With the "indelicate" passages of the original German omitted. AI 30457, Sabin 71301, Howes R 284. $ 50.00

1730. Ritter, Abraham. **HISTORY OF THE MORAVIAN CHURCH IN PHILA.** Phila: 1857. 282p. + Lithographed illus. Worn cloth. $ 36.00

1731. Rivinus, Emilie Markoe. **RIVINIANA. Records and Memoirs of the Rivinus Family, Collected on Both Sides of the Atlantic**. Phila: 1945. 80p. + Illus. + Ms. Notes. $ 20.00

1732. Robacker, Earl F. **PENNSYLVANIA DUTCH STUFF. A Guide to Country Antiques.** Phila: 1944. 163p. + Illus. Rarely seen in a complete Dust Jacket. Early classic. $ 30.00

1733. Robacker. **PENNSYLVANIA DUTCH STUFF. A Guide to Country Antiques**. Phila: 1961. 163p. + Illus. DJ. Still useful & informative. $ 14.00

1734. Robacker. **PENNSYLVANIA GERMAN LITERATURE. Changing Trends, 1683-1942.** Phila: 1943. 217p. + Letter from the author to *WST*. DJ. Really informative. $ 50.00

1735. Robacker. **TOUCH OF THE DUTCHLAND.** NY: 1965. 240p. + Photo Illus. DJ. Very interesting information. $ 25.00

1736. Roberts, Clarence V. **EARLY FRIENDS FAMILIES OF UPPER BUCKS, With Some Account of Their Descendants**... Phila: 1925. 680p. + Fine Illus. First Edition. $ 145.00

1737. Roberts & Schindel. **HISTORY OF EGYPT CHURCH.** Allentown: 1908. 71p. Illus. Oldest Reformed congregation in Lehigh County (1734). *WST*. $ 20.00

1738. Roberts, Elwood. **BIOGRAPHICAL ANNALS OF MONTGOMERY COUNTY, PA.** NY: 1904. Two volumes. 1086p. + Illus. 4to. Spines taped. $ 125.00

1739. Roberts, Ned H. **THE MUZZLE-LOADING CAP LOCK RIFLE.** Harrisburg: 1952. 308p. Illustrated. DJ. Folio. The best work on the subject. $ 75.00

1740. Rohrbaugh, Jacob Hartman. **NEW YEAR SERENADES. Greetings in the Pennsylvania German Dialect**. Macungie, Pa: 1945. 25p. Printed wraps. *WST*. $ 20.00

1741. Rohrer, Gertrude Martin. **MUSIC & MUSICIANS OF PENNSYLVANIA.** Phila: 1940. 121p. DJ. Important biographical Reference. $ 25.00

1742. Rondthaler, Edward. **LIFE OF JOHN HECKEWELDER...** Phila: 1847. 174p. + Fine frontis lithograph + *Manuscript note about Maria Heckewelder.* Edited by Dr. B. H. Coates. Spine taped. *Gilpin family copy.* Sabin 73081, Howes R 429. Moravian missionary and chronicler of the American Indian. $ 55.00

1743. Rose, H. W. **THE COLONIAL HOUSES OF WORSHIP IN AMERICA.** NY: 1963. 574p. Well illustrated. DJ. Slipcase. Includes architectural & historical info. on the most important churches and meetings houses in Pa. Notably those of the early Quakers, Mennonites, Brethren, and Lutherans. $ 80.00

1744. Rosenberger, Homer Tope. **ADVENTURES AND PHILOSOPHY OF A PENNSYLVANIA DUTCHMAN...** Bellefonte: 1971. 665p. Illus. DJ. $ 24.00

1745. Rosenberger, Jesse L. **THE PENNSYLVANIA GERMANS. A Sketch of Their History & Life, of the Mennonites, and Side Lights from the Rosenberger Family.** Chicago: 1923. 173p. + Illus. *WST.* $ 45.00

1746. Rosengarten, J. G. **THE GERMAN SOLDIER IN THE WARS OF THE UNITED STATES.** Phila: 1890. 298p. + *WST.* $ 42.00

1747. Ross, Alexander. [Greek Title] **PANSEBIA: or, A View of all Religions in the World...** Little Britain (London): 1672. 551p. Without the illustrated annex. 24mo. Later cloth. Ross [1591-1654] was an Anglican divine and mystic, who was a chaplain to King Charles I. Includes a short, but interesting section on Anabaptists. $ 100.00

1748. Roux de Rochelle, Jean B. G. **ETATS-UNIS D'AMERIQUE.** Bound With / Regnault's **Histoire des Antilles & Suite des Etats-Unis...** Bound With / Lacroix's **Possessions Anglaises dans L'Amerique du Nord...** Bound With / Denys' **LES CALIFORNIES...** Didot, Paris: 1837 & 1849. pp. 400, 108, 164, 158 + *124 Remarkable Engraved Plates*, which feature many Pennsylvania scenes. Handsome half leather binding. Howes R473 aa, Sabin 73516 / 68924. Roux de Rochelle was the French Minister to the U. S. 1829-31. $ 330.00

1749. (Rumberger). **LIFE AND CONFESSION OF FRANK H. RUMBERGER, One of the Troutman Murderers.** Harrisburg: 1882. 56p. Ills. Old tape repairs to wraps. McDade #842. Frank & Henry Rumberger tried to rob an old farmer, Dan Troutman, at his home near Uniontown in Dauphin County. He resisted and was shot. The brothers were hung. This work includes a history of the gallows in Harrisburg, 1854-1882. $ 60.00

1750. Rupp, Israel Daniel [1803-1878]. **A BRIEF BIOGRAPHICAL MEMORIAL OF JOH. JONAS RUPP, AND A COMPLETE GENEALOGICAL FAMILY REGISTER OF HIS LINEAL DESCENDANTS, 1756=1875.** West Phila: 1875. 292p. + Frontis + Publisher's Notice + *Manuscript genealogy of the Zehring Family.* $ 50.00

1751. Rupp. **A COLLECTION OF UPWARDS OF 30,000 NAMES OF GERMAN, SWISS, DUTCH, FRENCH, AND OTHER IMMIGRANTS IN PENNSYLVANIA. 1727=1776.** Harrisburg: 1856. pp. 24, 368, 37. Xlib. Library binding. Invaluable. $ 50.00

1752. Rupp. **A COLLECTION OF UPWARDS OF 30,000 NAMES...** Phila: 1876. 495p. + Ads + Centennial plates. This 2nd edition has the text in both English and German. *The Breinig family copy, of Breinigsville, Lehigh County. WST.* $ 60.00

1753. Rupp. **A COLLECTION OF UPWARDS OF 30,000 NAMES...** Balt: 1985. 583p. Indexed. Probably the best edition for modern use. $ 35.00

1754. Rupp. **HISTORY OF THE COUNTIES OF BERKS AND LEBANON: Containing a Brief Account of the Indians.** Reprint of the Lancaster, 1844 Edition. 600+p. With a new Name Index. Useful edition of this fine history. $ 44.00

1755. Rupp. **HISTORY OF LANCASTER COUNTY.** Reprint of the Lancaster, 1844 edition. 600+p. + New Name Index. $ 40.00

1756. Rupp. **HISTORY OF NORTHAMPTON, LEHIGH, MONROE, CARBON, & SCHUYLKILL COUNTIES...** Harrisburg: 1845. 658p. + Lithographed Plates. Nice full leather gilt. *WST.* $ 120.00

1757. Rupp. **[Greek Title] HE PASA EKKLESIA. AN ORIGINAL HISTORY OF THE RELIGIOUS DENOMINATIONS AT PRESENT EXISTING IN THE U.S.** Phila: 1844. 734p. Disbound. Scarce & very informative collection that contains a "*History of the Jews*" by Isaac Leeser; and Mennonite Histories by Christian and John Herr. $ 75.00

1758. Rush, Dr. Benjamin. **AN ACCOUNT OF THE MANNERS OF THE GERMAN INHABITANTS OF PA.** W/ Notes by Prof. I. Daniel Rupp. Phila: 1875. 72p. + Ill. $ 45.00

1759. Ruth, John L. **'TWAS SEEDING TIME.** Scottdale: 1976. 220p. Wraps. Mennonite view of the American Revolution. $ 10.00

1760. Sachse, Julius F. **DANIEL FALCKNER'S CURIEUSE NACHRICHT FROM PENNSYLVANIA. The Book that Stimulated the Great German Immigration to Pa. in the Early Years of the 18th Cent.** PGS, Lancaster: 1905. 256p. + Illus. New wraps. $ 40.00

1761. Sachse. **THE GERMAN PIETISTS OF PROVINCIAL PENNSYLVANIA, 1694=1708.** Phila: 1895. 504p. + Illus. Limited to only 500 copies. Invaluable work. $ 320.00

1762. Sachse. **THE GERMAN SECTARIANS OF PENNSYLVANIA, 1708-1800. A Critical & Legendary History of the Ephrata Cloisters & the Dunkers.** Two volumes. 1041p. + Illus. Limited to only 350 copies. Scarce & important companion to the "Pietists". $ 420.00

1763. Sachse. **JUSTUS FALCKNER, MYSTIC AND SCHOLAR. Devout Pietist in Germany, Hermit on the Wissahickon, & Missionary on the Hudson.** Phila: 1903. 141p. + Illus. Nice cloth binding. Limited to only 500 copies. $ 100.00

1764. Sachse. **LETTERS RELATING TO THE SETTLEMENT OF GERMANTOWN IN PENNSYLVANIA, 1683-4.** Lübeck & Phila: 1903. pp. 12, 33, 36. Full crimson crushed morocco. *"Ten facsimile copies of the Könneken Manuscript have been made & the plates destroyed... this book contains set No. 4, together with a translation of the four German Missives.* $ 220.00

1765. **ST. PAUL'S ENGLISH EVANG. LUTHERAN CHURCH. Memorial of 50 Years, 1836-1886.** York, Pa: 1886. 95p. + Frontis. Soft morocco binding $ 17.00

1766. Sappington, Roger E. **THE BRETHREN IN INDUSTRIAL AMERICA, 1865-1915.** Elgin, IL: 1985. 504p. Illus. Cloth. $ 25.00

1767. Sappington. **THE BRETHREN IN THE NEW NATION, 1785-1865.** Elgin, IL: 1985. 474p. Illus. Cloth. $ 17.00

1768. Schabalie, John Philip. **THE WANDERING SOUL...** Printed at the Virginian Office, Winchester: 1841. 471p. Full leather. 16mo. Translated from Dutch into German by B. B. Brechbill, and thence into English. $ 60.00

1769. Schaefer, J. C. **NEW MANUAL OF HOMOEOPATHIC VETERINARY MEDICINE...** Translated from the German and Augmented by Charles J. Hempel. Phila: 1880. 321p. + Ads + Folding Plate. $ 44.00

1770. Schaeffer, Charles E. **A REPAIRER OF THE BREACH. Memoirs of Bernard C. Wolff.** Lancaster: 1949. 117p. + Ill. Important figure in the history of Franklin & Marshall College, and the German Reformed Church. $ 12.00

1771. Schalk, Adolph. **THE GERMANS IN AMERICA.** Chi: 1973. 48p. $ 4.00

1772. Scheirer, David. **SCHEIRER FAMILY DIRECTORY & HISTORICAL FOREWORD.** Allentown: 1934. Excellent genealogy. Illus. 24mo. Printed wraps. *WST.* $ 25.00

1773. Schiffer, Herbert F. **EARLY PENNSYLVANIA HARDWARE.** Whitford, Pa: 1966. 64p. Illustrated by 192 line drawings. Wraps. $ 6.00

1774. Schiffer, Margaret B. **ARTS & CRAFTS OF CHESTER COUNTY, PA.** West Chester. 285p. + 289 Photo illustrations. $ 30.00

1775. Schiffer. **CHESTER COUNTY, PA. INVENTORIES.** West Chester. 402p. Ring Binder. Very useful reference. $ 22.00

1776. Schiffer. **FURNITURE AND ITS MAKERS OF CHESTER COUNTY, PA.** West Chester. 504p. + 183 Photo Illustrations. $ 35.00

1777. Schiffer. **HISTORICAL NEEDLEWORK OF PENNSYLVANIA.** NY: 1968. 160p. + Illus. DJ. 4to. Valuable reference. $ 30.00

1778. **SCHILLER'S "THE SONG OF THE BELL" & Other Poems.** Translated from or into the German by Thos. C. Zimmerman. Printed for private circulation only, Reading: 1896. 58p. Wraps. Xlib. Signed by Zimmerman, $ 20.00

1779. Schlabach, T. F. **PEACE, FAITH, NATION: Mennonites & Amish in 19th Century America.** Scottdale: 1988. 400p. $ 20.00

1780. Schmauk, Theodore E. **A HISTORY OF THE LUTHERAN CHURCH IN PA. 1638 - 1820...** Phila: 1903. 588p. + Illus. Cloth. Limited to 225 Copies signed by the author. This is called Vol. I, but this appears to be the only complete edition of the text issued as PGS Vol. XI. Invaluable reference. $ 140.00

1781. Schmucker, S. S. **DISCOURSE IN COMMEMORATION OF THE GLORIOUS REFORMATION...** NY: 1838. 137p. Ds. 32mo. Embossed publisher's cloth. $ 16.00

1782. Schmucker, Samuel M. **HISTORY OF ALL RELIGIONS...** Enlarged by Charles Drew. Phila: 1870. 352p. Embossed blue cloth gilt. Includes Mennonites, Etc. Etc. $ 40.00

1783. Schrock, Wilson & Rogers. **WONDERFUL GOOD COOKING.** Scottdale: 1974. 136p. Illus. Spiral bound. Recipes from the Ohio Amish country. $ 8.00

1784. Schultz, Christopher. **SHORT QUESTIONS CONCERNING THE CHRISTIAN DOCTRINE OF FAITH...** Translated from the German by I. D. Rupp. Schuenemann, Skippackville: 1863. pp. 12, 140. Unusual Schwenkfelder item. $ 40.00

1785. Schultz, Selina Gerhard. **A COURSE OF STUDY IN THE LIFE & TEACHINGS OF CASPAR SCHWECKFELD VON OSSIG [1489-1561]; A History of the Schwenckfelder Religious Movement [1518-1964].** Gottingen: 1964. 184p. Cloth. $ 20.00

1786. Schultz. **CASPAR SCHWECKFELD VON OSSIG [1489-1561]; Spiritual Interpreter of Christianity, Apostle of the Middle Way, & Pioneer in Modern Religious Thought.** Norristown: 1946. 453p. + Frontis. By the Editor of the "*Corpus Schwenckfeldianorum*". $ 50.00

1787. Schwarze, Dr. Wm. N. **THE MORAVIAN SETTLEMENT OF BETHLEHEM: Its Courage, Its Vision, & Its Ideals**. Newcomen: 1940. 24p. Printed wraps. $ 6.00

1788. **THE SCHWENKFELDIAN**. Magazine published by the First Schwenkfeldian Church. Phila: 1904=08. Selected run of over 30 issues. $ 30.00

1789. Scott, Job. **JOURNAL OF THE LIFE, TRAVELS, AND GOSPEL LABOURS OF JOB SCOTT**... Phila: 1814. 323p. Full leather. AI 32727. $ 35.00

1790. Scott, Kenneth. **ABSTRACTS FROM BEN FRANKLIN'S PENNSYLVANIA GAZETTE, 1728-84**. Balt: 1975. 720p. $ 40.00

1791. Scott & Clarke. **ABSTRACTS FROM THE PENNSYLVANIA GAZETTE, 1748-55**. Balt: 1977. 377p. $ 25.00

1792. Scott & Stryker-Rodda. **BURIED GENEALOGICAL DATA. A Complete List of Addressed Letters Left in the Post Offices of Phila., Chester, Lancaster, Trenton, New Castle, & Wilmington 1748-1780. Extracted from the Pa. Gazette**. Balt: 1977. 241p. Cloth. $ 20.00

1793. Seabrook, William. **THESE FOREIGNERS**. NY: 1938. 358p. DJ. Review Copy. The chapter on German Americans is the largest & most interesting. $ 25.00

1794. Seidensticker, Oswald. **THE FIRST CENTURY OF GERMAN PRINTING IN AMERICA, 1728-1830**. Reprint of the rare 1893 edition. Millwood, NY: 1980. 253p. Fundamental reference. $ 50.00

1795. Seipt, A. A. **SCHWENKFELDER HYMNOLOGY AND THE SOURCES OF THE FIRST SCHWENKFELDER HYMN-BOOK PRINTED IN AMERICA**. Phila: 1909. 112p. + Illus. Impressive bibliographic scholarship. *WST*. $ 80.00

1796. Sewel, William. **THE HISTORY OF THE RISE, INCREASE & PROGRESS OF THE CHRISTIAN PEOPLE CALLED QUAKERS**... 3rd Ed. Corrected. Isaac Collins, Trenton, NJ: 1774. 828p. Folio. Worn original full leather. Front board detached. Possibly bound by Robert Aitken. Sabin 79605, Evans 13607. Really the 2nd American Edition. This masterpiece of Quaker history was one of the largest jobs undertaken by the famed printer Collins, occupying him for over two years. See #1562 for an important Sewel manuscript item. $ 175.00

1797. Sewel. **THE HISTORY OF THE RISE, INCREASE, AND PROGRESS OF THE CHRISTIAN PEOPLE CALLED QUAKERS**... Phila: 1811. Two volumes. 1133p. AI 23920, Sabin 79609. Standard Quaker history. $ 40.00

1798. Shank, Esther H. **MENNONITE COUNTRY STYLE RECIPES & KITCHEN SECRETS. Collection of a Shenandoah Valley Cook**. Scottdale: 1987. 679p. $ 20.00

1799. Shelley, Donald A. **THE PENNSYLVANIA GERMAN STYLE OF ILLUMINATION**. NYU Doctoral Dissertation (1953). Re-Issued by the Pa. German Folklore Soc. as Vol. 23. Allentown: 1961. 375p. + Many Illustrations. Essential early work on Fraktur. $ 80.00

1800. Shenk, H. H. **A LEBANON COUNTY OLD BACKWOODS PREACHER = Moses Dissinger**. Lebanon Cty. Hist. Soc: 1915. pp. 414 - 439. Printed Wraps. Bush Meeting Evangelism. $ 12.00

1801. Shoemaker, Alfred L. **CHRISTMAS IN PENNSYLVANIA. A Folk=Cultural Study**. Pa Folklore Soc. Kutztown: 1959. 116p. Illus. Folio. $ 60.00

1802. Shoemaker. **EASTERTIDE IN PENNSYLVANIA. A Folk=Cultural Study**. Pa Folklore Soc. Kutztown: 1960. 96p. Illus. Folio. $ 60.00

1803. Shoemaker, Alfred L. **GERMAN PRESS OF LEHIGH COUNTY, 1807-1900**. Lehigh County Hist. Soc. Vol. 16. Allentown: 1947. 240p. Invaluable bibliographic checklist of Lehigh County imprints + Printer's biographies. $ 40.00

1804. Shoemaker. **MY OFF IS ALL** Pa Dutch Folklore Center, F & M, Lancaster: 1953. 36p. Printed Wraps. Pa. Dutch Humor. $ 12.00

1805. Shoemaker, et. al. **A PEEK AT THE AMISH**. Pa Dutch Folklore Center, F & M, Lancaster: 1954. 40p. Fine photographic illustrations by Charles S. Rice. Wraps. $ 20.00

1806. Shoemaker. **3 MYTHS ABOUT THE PENNSYLVANIA DUTCH COUNTRY**. Harrisburg: 1947. 32p. Illus. Printed wraps. *WST*. $ 14.00

1807. Shoemaker, et. al. **TOURIST GUIDE THROUGH THE DUTCH COUNTRY = 1954**. Pa. Dutch Folklore Center, Lancaster: 1954. 72p. Illus. Wraps. $ 10.00

1808. Shoemaker, et. al. **TOURIST GUIDE THROUGH THE DUTCH COUNTRY**. Pa. Dutch Folklore Center, Bethel, Pa: 1958. 100p. Illus. Wraps. $ 8.00

1809. Shoemaker, Yoder, et. al. **IN THE DUTCH COUNTRY**. F & M, Lancaster, Ca: 1951. 44p. Illustrated with photos by Rice. Colored wraps. 4to. Quite informative. $ 20.00

1810. Shoemaker, Yoder, et. al. **THE PENNSYLVANIA BARN**. F & M, Lancaster: 1955. 96p. Well illus. Wraps. Folio. $ 65.00

1811. Showalter, Mary Emma. **FAVORITE FAMILY RECIPES**. Selected from the Mennonite Community Cookbook. Scottdale: 1972. 129p. Wraps. $ 5.00

1812. Showalter. **MENNONITE COMMUNITY COOKBOOK**. Scottdale, Pa: 1978. 494p. Illus. Cloth. Classic collection of tantalizing recipes. $ 20.00

1813. (Shultze). **THE JOURNALS AND PAPERS OF DAVID SHULTZE, 1726-1797**. Translated and Edited by Andrew S. Berky. Pennsburg: 1952. Two Volumes. 580p. + Facsimiles. Remarkable Schwenkfelder record. See also: #798, #806, Etc. *WST*. $ 75.00

1814. Shumway, George. **PENNSYLVANIA LONGRIFLES OF NOTE**. York: 1977. 63p. Well illustrated. Wraps. $ 10.00

1815. Shumway. **RIFLES OF COLONIAL AMERICA**. York: 1980. Two Vols. $ 120.00

1816. Shumway, Durrell, & Frey. **CONESTOGA WAGON, 1750-1850**. York: 1966. 206p. Illus. Wraps. Fine study of technology & culture. $ 22.00

1817. Sibole, Rev. E. E. **HISTORICAL SKETCH, ST. JOHN'S EVANGELICAL LUTHERAN CHURCH, 1806-1906**. Phila: 1906. 136p. + Illus. Cloth. $ 15.00

1818. Silver, Rollo G. **TYPEFOUNDING IN AMERICA, 1787=1825**. Univ. Va: 1965. 139p. + Illus. Cloth backed bds. Though this is the best work on the subject, (and there is much on the later Sowers) the early German types are not treated fully enough. $ 30.00

1819. Simmendinger, Ulrich. **TRUE & AUTHENTIC REGISTER OF PERSONS WHO JOURNEYED FROM GERMANY TO AMERICA - 1709**. Balt: 1984. 20p. Wraps. Palatine settlers in New York's Mohawk Valley. First published in 1934. $ 8.00

1820. (Simmonetti, et. al.). **DESCRIPTIVE LIST OF THE MAP COLLECTION IN THE PA. STATE ARCHIVES**. Harrisburg: 1976. 178p. Cloth. DJ. $ 10.00

1821. Simpson, Henry. **THE LIVES OF EMINENT PHILADELPHIANS, Now Deceased...** Brotherhead, Phila: 1859. 993p. + 44 Fine engravings, by the best American artists. Thick 4to. Original cloth worn. The portraits by Sartain, and his contemporaries, are among their most expressive and powerful. Substantial and valuable reference. $ 80.00

1822. Singmaster, Elsie. **MARTIN LUTHER.** Phila: 1939. 138p. DJ. $ 10.00

1823. Singmaster. **WHEN SARAH WENT TO SCHOOL.** Boston: 1910. 188p. $ 12.00

CLASSIC STUDIES OF THE INDIANS ON THE PENNSYLVANIA FRONTIER

1824. Sipe, C. Hale. **THE INDIAN CHIEFS OF PENNSYLVANIA...** Butler, Pa: 1927. 569p. + Ill. Very important companion to the "*Indian Wars*" listed below. $ 120.00

1825. Sipe. **THE INDIAN WARS OF PENNSYLVANIA. An Account of Indian Events in Pa., The French & Indian War, Pontiac's War, Lord Dunsmore's War, The Revolution, Etc.** Harrisburg: 1929. 793p. + Map. Cloth. With / **The Supplement to the First Edition...** Harrisburg: 1931. 115p. Wraps. $ 160.00

1826. Siskind & Morgan. **BUCKS COUNTY. Photographs of Early Architecture**. Doylestown: 1974. 122p. Fine photos of architectural details. $ 14.00

1827. Skardon, Alvin W. **WILLIAM AUGUSTUS MUHLENBERG = CHURCH LEADER IN THE CITIES.** Phila: 1971. 343p. + Illus. DJ. $ 16.00

1828. Sloan, Samuel. **SLOAN'S HOMESTEAD ARCHITECTURE, Forty Designs for Villas, Cottages, & Farm Houses, with Essays on Style, Construction, Landscape Gardening, Furniture, Etc...** Phila: 1867. 355p. Illustrated by plates and figures. Second Edition. Classic text in the history of Victorian architecture and style. $ 125.00

1829. Smaby, Beverly P. **THE TRANSFORMATION OF MORAVIAN BETHLEHEM, From Communal Mission to Family Economy**. Phila: 1989. 288p. Illus. $ 35.00

1830. Small, A. E. & Sheek, J. F. **THE POCKET MANUAL OF HOMOEOPATHIC PRACTICE...** Phila: 1855. 126p. + Bookseller's ads. Embossed cloth. 32mo. $ 40.00

1831. Smith, Dr. Geo. **HISTORY OF DELAWARE COUNTY, PA.** Phila: (1907). 581p. + Maps & fine plates by Sartain. 1/2 morocco. It's often overlooked that this is a reissue of the original 1862 plates and sheets. Handsome copy of the best edition. Howes S 594. $ 120.00

1832. Smith, E. L. et. al. **ANTIQUES IN PENNSYLVANIA DUTCHLAND.** Lebanon: 1967. 42p. Illus. 4to. Wraps. $ 7.00

1833. Smith, et. al. **ARTS AND CRAFTS OF THE SHENANDOAH VALLEY.** Witmer, Pa: 1968. 44p. Illustrated. 4to. Wraps. $ 10.00

1834. Smith & Thompson. **TRADITIONALLY PENNSYLVANIA DUTCH.** NY: 1947. 81p. Charmingly illustrated. Signed by both authors. $ 24.00

1835. Smith, Richard Flanders. **PENNSYLVANIA BUTTER PRINTS**. Science Press, Ephrata: 1970. 36p. Well illus. Cloth. Limited to 400 copies. $ 35.00

1836. Smith, Samuel. **HISTORY OF THE COLONY OF NOVA-CAESARIA, OR NEW JERSEY...** Trenton, NJ: 1890. 613p. + Map. Cloth. XLib. Important scholarly reprint of the rare 1765 edition. $ 45.00

1837. Smith. **HISTORY OF THE PROVINCE OF PENNSYLVANIA.** Wm. M. Mervine, Editor. Pa. Colonial Soc. Phila: 1913. 231p. + List of members. Uncut & unopened. $ 50.00

1838. Smith, Willard H. **MENNONITES IN ILLINOIS**. Scottdale: 1983. 616p. $ 28.00

1839. **SMYSER FAMILY IN AMERICA**. York: 1947. 107p. + Illus. Wraps. $ 15.00

1840. Snader, Howard. **GLOSSARY OF 6167 ENGLISH WORDS & EXPRESSIONS AND THEIR BERKS COUNTY, PA. DUTCH EQUIVALENTS**. Reading: 1948. 64p. Worn wraps. Useful dialect reference. $ 18.00

1841. **SNIPSNAPS AND SNICKERINGS**. Dick & Fitzgerald, NY. Ca: 1865. 128p. + Ads. Printed wraps. Includes "Dutch Jokes". $ 24.00

1842. Snyder, C. A. **THE LIFE & THOUGHT OF MICHAEL SATTLER**. Scottdale: 1984. 264p. Anabaptist leader & martyr. $ 22.00

1843. Snyder, Henry L. **OLD ZIONSVILLE**. Miami: 1947. 63p. Memories of Pennsylvania German Lehigh County. *WST*. $ 22.00

1844. (Soderlund, Jean R.). **WILLIAM PENN & THE FOUNDING OF PENNSYLVANIA, 1680 - 1684. A Documentary History**. U of P, Phila: 1983. 416p. Illus. $ 20.00

1845. **THE SOLDIER'S POCKET BOOK**. Presbyterian Board of Pub. Phila: 1862. 64p. 24mo. Cloth wraps. Distributed to Civil War Soldiers. *This copy owned by C. Penrose Sherk, Co. E, 127th Pennsylvania Volunteers*. $ 32.00

1846. Spangler, Edward W. **THE ANNALS OF THE FAMILIES OF CASPAR, HENRY, BALTZER AND GEORGE SPENGLER, WHO SETTLED IN YORK COUNTY, 1729 - 1751**. York: 1896. 605p. + Illus. Crimson cloth gilt. Important historic genealogy, filled with great accounts of little known incidents in York County and Pa. German history. $ 150.00

1847. (Spears, J. F.). **THE HOUSE OF DERR. Pennsylvania's Contribution to the World of Primitive Art. A True Story of Three Brothers in the Summer Hills of Berks County, Pa.** Lebanon: 1973. 187p. Well illus. Early makers of metal, tin, & tole ware. $ 30.00

1848. Spotts, Charles D. **STORY OF LEATHER TANNING IN LANCASTER COUNTY**. Lancaster: 1973. 57p. Illus. Ds. Wraps. $ 14.00

1849. Springer & Klassen. **MENNONITE BIBLIOGRAPHY**. Scottdale: 1977. Two volumes. Over 1000p. Over 28000 entries. Essential. $ 160.00

1850. Stanton. **JOURNAL OF THE LIFE AND TRAVELS... OF DANIEL STANTON**. Crukshank, Phila: 1772. pp. 17, 184 + Errata. Contemporary full roan. Detailed Quaker journal of travels in America and the West Indies. Includes a first-hand account of the Indian Treaty negotiations at Bethlehem, 1756-9. Evans 12565, Sabin 90387. $ 145.00

1851. Stapleton, A. **A WONDERFUL STORY OF OLD TIME EVANGELICAL EVANGELISM, Being an Account of the Life & Time of Rev. Jacob Albright...** Harrisburg: 1917. 143p. + Illus. Scarce history of the Evangelical Association. $ 50.00

1852. Stapleton. **MEMORIALS OF THE HUGUENOTS IN AMERICA. With Special Reference to their Emigration to Pa**. Carlisle: 1901. 164p. + Illus. Cloth wraps. $ 40.00

1853. (Stein, Kurt M.). **GEMIXTE PICKLES. By K. M. S.** Chicago: 1927. 94p. Poetic humor written in a pidgin German American dialect. This is very curious, but fun to read. $ 22.00

1854. Steinfelt, B. **THE AMISH OF LANCASTER COUNTY. A Brief but Truthful Account of the Actual Life & Customs of the Most Unique Class of People in the U. S.** Lancaster: 1937. 32p. + Photos. Wraps. $ 12.00

1855. Stetzel, Henry. **A BRIEF BIOGRAPHY OF MOSES DISSINGER, Preacher of the Evangelical Association.** Allentown: 1892. 27p. Wraps. *WST.* $ 20.00

STEUBEN'S MILITARY MANUAL

1856. (Steuben, Baron von). **REGULATIONS FOR THE ORDER AND DISCIPLINE OF THE TROOPS OF THE UNITED STATES.** Phila: 1800. 151p. + Eight folding engraved plates. Evans 38806. $ 220.00

1857. **STEUBEN SOCIETY OF AMERICA.** Collection of Seven German & English Promotional & Informational Pamphlets. (NY: 1935). *WST.* $ 30.00

1858. Stevens, Sylvester K. **PENNSYLVANIA - The Heritage of a Commonwealth.** West Palm Beach: 1968-9. Four Volumes. Illus. Fine modern historical & biographical work that replace many older "classics". $ 60.00

1859. Stevens & Kent. **WILDERNESS CHRONICLES OF NORTHWESTERN PA.** WPA/HMC, Harrisburg: 1941. 342p. + Map. Cloth. Invaluable study of the French & English on the frontier. $ 30.00

1860. Stevens, Thaddeus [1792-1868]. **FREE-MASONRY UNMASKED: Or Minutes of the Trial of a Suit in the Court of Common Pleas of Adams County, Thaddeus Stevens, Esq. was Plaintiff, and Jacob Lefever, Defendant.** Middleton, Gettysburg: 1835. 93p. Curious woodcut on title. Original leather backed paper boards. AI 34380. Very important and influential Anti-Masonic document. $ 70.00

1861. Stiles, Henry Reed. **BUNDLING. Its Origin, Progress & Decline in America.** (Chicago? 1920?). Privately Issued for Subscribers Only. 146p. *WST.* $ 26.00

1862. Stiles. **BUNDLING. Its Origin, Progress & Decline in America.** Book Collector's Assoc. NY: 1934. 146p. + Plates from the Paramount production of "*The Pursuit of Happiness*" *!!* DJ. Motion Picture edition. The movie itself must be quite curious. $ 22.00

1863. Stocker, Harry E. **A HISTORY OF THE MORAVIAN CHURCH IN NEW YORK CITY.** NY: 1922. 389p. Ill. *WST.* $ 30.00

1864. Stoeffler, F. Ernest. **GERMAN PIETISM DURING THE EIGHTEENTH CENTURY.** Leiden: 1973. 281p. Invaluable reference. $ 44.00

1865. (Stoever, John Caspar). **EARLY LUTHERAN BAPTISMS & MARRIAGES IN SOUTHEASTERN PENNSYLVANIA, 1730 = 1779.** Indexed by Eliz. P. Bentley. Balt: 1988. 107p. Valued collection of genealogical information, first published in 1896. $ 20.00

1866. **THE STOLEN CHILD = Henry von Eichenfels.** Translation into English by Bachman & Miller. Gordonville: 1966. 40p. Wraps. $ 10.00

1867. Stoltzfus, Grant M. **MENNONITES OF THE OHIO & EASTERN CONFERENCE.** Scottdale: 1969. 459p. DJ. 1st Edition. Now Out of Print. $ 40.00

1868. Story, Thomas. **A JOURNAL OF THE LIFE OF THOMAS STORY...** Newcastle Upon Tyne: 1747. pp. 4, 768, 8. Folio. Full contemporary leather binding, need re-backing. Internally, a crisp copy of the First Edition. One of the most important journals of Quaker travel. Sabin 92324. Story [1670-1742] sailed for Pa. in 1698, and stayed for 16 years. $ 150.00

1869. Stoudt, John Baer. **THE FOLKLORE OF THE PENNSYLVANIA GERMANS.** Campbell, Phila: 1916. 155p. Illus. Cloth. Author's off-print from PGS Vol. 23, Pt. II. Very scarce in this form. *WST.* $ 95.00

1870. Stoudt. **THE LIBERTY BELL IN ALLENTOWN, and Allentown's Liberty Bell.** Allentown: 1927. 61p. Illus. Cloth. *WST.* $ 22.00

1871. Stoudt. **THE LIBERTY BELLS OF PENNSYLVANIA.** Phila: 1930. 205p. + Illus. Cloth gilt. Signed presentation from Stoudt to *WST.* Still the best study of the historic "Great Bells of Pennsylvania." $ 50.00

1872. Stoudt. **THE LIFE AND TIMES OF COLONEL JOHN SIEGFRIED.** Northampton: 1914. 62p. + Illus. Important details on Indians, Mennonites, War, etc. $ 40.00

1873. Stoudt, John Joseph. **EARLY PENNSYLVANIA ARTS & CRAFTS.** NY: 1964. 364p. + Excellent illustrations. DJ. Folio. Useful study. $ 40.00

1874. Stoudt. **PENNSYLVANIA FOLK-ART. An Interpretation.** Schlecter's, Allentown: 1948. 403p. Illus. With the rarely seen Dust Jacket. "Second Edition" of "*Consider the Lillies*". $ 80.00

1875. Strassburger, Ralph Beaver. **THE STRASSBURGER FAMILY & ALLIED FAMILIES OF PENNSYLVANIA.** Gwynedd Valley, Pa: 1922. 520p. + Plates. Large 4to. Classic historical genealogy. $ 60.00

1876. Strassburger & Hinke. **PENNSYLVANIA GERMAN PIONEERS. A Publication of the Original Lists of Arrivals In the Port of Phila. 1727-1808.** PGS, Norristown: 1934. Three volumes. Cloth. The original edition of this very valuable reference, published by the Pa. German Society. See #2043. $ 260.00

1877. Strassburger & Hinke. **PENNSYLVANIA GERMAN PIONEERS...** Balt: 1980. 2 Vols. Cloth. Lists nearly 30,000 names in the index. Reprint of the above. O.P. $ 150.00

1878. Studder, Gerald C. **CHRISTOPHER DOCK: COLONIAL SCHOOLMASTER.** Scottdale: 1967. 448p. + Illus. Biography and Writings of the "Father of American Pedagogy". Now, Out of Print. $ 32.00

1879. **STURM'S REFLECTIONS ON THE WORKS OF GOD & HIS PROVIDENCE THROUGHOUT ALL NATURE.** Joseph Funk & Sons, Mountain Valley, Virginia: 1848. 490p. + Curious woodcut plates on yellow paper. Disbound. Originally issued in German, this work is a curious, but appealing, naturalistic day-book. The publisher, Joseph Funk [1778-1862], was known as the Mennonite "Father of Song in Northern Virginia". All books from his press are rare. $ 95.00

1880. **THE SUNDAY SCHOOL HYMN BOOK.** Ashmead for the Sunday & Adult School Union, Phila: 1822. (125p.) 32mo. Attractive full leather. AI 10378.
Manuscript presentation from the Lebanon Sunday School Society. $ 30.00

1881. Swank, Scott T. et. al. **ARTS OF THE PENNSYLVANIA GERMANS.** Winterthur / PGS: 1983. 309p. Highly Illus. Cloth. DJ. $ 44.00

T

1882. Taylor, F. R. **LIFE OF WILLIAM SAVERY OF PHILADELPHIA, 1750 - 1804**. NY: 1925. 474p. + Illus. XLib. Important record. $ 22.00

1883. Tepper, Michael. **NEW WORLD IMMIGRANTS. A Consolidation of Ship Passenger Lists from Periodical Literature**. Balt: 1988. Two volumes. 1170p. Identifies over 27,500 immigrants. $ 60.00

1884. Tepper & Bentley. **PASSENGER ARRIVALS AT THE PORT OF PHILADELPHIA, 1800-19**. Balt: 1986. 913p. 40000 English, Irish, & Germans. $ 45.00

1885. Thaeler, A. D. **THE STORY OF THE CHRISTMAS PUTZ**. (Bethlehem): 1927. 20p. Illus. Printed wraps. Pennsylvania German religious art. *WST*. $ 16.00

1886. Thomas, Augusta Dillman. **THE BOWMANS. A History of Hans Dieterick Bauman & His Descendants**. Allentown: 1934. 466p. + Chart + Bowmanstown Inserts. Illus. $ 60.00

1887. Thomas, Augusta Dillman. **ONE CROWDED HOUR**. Schlechter's, Allentown: 1940. 173p. Depicts the experiences of a Pa. German at the West Chester Normal School. $ 14.00

1888. Thomas, Edith M. **MARY AT THE FARM & BOOK OF RECIPES Compiled During Her Visit Among the "Pennsylvania Germans"**. Norristown: 1915. 440p. + Illus. + Letters from Thomas to *WST*. Signed. Attractive copy of this early monograph. $ 75.00

1889. Thomas. **MARY AT THE FARM & BOOK OF RECIPES Compiled During Her Visit Among the "Pennsylvania Germans"**. Harrisburg: 1928. 423p. + Signed by Thomas. 2nd Edition. *WST*. $ 60.00

1890. Thomas, Robert. **A CENTURY OF METHODISM IN GERMANTOWN**. Germantown: 1895. 76p. Illus. Crimson cloth. $ 24.00

1891. **THE THREE EARLS**... New Holland: 1876. 115p. Old ink stain. Excellent contribution to Lancaster County history. $ 30.00

1892. Tolles, Frederick B. **MEETING HOUSE AND COUNTING HOUSE. The Quaker Merchants of Philadelphia, 1682-1763**. Chapel Hill: 1948. 292p. $ 24.00

1893. Tolzmann, Don Heinrich. **GERMAN-AMERICAN LITERATURE**. Metuchen, NJ: 1977. pp. 12, 328. Cloth. Valuable articles on Beissel, Harbaugh, Fisher, et. al. $ 24.00

1894. Toews, John A. **A HISTORY OF THE MENNONITE BRETHREN CHURCH; Pilgrims & Pioneers**. (Scottdale): 1975. 513p. $ 16.00

1895. Torrey, Jesse Jr. **A MENTAL MUSEUM FOR THE RISING GENERATION**... Desilver, Phila: 1829. pp. 360, 12 + Hand colored woodcut frontis. Printed boards with a printer/stationer ad for Desilver. Includes "The Constitution of the First Free Circulating Library" in America. Barnitz ownership. Ds. AI 40661. $ 30.00

1896. **TRINITY LUTHERAN CHURCH RECORDS, Lancaster, Pa. 1730-67**. Translated and Edited by Debra D. Smith & Frederick S. Weiser. (Lititz: 1989). 484p. $ 40.00

1897. Troxel, William S. ("Pumpernickle Bill"). **AUS PENNSYLFAWNIA. An Anthology of Translations into the Pennsylvania German Dialect**. Phila: 1938. 60p. Tall 8vo. Brilliant decorated cloth. Text in English and Dialect. Pumpernickle's own copy. *WST*. $ 40.00

V 1898. Vaux, Roberts. **MEMOIRS OF THE LIFE OF ANTHONY BENEZET.** Phila: 1817. pp. (8), 136 + Frontis of the famed 1757 Indian Medal + Benezet facsimile autograph. Sabin 98704, AI 42769. $ 50.00

1899. Verheyden, A. L. E. **ANABAPTISM IN FLANDERS.** Scottdale: 1961. 126p. $ 16.00

1900. (Vinegar). **A COMPLETE TREATISE ON THE MANUFACTURE OF VINEGAR from Cider, Malt, Wine, Sugar, Sorghum, Molasses, Etc... & Convert It Into Sparkling Champagne Wine.** Pearsol & Geist, Lancaster: 1874. 36p. 12mo. Stiff orange cloth bds. Scarce. $ 75.00

1901. Voltaire. **LETTERS CONCERNING THE ENGLISH NATION...** London: 1741. 255p. + Index & Ads. Disbound. *Thomas Partington's copy.* The first four letters are on Quakers, Penn, & Pennsylvania. Sabin 100751. $ 150.00

W 1902. Wagenen, Jared Van Jr. **THE GOLDEN AGE OF HOMESPUN.** Cornell: 1953. 280p. Illus. DJ. Good account of many early American crafts & trades. $ 20.00

1903. Wagner, A. E. **HISTORY, GOVERNMENT & GEOGRAPHY OF CARBON COUNTY.** Allentown: 1910. 181p. + Brilliant Engraved Frontis of Asa Parker. *WST.* $ 38.00

1904. Walker, L. Burd. **THE "BURD PAPERS". EXTRACTS FROM (PENNSYLVANIA) CHIEF JUSTICE WILLIAM ALLEN'S LETTER BOOK. Including: Pamphlets in the Controversy with Franklin.** (Phila: 1897). 136p. + Fine Rosenthal engraved frontis. Uncut and unopened. Remarkable historical record. Exciting reading. $ 24.00

1905. Wallace, Paul A. W. **THE MUHLENBERGS OF PA.** Phila: 1950. 358p. + Illus. Cloth. Xlib. Fine study of a remarkable family. $ 15.00

1906. Walters, Raymond. **BETHLEHEM. Long Ago & Today.** Bethlehem: 1923. 159p. + Illus. Details the Moravian community, etc. $ 16.00

1907. Walton, Joseph S. **CONRAD WEISER, & THE INDIAN POLICY OF COLONIAL PA.** Phila: 1900. 420p. + Illus. Very XLib. Worn. Weiser also played a leading part in the early struggles for the Ohio Valley. Howes W78. $ 32.00

1908. Wanner, A. **THE FAMILY; Marriage Relation & Religious Training of Children.** Chambersburg: 1853. 238p. Wanner was pastor of the German Reformed Church, Washingtonville, Ohio. $ 22.00

1909. Weaver, M. G. **A HISTORY OF NEW HOLLAND, PA. 1728-1928.** New Holland: 1928. 175p. Illus. Printed wraps. $ 30.00

1910. Weeks, Lyman H. **HISTORY OF PAPER MANUFACTURING IN THE UNITED STATES, 1690=1916.** Reprint of the 1916 Edition. NY: 1969. 357p. Foremost history of this important early American industry. $ 40.00

1911. Weekes, Refine. **THE LIFE OF WILLIAM PENN, & Other Poems...** St. Clairsville, Ohio: 1836. 168p. Full leather. Ds. $ 40.00

1912. (Weiser, Charles W.). **SIM SCHMALZGSICHT'S OWN MAGAZINE. The Only Pennsylvania German Humorous Publication in the U.S.** Allentown: 1913. Four Issues (All that were published). Crisp condition. Nicely bound in cloth. Perhaps the single greatest influence on the creation of "Pumpernickle Bill". *WST.* $ 80.00

1913. Weiser, C. Z. **THE LIFE OF (JOHN) CONRAD WEISER, THE GERMAN PIONEER, PATRIOT, & PATRON OF TWO RACES**. Reading: 1899. 140p. $ 38.00

1914. Weiser, Frederick F. **FRAKTUR. PENNSYLVANIA GERMAN FOLK ART**. Science Press (Ephrata): 1973. 103p. Beautifully produced and illustrated. Oblong 4to. Cloth. Uncommon and eagerly sought after. $ 145.00

1915. Weiser & Heaney. **THE PENNSYLVANIA GERMAN FRAKTUR COLLECTION OF THE FREE LIBRARY OF PHILA**. PGS (Vols. 10-11), Breinigsville: 1976-7. *Rare "Deluxe Edition"*. Two Volumes. Oblong folio. Specially bound and boxed. Signed by the designer and authors. No. 193 of only 500 copies. $ 220.00

1916. Weiser & Neff. **THE ACCOUNT BOOK OF CONRAD WEISER, BERKS COUNTY, PA, 1746-1760**. PGS, Breinigsville: 1981. 184p. Folio. Wraps. $ 18.00

1917A. Weiss. **THE LETTER BOOK OF JACOB WEISS, Deputy Quartermaster General of the Revolution**. M. J. Boyer, Editor. Lehigh Cty. Hist. Soc. Allentown: 1956. 136p. $ 20.00

1917B. Weld, Isaac. **VOYAGE AU CANADA, 1795-1797...** Paris: (1803). Three volumes. Well illustrated with maps and plates. Worn full leather. Ds. Howes W235, Sabin 102544. Scarce edition of this important account of American travel, which includes a sojourn with the Moravians in Bethlehem, Pennsylvania. $ 325.00

1918. Wenger, John C. **HISTORY OF THE MENNONITES OF THE FRANCONIA CONFERENCE**. Telford, Pa: 1937. 523p. + Illus. *WST*. $ 75.00

1919. Wenger. **THE MENNONITE CHURCH IN AMERICA**. Scottdale: 1967. 384p. One of the best modern histories of the "Old Mennonites". $ 20.00

1920. Wentz, Abel Ross. **HISTORY OF THE GETTYSBURG THEOLOGICAL SEMINARY...** 1826-1926. Phila: (1926). 624p. Illus. Fine historical & biographical reference. $ 22.00

1921. Wentz. **THE LUTHERAN CHURCH IN AMERICAN HISTORY**. Philadelphia: 1933. 465p. Fundamental history. $ 16.00

1922. Wentz, Stephen. **BURIAL RECORD OF ST. PAUL'S CHURCH GRAVEYARD & CEMETERY, Cherryville, Northampton County, Pa.** (Easton: 1888). 24p. Cloth wraps. Lists over 1000 names 1756-1888. *WST*. $ 32.00

1923. Weygandt, Cornelius. **PHILADELPHIA FOLKS: Ways & Institutions In & About the Quaker City**. NY: 1938. 357p. + Illus. DJ. Charming. $ 16.00

1924. Weygandt. **THE PLENTY OF PA. Samples of Seven Cultures Persisting from Colonial Days**. NY: 1942. 319p. + Illus. Cloth. XLib. $ 12.00

1925. Weygandt. **THE RED HILLS. A record of Good Days Outdoors & In, With Things Pa. Dutch**. Phila: 1929. 251p. + Illus. Interpretative account of the Pennsylvania Germans. The first edition sold out in just three weeks. *Signed by Weygandt*. $ 40.00

1926. Weygandt. **THE WISSAHICKON HILLS: Memories of Leisure Hours Out of Doors in an Old Countryside**. Phila: 1930. 366p. + Illus. $ 20.00

1927. Whisker, James B. **GUNSMITHS OF ADAMS, FRANKLIN & CUMBERLAND COUNTIES, PA**. Bedford, Pa: 1989. 126p. Well illustrated. 4to. $ 35.00

1928. Whisker. **GUNSMITHS OF WEST VIRGINIA**. Bedford, Pa: 1987. 128p. Illus. 4to. Cloth. Many of these Gunsmiths came from Pennsylvania. $ 35.00

1929. Whisker & Vaughn. **THE GUN MAKERS & GUNSMITHS OF WESTERN PA.** Bedford, Pa: 1982. 103p. Illus. 4to. Wraps. Limited to 500 copies. $ 40.00

1930. Whisker & Chandler. **ARMS MAKERS OF EASTERN PA. The Colonial Years to 1790.** Bedford, Pa: 1984. 100+p. Illus. 4to. Wraps. $ 28.00

1931. Whisker & Chandler. **PENNSYLVANIA GUNMAKERS (A Collection)**. Bedford, Pa: 1984. 177p. Illus. 4to. Cloth. Limited to 1000 copies. $ 60.00

1932. Whisker & Metzgar. **GUNSMITHS OF WESTERN PA.** Vol. I. Bedford: 1988. 190p. Illus. Cloth. $ 35.00

1933. Wickersham, James P. **A HISTORY OF EDUCATION IN PA...** Lancaster: 1886. 683p. Illus. Includes the German schools. Review copy for A. R. Horne. *WST.* $ 40.00

1934. Wildes, Harry Emerson. **WILLIAM PENN.** NY: 1974. 469p. DJ. $ 12.00

1935. Wiley, Samuel T. **BIOGRAPHICAL & PORTRAIT ENCYCLOPEDIA of the 19th Congressional District - Cumberland, York, & Adams Counties.** Reprint of the 1897 edition. 780p. Illus. Includes a very useful new surname index. $ 60.00

1937. Wilkinson. et. al. **BIBLIOGRAPHY OF PENNSYLVANIA HISTORY.** Harrisburg: 1957. 826p. This important bibliography is now out of print. Absolutely essential to any reader of this catalog, and enthusiast of Pennsylvania history. $ 22.00

1938. **WILLIAM PENN THE POLITICIAN, His Relations with the English Government.** Cornell: 1965. 267p. DJ. $ 12.00

1939. **WILLIAM PENN MEMORIAL IN LONDON.** NY: 1911. 110p. Illus. Cloth. $ 20.00

1940. Williams, David G. **BRIDGES - and Those of the Lower Jordan Valley...** Lehigh Cty. Hist. Soc. Vol. 20, Allentown: 1954. 70p. + Plans + Other articles of interest. $ 24.00

1941. Williams. **THE LOWER JORDAN VALLEY PENNSYLVANIA GERMAN SETTLEMENT**. Lehigh Cty. Hist. Soc. Vol. 18, Allentown: 1950. 180p. + Plates. Especially important as an architectural and cultural reference. $ 40.00

1942. (Williamson). **THE CASE OF PASSMORE WILLIAMSON...** Phila: 1856. 191p. + *Broadside "Letter of Sympathy" from Charles Sumner.* Original cloth. Williamson tried to save a young black girl & her two children, but was arrested & forced by this court to give them up to their "owner". "The case caused much excitement in the time" = Sabin 10696. $ 60.00

1943. Wilson, Yorick. **THE GENTLEMAN'S VETERINARY MONITOR, & STABLE GUIDE.** M'Culloch for Johnson & Warner, Phila: 1810. 142p. 24mo. Leather backed marbled boards. AI 22069. Scarce American Farrier's guide. $ 100.00

1944. Winebrenner, John [1797-1860]. **A PRAYER MEETING & REVIVAL HYMN BOOK...** M'Kinley, Harrisburg: 1825. (304p.) 32mo. Full leather. Worn. AI 23352/3. 1st Ed. $ 20.00

1945. Winebrenner. **A PRAYER MEETING & REVIVAL HYMN BOOK...** Wiestling, Harrisburg: 1827. 32mo. Full leather. AI 31787. $ 22.00

1946. Winebrenner. **A PRAYER MEETING & REVIVAL HYMN BOOK...** Winebrenner, Harrisburg: 1837. 32mo. Full leather. *Apparently Not in AI.* $ 22.00

1947. (Wingate, Robert Bray). **PENNSYLVANIA IMPRINTS, 1689=1789.** Harrisburg: nd. 52p. 4to. Wraps. Holdings of Early Imprints in the State Library. $ 8.00

1948. Winters, Roy Lutz. **RELIGIOUS LIFE OF THE PA. GERMAN PIONEERS; and The First Stoevers**. Lebanon Cty. Hist. Soc: 1932. pp. 159-206. Illus. Printed wraps. $ 12.00

1949. Wolf, Edmund Jacob. **THE LUTHERANS IN AMERICA...** NY: 1889. 544p. $ 22.00

1950. Wollenweber, Ludwig A. **MOUNTAIN MARY: An Historical Tale of Early America.** Translated by John Joseph Stoudt. York: 1974. 78p. Wraps. $ 10.00

1951. Wood, Jerome H. **CONESTOGA CROSSROADS. LANCASTER, PA. 1730-1790.** Harrisburg: 1979. 305p. Illus. DJ. $ 12.00

1952. (Wood, Ralph). **THE PENNSYLVANIA GERMANS.** Princeton: 1943. 299p. Excellent essays by the most prominent authors in the field. $ 24.00

1953. Woods, Jennifer. **HOW TO MAKE PASTE PAPERS.** Library Co. of Phila: 1988. 12p. Handmade paste paper wraps. 24mo. Many 19th century Pennsylvania German books were bound in attractive paste papers. $ 8.00

1954. Woolman, John. **JOURNAL OF JOHN WOOLMAN...** Phila: 1869. 372p. $ 12.00

1955. Woolman. **JOURNAL OF JOHN WOOLMAN...** With an Introduction by John Greenleaf Whittier. Boston: 1882. 315p. XLib. $ 12.00

1956. Woolman. **THE WORKS OF JOHN WOOLMAN.** Crukshank, Phila: 1774. 436p. With separate title pages. Contemporary full leather binding. Includes his: "*Considerations on the Keeping of Negroes*". *First American Edition*". Howes W669aa, Evans 13782, Sabin 105211. The works of Woolman [1720-1772] were considered among the most pleasing and salutary efforts of the 18th century. $ 200.00

1957. Woolman. **THE WORKS OF WOOLMAN.** Phila: 1818. 321p. AI 46865. $ 30.00

1958. WPA. **A CHECKLIST OF PENNSYLVANIA NEWSPAPERS. Philadelphia County**. Pa. Historical Survey, Harrisburg: 1944. 323p. Cloth. $ 12.00

1959. WPA. **THE HARMONY SOCIETY IN PENNSYLVANIA.** Federal Writer's Project, Phila: 1937. 38p. Illus. Printed wraps. Rappite Colony in Pa. $ 24.00

1960. Wright, Thomas. **A HISTORY OF THE RISE & PROGRESS OF THE PEOPLE CALLED QUAKERS, IN IRELAND, 1653-1700.** Continued to 1751 by John Rutty. London: 1811. 328p. Disbound. $ 35.00

OBLONG SHAPED NOTE SONG BOOKS

1961. Wyeth, John. **WYETH'S REPOSITORY OF SACRED MUSIC...** Harrisburg: 1818. Two volumes in one. pp. 132, 132. *Oblong shaped note songbook.* AI 46885. Many other shaped note tune books are listed in Part I. $ 100.00

1962. Wyeth. **WYETH'S REPOSITORY OF SACRED MUSIC...** 2nd Part. Harrisburg: 1820. 132p. *Oblong shaped note songbook.* AI 4347. Nice condition. $ 100.00

1963. Wyeth. **WYETH'S REPOSITORY OF SACRED MUSIC...** Harrisburg: 1834. 144p. *Oblong shaped note songbook.* Taped spine. AI 29835. $ 95.00

Y 1964. (Yeager). **BRIEF STORY OF HISTORIC EPHRATA.** Ephrata. Ca: 1920. 48p. + Illus. Later wraps. 16mo. Useful little history. $ 12.00

1965. Yearsley, Ann. **THE ROYAL CAPTIVES...** William Woodward, Phila: 1795. pp. 8, 273. Last page mounted. Original full leather. Evans 29934. $ 60.00

1966. Yoder, Don. **PENNSYLVANIA GERMAN IMMIGRANTS, 1709-86. Lists Consolidated from the Pa. German Folklore Society Yearbooks.** Balt: 1989. 394p. Indexed. $ 30.00

1967. Yoder. **PENNSYLVANIA SPIRITUALS.** Lancaster: 1961. 528p. $ 24.00

1968. Yoder. **RHINELAND EMIGRANTS. Lists of German Settlers in Colonial America.** Balt: 1985. 182p. Illus. Useful reference extracted from Pa. Folklife Magazine. $ 24.00

1969. Yoder, John H. **THE LEGACY OF MICHAEL SATTLER.** Scottdale: 1973. 208p. Early Anabaptist leader. $ 14.00

1970. Yoder, Joseph W. **AMISH TRADITIONS.** Huntingdon, Pa: 1950. 215p. $ 26.00

1971. Yoder. **ROSANNA OF THE AMISH.** Huntingdon, Pa: 1940. 319p. Illus. DJ. *WST*. Very popular Amish book. $ 22.00

1972. Yoder. **ROSANNA OF THE AMISH.** Scottdale: 1983. 256p. Wraps. $ 5.00

1973. Yoder. **ROSANNA'S BOYS.** Huntingdon: 1948. 345p. Signed by Yoder. $ 30.00

1974. York. **A BOOK OF VIEWS, ILLUSTRATING YORK COUNTY'S SESQUI - CENTENNIAL CELEBRATION, September 3-6, 1899.** York: 1899. Oblong cloth gilt. Great pictures and advertisements. $ 24.00

1975. **YORK'S CENTENARY MEMORIAL ...** York: 1887. 226p. + Illus. Quite worn. XLib. History of York's Centennial celebration. $ 20.00

1976. **YORK COUNTY AND THE WORLD WAR (I).** (York: 1920). 424p. Illustrated. Lists every person from York who served in World War I. $ 25.00

1977. **YORK COUNTY'S HISTORICAL HERITAGE, As Capital of the U. S. 1777-8.** York Gazette: 1959. 48p. Well Illustrated. Wraps. Folio. $ 12.00

1978. **YORK MEMORIAL SOUVENIR. 150th Anniversary of York as the Capital of the United States of America.** York: 1927. 64p. Folio. Wraps. $ 20.00

1979. **YORK, PENN'A. PICTURESQUE & INDUSTRIAL.** In Commemoration of the 51st Conclave of the Grand Commandery, Knights Templar (Pa.). York: 1904. Oblong. Cloth. Wonderful architectural record & York's most extensive photo view book. Fascinating ads. Mainly by Charles McElhinny. $ 22.00

1980. **YORK, PENNSYLVANIA. Financial, Manufacturing, Historic, To-Day.** Phila: 1904. 76p. Folio. Highly illus. Handsome wraps. By the best historians. Great ads! $ 32.00

1981. **YOUR FRIEND, WILLIAM PENN.** Phila: 1944. 24p. Wraps. $ 2.00

1982. **ZELL'S DESCRIPTIVE HAND ATLAS OF THE WORLD**. By John Batholomew. T. E. Zell, Phila: 1873. Nearly 300p. of descriptive text. + 57 Colored Maps & Plans. 1/2 Leather. Small Folio. $ 185.00

1983. Zentler, Conrad. **A COLLECTION OF DIALOGUES AND PHRASES IN GERMAN & ENGLISH.** Zentler, Phila: 1823. 228p. No German Tp. Text in German & English. Disbd. Extensive manuscript ownership of: "*Abraham Weiss, Upper Milford Twp., Lehigh County, 1827 & 1832*". AI 15005, Seid. p. 220. *WST.* $ 50.00

1984. Zimmerman & Wolfert. **GERMAN IMMIGRANTS, Lists of Passengers Bound From Bremen to New York, 1847=63**. Balt: 1986-88. 3 Volumes. $ 75.00

1985. Zimmermann, Johann Georg von [1728=95]. **SOLITUDE CONSIDERED WITH RESPECT TO ITS INFLUENCE UPON THE MIND AND THE HEART...** Phila: 1793. pp. (4), 7, 328. Disbound. *First edition in English*. Evans 26528. Very popular among the Pennsylvania Germans and Quakers. $ 90.00

1986. Zimmermann. **SOLITUDE CONSIDERED...** Johnson & Preston, Wilmington: 1797. pp. 4, 5, 298. Contemporary full leather. Evans 33261, Rink 479. $ 50.00

1987. Zimmermann, Thos. C. **OLLA PODRIDA. Addresses, Translations, Poems, Hymns, & Sketches of Out-Door Life**. Reading: 1903. Two volumes. 729p. 24mo. Includes interesting Pennsylvania German historical articles, & poems in the dialect. *WST.* $ 40.00

1988. **ZION (STONE) CHURCH HISTORY**. Allentown: 1936. 128p. Stone Church near Kreidersville, Pa. was built in 1836. *WST.* $ 16.00

1989. Zollers, George D. **THRILLING INCIDENTS ON SEA & LAND...** Mt. Morris, Il: 1902. 400p. Illus. Full roan. A Brethren's exciting adventures around the world. $ 20.00

PART THREE

KEYSTONE TEN

= "*Die Alte Zeite*" =

PART III

PUBLICATIONS AND PROCEEDINGS OF THE PENNSYLVANIA GERMAN SOCIETY AND THE PENNSYLVANIA GERMAN FOLKLORE SOCIETY.

Device Used By Anthony Armbruster, Philadelphia: 1764

KEYSTONE TEN = "Die Alte Zeite"
PART III

PUBLICATIONS OF THE PENNSYLVANIA GERMAN SOCIETY AND THE PENNSYLVANIA GERMAN FOLKLORE SOCIETY

PENNSYLVANIA GERMAN SOCIETY PUBLICATIONS

We are very pleased to be able to offer, individually, a complete set of the remarkable historical series issued as the Proceedings, Addresses, Papers, and Publications of the Pennsylvania German Society. Many of the most important early scholarly monographs about the Germans in America first appeared in this series. Though not mentioned in the descriptions below: *Most of these volumes were published in editions limited to less than 300 - 700 copies.*

2001. **Vol. I.** Includes: **SKETCH OF THE ORIGIN OF THE PENNSYLVANIA GERMAN SOCIETY, With the Proceedings & Addresses at Its Organization.** Lancaster: 1891. 94p. Ill. New Wraps. $ 95.00

2002. **Vol. II.** Includes: Egle. **THE PENNSYLVANIA GERMAN: His Place in the History of Pennsylvania** // + Other Papers. Lancaster: 1892. 132p. + *Original Invitations & Menus for the 1892 Meeting.* New wraps. *WST.* $ 95.00

2003. **Vol. III.** Includes: Nead. **THE PENNSYLVANIA GERMAN IN HISTORY** // Heckman. **PENNSYLVANIA GERMANS AT THE BATTLE OF LONG ISLAND // BIRTH & BAPTISMAL RECORDS OF TRINITY LUTHERAN CHURCH, Lancaster** // + Numerous Other Articles of Interest. (Lancaster): 1893. 1/2 Morocco. 292p. $ 150.00

2004. **Vol. IV.** Includes: De Schweinitz. **THE GERMAN MORAVIANS IN PENNSYLVANIA // BIOGRAPHICAL SKETCHES // BIRTH & BAPTISMAL RECORDS** // + Other Papers... PGS, (Lancaster: 1894). 252 [of 292p.]. + *Numerous original inserts relating to the 1894 meeting.* New Wraps. *WST.* $ 75.00

2005. **Vol. V.** Includes: **BIRTHS & BAPTISMAL REGISTERS** // + Numerous Other Important Papers on Conrad Weiser, et. al. Reading: 1895. 266p. New Wraps. $ 90.00

2006. **Vol. VI.** Includes: Sachse. **THE TRAPPE RECORDS // TRINITY LUTHERAN CHURCH REGISTER** // Reichel. **SKETCH OF THE OLD SUN INN** // + Other Papers. Lancaster: 1908. 283p. + Illus. + *The Original Program for the Meeting.* New Wraps. $ 100.00

2007. **Vol. VII.** Includes: Sachse. **THE FATHERLAND: Showing the Part it Bore in the Discovery, Exploration and Development of the Western Continent // Title Pages (in Facsimile) of the Books & Pamphlets that Influenced German Emigration to Pa** // + Other Papers. Reading: 1907. 576p. + Illus. New Wraps. Extremely scarce. $ 180.00

2008. **Vol. VIII.** Includes: Jacobs. **THE GERMAN EMIGRATION TO AMERICA, 1709-40** // Nead. **INDEX TO NAMES IN VOLS. I-VI** // & Richards. **THE DISCOVERERS OF AMERICA WERE GERMAN.** PGS, Lancaster: 1898. pp. 26, 222, 100, 28 + Illus. + *The Original Program for the Annual Banquet.* New Wraps. *WST.* $ 125.00

2009. **Vol. IX.** Includes: Pennypacker. **THE SETTLEMENT OF GERMANTOWN, PA. and the Beginning of German Immigration to North America** // & Richards. **THE GERMAN IMMIGRATION FROM NEW YORK PROVINCE INTO PA.** PGS, Lancaster: 1899. 468p. + Illus. + *Original Program for the Annual Meeting.* New Wraps. Howes P 213. $ 120.00

2010. **Vol. X.** Includes: Schantz. **THE DOMESTIC LIFE & CHARACTERISTICS OF THE PA. GERMAN PIONEER** // Falkenstein. **THE GERMAN BAPTIST BRETHREN** // Hark. **EN HONDFULL FARSCH** // & Richards. **DESCENDANTS OF HENRY MELCHIOR MUHLENBERG.** PGS, Lancaster: 1900. pp. 46, 328, 148, 89 + Illus. Cloth. *WST.* $ 100.00

2011. **Vol. XI.** Includes: Schmauk. **HISTORY OF THE LUTHERAN CHURCH IN PA. 1638 - 1800** // Dubbs. **THE REFORMED CHURCH IN PA.** PGS, Lancaster: 1902. pp. 50, 355, 357 + Illus. Cloth. Contains an abundance of valuable information. *WST.* $ 140.00

2012. **Vol. XII.** Includes: Sachse. **THE MUSIC OF THE EPHRATA CLOISTER** // Schmauk. **HISTORY OF THE LUTHERAN CHURCH IN PA. 1638-1820** // & Grumbine. **THE PA. GERMAN DIALECT.** PGS, Lancaster: 1903. pp. 72, 108, 588, 139 + Illus. Wraps. $ 140.00

2013. **Vol. XIII.** Includes: Kriebel. **THE SCHWENKFELDERS IN PA** // Rosengarten. **AMERICAN HISTORY FROM GERMAN ARCHIVES Relating to German Soldiers in the Revolution; & Franklin's Visit to Germany** // & Richardson. **PICTURESQUE QUALITY OF THE PA. GERMAN.** PGS, Lancaster: 1904. pp. 36, 232, 93, 27 + Illus. Wraps. $ 135.00

2014. **Vol. XIV.** Includes: Sachse. **DANIEL FALCKNER'S CURIEUSE NACHRICHT FROM PA. The Book that Stimulated German Immigration to Pa.** PGS, Lancaster: 1905. Over 400p. Illus. Original Wraps. *WST.* $ 125.00

2015. **Vol. XV.** Includes: Richards. **THE PA. GERMAN IN THE FRENCH & INDIAN WAR** // & Keyser. **OLD HISTORIC GERMANTOWN.** PGS, Lancaster: 1906. pp. 54, 558, 77 + Illus. Wraps. $ 80.00

2016. **Vol. XVI.** Includes: Sachse. **WRECK OF THE SHIP NEW ERA** // Richards. **GOVERNOR JOSEPH HEISTER & THE HEISTER GENEALOGY** // & **RECORD OF INDENTURES... Apprentices, Servants Etc. Phila. 1771-3.** PGS, Lancaster: 1907. pp. 55, 51, 325 + Illus. Original wraps. Extremely important records. *WST.* $ 80.00

2017. **Vol. XVII.** Includes: Richards. **THE PENNSYLVANIA GERMAN IN THE REVOLUTIONARY WAR** // & Heller. **GUN MAKERS OF OLD NORTHAMPTON.** PGS, (Lancaster: 1908). pp. 58, 542, 14 + Illus. original wraps. *WST.* $ 80.00

2018. **Vol. XVIII.** Includes: Sachse. **DIARY OF A VOYAGE FROM ROTTERDAM TO PHILA. IN 1728** // Arfwedson. **A BRIEF HISTORY OF THE COLONY OF NEW SWEDEN** // Sachse. **MISSIVES TO FRANCKE FROM DAN & JUSTUS FALCKNER** // Koons. **HARBAUGH'S HARFE** // & **RECORDS OF THE WILLIAMS TOWNSHIP CONGREGATION.** PGS, (Lancaster: 1909). 264p. + Illus. Original wraps. $ 75.00

2019. **Vol. XIX.** Includes: Schmauk. **RUSH'S ACCOUNT OF THE MANNERS OF THE GERMAN INHABITANTS OF PA** // & Miller. **EARLY GERMAN AMERICAN NEWSPAPERS.** PGS, Lanc: 1910. pp. 42, 128, 107. Original wraps. Very useful. $ 60.00

2020. **Vol. XX.** Includes: Kline. **THE LUTHERAN CHURCH IN NEW HANOVER, (Falckner Swamp) Montgomery County.** PGS, Lancaster: 1911. pp. 58, 444 + Illus. Original Blue Wraps. Important genealogical record. *WST.* $ 75.00

2021. **Vol. XXI.** Includes: Sachse. **THE WAYSIDE INNS ON THE LANCASTER ROADSIDE** // & Schultz. **GUIDE TO THE OLD MORAVIAN CEMETERY OF BETHLEHEM, 1742-1910** // & **BEISSEL'S 99 MYSTICAL PROVERBS, A Unique Manuscript by Peter Miller.** PGS, Lancaster: 1912. pp. 66, 77, 218p. + Illus. *WST.* $ 60.00

2022. **Vol. XXII.** Includes: Sachse. **THE WAYSIDE INNS ON THE LANCASTER ROADSIDE, BETWEEN PHILA. & LANCASTER** // & Nead. **THE PENNSYLVANIA GERMAN IN THE SETTLEMENT OF MARYLAND.** PGS, Lancaster: 1914. 413+p. + Illus. Wraps. $ 55.00

2023. **Vol. XXIII.** Includes: Sachse. **QUAINT OLD GERMANTOWN IN PA.** PGS, Lancaster: 1915. pp. 56, 7, + Over 60 plates. Original Wraps. $ 34.00

2024. **Vol. XXIII-Supplement.** Includes: Stoudt. **FOLKLORE OF THE PENNSYLVANIA GERMAN.** PGS, Lancaster: 1915. 155p. Original Wraps. *WST.* $ 75.00

2025. **Vol. XXIV.** Includes: Wentz. **THE BEGINNINGS OF THE GERMAN ELEMENT IN YORK COUNTY, PA.** Lancaster: 1916. 217p. Original Wraps. *WST.* $ 50.00

2026. **Vol. XXV.** Includes: Sachse. **THE DIARIUM OF MAGISTER JOHANNES KELPIUS** // & Sachse. **CONDITIONS OF PENNSYLVANIA IN THE YEAR 1755. THE BRADDOCK EXPEDITION. Translation of a French Pamphlet.** PGS, Lancaster: 1917. pp. 55, 100, 38, 48 + Illus. Original Wraps. *WST.* $ 50.00

2027. **Vol. XXVI.** Includes: Richards. **VALLEY FORGE & THE PA. GERMANS.** // & Reichard. **PENNSYLVANIA-GERMAN DIALECT WRITINGS & THEIR WRITERS.** PGS, Lancaster: 1918. pp. 73, 32, 400 + Illus. Original wraps. *WST.* $ 120.00

2028. **Vol. XXVII.** Includes: Hinke. **HISTORY OF THE GOSHENHPOPPEN REFORMED CHARGE (1719-1819)** // & Knipe. **PA. GERMAN IN THE CIVIL WAR.** PGS, Lancaster: 1920. pp. 61, 271, 52. *WST.* $ 50.00

2029. **Vol. XXVIII.** Includes: Hinke. **CHURCH RECORDS OF THE GOSHENHPOPPEN REFORMED CHARGE (1731-1833).** Lancaster: 1922. pp. 17, (272-490). Wraps. $ 50.00

2030. **Vol. XXIX.** Includes: Knauss. **SOCIAL CONDITIONS AMONG THE PENNSYLVANIA GERMANS IN THE EIGHTEENTH CENTURY.** PGS, Lancaster: 1917. pp. 16, 217. Illustrated. Wraps. *WST.* $ 60.00

2031. **Vol. XXX.** Includes: Lambert. **A DICTIONARY OF THE NON-ENGLISH WORDS OF THE PENNSYLVANIA-GERMAN DIALECT, With an Appendix.** PGS, Lancaster: 1924. pp. 68, 31, 193. Original Wraps. *WST.* $ 34.00

2032. **Vol. XXXI.** Includes: Hinke. **HISTORY OF THE TOHICKON UNION CHURCH.** Meadville: 1925. 483p. Original blue wraps. Important genealogical information. $ 60.00

2033. **Vol. XXXII.** Includes: Richards. **THE WEISER FAMILY** // Richards. **THE PA. GERMAN IN THE BRITISH MILITARY PRISONS OF THE REVOLUTIONARY WAR** // Dapp. **EVOLUTION OF AN AMERICAN PATRIOT = JOHN HENRY MILLER.** PGS, Lancaster: 1924. pp. 45, 33, 68, 115 + Illus. Wraps. The genealogies of the Weiser family are especially useful. *WST.* $ 48.00

2034. **Vol. XXXIII.** Includes: Lick & Brendle. **PLANT NAMES AND PLANT LORE AMONG THE PENNSYLVANIA-GERMANS** // & Zundel. **FORT ALLEN IN WESTMORELAND COUNTY** // + Other Articles. PGS, Lancaster: 1926. pp. 86, 38, 300. Illus. Wraps. $ 120.00

2035. **Vol. XXXIV.** Includes: Smith, Edgar Fahs. **EMINENT PENNSYLVANIA GERMANS** // & Hinke. **DIARIES OF MISSIONARY TRAVELS AMONG THE GERMAN SETTLERS IN AMERICA, 1743-8** // + Others. PGS, Lancaster: 1929. 131p. Wraps. $ 40.00

2036. **Vol. XXXV.** Includes: Smith. **THE MENNONITE IMMIGRATION TO PA.** PGS, Norristown: 1929. 412p. + Illus. Original blue wraps. *WST.* $ 85.00

2037. **Vol. XXXVI.** Includes: Fogel. **PROVERBS OF THE PENNSYLVANIA GERMAN** // + Others. PGS, Lancaster: 1929. pp. 45, 222. Original wraps. Important dialect and cultural record. Is there any interest in a new, more comprehensive version of this? $ 75.00

2038. **Vol. XXXVII.** Includes: Stoudt. **THE LIBERTY BELLS OF PENNSYLVANIA.** PGS, Norristown: 1930. pp. 31, 204 + Illus. Original wraps. *WST.* $ 40.00

2039. **Vol. XXXVIII.** Includes: Livingood. **EIGHTEENTH CENTURY REFORMED CHURCH SCHOOLS.** PGS, Norristown: 1930. pp. 22, 313 + Illus. Original wraps. Fine study of the Lutheran Church & education in Pa. *WST.* $ 45.00

2040. **Vol. XXXIX.** Includes: Fegley. **AMONG SOME OF THE OLDER MILLS OF EASTERN PA.** // & Roberts. **GERMANIC IMMIGRANTS NAMED IN EARLY PENNSYLVANIA SHIP LISTS** // + Others. PGS, Norristown: 1930. 165p. + Great photo illustrations of mIlls, etc. Original blue wraps. *WST.* $ 100.00

2041. **Vol. XL.** Includes: Maurer. **EARLY LUTHERAN EDUCATION IN PENNSYLVANIA** // & Hinke. **THE LISTS OF IMMIGRANTS ENTERING PA. 1727 TO 1808.** PGS, Norristown: 1932. pp. 32, 294 + Illus. Original Wraps. *WST.* $ 40.00

2042. **Vol. XLI.** Includes: Brumbaugh. **COLONIAL ARCHITECTURE OF THE PA. GERMANS,** Etc. PGS, Norristown: 1933. pp. 23, 44, 60 + 105 Photo Plates of Houses. Wraps. Preserves much important architectural information. $ 100.00

2043. **Vols. XLII, XLIII, XLIV.** Includes: Strassburger & Hinke. **PENNSYLVANIA GERMAN PIONEERS. A Publication of the Original Lists of Arrivals In the Port of Phila. 1727-1808.** PGS, Norristown: 1934. Three volumes. Cloth. Extremely important reference. $ 260.00

2044. **Vol. XLV.** Includes: Brendle & Unger. **FOLK MEDICINE OF THE PENNSYLVANIA GERMANS.** PGS, Norristown: 1935. pp. 48, 303 + Illus. Original wraps. Important study of Folk Medicine and Pharmacy. *WST.* $ 140.00

2045. **Vol. XLVI.** Includes: Borneman. **PENNSYLVANIA GERMAN ILLUMINATED MANUSCRIPTS. A Classification of Fraktur-Schriften & An Inquiry into their History & Art.** PGS, Norristown: 1938. 58p. + 38 Color Plates. Oblong folio. Nice copy of the first, and best, edition of this scarce and very eagerly sought after monograph. *WST.* $ 380.00

2046. **Vol. XLVII.** Includes: Landis. **EARLY KITCHENS OF THE PENNSYLVANIA GERMANS** // & Graeff. **RELATIONS BETWEEN THE PA. GERMANS & THE BRITISH, 1750-76.** PGS, Norristown: 1939. pp. 37, 130, 271. Original wraps. Great content. $ 100.00

2047. **Vol. XLVIII.** Includes: Reichard. **PENNSYLVANIA GERMAN VERSE. A Dialect Anthology.** PGS, Norristown: 1940. 239p. Wraps. *WST.* $ 50.00

2048. **Vol. XLIX.** Includes: Bachman. **THE OLD ORDER AMISH OF LANCASTER COUNTY.** PGS, Norristown: 1942. pp. 30, 297 + Illus. Original wraps. *WST.* $ 100.00

2049. **Vol. L.** Includes: Brendle & Troxell. **PENNSYLVANIA GERMAN FOLK TALES, LEGENDS, Etc. In English & the Dialect.** PGS, Norristown: 1944. pp. 24, 238. Wraps. *WST.* $ 45.00

2050. **Vol. LI.** Includes: Kieffer. **HENRY HARBAUGH, Pennsylvania Dutchman, 1817-1867.** PGS, Norristown: 1945. pp. 9, 365 + Illus. Wraps. *WST.* $ 40.00

2051. **Vol. LII.** Includes: Rupp. **BIRD NAMES & BIRD LORE AMONG THE PA. GERMANS.** PGS, Norristown: 1946. 337p. Original wraps. "A compendium with which there is no work to compare for any other state, nor for any other country" = The Auk. $ 140.00

2052. **Vol. LIII.** Includes: Hocker. **THE SOWER PRINTING HOUSE OF COLONIAL TIMES** // & Winters. **JOHN CASPER STOEVER.** PGS, Norristown: 1948. pp. 125, 171. Excellent history of the Sauer printing family. *WST.* $ 100.00

2053. **Vol. LIV.** Includes: Borneman. **PENNSYLVANIA GERMAN BOOKPLATES.** PGS, Phila: 1953. 169p. + 24 Plates in Color. Decorated Cloth. Classic study. $ 125.00

2054. **Vol. LV.** Includes: Berky. **PRACTITIONER IN PHYSICK. A Biography of Abraham Wagner, 1717-1763.** PGS, (Pennsburg: 1954). 175p. + Illus. 4to. This includes a superb collection of early remedies. $ 40.00

2055. **Vol. LVI.** Includes: Berky. **THE SCHOOLHOUSE NEAR THE OLD SPRING.** PGS, Norristown: 1955. 173p. $ 40.00

2056. **Vol. LVII.** Reaman, G. Elmore. **THE TRAIL OF THE BLACK WALNUT.** NY: 1957. 256p. + Illus. DJ. First Edition. Pa. Mennonites in Upper New York & Canada. $ 60.00

2057.**Vol. LVIII.** Includes: Rubincam. **WILLIAM RITTENHOUSE, AMERICA'S PIONEER PAPER MANUFACTURER & MENNONITE MINISTER** // & Brendle. **MOSES DISSINGER, EVANGELIST & PATRIOT.** PGS, (Scottdale: 1959). 192p. + Illus. $ 40.00

2058. **Vol. LIX.** Includes: Korson. **BLACK ROCK. MINING FOLK LORE OF THE PENNSYLVANIA DUTCH.** PGS, (Balt: 1960). 453p. Illus. DJ. Cloth. $ 45.00

2059. **Vol. LX.** Includes: Bachman. **THE OLD ORDER AMISH OF LANCASTER COUNTY.** PGS, Lancaster: 1961. 297p. DJ. $ 120.00

2060. **Vol. LXI.** Includes: Buffington. **THE REICHARD COLLECTION OF EARLY PA. GERMAN DIALOGUES & PLAYS.** PGS, Lancaster: 1962. 439p. Cloth. $ 40.00

2061. **Vol. LXII.** Includes: Buffington. **"DUTCHIFIED GERMAN" SPIRITUALS.** PGS, Lancaster: 1965. 239p. Cloth. $ 35.00

2062. **Vol. LXIII.** Includes: Rosenberger. **THE PENNSYLVANIA GERMANS, 1891-1965.** PGS, Lancaster: 1966. 619p. Illus. Cloth. $ 50.00

PENNSYLVANIA GERMAN FOLKLORE SOCIETY PUBLICATIONS

2063. **PENNSYLVANIA GERMAN FOLKLORE SOCIETY PUBLICATIONS. A Complete Run of All Twenty Eight Volumes. Allentown: 1936-1966. Uniformly bound in linen cloth. Sold as a collection only [but see below for the whole series offered as individual volumes]. The publications of the Pennsylvania German Folklore Society form a unique resource for information on the history, crafts, lore, and culture of the Germans in America. Complete runs are now very difficult to put together. $1600.00**

2064. VOL. I. Includes: Ziegler. **DRAUSS UN DEHEEM, Gedichte in Pennsylvanisch Deitsch** // Drowns. **THE HOUSE OF THE MILLER ON THE MILLBACH, The Architecture, Arts, & Crafts of the Pa. Germans** // & Hinke & Stoudt. **A LIST OF GERMAN IMMIGRANTS TO THE AMERICAN COLONIES FROM ZWEIBRUECKEN IN THE PALATINATE.** Allentown: 1936. 138p. *WST.* $ 75.00

2065. VOL. II. Includes: Stoudt. **CONSIDER THE LILIES HOW THEY GROW. INTERPRETATION OF THE SYMBOLISM OF PENNSYLVANIA GERMAN ART.** Allentown: 1937. 333p. + Illus. Significant and articulate work on fraktur and other folk arts. $ 95.00

2066. VOL. III. Includes: Beckel. **EARLY MORAVIAN MARRIAGE CUSTOMS IN BETHLEHEM** // Landis. **CONESTOGA WAGONS & THEIR ORNAMENTAL IRONING** // Etc. Allentown: 1938. 254p. + Illus. *WST.* $ 62.00

2067. **VOL. IV**. Includes: Barba. **LEWIS MILLER, PA. GERMAN FOLK ARTIST** // ETC. Allentown: 1939. 125p. Highly illustrated. *WST*. $ 75.00

2068. **VOL. V**. Includes: Heckewelder. **NAMES GIVEN BY THE LENNI LENAPE OR DELAWARE INDIANS TO RIVERS, STREAMS, AND PLACES** // Ziegler. **THE EPHRATA PRINTING PRESS**. Allentown: 1940. 122p. + Illus. *WST*. $ 65.00

2069. **VOL. VI**. Includes: Nitzsche. **THE CHRISTMAS PUTZ OF THE PA. GERMANS** // + Other Important Articles on Pa. German Christmas History, Customs, & poetry. Allentown: 1941. 190p. + Illus. *WST*. $ 60.00

2070. **VOL. VII**. Includes: Landis. **LANCASTER RIFLES** // ETC. Allentown: 1943 174p. + Illus. Exceptional study of "Kentucky" Rifles. *WST*. $ 75.00

2071. **VOL. VIII**. Includes: Graeff. **CONRAD WEISER, PENNSYLVANIA PEACEMAKER**. Allentown: 1945. 407p. + Illus. *WST*. $ 75.00

2072. **VOL. IX**. Includes: Landis. **LANCASTER RIFLE ACCESSORIES** // Etc. Allentown: 1946. 243p. + Illus. Fine companion to Vol. 7. $ 50.00

2073. **VOL. X**. Includes: Ludwig. **THE INFLUENCE OF THE PA. DUTCH IN THE MIDDLE WEST** // & Yoder. **WUERTTEMBERG EMIGRANTS**. Allentown: 1945=7. 246p. $ 40.00

2074. **VOL. XI** Includes: Graeff. **THE PENNSYLVANIA GERMANS IN ONTARIO**. // & Kauffmann. **COPPERSMITHING IN PA**. Allentown: 1946. 150p. Illus. $ 34.00

2075. **VOL. XII**. Includes: Moll. **AM SCHWARZE BAER** // Langmuth & Yoder. **PA. GERMAN PIONEERS FROM WERTHEIM**. Allentown: 1947=8. 306p. XLib. $ 45.00

2076. **VOL. XIII**. Includes: Reinert. **COVERLETS OF THE PENNSYLVANIA GERMANS**. / & Kuder. **THE PRACTICAL FAMILY DYER**. / & Buffington. **LINGUISTIC VARIANTS OF THE PA. GERMAN DIALECT**. Allentown: 1948=9. 256p. Extremely important. $ 160.00

2077. **VOL. XIV**. Includes: Stoeffler. **MYSTICISM IN THE GERMAN DEVOTIONAL LITERATURE OF COLONIAL PENNSYLVANIA**. Allentown: 1950. 195p. $ 50.00

2078. **VOL. XV**. Includes: Gilbert. **PENNSYLVANIA GERMAN WILLS**. Allentown: 1950=1. 139p. Wills & Vendue lists are great storehouses of information. $ 42.00

2079. **VOL. XVI**. Includes: Stoudt. **PENNSYLVANIA GERMAN FOLKLORE** // **GERMAN IMMIGRANTS TO AMERICA FROM THE PALATINATE** // **LATER POEMS OF JOHN BIRMELIN** // Etc. Allentown: 1953. 213p. Illus. $ 45.00

2080. **VOL. XVII**. Includes: Reichman & Doll. **EPHRATA AS SEEN BY CONTEMPORARIES**. Allentown: 1952=3. 211p. + Illus. Valuable accounts. $ 60.00

2081. **VOL. XVIII**. Includes: Barba. **PENNSYLVANIA GERMAN TOMBSTONES, A Study in Folk Art**. Allentown: 1954. 232p. Illus. $ 40.00

2082. **VOL. XIX**. Includes: Dundore. **THE SAGA OF THE PENNSYLVANIA GERMAN IN WISCONSIN** // & Buffington. **HERBERT MEYER: An Early Pennsylvania German Poet**. Allentown: 1954=5. 176p. Illus. $ 40.00

2083. **VOL. XX**. Includes: Stoudt. **PENNSYLVANIA GERMAN POETRY, 1685-1830**. Allentown: 1955=6. 380p. Illus. $ 45.00

2084. **VOL. XXI**. Includes: Dornbusch. **PENNSYLVANIA GERMAN BARNS**. Allentown: 1958. 312p. Highly illustrated. Now very scarce. Important. $ 175.00

2085. **VOL. XXII**. Includes: Nitzsche. **MARRIAGE BY LOT. A Novel Based on Moravian History**. Allentown: 1957=8. 154p. DJ. Pa. German marriage based on the casting of lots and other drawing of straws. $ 40.00

2086. **VOL. XXIII.** Includes: Shelley. **THE FRAKTUR WRITINGS OR ILLUMINATED MANUSCRIPTS OF THE PENNSYLVANIA GERMANS.** Allentown: 1958=9. 357p. + Many Illus. Essential work on Fraktur. $ 75.00

2087. **VOL. XXIV.** Includes: Smith. **THE AMISH OF TODAY. Analysis of Their Beliefs, Behavior & Contemporary Problems.** Allentown: 1960=1. 347p. $ 50.00

2088. **VOL. XXV.** Includes: Ernst. **EPHRATA, A HISTORY.** Allentown: 1961=3. 354p. Very useful history. Essential reading. $ 50.00

2089. **VOL. XXVI.** Includes: Smith, Stewart, & Kyger. **THE PENNSYLVANIA GERMANS OF THE SHENANDOAH VALLEY.** Allentown: 1964. 278p. + Illus. Good sections on Virginia Fraktur and Virginia Imprints. $ 90.00

2090. **VOL. XXVII.** Includes: Buffington & Barba. **A PENNSYLVANIA GERMAN GRAMMAR.** Allentown: 1964. 170p. Becoming avidly sought after and consulted. $ 60.00

2091. **VOL. XXVIII.** Includes: Stoudt. **PENNSYLVANIA GERMAN FOLK ART.** Allentown: 1966. 386p. + Illus. $ 60.00

PENNSYLVANIA GERMAN SOCIETY
== NEW SERIES ==
COMBINED PUBLICATIONS

2092. **Vol. 1.** Includes: Wood. **THE FOUR GOSPELS. Translated Into Pennsylvania German Dialect** // & Weiser. **DANIEL SCHUMACHER'S BAPTISMAL REGISTER.** Allentown: 1968. 407p. + Colored illustrations of Schumacher's Fraktur art. Cloth. $ 40.00

2093. **Vol. 2.** Includes: Treher. **SNOW HILL CLOISTER** // & Barba. **THE DIALECT POEMS OF RALPH FUNK.** Allentown: 1968. 328p. Illus. $ 35.00

2094. **Vol. 3.** Includes: Biever, Barba, Buffington, et. al. **FOUR PENNSYLVANIA GERMAN STUDIES.** Allentown: 1970. 179p. Illus. Including fine studies on the Archaeology of the Ephrata Cloister; and Rachel Bahn, the York Poetess. $ 30.00

2095. **Vol. 4.** Includes: Gingerich, Melvin. **MENNONITE ATTIRE THROUGH FOUR CENTURIES.** Breinigsville: 1970. 192p. Illustrated. Polka-Dot Cloth. Important. $ 60.00

2096. **Vol. 5.** Includes: **SELECTIONS FROM ARTHUR D. GRAEFF'S SCHOLLA.** Breinigsville: 1971. 202p. Cloth. PA German Tales & Memories. $ 20.00

2097. **Vol. 6.** Long. **THE PENNSYLVANIA GERMAN FAMILY FARM.** PGS, Breinigsville: 1972. 518p. Illus. Cloth. Fascinating text and illustrations. Already a classic. $ 100.00

2098. **Vol. 7.** Includes: Klinefelter. **THE ABC BOOKS OF THE PA. GERMANS** // & Heckman. **ABRAHAM HARLEY CASSEL, 19TH CENTURY GERMAN AMERICAN BOOK COLLECTOR** // & Braun & Weiser. **MARRIAGES AT THE HOLY TRINITY EVANG. LUTHERAN CHURCH 1748-67.** Breingsville: 1973. 299p. Illus. Cloth. These studies are all of great value, notably that on the ABC books. $ 35.00

2099. **Vol. 8.** Buffington. **PENNSYLVANIA GERMAN SECULAR FOLKSONGS.** PGS, Breinigsville: 1974. 182p. Cloth. $ 20.00

2100. **Vol. 9.** Gilbert. **BILDER UN GEDANKE. A Book of Pennsylvania German Verse.** PGS, Breinigsville: 1975. 119p. Cloth. $ 20.00

2101. **Vols. 10-11.** Weiser & Heaney. **THE PENNSYLVANIA GERMAN FRAKTUR COLLECTION OF THE FREE LIBRARY OF PHILA.** PGS, Breinigsville: 1976-7. Two Volumes. Oblong folio. Well illustrated. Cloth. Wonderful treatise. Essential to the study of German American Fraktur. $ 60.00

2102. **Vol. 12.** Fabian. **THE PENNSYLVANIA GERMAN DECORATED CHEST.** NY: 1978. 230p. Well illustrated. Cloth. DJ. Hotly sought after. $ 150.00

2103. **Vols. 13 & 15.** Glatfelter, Charles H. **PASTORS & PEOPLE. German Lutheran & Reformed Churches in the Pennsylvania Field, 1717-93.** PGS, Breinigsville: 1980-1. 2 Volumes. Illus. Cloth. First class biographical and historical reference. $ 60.00

2104. **Vol. 14.** Includes: **EBBES FER ALLE-EBBER, EBBES FER DICH. Something For Everyone, Something For You.** Breinigsville: 1980. Illus. Cloth. Contains nine lively and useful Studies on: Dialect, York County Gunsmiths, Furniture, Fraktur, Etc. $ 25.00

2105. **Vols. 16 & Vol. 19.** Burgert. **18TH CENTURY EMIGRANTS FROM GERMAN-SPEAKING LANDS - Vols. I [Northern Kraichgau] & II [Western Palatinate].** PGS, Breinigsville: 1983-5. 462p. Illus. Cloth. Fine reference. $ 80.00

2106. **Vol. 17.** Swank, et. al. **ARTS OF THE PENNSYLVANIA GERMANS.** PGS / Winterthur: 1984. 309p. Well illustrated. 4to. Really excellent. $ 40.00

2107. **Vol. 18. THIS WAY I PASS MY TIME - Pennsylvania German Decorated Hand Towels.** By Ellen J. Gehret, in Cooperation with Tandy Hersh, Alan G. Keyser, and Frederick S. Weiser. PGS, Birdsboro, Pa: 1985. 292p. Highly illustrated. Sm. folio. Cloth. DJ. A comprehensive contribution to the study of Pa. German needlework and iconography. $ 45.00

2108. **Vol. 20. FARMING, ALWAYS FARMING. A Photographic Essay of Rural Pa. German Land & Life, Made by H. Winslow Fegley [1871-1944].** PGS, Birdsboro: 1987. 312p. Great photo illus. Oblong 4to. DJ. $ 35.00

2109. **Vol. 21-22. THE FIRST CENTURY OF GERMAN LANGUAGE PRINTING IN THE U.S.A. A Bibliography.** Two Volumes. An eagerly awaited reference, that is sure to live up to expectations. Call for latest pricing.

PART FOUR

KEYSTONE TEN

= "*Die Alte Zeite*" =

PART IV

GERMAN AMERICAN BROADSIDES, MANUSCRIPTS, AND EPHEMERA.

Device Used By Der Brüderschaft, Ephrata: 1748 & 1763.

KEYSTONE X = "Die Alte Zeite"

PART IV

GERMAN AMERICAN BROADSIDES, MANUSCRIPTS, AND EPHEMERA

2150. **EINE ACTE um desto füglicher und besser die öffentliche Wege und Landstrassen...** Special supplement to the "Pennsylvanischen Berichte". Christoph Saur, Germantown, Circa: 1748-62. 2p. 8.5" x 14". *Broadsheet* printing of an Act of the Provincial Assembly on building better Roads and Highways (the Lancaster Turnpike?). Rare. $ 75.00

2151. **AUCTION ACCOUNT OF A PUBLIC VENDUE HELD AT THE DWELLING HOUSE OF PHILLIP ACHENBACH, Bloom Township, (Cumberland County?), Pa.** Oct. 9, 1823. 12p. *Manuscript* record that details the Conditions of Sale, objects sold, with buyer's names, and prices paid. This sale realized over $1000.00. The horses brought the highest prices. An "Eight Day (Tall Case) Clock" went for $50.05. Important and useful period record for scholars of material culture, antiques, and ancillary artifacts. $ 140.00

2152. **DER BAURSTAND.** (Ephrata? Ca: 1810). *Poetic Broadside* in praise of Peasants and Farmers; enumerating the debts that all men owe to them. 7" x 10". Repaired at fold. Curious and lively text that articulates the strong agrarian feelings of German Americans. $ 100.00

2153. **EIN BITTEND LIED, AN DEN SCHÖPFER...** *Poetic Broadside Song* in twelve stanzas. 6.5" x 7". (Lancaster? Circa: 1800). $ 40.00

LETTERS FROM GOD = HIMMELS BRIEF

2154. **EIN BRIEF, so aus den Wolken Herab und in die Stadt Magdeburg niedergelassen worden ist...** Published by Ezechiel Hermann. Ca: 1800. *Poetic Broadside*. 7.5" x 11.5". Slight loss from the typographic border. One of the earliest American broadside versions of this famous religious "*Letter from Heaven*", delivered at Magdeburg in 1783. It was apparently used in many Pennsylvania German homes as a talisman to ward off evil, and as a persistent cautionary warning to righteous behavior and faith. $ 145.00

2155. **EIN BRIEF, so von Gott selbst geschrieben und zu Magdeburg niedergelassen worden ist...** (Reading?, Ca: 1820). *Poetic Broadside*. 7" x 9". Greek key typographic border. Ds. Fine small broadside, perhaps intended to be carried, rather than posted. $ 70.00

2156. **EIN BRIEF, so von Gott selbst geschrieben und zu Magdeburg niedergelassen worden ist...** (Lancaster?, Ca: 1840). *Poetic Broadside*. 8.7" x 11.5". Typographic border. Attractive and wide margined. $ 50.00

2157. **CERTIFICATE OF BIRTH & BAPTISM.** Attractive blank form in English. Printed in Hanover or Chambersburg, Pa. Ca: 1815. 15" x 12". Illustrated by eight printer's ornaments & two typographic borders. Based on the Pennsylvania German *Taufschein*. Unusual. $ 75.00

To these two Parents; as
and his Wife a born
was born a the
Day of in the year of our
Lord This child was born in
in County, in the state
of in North-America; was
baptised by the Rev. and
received the name of
Witness present at the act of the
holy Baptism:

"YOUR SONS AND DAUGHTERS SHALL PROPHESY"

2158. (Childs). **THE VISION OF ISAAC CHILDS, which He Saw Concerning the Land of his Nativity (Pennsylvania).** *Rare manuscript* of a remarkable mystical Quaker work. Apparently scribed by Ann Baldwin (Chester County?): 1775. Also signed by Joshua B. Sharpless, Downingtown, Pa. 16p. 4to. Plain wraps. On paper made by Frederick Bicking, Mill Creek, Lower Merion Twp. Montgomery County, Pa. First printed in 1766 (Evans 10258) [See also the Reading, 1791, German edition =Part I #263]. This little known Quaker prophetic dream / vision must have had compelling metaphysical power. The text of the manuscript does not exactly follow the published version. Unique. $ 385.00

THE WONDERFUL LEGEND OF CONCORDIA

2159. Concordia. **DIE WUNDERBARE CONCORDIA; EINES COMMANDANTEN TOCHTER, WELCHE 120 JAHRE ENTFÜHRET WAR, UND MEYNTE ES WÄRE NUR ZWEY STUNDEN GEWESEN.** (Heinrich Merklein, Chambersburg. Ca: 1815). *Poetic Broadside.* 9" x 14.5". Repaired at fold. Lovely hand colored idealized portrait of Concordia framed in floral wreaths. Handsome and rare printing of the curious and very popular tale of Concordia who, like Rip Van Winkle, slept for 120 years. $ 275.00

2160. Concordia. **EINE WUNDERBARE GESCHICHTE VON CONCORDIA, eines Commandanten Tochter, welch 120 Jahren entführet war, und meynte es wären nur etliche Stunden.** (Bauman, Ephrata, Ca: 1811). *Poetic Broadside,* with a central woodcut of Concordia as an Angel. 8.5" x 12". Worn and mounted, with loss from Concordia's skirt. Scarce early version. $ 100.00

2161. (Cox, Susanna). **NEUES TRAUERLIED, Enthaltend die Geschichte der Susanna Cox, die in Reading wegen Ermordung ihres Kindes hingerichter wurde...** (Reading? Ca: 1840). *Poetic Broadside.* 8.5" x 11.5". Numerous old tape repairs. Very popular cautionary tale about infanticide and criminal justice. $ 50.00

2162. (Cresson, Caleb). **DYING SAYINGS OF MARY ARMITT, who Deceased at Philadelphia, 1791. Aged 83 Years.** *Quaker Manuscript* written by Caleb Cresson, for his friend Alice Needham. Philadelphia, Ca: (1791). 26p. Pious Quaker thoughts and devotions, taken down, surreptitiously, but with great care. Never publisahed?? $ 200.00

2163. **AN DIE DEMOCRATISCHEN ERWAHLER VON YORK COUNTY.** (York. Ca: 1810). 11 x 17.5". Deckle edged paper of local manufacture. *Political broadside,* presenting arguments against the Congressional candidate, Adam König. Handsome political display piece. $ 150.00

2164. **DRINGENDER ZURUF, Eines treuen Lehrers bey Einsegnung der Kinder.** (Lancaster? Ca: 1840). 10" x 15". Repaired with slight loss. Typographic border. *Poetic Broadside,* likely issued as a Confirmation song. $ 65.00

2165. Egelmann, C. F. **GEBURTS = UND TAUFSCHEIN.** Stipple Engraved *Taufschein,* printed by Egelmann, Reading, Circa: 1820. 10" x 12". Crisp, unused example. Edition with clouds. See: Shelley "*Fraktur*". Powerfully designed, and handsomely printed. Sadly, our illustrations do little justice to these broadsides. $ 150.00

This Indenture

2166. **EPHRATA PRINTED DEED.** ***This Indenture***, made July 5, 1768, between John Mergel of Wilmington and George Mergel (Merkel) of Cogollico (Cocalico) Twp. Lancaster County... For a tract of land (180 acres) along the Cocalico Creek. Printed form filled out in manuscript, and signed by Edward Carpenter, as well as Johannis Mergel, Joseph Meays, et. al. 15.5" x 19.75". Repaired at folds. Printed at the Cloister Press on paper made at the Ephrata paper mill. John Mergel was a "house father" associated with the Cloisters. Handsome Ephrata display piece. $ 200.00

2167. **EPHRATA PRINTED DEED.** ***This Indenture***, made April 3, 1773, Walter Newman and Stefan Rudolf, both of Heidelberg Twp. Lancaster County... For a lot (#23) in Newbury Town, Heidelberg Twp. Printed form filled out in manuscript, very similar to the deed above. Very well preserved example of the "Job Printing" of the Cloister Press, and their use of Ephrata made paper. $ 175.00

2168. **EPHRATA PRINTED DEED.** ***This Indenture***, made March 6, 1790, between John Gunckel and Jacob Peffley, of Bethel Twp. Dauphin County... For a 56 acre tract of land in Bethel Twp. Printed form filled out in manuscript, and signed by Thomas Clark, as well as Baltzer Stein, and Mr. & Mrs. Gunkle. 17" x 21". The woodcut title block was used by several Lancaster and Ephrata printers. $ 120.00

2169. (Foster, Stephen). **O, SUSANNA! Das bekannte Lied eines verliebten Negers.** (Lancaster? Ca: 1850). 4.75" x 9.75". Slight loss of typographic border. Stained. Rare Pennsylvania German *Broadside* printing of this famous song. $ 50.00

2170. (Gerberich). **UEBER DEN TOD VON EPHRAIM GERBERICH.** *Broadside Eulogistic Poem*. Lancaster? Circa: 1860. 4.75" x 5.75". $ 22.00

2171. **GEBURTS=UND TAUFSCHEIN.** Printed by Leisenring, Trexler & Co. Allentown. Ca: 1872. Attractive, blank, color printed *Birth and Baptismal Certificate*. 13" x 17". Fine condition. Ideal candidate for modern reproduction. $ 60.00

2172. **GEISTLICHER IRRGARTEN.** *Spiritual Labyrinth Broadside*. (Reading? Ca: 1805). 13" x 16". One small hole. Printed on paper made by Abraham Levan, whose mill was near Kutztown. Handsome mystical labyrinth, of the type so popular in Ephrata. $ 275.00

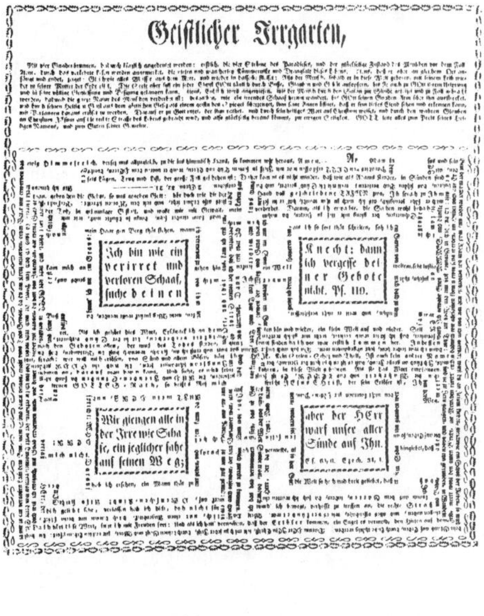
Geistlicher Irrgarten,

Ich bin wie ein verirret und verloren Schaaf, suche deinen

Knecht; denn ich vergesse deiner Gebote nicht. Ps. 119.

Wir giengen alle in der Irre wie Schafe, ein jeglicher sahe auf seinen Weg;

aber der HErr warf unser aller Sünde auf Ihn.

2173. **GEMEINDE = ORDNUNG der Evang. Luth. Zion's Kirche, in Ober = Milford Twp. Lecha County, Pa.** (Allentown: 1877). 12.5" x 9.5". *Broadside*. Three columns. $ 26.00

2174. **GOTTESVERTRAUEN.** *Poetic Devotional Broadside* in 12 stanzas. (Philadelphia? Circa: 1867). 6.5" x 8". $ 22.00

2175. **GÜLDIN FAMILY REGISTER.** *Partially Printed and Manuscript German Form*, recording births in the family, from the 1830's-1870's. 3p. 4to. $ 34.00

2176. **EIN GUTER ABROBIRTER SEGEN IN FEUERSBRUNT. Dieses hat ein Christlicher Zigeuner König aus Egypten erfunden...** H. D. Laubach, Hellertown, Ca: 1889. 8.5" x 12". *Broadside with typographic border.* Repaired at folds. A Christian Gypsy King from Egypt, gives a blessing to preserve the user from fire. $ 150.00

2177. (Guth, Christian). **EIN GEISLICHES LIED, Gedichet von einem Prediger auf seinem Siechbett...** (Allentown, Ca: 1860). 5" x 8". *Poetic Broadside.* The author's name is revealed through an acrostic in the broadside's text. $ 40.00

2178. Harbaugh, Henry. **CENTENARY HYMN.** *Poetic English Broadside.* 5" x 9". (Mercersburg? Circa: 1860). $ 30.00

2179. **JESUS MEIN VERLANGEN.** (Allentown? Ca: 1840). 5.5" x 11". *Poetic Broadside* in six stanzas. Stained. $ 28.00

2180. **JOSEPH UND SEINE BRÜDER.** (Chambersburg? Ca: 1830). *Poetic Broadside* in eight stanzas. 6.5" x 9". Another version of the popular tale of Joseph & his Brothers. $ 40.00

2181. **LANDS FOR SALE.** C. Schlichting, York: 1803. 7.5 x 13". Frayed with slight loss. Very scarce *Broadside in English & German*, signed in type by Charles W. Hartley. A offer of several tracts of land in Bald Eagle Township, Center County, Pennsylvania. This is apparently one of the earliest items printed by Schlichting. $ 120.00

2182. **EIN LIED AUF ALLE HANDWERKER.** *Poetic Broadside* with a typographic border and rococo headpiece. 8" x 11". (Lancaster? Ca: 1810). The text celebrates and commends all sorts of crafts and trades. Really quite interesting. $ 120.00

2183. Mayer, Benjamin. **LETTER FROM THE EPHRATA PRINTER BENJAMIN MAYER, TO JOHANN PETER MILLER.** (Ephrata, Ca: 1790). *German Manuscript Letter* on Ephrata watermarked paper. 1p. Folio. Mayer asks Miller for his understanding and forgiveness for his actions in some unspecified transaction. Unusual and interesting Ephrata document. $ 125.00

2184. **MEDICAL RECIPE.** (Philadelphia? Ca: 1800). *German Manuscript Prescription.* Apparently, for an intestinal purge to cure a fever. $ 40.00

Vorbereitung.

Gnade und Friede / Heyl und Freude / Segen und Leben / sey mit uns allen von JESU Christo / dessen heilsahme Gnade uns erschienen / und Frieden auf Erde gebracht / dessen Heyl bis an der Welt Ende / und unsere Hertzen erfüllet mit Freude und Wonne / der den Fluch in Segen verwandelt / und uns das geistliche und ewige Leben giebet! Demselben samt seinem himmlischen Vater und dem heiligen Geist sey Preiß / Ehr und Danck / jetzt und in Ewigkeit! Amen.

Ihr andächtige und durch Christum den neugebohrnen Heylands erlösete Seelen. Es ist und bleibt die Menschwerdung und Geburt unsers Herrn JEsu Christi ein grosses Geheimniß der Gottseligkeit / 1. Tim. III. 1. Welches / da es von der Welt verschwiegen gewesen / Röm. XVI.

EXTRAORDINARY CALLIGRAPHIC BOOK

2185. Mickler, Carl Gotthard. **ZUM ÜBEN DES SCHREIBENS, und zum sammlen des geschrieben.** Np. 1816. 4to. *Manuscript in Gothic and Roman letter.* Colored titles; followed by five pages of ABC's; 53 pages of Biblical quotations, and excerpts from works by Johann Christian Hagemann (1720) and Michael Scotus (1717); + a folding folio mystical broadside = all in a hand that can only be described as *"almost like type set"*. The skill and execution must be seen to be believed. Also includes a portrait drawing of Johann Arndt, and a full page allegorical plate of a "Soldier of God". Must be seen to be fully appreciated. $ 425.00

2186. Miller, John. **ACCOUNT OF THE ESTATE OF JOHN MILLER.** Cocalico Township, Lancaster County: 1823. *Folio Manuscript Executors' Record*, signed by John Bachman, Jr. 13" x 16". On paper made by Samuel Boyer, Oley, Pa. Lists many prominent persons including the printer - Peter Montelius. $ 50.00

TRAGIC HOMICIDE IN LEBANON COUNTY

2187. (Miller, Joseph). **EIN NEUES LIED, VON DER MORD=GESCHICHTE DES JOSEPH MILLER...** *Poetic Broadside* with a typographic border. (Lebanon, Ca; 1822). 7.5" x 18". The sad tale of Joseph Miller, who lived in Myerstown, Lebanon County. In 1822 he murdered his pregnant wife and two children, and then hung himself. Rare. $ 280.00

2188. **MUSIC BOOK.** *Manuscript Music Book.* Created by John Philip Wind. (Lehigh County? Ca: 1800). Bound in contemporary leather backed marbled boards. Oblong. Nearly 100 tunes (without words) + Index of First Lines. Most are German language religious songs, perhaps of Moravian usage. There is also a "Hornpipe" and one other English song = "Gen. Washington's March". Owned later (1843) by Samuel Snyder. Original German American manuscript music books have become quite rare. $ 320.00

2189. New York World's Fair. **PENNSYLFAWNISCH DEITSCHER DAWG.** Cardboard badges issued for Pennsylvania Dutch Days at the World's Fair, Sept. 28, 1940. Shows a picture of a Pennsylvania "Dutchman", patterned on "Pumpernickle Bill". WST. $ 10.00

2190. **NORTH WHITEHALL TOWNSHIP, LEHIGH COUNTY, PERSONAL PROPERTY TAX RECORDS.** *Manuscript Record Book.* 1834-5. 47p. 16mo. Plain wraps. The names of all the property owners are written in German script, with the State & County tax due. The copy of John (Jacob) Scheirer, Township Tax Collector. $ 80.00

2191. **NORTH WHITEHALL TOWNSHIP, LEHIGH COUNTY, POOR TAX RECORDS.** *Manuscript Record Book.* 1816. 23p. 16mo. Plain wraps. Ds. The names are, for the greater part, written in English this time. Valuable cultural and genealogical records. $ 75.00

2192. **PALATINA/TUS AD RHENUM.** *Map by Joannes Jansson*, Amsterdam. Ca: 1650. 21 x 17.5". Very handsome map of the Palatinate with contemporary coloring and very attractive cartouches. Text on verso. Homeland for early German emigrants. $ 300.00

VERY EARLY AND SIGNIFICANT GERMANTOWN LAND GRANT

2193. Penn, William. **GRANT OF LAND IN GERMANTOWN.** 500 Acres Granted to Leonart Aretz (Arents) [See below]. Large *Manuscript Document on Vellum.* 24.75" x 13". (Philadelphia 1707/8). Calligraphic manuscript in old English. *Signed by Edward Shippen, Griffith Owen, Thomas Story, & James Logan*, without seals. The ink is somewhat faded, therefore a transcript is provided. Lenart Arents van Aken, was one of the group of thirteen Crefeld (Krefeld) Mennonite / Quaker families (mostly weavers), who formed the first permanent German settlement in America (1683). His wife was a sister of Wilhelm and Jan Strepers who, in 1683, bought 5000 acres from Penn. The text clearly details parts of this transaction, as well as Arents' own 1683 purchase of land (making him one of the first six Crefeld purchasers of land in America). An illuminating artifact of the earliest German settlement in America. $ 650.00

AMERICA'S FIRST COMMERCIAL COLOR PRINTER

2194. Peters. **GEBURTS = UND TAUF = SCHEIN.** Color Printed, Woodblock Illustrated Blank *Birth and Baptismal Certificate*. Engraved and printed by G. S. Peters, Harrisburg. Ca: 1830. 13" x 16.25". Slight border loss. $ 275.00

2195. Peters. **GEBURTS=UND TAUF=SCHEIN.** Color Printed, Woodblock Illustrated *Birth and Baptismal Certificate* for Johannes D. Bechtel (1851), Tulpenhocken Twp., Berks County, Pa. Engraved and printed in colors by G. S. Peters, Harrisburg. Ca: 1850. 13" x 16.25". A fine, crisp example. $ 320.00

2196. Peters. **THE HISTORY OF JOSEPH & HIS BRETHREN.** G. S. Peters, Harrisburg. Ca: 1829. 18 x 22". *Broadside.* Illustrated by fifteen, uncolored, but boldly struck woodcuts, similar to those that appear in the famous Peters chapbook. Verses in English. Old repairs. Foxed. $ 500.00

POW WOW MANUSCRIPTS

2197. Pow Wow. **FORMULAS, RECIPES, INCANTATIONS, PRAYERS, & CURSES TO CURE MAN & BEAST.** *German American Manuscript.* Lancaster County, Ca: 1840. 86p. + Slips of paper with mystical alphabetic formulas. Leather wallet binding. Extensive collection of cures. Rare. $ 340.00

2198. Pow Wow. **FORMULAS, RECIPES, ETC.** *Manuscript in English and German.* Lehigh County, Ca: 1860. 12p. + Printed and manuscript formulae + folded and singed "*S A T O R*" slips + (Silver?) nails! A Pow Wow Doctor's Kit. $ 160.00

IMPORTANT AMERICAN PACIFIST STATEMENT ON THE EVE OF REVOLUTION

2199. Quaker Broadsheet. **TO THE REPRESENTATIVES OF THE FREEMAN OF THE PROVINCE OF PENNSYLVANIA IN GENERAL ASSEMBLY MET. The Address of the People Called Quakers.** Philadelphia: 1775. 2p. Folio. *Broadsheet.* Signed in type by John Pemberton, and in manuscript by James Moon. Evans 14053. Greatly alarmed by the agitation of Revolution and war, the Society of Friends asserts that their "Liberty of Conscience" should not be subverted by the growing breach with the Crown. They argue persuasively that their exemption from warlike services has been respected for nearly one hundred years, and is reaffirmed by Penn's Charter and the English Constitution. Many German non-resistant sects in Pennsylvania claimed the same rights, privileges, and freedoms. $ 320.00

FROM THE FOUNDATIONS OF AMERICAN LUTHERANISM

2200. **ST. MICHAEL'S & ZION'S CHURCH = ORIGINAL MANUSCRIPT PEW REGISTER INDEX.** Phila. Circa: 1770. 45+p. *German Manuscript.* Oblong folio. St. Michael's, was the first Evangelical Lutheran Church in America (1748). When built, it was regarded as too large and costly a structure for such a small congregation; but it was soon outgrown, and Zion's Church was built at 4th & Cherry Streets to house the greater portion of the congregation. Consecrated before a huge throng in 1769, Zion's Church was long regarded as the finest house of worship in America. This rare register records the distribution of the congregation between the two churches. The most important figures of the early American Lutheran community are all listed, with their occupations, chosen church, and pew number. Included too, is the Pew receipt and application book for Zion's Church, 1834=53, with fascinating details about charity cases, etc. Magnificent documents from an eventful period in American church history. $ 500.00

2201. (Sauer). **EIN LIED, Von einem 10jährigen Knaben, Namens Daniel Sauer, welches auf Begehren seiner Freunde zum Druck befordert wurde - 1831**. (Sower? Norristown? 1831). *Poetic Broadside*. Typographic border. 4" x 10.5". Probably issued for the young Sauer's confirmation. $ 50.00

2202. **EIN SCHÖN JESUS = LIED**. (Lancaster? Ca: 1860). 7.25" x 11.5". *Poetic Broadside*, in nine stanzas. $ 24.00

TWO IMPORTANT SCHWENKFELDER MANUSCRIPTS.

2203. Schwenkfelder. **COMPENDIUM, das ist Kurtze Zusammenfassung und Inbegriff diver Christlichen Glaübens = Lehren...** von C. S. *Manuscript in German*, describing Schwenkfelder belief. Closely written on 515 pages + manuscript inserts. (Montgomery County, Pa: 1783-8). Probably authored and scribed by Christopher Schultz [1718-89], one of the most illustrious and influential of all Schwenkfelder pioneers. Contemporary full leather binding in fine condition. Small 4to. In addition to their several printed works, Schwenkfelder hymns, prayers, and theological writings, circulated mainly in manuscript form. It was through these laboriously produced manuscripts that the faith was refined, preserved, and promoted. They are powerful historical and cultural documents. $1800.00

2204. Schwenkfelder. **EIN SCHÖN CHRISTLICHES GEISTLICHES GEBETBÜCH, bestehend In neünzehn Classen oder Theilen... von dem Seeligen Caspar Schwenkfeldt...** Michel Hiller, George Frell, et. al. *German Manuscript* Collection of prayers and commentary. Neatly written on thick paper. (Montgomery County, Pa. Ca: 1760). 549p. Some page repairs. Small 4to. Contemporary full leather binding by Rev. Christopher Hoffman, with original decorated brass corner bosses. The scribe / author of this manuscript may also be Christopher Hoffman [1727-1804], an eminent Schwenkfelder minister, copyist, hymnologist, and bookbinder. One cannot fail to be impressed by the piety, industry, and art required to produce the corpus of Schwenkfelder manuscripts. Pennypacker called them "... a record of midnight toil and anguish of the soul; historic accretions of profound thinking; rubies and diamonds for the adornment of God's spiritual temple and kingdom." Rarely found today in private hands. $2000.00

2205. (Stein, Johannes). **ZURUF EINES LEHRERS, an seine Confirmanten; Am Tage der Confirmation**. (Lancaster? Ca: 1855). 7" x 11". *Poetic Broadside*, in five stanzas. $ 28.00

2206. **STERB = UND LEICHEN = GESANG**. Mel. Werde munter mein gemüthe, &c. (Allentown? Ca: 1820). *Poetic Eulogistic Broadside*, in eleven stanzas. 6.5" x 12". Repaired at folds. $ 40.00

2207. **TAUF = ZEDEL**. Color Printed *Christening Note*. 6.5 x 6.5". Ca: 1820. Nicely framed. Possibly printed in Northern Alsace, or in the Palatinate. Very popular among the Pennsylvania immigrants. They were intended to be folded around money & given for the baby's future (or sometimes as a wedding gift). Rarely encountered today. Attractive. $ 150.00

2208. Trade Token?. **GENERAL WASHINGTON / Composit^{S} Spiel Marke**. Penny sized, copper coin, showing a full bust view of Washington / and on the obverse a profile head of the Goddess Liberty. Rare German American *Trade Token, or "Play Money"*. $ 42.00

2209. Valentine Poems. **MEIN EINZIGER TROST AUF ERDEN...** (Reading? Ca: 1810). Worn. Verses within typographic borders. Probably meant to be folded up and given to loved one. Scarce. $ 50.00

Vereinigung der Kinder im Gebet.

Mel. Herr Jesu Christ dich 2c.

Kommt laßt uns Jesum suchen bald,
Wir werden sonsten hart und kalt;
Jetzt ist die angenehme Zeit,
Zu sorgen für die Ewigkeit.

Bey Jesu hat man's wahrlich gut,
Er liebt uns sehr—er gab sein Blut,
Für uns am Kreutz; damit man frey,
Von Sünde, Tod und Hölle sey.

Drum laßt uns ihm, dem guten Herrn
Von ganzem Herzen folgen gern.
Der Sünde laßt uns sagen ab,
Und fromm seyn biß ins kühle Grab.

Dann gehts uns gut in dieser Zeit,
Und dort hernach in Ewigkeit.
Er, Jesus führt uns ein zur Ruh,
Und urtheilt uns das Kleinod zu!

Joseph Schnee, Drucker.

2210. **VEREINIGUNG DER KINDER IM GEBET**. Joseph Schnee (Lebanon: 1813). Lovely little *Poetic Broadside* that shows two children (Samuel?) kneeling in prayer, on either side of the text. 13" x 8". Slight loss of typographic border. Scarce. $ 175.00

2211. **EIN VORTREFFLICHES MITTEL GEGEN WASSERSUCHT**. *Medical Formula Broadside*, for a remedy against dropsy. (Lehigh County? Ca: 1850). 5.75" x 6". $ 40.00

2212. Weiser, Conrad. **ADMINISTRATION BOND MEMORANDUM FOR THE ESTATE OF HENRY MOYER (MEYER)...** *Manuscript*, written in the hand of, and signed by Conrad Weiser, 1744. 1p. 4to. Signed also by Francis Lawyenberger, Batholmeus Sheffer, and John Shupp - who testified that Moyer (of Heidelberg Twp. Lancaster County) on his deathbed, left his estate to his wife. Interesting example of the work that Weiser did in his community as a scrivener and "Justice of the Peace". Rare. $ 145.00

2213. **ZU MEINEIN 90TEN JAHRESTAGE. Den 19ten Maerz 1867**. (Philadelphia? 1867). *Poetic Broadside*, in 12 stanzas. 6" x 8". The unnamed subject of this birthday celebration was born in 1777. $ 38.00

2214. **ZWEY SCHÖNE LIEDER**. (Heinrich Merklein, Chambersburg. Ca: 1815). *Poetic Broadside*, with a hand colored headpiece, showing a flying angel, holding branches in each hand. 6.75" x 9.25". Attractive. $ 120.00

SOME DESCRIPTIVE ABBREVIATIONS USED IN KEYSTONE TEN

= *"Die Alte Zeite"* =

Acidic	On paper high in acidity. Brittle and browned.
Ads.	Advertisements.
Bds.	Boards. Front or Back Covers.
Cloth	Bound in Cloth. Hard Bound.
Disbd.	Disbound. Binding worn, detached, or missing.
Ds.	Damp Stained. Age Stained.
Folio	Large Sized Book. Usually over 12" tall.
Fxd.	Foxed. Browned.
HSH.	Associated with the Collector, Henry Savley Heilman
Ill.	One Illustration.
Illus.	Illustrations. Illustrated.
Miniature.	Less than 3" Tall.
Ms.	Manuscript.
pp.	Pagination
Wraps	Paper Bound. Soft Bound. Pamphlet.
WST.	From the Collection of William. S. Troxell, "Pumpernickle Bill".
XLib.	Owned and marked by a Library. Withdrawn. Also: XL.
4to.	Quarto. Usually a square shaped book. Approximately 10".
8vo.	Octavo. 7" to 9" Tall. Not usually mentioned in descriptions.
12mo.	Duodecimo. 6" to 8" Tall. Not usually mentioned in descriptions.
16mo.	Sextodecimo. 5" to 7" Tall. Rarely mentioned in descriptions.
24mo.	Vigesimoquarto. 4" to 6" Tall. Usually somewhat square shaped.
32mo.	Trigesimosecundo. 3" to 5" Tall.
48mo.	Fortyeightmo. Less than 4" Tall.

Ron Lieberman
THE FAMILY ALBUM
RD 1, BOx 42
Glen Rock, PA 17327
U.S.A.
Phone: (717) 235-2134